Palgrave Studies in Economic History

Series Editor
Kent Deng
London School of Economics
London
United Kingdom

Palgrave Studies in Economic History is designed to illuminate and enrich our understanding of economies and economic phenomena of the past. The series covers a vast range of topics including financial history, labour history, development economics, commercialisation, urbanisation, industrialisation, modernisation, globalisation, and changes in world economic orders.

More information about this series at
http://www.springer.com/series/14632

David Hall

Emerging From an Entrenched Colonial Economy

New Zealand Primary Production, Britain and the EEC, 1945–1975

palgrave
macmillan

David Hall
Victoria University of Wellington
Wellington, New Zealand

Palgrave Studies in Economic History
ISBN 978-3-319-53015-4 ISBN 978-3-319-53016-1 (eBook)
DOI 10.1007/978-3-319-53016-1

Library of Congress Control Number: 2017935474

Cover illustration: DPK-Photo / Alamy Stock Photo

Printed on acid-free paper

This Palgrave Macmillan imprint is published by Springer Nature
The registered company is Springer International Publishing AG
The registered company address is: Gewerbestrasse 11, 6330 Cham, Switzerland

For Margaret, Stephen, Susan and Evelyn whose support made this work possible

Preface

This book is based on the research I first conducted during my PhD studies in the School of History, Philosophy, Political Science and International Relations at Victoria University of Wellington, New Zealand. Those studies took place with considerable assistance from my supervisors Professor Jim McAloon and Professor Steve Behrendt. Jim gave essential guidance on the key New Zealand issues and personalities to which the book gives prominence. Steve, through his rigorous approach to how English should be written, made my writing far more concise and clear. Dr Malcolm McKinnon also provided key guidance in the final stages of the work. There has also been substantial and patient help from the staff at the New Zealand National Archives, National Library, Alexander Turnbull Library, Macmillan Brown Library and the Hawke's Bay Museum-Theatre-Gallery. Rod and Dee Fry, through their hospitality and by introducing me to their acquaintances in the Motueka farming community, have given me a far more thorough insight into New Zealand farming than I could ever have acquired from paper studies. The studies have benefitted from valuable conversations with John Acland, Jim Bolger, Roger Buchanan, Brian Chamberlin, Professor Brian Easton, Rod Fry, Jared Fry, Paul Heyward, Evan Heyward, Tom Inglis, Brian Lynch, Sir Geoffrey

Palmer, Dr Judith Simon, Ian Stewart, Neil Taylor and Dr John Wood. Professor Natalie Chablin at the University of Canterbury encouraged those conversations and provided financial support to conduct them as part of our joint work on New Zealand perceptions of the European Union.

Contents

Abbreviations

ANZ	Archives New Zealand
ANZUS	Australia, New Zealand and United States (Security Treaty)
ATL	Alexander Turnbull Library
CAP	Common Agricultural Policy (of the European Economic Community)
CCEFQ	Cabinet Committee on Economic and Financial Questions
CCEFP	Cabinet Committee on Economic and Financial Policy
CEC	Cabinet Economic Committee
EEC	European Economic Community
FAO	(United Nations) Food and Agriculture Organisation
GATT	General Agreement on Trade and Tariffs
GNP	Gross National Product
GNI	Gross National Income
IFAP	International Federation of Agricultural Producers
IWS	International Wool Secretariat
JO	Joint Organisation (for disposal of wool stockpile left over from World War II)
MBL	Macmillan Brown Library, University of Canterbury
MTG	Museum, Theatre, Gallery (Hawke's Bay)
NZDYB	New Zealand Digital Yearbooks (Statistics New Zealand)
OECD	Organisation for Economic Co-operation and Development
OEEC	Organisation for European Economic Cooperation
UNCTAD	United Nations Conference on Trade and Development
WCL	Wellington Central Library

List of Figures

List of Tables

1

Introduction

1.1 General

In 1974 the Organisation for Economic Cooperation and Development (OECD) reported on Agricultural Policy in New Zealand as part of its objective to review that topic in all member states. The OECD identified the importance of agriculture for New Zealand and pointed out the comparative advantage that made New Zealand heavily dependent on agriculture for export earnings:

> Several features of the New Zealand climate favour the intensive grassland farming upon which New Zealand agriculture is based. Rainfall is, in general, adequate and reliable and there is abundant sunshine. Winters are sufficiently mild for sheep and cattle to remain in the open and pasture growth continues throughout the year.[1]

New Zealand had been populated through the nineteenth and twentieth centuries by immigration mainly from Britain and strong familial

[1] Agricultural Policy in New Zealand, OECD Report, February 1974, 9, Archives New Zealand (ANZ).

D. Hall, *Emerging from an Entrenched Colonial Economy*, Palgrave Studies in Economic History, DOI 10.1007/978-3-319-53016-1_1

and sentimental links encouraged New Zealand to build a strong trading relationship and dependence on selling farm produce to Britain.[2] New Zealand fostered the image that British consumers when buying New Zealand produce were buying food produced by Britons.[3] New Zealand's location in the southern hemisphere was also an advantage in that produce was available during seasons of shortages in produce from northern hemisphere agriculture.

In the mid-twentieth century the relationship with Britain began to change and this book analyses how New Zealand's primary production adapted to changes in overseas trading from 1945 when the main market, by far, was Britain, until 1975 when markets were mainly Asian/Pacific. In the decades after World War II, Britain increased its own agricultural production to replace food imports; its textile industry declined reducing the need for raw wool; and, in 1973, Britain became a member of the European Economic Community (EEC), an organisation that had strong protection for its domestic farming against suppliers from outside the Community. Those changes in Britain, and changes in New Zealand's perception of its relationship with Britain, made adaptation essential within New Zealand's primary production.

The diplomatic and political developments during that period of change have been well covered by others whose work is cited at the appropriate places in the book. Because of its key role as an earner of overseas revenue, a failure to change within primary production would have stymied the diplomatic and political forces for change. New Zealand's comparative advantage as an efficient producer of agricultural produce made it dependent on primary production for export; it did not have sufficient advantage in other areas to move easily away from that dependence. The book analyses mainly change, or the lack of change, within the three most important primary production sectors

---

[2] James Belich, *Paradise Reforged: A History of New Zealanders from the 1880s to the Year 2000* (Auckland: Penguin Books [NZ], 2001), 29–30; Felicity Barnes, *New Zealand's London: A Colony and Its Metropolis* (Auckland: Auckland University Press, 2012), 124. 'Britain' is used as shorthand for the United Kingdom of Great Britain and Northern Ireland. When reporting remarks by others sometimes 'Great Britain', 'the United Kingdom' or 'England' may be used but they all refer to the same country.

[3] Barnes, 157.

in New Zealand, meat, dairy and wool, and, especially, change for the individuals and organisations that made up the sectors – producers within the farm gate, those handling the produce between the farm gate and exporters, for instance, wool brokers and freezing and dairy factories, and those representing, informing and supporting primary producers, mainly Federated Farmers and statutory boards, boards that producers insisted should be producer-controlled. The various primary production elements and the connections between them and with the government as they stood in 1961 are shown schematically in Fig. 1.1.

The boards facilitated exporting and were sensitive to New Zealand's overseas markets. Federated Farmers had strong links with international bodies and overseas farming organisations and often pressed for change earlier than the boards. Produce processors, especially dairy and freezing factories, were responsive to changes in overseas markets through immediate contact with market returns. Producers within the farm gate (called farmers from now on) were the most isolated from overseas markets, and relied on feedback from the boards, Federated Farmers and processors to relay the need for change. Because the boards were intended to be producer-controlled, major changes to marketing needed approval from farmers. Primary production's importance as the main earner of overseas revenue made government take a keen interest in the industry, with representation on the boards, thereby creating the suspicion that the boards were not controlled fully by producers. That made the boards' task of encouraging change more difficult. Federated Farmers more directly represented farmers but did not have a statutory role in facilitating exports or liaising with government.

The individual elements of primary production were (and are) multi-dependent variables and could not change independently: adaptation required change throughout. For example, increased production by meat farmers needed to be matched by increased throughput in freezing factories. That increased throughput needed to be matched by increased shipping to take the products to overseas markets. And that increased shipping needed to be matched by increased overseas markets with end users who needed, and could afford, the products. The arrangements also worked in reverse – if buyers identified additional customers for, say, beef, then dairy farmers and freezing factories were

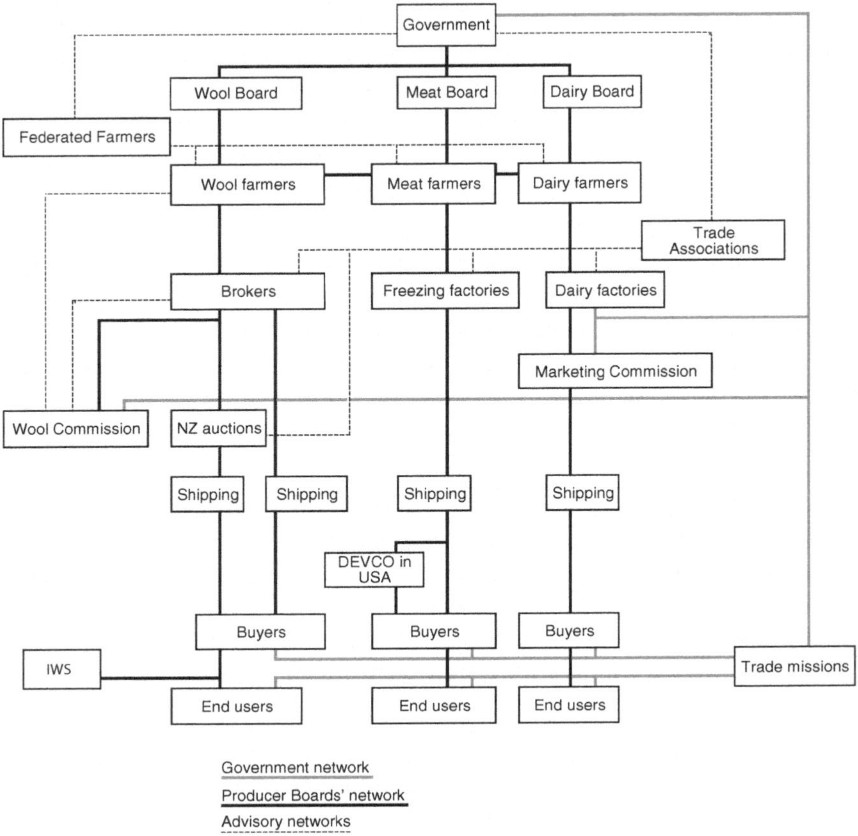

Fig. 1.1 Organisational schematic of primary production in New Zealand in 1961

encouraged to change to beef production. The industry's diverse components worked together, sometimes reluctantly, to achieve the adaptation that took place between 1945 and 1975. New Zealand changed from being 'an English farm in the Pacific' and the 'town supply district of London' to 'an independent nation depending more than ever on our own resources'.[4] Customers for New Zealand's primary produce increased significantly, and primary production in New Zealand needed to adapt to meet the demands of new customers rather than continue, unchanged, its long-term trading with Britain, a customer who had fallen on hard times and struggled to pay for food and wool imports. Once the sentimental links binding New Zealand to Britain started to decline it became incongruous that New Zealand's main customer remained the most distant geographically with billions of potential customers much closer at hand.

The need to cope with trading mainly with a customer on the other side of the world meant that shipping was important and a striking example of path dependence for New Zealand primary production was the dependence on a 'Conference' of four British shipping lines that carried New Zealand exports.[5] The arrangement had first started in the nineteenth century and was reinforced during World Wars I and II when Britain procured all New Zealand's exportable surpluses of food and wool and paid the shipping costs. After the bulk purchase arrangements ended in 1954 the arrangement with the Conference continued but with New Zealand now paying shipping costs which were about 10%–15% of the value of exports. There were occasional proposals from New Zealand primary producers that alternatives to the Conference should be sought, including setting up a New Zealand shipping company, but those usually foundered on the uncertainties of moving away from the well-established arrangement with the British companies.[6] One advantage for New Zealand was that the strength of the British merchant and naval fleet during wartime enabled trade with New Zealand to be maintained despite the considerable shipping losses through enemy action.[7] An advantage during the decades following World War II was that the Conference

[4] The three quotes are, respectively, from Harold Macmillan, *At the End of the Day* (London: Macmillan, 1973), 349; Belich, 30; and John Ormond, 'We Are Now More Alone', *Straight Furrow*, 20/10/1971, 19.

[5] 'Shipping Companies Have Served New Zealand Well', *Straight Furrow*, 01/02/1957, 39.

[6] 'Shipping Our Produce', *Straight Furrow*, 01/11/1961, 3.

[7] 'Shipping Companies Have Served New Zealand Well', *Straight Furrow*, 01/02/1957, 39.

provided dedicated, refrigerated shipping for the New Zealand trade. Shipping was phased to deploy the ships most efficiently taking into account the seasonal nature of New Zealand produce and with regular joint reviews of the arrangements, including an independent review of the appropriate charges.[8] But difficulty in arranging suitable alternative shipping at first inhibited the growth of trade with Asia even though Asian markets were far closer to New Zealand.[9]

Figures 1.2 and 1.3 demonstrate the significant change in New Zealand's customers and in the balance in export earnings between 1949, when the main disruption caused by World War II had ended, and 1975. Primary production still dominated exports in 1975 but the countries buying the produce had changed. Britain remained the main single customer, but the percentage of exports sold to Britain had decreased significantly, whilst exports to Asia and countries

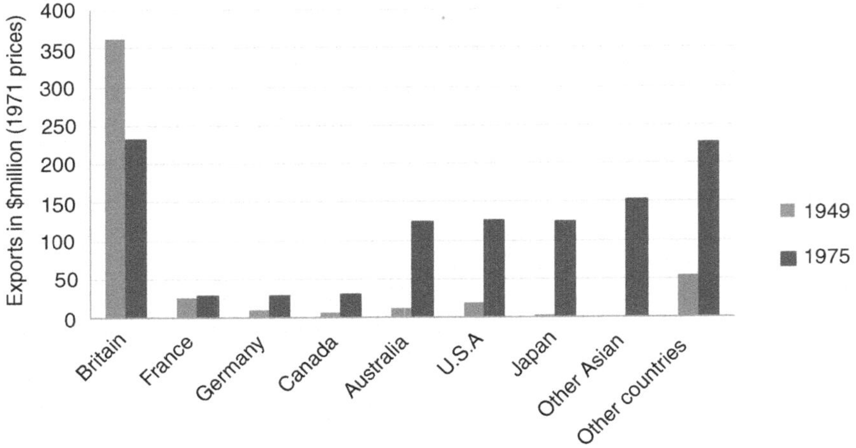

Fig. 1.2 Destinations of New Zealand exports in 1949 and 1975 (New Zealand digital yearbook [NZDYB])

[8] 'Keep Shipping Costs Down', *Straight Furrow*, 20/05/1964, 19.

[9] 'Expansion of Trade with the East', *Straight Furrow*, 01/08/1957, 23.

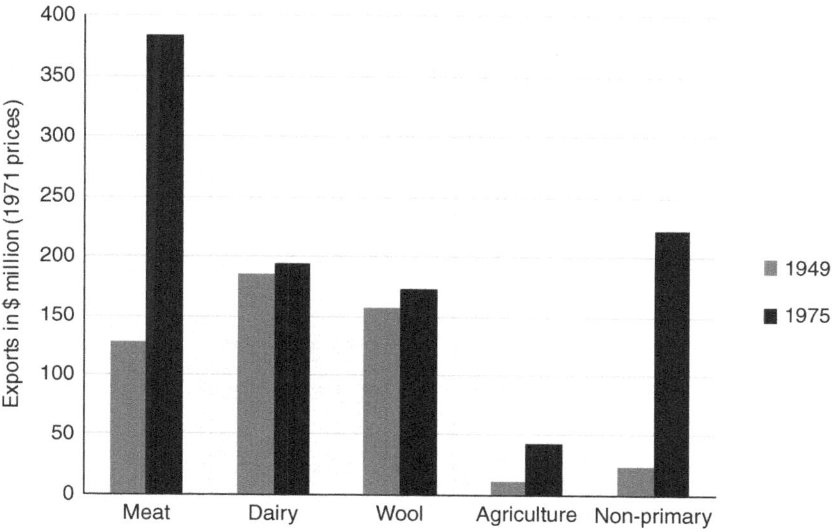

Fig. 1.3 New Zealand exports by commodity in 1949 and 1975 (NZDYB)

bordering the Pacific Ocean expanded. Exports doubled in value in real terms between 1949 and 1975 because farm production increased for all commodities, except cheese, with the largest increases in beef, milk powder and casein. That was achieved with fewer but bigger farms (Table 1.1). Another significant change through the period is in the growth of secondary industry; that is not discussed here but covered thoroughly by Carol Neill, and John Singleton and Paul Robertson.[10] Through the 1950s, 1960s and into the 1970s, the meat and dairy industries responded to the need for change and voluntarily decolonised.

Farming procedures changed to achieve high productivity and quality, and the balance of farm produce changed. Sheep farmers could concentrate efforts on either meat or wool, dairy farmers on either Friesian cattle which were better for milk powder production or the high-fat producing Jerseys which were better for butter and cheese. Both sheep

[10] Carol Neill, *Trading Our Way: Developments in New Zealand's Trade Policy 1930s to 1980s*, Doctoral Book, Massey University, Palmerston North, 2010, 139–288; John Singleton and Paul Robertson, *Economic Relations Between Britain and Australasia 1945–1970* (Basingstoke: Palgrave, 2002), 75–98.

Table 1.1 Commodity production, number of farms and farms' areas

(Statistics NZ, NZDYB, Appendices to the *Journals of the House of Representatives*)

	Lamb and mutton	Beef	Butter	Cheese	Milk powder	Casein	Wool	Number of farms	Average area, hectares	Total area (000) hectares
	(000) tonnes	(000) tonnes	(000) tonnes	(000) tonnes	(000) tonnes	(000) tonnes	(000) tonnes			
1951	291	95	182	109	54	7	179	90,230	194	17,505
1956	368	210	203	96	63	15	184	84,705	203	17,195
1961	470	207	213	98	77	30	233	73,166	242	17,706
1966	469	270	253	100	128	53	277	69,896	251	17,544
1971	564	372	230	105	182	54	288	64,882	269	17,453
1976	513	599	256	105	254	53	312	67,774	313	21,213

and dairy farmers also had the option of change to beef production. The rate at which such changes took place determined how rapidly that adaptation to new markets and new products could happen.

1.2 Primary Producers: A Conservative or Innovative Community?

Barry Gustafson explains the importance of primary production during the mid-twentieth century by pointing out how, for Sir Keith Holyoake, a farmer who became Minister for Agriculture in the 1950s and Prime Minister in the 1960s, his 'approach to the economy was based on a number of simple beliefs. One was that farming was the backbone of the economy', and to achieve exports' expansion 'the pastoral industry was seen as the only major option'.[11] But many writers give examples of primary production practices that could be changed only with difficulty, leaving an impression of primary industries as overly conservative and path dependent, continuing with practices established in the first half of the twentieth century. Family farms passing through the generations dominated farming and Roger Buchanan aptly summarises that the rule was, '"do what father did" rather than rational consideration of what would most cost effectively meet market requirements'.[12] Another force for conservatism was:

> Europe and the UK were easy for us in our early days because they were 'us', the same. We all come from Mother England. The relationship with England from New Zealand has been in place since the 1840s. Companies have traded right through; it was really easy.[13]

Jim McAloon gives one example of 'long-established, deep-rooted mental attitudes and settled practices':

[11] Barry Gustafson, *Kiwi Keith: A Biography of Keith Holyoake* (Auckland: Auckland University Press, 2007), 314.

[12] Roger Buchanan, *The Last Shepherd: Anecdotes and Observations from Five Decades in the Wool Industry* (Wellington: Ngaio Press, 2012), 113.

[13] A farmer speaking to the author in 2014.

> J D Ormond, a Hawke's Bay farmer and Meat Board chairman, told the Cabinet Committee on Economic Policy that even with increased Argentinean and Australian production, New Zealand had a right to the British market and, in fact, should claim a greater percentage than was talked of in the old days.[14]

Sir John (Jack) Marshall says that in the 1950s

> [t]he need to broaden the base of our own economy and to expand and diversify our export trade was becoming more and more urgent if we were to survive in a highly competitive world. This was the challenge which faced me as the first Minister of Overseas Trade, a post which I held for the next eleven years . . . The task was made even more formidable because we had to change long-established, deep-rooted mental attitudes and settled practices at all levels of industry and commerce.[15]

He says, also,

> the term of the second National Government from 1960 to 1972 was a period of industrial revolution during which . . . the farming industries, were brought face to face with the cold, hard world of international trading.[16]

Bruce Curtis and James Reveley conclude that the Meat Board 'sustained inefficient practices . . . by the desire to maximise the number of family-labour farmers . . . including some relatively inefficient farmers'.[17] Singleton and Robertson see New Zealand as reluctant to revise its policies in the light of changes in the international economic environment during the 1950s and 1960s, and New Zealand 'persisted in the supply of a narrow range of export commodities, including sheepmeat and dairy products, which had few outlets except Britain'. In consequence

---

[14] Jim McAloon, *Judgements of All Kinds* (Wellington: Victoria University Press, 2013), 99.

[15] John Marshall, *Memoirs Vol II; 1960–1988* (Auckland: William Collins Ltd., 1989), 48.

[16] Marshall, 29.

[17] Bruce Curtis and James Reveley, 'Producers, Processors and Unions: The Meat Producers Board and Labour Relations in the New Zealand Meat Industry 1952–71', *Australian Economic History Review*, 41, 2, July 2001, 155.

New Zealand did not fulfil its potential and growth was constrained by 'institutional sclerosis'.[18] Gustafson reports the British High Commissioner warning the Commonwealth Office, 'the [New Zealand] small farmer has become used to the idea that the world owes him a comfortable living'.[19] William Sutch noted a reluctance to change within New Zealand: 'The need for long-term market diversification and the changes necessary to achieve it are not fully appreciated by the farming electors who determine the policies of the farm-producer boards.'[20] He illustrated this with a specific example – 'a protest by the Federated Farmers Auckland Branch against vineyards being extended into grass areas'.[21]

Those impressions of overly-conservative primary production are countered by meat and dairy producers' recollections of responses to the need for change. Those suggest, rather than a reluctance to change, the industries were innovative communities that sought diversification and new markets soon after World War II, and in some cases, before. Meat and dairy producers' versions of their response to the need for change are in producer boards' histories written mainly by those who had worked for the boards. The histories, written in celebration of major anniversaries, give prominence to positive aspects of the boards' activities. Dai Hayward, who edited the Meat Board history, had been the Board's export promotion executive and the book comprises personal reminiscences. The book rebuts suggestions that the Meat Board did not respond to changes in international markets; Hayward contends that the Board began to encourage diversification into markets other than Britain well before concerns arose over Britain's potential EEC membership.[22]

Those writing about the dairy industry stressed the industry's innovations. Arthur Ward edited the Dairy Board history published to coincide with the Board's 50th anniversary, and Ward gives a positive view of

---

[18] Singleton and Robertson, 2 and 24.

[19] Gustafson, *Holyoake*, 294.

[20] William Sutch, 'Colony or Nation?', in Michael Turnbull (ed.), *Economic Crises in New Zealand from the 1860s to the 1960s* (Sydney: Sydney University Press, 1968), 166.

[21] *New Zealand Herald*, 03/02/1965, reported in Sutch, 1968, Note 1 167.

[22] Dai Hayward, editor: *Golden Jubilee: The Story of the First Fifty Years of the New Zealand Meat Producers Board 1922–1972* (Wellington: Universal Printers, 1972), 134.

how the industry faced the need for change. Ward played an integral role in the Board's activities for 40 of those 50 years, including being General Manager through the 1950s and 1960s. He rebuts the view that the Board did nothing to foster markets other than Britain, reporting efforts to find new markets 'during the 1910–1920 period, and systematically thereafter', whilst noting that Britain remained the only major country that imported butter and cheese.[23] A demonstration of considerable change in the dairy industry is given, also, by Clive Lind in tracing thoroughly New Zealand dairying through the twentieth century and into the twenty-first century.[24]

Writers on the wool industry give a balanced interpretation of how the industry coped with change. Bill Carter and John MacGibbon wrote the most comprehensive history of the New Zealand wool industry from its origins in the mid-nineteenth century, a history informed by Carter's direct involvement in industry in the mid-twentieth century.[25] Three other books, written by those with inside knowledge of the wool industry, are those by Edward Greensmith, Roger Buchanan and Rex Weber. Greensmith wrote the New Zealand Wool Commission history based on his experiences as the Commission Chairman and, from 1955 to 1962, Treasury Secretary.[26] Buchanan's biography describes how he grew up on a sheep farm and worked for the Wool Commission and Wool Board, eventually becoming the final Wool Board chairman.[27] Weber's autobiography describes his life as a wool merchant with strong insight into farmer attitudes.[28] Greensmith reports in fine detail the domestic changes and resistance to change through the 1950s and 1960s.

[23] Arthur Ward, *A Command of Co-operatives* (Wellington: New Zealand Dairy Board, 1975), 207.

[24] Clive Lind, *Till the Cows Came Home* (Wellington: Steele Roberts, 2013).

[25] Bill Carter and John MacGibbon, *Wool: A History of New Zealand's Wool Industry* (Wellington: Ngaio Press, 2003).

[26] Edward Greensmith, *The New Zealand Wool Commission* (Wellington: New Zealand Wool Marketing Corporation, 1996).

[27] Roger Buchanan, *The Last Shepherd: Anecdotes and Observations from Five Decades in the Wool Industry* (Wellington: Ngaio Press, 2012).

[28] Rex Weber, *Wool Man* (Queen Charlotte Sound: Cape Catley Ltd, 1992).

In describing the long-term outcome following resistance to reform in the late 1960s and early 1970s, Buchanan and Weber give better insight into personalities and their human responses than Greensmith, and bring out well the causes of opposition to change. Buchanan in particular demonstrates that, for farmers, the importance of activities decreased in their eyes with distance from the farm gate at which those activities took place.

A primary production sector that was growing through the 1970s, and partly accounts for the increase in agriculture exports shown in Fig. 1.3, was horticulture, for instance, the growing of fruit and hops. The changes that took place in horticulture belie the impression that primary producers were reluctant to change. An example is horticulture in the region surrounding Motueka. In the 1950s and 1960s apples, pears, tobacco and hops were the main products and for the last two New Zealand production was dominated by growers in the Motueka region.[29] For apples and pears consumers' tastes changed and growers were constantly faced with decisions on when to transfer to new varieties, such changes needing four or five years to reach fruition. The other pressure for change came from evolution of hygiene standards with a continuing need to reduce minimum residue levels from sprays.

In the 1960s and early 1970s hop producers had little reason for change. Their hops were sold domestically to New Zealand breweries with little change from year to year. But in the 1970s hop producers began to explore international opportunities and secured orders from Japan, the USA and Europe. New technology was introduced, for example, pelletisation that created a product more attractive to overseas buyers. Research at the Hop Research Institute in Riwaka helped eliminate disease, encouraged production of seedless hops and introduced mite control using predators rather than sprays. By the 1990s hop producers were able to triple their production and exports.[30]

---

[29] Jim McAloon, Hops, Tobacco and Hemp, Te Ara – the Encyclopedia of New Zealand, accessed 19 January 2015.

[30] Jim McAloon, Hops, Tobacco and Hemp, Te Ara – the Encyclopedia of New Zealand, accessed 19 January 2015.

Even more important than hops for the Motueka region in the middle of the twentieth century was tobacco. Tobacco at that time was a cash crop – there were secure annual orders from the manufacturers of cigarettes in New Zealand. The government policy was that New Zealand should be near self-sufficient in growing the tobacco manufactured into cigarettes in New Zealand.[31] But in the GATT negotiations of the 1970s New Zealand agreed that more tobacco could be exported to New Zealand from the USA in return for nil duty on New Zealand carpet wool imported into the USA.[32] In the 1970s the percentage of New Zealand tobacco used by manufacturers began to fall and oversupply became a serious problem in the industry.[33] The government decided to offer tobacco growers the opportunity to move out of tobacco growing into alternative crops by providing $7000 per Ha to those who wished to do so.[34] Many tobacco growers took the opportunity changing to kiwifruit growing which was becoming a significant export product.

Horticulture contributed less than 10% to New Zealand's exports in the decades after World War II; how the export sectors that contributed more than 70%, meat, dairy and wool, faced up to the need for change from the dependency established through the quasi-colonial relationship with Britain is the main theme of this book.

1.3 Chapter Themes

Specifically, the book analyses whether primary producers of meat, dairy and wool recognised their over-dependence on Britain and that that could not last. How did producers respond to the re-building of Britain's agriculture and Britain's attempts to join the EEC between 1961 and 1971? How did producers respond once restrictions imposed first by Britain and then by the EEC became a reality in the 1960s and 1970s? Did primary producers

[31] Right Hon. Sir Keith Holyoake, *NZPD*, 1974, Vol. 392, p. 3395.

[32] Hon. B.E. Talboys, *NZPD*, 1974, Vol. 392, p. 3404.

[33] Rt. Hon. L.R. Adams-Schneider, *NZPD*, 1981, Vol. 441, p. 3645.

[34] Rt. Hon. L.R. Adams-Schneider, *NZPD*, 1981, Vol. 440, p. 3228.

comprise a force for change or conservatism; if the former how did changes take place, if the latter, what eventually forced change? Did market diversification arise from a sudden realisation that change became essential in the 1970s, with New Zealand shaken from an entrenched colonial attitude by Britain becoming a member of the EEC, or, did the realisation develop over many years, from the 1940s when New Zealand's growing international contacts encouraged moves into new markets and products, and encouraged a breaking away from dependence on Britain? How much did New Zealand's wishes for growing independence drive diversification whatever the changes in Britain?

The book analyses whether chance or deliberate policy drove the diversification, and, whether for conservatism or change, how far producers influenced government decisions. Marshall, when discussing EEC negotiations, says, 'We also recognised that . . . it was essential that the farmers, represented by the producer boards, should be consulted whenever their interests were involved.'[35] Singleton and Robertson say, 'The dairy farmers had great influence over the ruling National Party.'[36] Gustafson reports the British High Commissioner as writing:

> New Zealand is still in essence a large farm supplying mainly the United Kingdom market; and a threat to this market sends the whole country instinctively to panic stations. Mr Holyoake and his Ministers echo and magnify these dangers and fears, for the National Party rests on the farm interest for its central support.[37]

Mick Calder and Janet Tyson report the Meat Board Chairman, John Ormond, when accompanied by Jack Acland, the Wool Board Chairman, at a meeting with the Minister of Finance, Robert Muldoon, telling Muldoon that they as Board Chairman rather than Muldoon 'control this country'.[38] Did Ormond exaggerate or reflect the strength of

---

[35] Marshall, 62.

[36] John Singleton and Paul Robertson, 'Britain, Butter and European Integration, 1957–1964', *Economic History Review*, L, 2, 1997, 336.

[37] Gustafson, *Holyoake*, 294.

[38] Mick Calder and Janet Tyson, *Meat Acts: The New Zealand Meat Industry 1972–1997* (Wellington: Meat New Zealand, 1999), 11.

farmer influence on government between 1945 and 1975 when more than three-quarters of New Zealand's exports were produced by farmers?

The structure used to answer those questions is that Chapter 2 analyses the changing relationship with Britain, whilst noting the development of domestic arrangements for New Zealand primary produce to reflect its importance as the main source of profitable exports. Chapter 3 analyses Britain's growing engagement with the EEC, the responses in New Zealand, and the actual and perceived impact when Britain became a member in 1973. Chapters 4–9 analyse change, or lack of change, in the New Zealand meat, dairy and wool industries, by far the dominant primary produce sectors in New Zealand between 1945 and 1975. Especially noted for each of New Zealand's meat, dairy and wool industries are the influences of Britain's engagement with the EEC.

1.4 Sources

Unlike earlier studies of economic and political change, the main sources for this analysis are documents that best represent the voices of producers rather than the voices of diplomats and politicians, for instance, documents of Federated Farmers, the Meat Board, Wool Board, Wool Commission, Dairy Board and Dairy Commission. For Federated Farmers, the organisation's monthly, later fortnightly, magazine, *Straight Furrow* (called *NZ Farmer* since April 2015), is cited frequently; that magazine reports most major activities carried out by the other organisations, and also summarises succinctly key issues, often with the objective to inform rather than persuade. It has an editorial bias in that it speaks for Federated Farmers but has the advantage that it illustrates farmers' key concerns usually earlier than the statutory organisations recognised those concerns. Its content demonstrates the diversity of opinion amongst primary producers far better than the bland, bureaucratic documents produced by the statutory organisations, which tend to report consensus and not the debate leading to consensus. *Straight Furrow* editorials, articles and letters together with reports of Federated Farmers meetings most closely represent farmers' voices.

Other sources informing this study are those from industries that processed raw produce and connected farmers with buyers, for instance, freezing works, dairy factories and woolbrokers. Government and parliamentary papers are used only when they refer specifically to primary production. Papers from four key individuals are used: Sir Keith Holyoake, Sir John Ormond, Sir Jack Acland and Sir John (Jack) Marshall. Holyoake was the most influential politician on primary production through the 1950s and 1960s. He was a farmer who became Minister for Agriculture in 1950 and then Prime Minister for a short period in 1957 and from 1960 until 1972. Ormond dominated the Meat Board as Chairman from 1951 to 1972 and was the most vociferous opponent in New Zealand to Britain's attempts to become an EEC member. Acland, Ormond's brother-in-law, was Chairman of the Wool Board from 1960 to 1972, a member of the Wool Commission and a director of the International Wool Secretariat (IWS). Marshall was Holyoake's Deputy Prime Minister and Overseas Development Minister in the 1950s and 1960s. He led New Zealand's EEC negotiations and was Prime Minister for a short period in 1972.

2

Changing Relationships

2.1 Introduction

Chapter 2 first reviews the development of New Zealand primary production from its beginnings as a key source of exports. Then it examines how over-dependence on Britain grew through a combination of sentimental links, the difficulties in global economics that encouraged the British Empire and Commonwealth countries to protect themselves through preferential trade arrangements, and, finally, through the disruption of World War II that encouraged Britain to procure all New Zealand's meat, dairy and wool production surplus to domestic needs. The weakening of the trading links after World War II is then noted, particularly the influences that encouraged New Zealand to broaden its trading outlook and for Britain to approach the EEC.

2.2 Primary Production up to 1945

Wool, wheat and gold comprised the first exports from New Zealand following early European settlement, but after ship refrigeration started in 1882 significant exports of pastoral products to Britain began. After

D. Hall, *Emerging from an Entrenched Colonial Economy*, Palgrave Studies in Economic History, DOI 10.1007/978-3-319-53016-1_2

World War I disrupted markets, the New Zealand government began setting up producer boards to better organise exports. When markets were again disrupted during the Depression in the 1930s, the British Empire and Commonwealth countries protected themselves through a series of preferential agreements ('Imperial Preferences'). World War II threatened Britain's supplies of food and wool and it contracted to purchase all New Zealand's exportable surplus. The contracts proved profitable and provided a sound basis for New Zealand's primary production following the War.

The introduction of ship refrigeration between New Zealand and Britain in 1882 allowed meat and dairy produce to be maintained in prime condition during the long sea voyage to Britain, and enabled significant exports of pastoral produce in addition to the exports of wool, wheat and gold that had developed following the influx of European settlers in the mid-nineteenth century.[1] Britain, exceptionally amongst the major developed nations in the nineteenth and early twentieth centuries, maintained free trade that gave its population cheap food at the expense of damage to its domestic agriculture.[2] Britain as the most diverse and successful nineteenth-century industrial nation provided the goods needed for New Zealand's development.

Land reforms by the Liberal governments in the 1890s established the nature of New Zealand farms that provided the exports in the twentieth century.[3] Farms mainly within the range 120–400 hectares followed those reforms because the Liberals sought to introduce close settlement for the most extensive estates. They also sought to prevent financial insecurity through farms becoming too small and unable to make an effective contribution to the national economy. In addition to land reform the Liberals introduced quality control by the state to ensure high produce standards for export - one example of how the state in

---

[1] John Bell Condliffe, *New Zealand in the Making: A Study of Economic and Social Development* (London: George Allen and Unwin Ltd., 1959), 152; Condliffe, 149.

[2] David Thomson, *The Pelican History of England: England in the Nineteenth Century* (Harmondsworth: Penguin Books Ltd., 1977), 195.

[3] Tom Brooking, *Lands for the People? The Highland Clearances and the Colonization of New Zealand: A Biography of John Mackenzie* (Dunedin: University of Otago Press, 1996), 254.

New Zealand played a key role in directing the country's activities from the nineteenth century.[4] Primary producers were described at various times as the 'backbone of the economy', the 'backbone of the New Zealand economy', and, even into the 1950s 'underpinned the viability of the New Zealand economy'.[5] Those comments reflected the contribution made to earning overseas income – that contribution remaining at more than 75% even at the end of the period analysed in this book. They did not reflect the contribution that agriculture made to Gross National Income (GNI) or employment; it contributed less than 10% of GNI and employed less than 15% of the workforce. Mechanisation of farming in New Zealand started in the 1930s and that enabled production to be maintained even during the significant demands of war on manpower but it meant also that alternatives to primary production were needed to maintain the government's policy of full employment.[6]

The economic uncertainties following the global disruption of markets by World War I made New Zealand governments set up producer organisations to facilitate exports for national benefit, and to provide better income security for the primary producers themselves.[7] In the 1920s Meat and Dairy Boards were set up and in the 1930s a Wool Committee added, becoming the Wool Board in 1944. In 1944–1946 farmers themselves, by bringing together the diverse organisations that had previously represented them, set up their own, strong, representative body, Federated Farmers.[8] Federated Farmers district, provincial and national meetings made the organisation closer to farmers than the

---

[4] Michael Bassett, *The State in the New Zealand: Socialism Without Doctrines?* (Auckland: Auckland University Press, 1998), 92.

[5] The three quotes are from Brooking, 82; Barry Gustafson, *Kiwi Keith: A Biography of Keith Holyoake* (Auckland: Auckland University Press, 2007), 314; Jim McAloon, *Judgements of All Kinds* (Wellington: Victoria University Press, 2013), 79, respectively.

[6] John Baker, *The New Zealand People at War: The War Economy* (Wellington: Historical Publications Branch, 1965) 15.

[7] Dai Hayward, editor: *Golden Jubilee: the Story of the First Fifty Years of the New Zealand Meat Producers Board 1922–1972* (Wellington: Universal Printers, 1972), 8.

[8] 'To Unite Farmers. New Organisation', *Evening Post*, Vol. CXXXVIII, Issue 135, 05/12/1944, 4; Phillip Herman, *A History of Federated Farmers*, Doctoral Book, Victoria University of Wellington, Wellington, 1974. Herman describes the difficulties in building a national organisation whilst satisfying provincial concerns for retaining local authority.

boards, which depended more on networking by the relatively few members to give and receive feedback. Federated Farmers considered itself to be the farmers' prime representative but more frequently government used the statutory boards to represent community views. Unsurprisingly, tension between Federated Farmers and the boards became permanent in producer politics.

In the early twentieth century the trading relationship between the two countries gave New Zealand a reliable and consistent market for its primary produce, and gave Britain a reliable and consistent market for its industrial exports together with reliable food and wool supplies. But the 1930s Depression made international trading unreliable. Britain 'gave up free trade in 1932' with Britain and Commonwealth countries mitigating the impact of the Depression by meeting at Ottawa, and agreeing trade arrangements based on 'Imperial Preference', a version of proposals for Empire tariff reform that had been advocated in both Britain and New Zealand since the start of the twentieth century.[9] Through those agreements Britain restricted imports from non-Commonwealth countries but continued to accept imports duty-free from Commonwealth countries, such as New Zealand, in return for preferential treatment of British exports.

Despite the Ottawa agreements, doubts grew in the later 1930s whether Britain could absorb New Zealand's produce in the long term. The trading difficulties which had led to the Ottawa agreements made New Zealand's trade 'more vulnerable' and it could 'no longer take for granted its trade with Britain'.[10] Britain introduced short-term quotas for New Zealand beef from 1935 and only 'very strong protests' by New Zealand stopped Britain introducing quotas for butter and cheese.[11] Walter Nash, New Zealand's Finance Minister from 1935,

[9] John Singleton and Paul Robertson, *Economic Relations between and Australasia 1945–1970* (Basingstoke: Palgrave, 2002), 7; Thomson, 1977: 199; Carol Neill, *Trading Our Way: Developments in New Zealand's Trade Policy 1930s to 1980s*, Doctoral Book, Massey University, Palmerston North, 2010, 44/45. Neill reports New Zealand's Prime Minister, William Massey, as an advocate of Imperial Preference from well before the Ottawa Conference.

[10] Neill, 51.

[11] Baker, 14.

had recognised in 1934 that 'the ultimate saturation of the British Market with products now exported to it from New Zealand will compel the reorganisation of our primary producers'.[12] But World War II intervened and postponed the saturation of the British market by at least two decades.

Nash, as Minister of Finance in the New Zealand's first Labour government, introduced a guaranteed price scheme for dairy farmers in 1936. To support that scheme he wanted 'a bilateral deal with Britain that would enable him to even out prices at a high level for a period of years'.[13] Nash sought fixed contracts for New Zealand's primary produce but was unsuccessful until World War II threatened disruption of British trading with others and made New Zealand's produce more important for Britain. Britain then agreed to purchase all primary produce surplus to New Zealand's domestic needs.[14] That bulk purchase proved 'of inestimable value' in giving security to New Zealand's primary production and very profitable.[15] Even into the 1970s when lamb prices fell the Meat Board could 'bolster returns' to producers using the '$100 million . . . legacy of the wartime UK Bulk Purchase agreement'.[16] New Zealand profited from the agreements financially but they tied New Zealand even more strongly to the British market – New Zealand needed British permission to sell in other markets.

2.3 After World War II

Their joint contributions to World War II ensured close, sentimental, relations between Britain and New Zealand, but bulk purchase of food and wool during the War made New Zealand over-dependent on trade with Britain. The relationship resembled that of a colony rather than an

[12] Keith Sinclair, *Walter Nash* (Auckland: Auckland University Press, 1976), 134.

[13] Sinclair, 127.

[14] Sinclair, 189.

[15] Hayward, 84.

[16] Mick Calder and Janet Tyson, *Meat Acts: The New Zealand Meat Industry 1972–1997* (Wellington: Meat New Zealand, 1999), 17.

independent dominion. The War had given New Zealand a false reprieve from the uncertainties in future trading with Britain that threatened in the 1930s, but uncertainties soon reappeared and primary producers became disillusioned and thought Britain exploited New Zealand's goodwill. Also, Britain's precarious financial status encouraged it to develop its own agriculture to reduce food imports. New Zealand sought increased independence from Britain, both politically and economically, but faced the dilemma that reducing preferences for British exports to New Zealand might encourage Britain to opt for European unification rather than continuing to prioritise Commonwealth trade. By the 1960s, the New Zealand government and most primary producers accepted the inevitability of changing to new markets.

Victory during World War II saw expressions of intense admiration in both Britain and New Zealand and the relations between the two were possibly at their closest. On Waitangi Day in 1945, celebrating the signing of the Treaty in 1840 through which Britain took over sovereignty of New Zealand from the indigenous, Maori, population, *The Times* in London carried a major article in which it eulogised New Zealand's contribution to the War and the strong ties between Britain and New Zealand. *The Times* reported that

> the New Zealand Prime Minister at the outbreak of war had said: 'Where Britain goes we go, where she stands we stand.' New Zealanders have never swerved from this declaration of national spirit . . . New Zealand has provided huge shipments of food for allied forces in the Pacific . . . and sent heavy cargoes of food to Britain by making ungrudging sacrifices of luxuries in a land of plenty.[17]

In celebrating Victory-in-Europe in May 1945 *Straight Furrow* similarly eulogised Britain and the British people

> viewed in retrospect there can be few more glorious pages in British history than those of 1940–41 when Britain stood alone against the Axis

[17] 'New Zealand's Day', *The Times*, 06/02/1945, 3, ATL.

powers . . . in the ultimate the deciding factor in this war has been the solid character of the people of Britain.[18]

Straight Furrow reported the Federated Farmers President telling farmers 'History had probably never before recorded the case of a nation . . . willing to go hungry itself in order to save its enemies from starvation . . . Britain did just that', adding 'amidst loud applause' – 'that is the race we proudly spring from'.[19] He was referring to Britain cutting its own people's rations to feed the famine-threatened populace of defeated Germany.[20]

Britons and New Zealanders considered the British Empire and Commonwealth to be a great power, perhaps even the greatest power, and undoubtedly a force for good in the world. New Zealand saw itself making a prime contribution, using its advantages from climate to provide food for Britain, 'home' for Dominions such as New Zealand. In World War II's aftermath, New Zealand's most significant market by far was Britain and primary produce dominated New Zealand's exports (Figs 1.2 and 1.3). It is clear from Fig. 1.2 why Keith Sinclair concluded that 'New Zealand . . . was singularly vulnerable and paralysingly dependent on Britain'.[21]

In 1945 New Zealand's trading role, despite the country's independent status as a Dominion, resembled a dependent colony providing raw materials for Britain. Robert Muldoon, New Zealand's Finance Minister from the 1960s, and Prime Minister and Finance Minister in the 1970s and early 1980s, reports how New Zealand 'became and remained Britain's offshore farm' between 1830 and World War II.[22] In 1945 the Ministry of Agriculture used producers' pride in that status to encourage increased productivity, exhorting producers that 'there

[18] 'Victory in Europe', *Straight Furrow*, 15/05/1945, 3, ATL.

[19] 'Britain's Help to Germany', *Straight Furrow*, 16/09/1946, 3, ATL.

[20] Alan Bullock, *Ernest Bevin: Foreign Secretary, 1945–1951* (London: William Heinemann Ltd., 1983), 232.

[21] Sinclair, 135.

[22] Robert Muldoon, *The New Zealand Economy: A Personal View* (Auckland: Endeavour Press Ltd., 1985), 11.

must be no let up if New Zealand is to continue to play the important role of dairy farm to Great Britain'.[23] A 'colonial economy remained entrenched' after World War II because New Zealand stinted its own importing to assist Britain's recovery 'out of sentiment and self-interest'.[24] Boris Schedvin claims that New Zealand suffered from the 'staples trap', a common feature leading to dependence amongst former settler colonies on decisions made early in the history of the colonies. In New Zealand's case, successful staples' exports such as meat and dairy products in the late nineteenth and early twentieth centuries, together with its relatively small population and location, made it difficult for New Zealand to adapt to meet the changing international situation.[25]

Felicity Barnes argues that New Zealanders strove to demonstrate that their country was distinct from 'exotic' colonies and that it was 'emphatically a white country populated by British people' but many historians agree that New Zealand's dependence on Britain amounted to colonisation.[26] James Belich calls New Zealand's dependence on the British market 'recolonisation' because 'New Zealand became a town-supply district of London. London became the cultural capital of New Zealand.'[27] Barnes expands on that theme that New Zealand became an integral part of London despite its geographic location.[28] McAloon suggests that the term recolonisation was

> a summary description for the economic, cultural and political domination of New Zealand by Great Britain, a domination which was driven by refrigeration and narrowed the New Zealand economy massively.[29]

[23] Department of Agriculture, 'New Zealand Is Britain's Dairy Farm', *Straight Furrow*, 15/11/1945, 32, ATL.

[24] McAloon, 54.

[25] Boris Schedvin, 'Staples and regions of the Pax Britannica', *Economic History Review*, 43, 4, 1990, 533–59.

[26] Felicity Barnes, *New Zealand's London: A Colony and Its Metropolis* (Auckland: Auckland University Press, 2012), 151.

[27] Belich, 29–30.

[28] Barnes, 124.

[29] McAloon, 15.

Stuart Ward has defined the equivalent relationship between Australia and Britain as 'the British Embrace', a relationship that he considered to be unhealthy, claiming that Australian leaders such as Menzies 'put Australia to sleep through . . . fawning obsequiousness . . . to his beloved Britain'.[30] The economic narrowing in New Zealand bothered William Sutch; he questioned New Zealand's status – a colony or a nation?[31] In Sutch's view:

> the discovery of refrigeration diverted activities towards grassland farming, and since then our whole economic structure and our state and private institutions have been directed primarily towards grassland farmers. Other activities have had to fit into this pattern. The pattern has never been a healthy one.[32]

Following World War II, New Zealand had become 'paralysingly dependent' on a country for which the twentieth-century World Wars had changed its status profoundly for the worse. Michael Stewart succinctly describes the change:

> With stunning suddenness, the Second World War transformed Britain from a great power to a minor one, from a creditor to a debtor, from the ruler of an Empire to a member of the Commonwealth.[33]

For individual Britons, victory in World War II disguised that the war's expense had lost Britain its pre-eminent position as the world's banker and had turned Britain into the world's largest debtor.[34] To Edward Heath, British Prime Minister from 1970 to 1974, Britain tried to act as

[30] Stuart Ward, *Australia and the British Embrace: Demise of the Imperial Ideal* (Victoria: Melbourne University Press, 2001), 11.

[31] William Sutch, 'Colony or Nation?', in Michael Turnbull (ed.), *Economic Crises in New Zealand from the 1860s to the 1960s* (Sydney: Sydney University Press, 1968), 182.

[32] Sutch, 182.

[33] Michael Stewart, *Keynes and After* (Harmondsworth: Penguin Books, 1975), 185.

[34] D. Urwin, *A Political History of Western Europe since 1945* (Harlow: Pearson Education, 1997), 24.

a major imperial power for a decade after World War II.[35] A British senior diplomat recalled:

> We emerged from World War Two as co-victors with the United States. I think this gave the country . . . the illusion that we were somehow on par with the United States. That of course was a total illusion.[36]

To David Thomson:

> If war had been avoided in 1939, Britain would [still] have had to face tasks of economic overhaul and social reconstruction. . . . The problems of post-war Britain were to a large extent the endemic problems of twentieth-century Britain – of old and famous industries struggling to survive in unfavourable conditions.[37]

But the war made matters worse because Britain had spent 'vast overseas assets and incurred large foreign debts' to pay for the war, including purchases in dollars equivalent to the cost of sixteen years of imports from the USA.[38] Eighteen million tons of shipping had been lost from Britain's merchant fleet and only two-thirds had been replaced. Britain had become geared to war production and had coped during the war only because

> all essential supplies which would normally be paid for by dollars or hard currency were in effect obtained free from the United States' through the Lend-Lease arrangement.[39]

[35] Edward Heath, *The Course of My Life: My Autobiography* (London: Hodder and Stoughton, 1999), 147.

[36] Gustafson, *Holyoake*, 290.

[37] Thomson, 217.

[38] Keith Robbins, *The Eclipse of a Great Power: Modern Britain 1870–1992* (Harlow: Longman, 1994), 214.

[39] J. M. Livingstone, *Britain in the World Economy* (Harmondsworth: Penguin Books Ltd., 1971), 44.

Post-war Britain needed to return to earning its living through exports. But those were insufficient to enable Britain to procure essential imports, for instance, food. Britain needed its exports to reach 175% of the pre-war annual level within five years to be able to rebuild its reserves and pay its wartime debts.[40] Britain had become dependent financially on the USA, demonstrating its financial dependence through its need to secure a major loan from the USA to bolster its financial position in 1945 when Lend-Lease ended.[41] Britain saw its relations with the USA as a 'special relationship' but in 1956, when Britain attempted to take the Suez Canal from Egypt by force, the one-sidedness of the relationship became even more obvious than during the financial negotiations of 1945. The USA opposed the Suez action and forced Britain to withdraw finally destroying any remaining illusion within Britain that Britain was on par with the USA.[42]

Britain's fear of blockade during World War II first gave a 'fresh impetus' to rebuilding its domestic agriculture, and when the war ended Britain reaffirmed the rebuilding because its financial penury threatened purchase of essential food imports.[43] Britain could reduce import spending by becoming more self-sufficient in growing its own food, and introduced legislation to that effect in 1947. A British MP, Captain Crookshank, summarised for the British House of Commons: 'we must have a highly productive home agriculture to conserve foreign exchanges'.[44] Despite political bickering over detail, all the main British political parties supported the policy. The policy made little difference in the short term but implied that in the long term (perhaps two decades) food imports from countries such as New Zealand would be reduced.

When Britain's Empire mutated into the Commonwealth that mutation disguised that Britain had lost its identity as a major imperial power.

---

[40] Robbins, 214.

[41] Peter Clarke, *The Last Thousand Days of the British Empire* (London: Penguin, 2007), 430.

[42] Robert Rhodes James, *Anthony Eden* (London: Weidenfield and Nicholson Ltd., 1986), 584.

[43] Thomson, 209.

[44] 'Government Policy For Agriculture', *The Times*, 28/01/1947, 8.

After World War II, the British at first still 'viewed their economic ties with the Commonwealth as of greater value than their ties with Europe'.[45] In addition, the 'Sterling Area' tied the Commonwealth together. Within the Sterling Area

> trade was financed by sterling accounts [kept in London] that could not be converted into dollars to buy non-empire goods. Britain purchased food from the dominions, which used their receipts to buy British manufactures.[46]

Dollar shortages restricted purchase of goods from the USA after World War II and made the Sterling Area especially important.[47]

The USA resented the discrimination against itself inherent in the Sterling Area and Imperial Preference arrangements and, during the discussions leading to the General Agreement on Trade and Tariffs (GATT) after World War II, the USA offered tariff reductions to persuade Commonwealth countries to abandon Imperial Preferences.[48] But its agricultural community forced it to retain protection against imports from countries such as New Zealand, thereby weakening the case for eliminating the preferences. In addition, the Dominions were determined to keep the preferences; Nash, who led the New Zealand delegation at the GATT discussions, welcomed potential USA tariff relaxation but expressed even more relief that 'the full slate of American requests to eliminate preferences had been denied'.[49]

In 1948 in New Zealand an 'Aid for Britain' campaign demonstrated an underlying unease. The New Zealand government 'stage-managed'

[45] Singleton and Robertson, *Relations*, 146.

[46] T. W. Zeiler, *Free Trade, Free World; the Advent of GATT* (Chapel Hill: The University of North Carolina Press, 1999), 22.

[47] Peter Cain and Anthony Hopkins, *British Imperialism: 1688–2000* (Harlow: Pearson Education Ltd., 2002), 408.

[48] Zeiler, 105.

[49] Zeiler, 123.

the start of the campaign to be seen as responding to British calls for help with its food shortages but 'keeping faith with . . . the needs of the British increasingly seemed outdated'.[50] The New Zealand government reluctantly supported the Aid for Britain campaign: 'ministers and officials were becoming increasingly exasperated' by Britain's demands for help to overcome its financial difficulties.[51] The Aid for Britain campaign successfully encouraged many individuals to contribute food parcels but dairy production did not increase, certainly not by the 25% the campaign chairman told Britain would be possible.[52] The Awahura Co-operative Dairy Company decided specifically to take no action, perhaps a typical response.[53] A decrease in meat exports to Britain accompanied the exhortations for the Aid for Britain campaign.[54] Admiration for Britain amongst producers turned into disillusion, especially when they learnt they received less for their exports than other countries.[55]

Trade discussions in the late 1940s demonstrated the growing eagerness of New Zealand, Australia, Canada and South Africa to become less dependent on Britain. But 'Britain hoped to continue to dominate the Commonwealth . . . while the Dominions sought greater autonomy' both within and outside the association.[56] McAloon's interpretation is that after World War II: 'New Zealand was, out of sentiment and self-interest, committed to assisting British industrial recovery' but 'New Zealand ministers and officials became increasingly irked by

[50] McAloon, 70; Michael Bassett, *The State in New Zealand 1840–1984: Socialism Without Doctrines?* (Auckland: Auckland University Press, 1998), 319.

[51] McAloon, 70.

[52] 'Time to Put Aside Personal Recriminations', *Straight Furrow*, 15/10/1949, 1, ATL.

[53] *Minutes of the Awahuri Co-operative Dairy Company*, Minute Book, 1947, Massey University Archives, 154.

[54] Malcolm McKinnon, *The Impact of War: A Diplomatic History of New Zealand's Economic Relations with Britain, 1939–1954*, Doctoral Book, Victoria University Wellington, Wellington, 1981, 318.

[55] McKinnon, *Impact*, 321.

[56] Francine MacKenzie, *Redefining the Bonds of Commonwealth 1939–1948* (New York: Palgrave Macmillan, 2002), 12. MacKenzie uses the international discussions of trade relationships between 1939 and 1948 to illustrate how New Zealand, Australia, South Africa and Canada sought to establish their roles as independent countries in those discussions.

London's demands'.[57] Changes in political relationships accompanied developments in Commonwealth trading relationships. In the 1946 'Canberra Agreement', Australia and New Zealand demonstrated how they saw future relations between South Pacific countries, the first time such an agreement did not include Britain.[58] Clearly, New Zealand needed to rely on Britain to buy its exports but, after British failures against the Japanese in World War II, New Zealand could no longer rely on Britain for security.[59] In 1952 New Zealand and Australia reduced their dependence on Britain further by moving away from their close military connections with Britain and relying on the USA for their security through the ANZUS pact.[60]

'Centrifugal forces' in the 1950s weakened Commonwealth trade with Britain and those included

> a rising current of tension in relations with Britain over issues such as the payment of subsidies to UK farmers, industrial protection in Australia and New Zealand, the inability of Britain to satisfy the dominions' thirst for capital.[61]

Centrifugal forces grew when bulk purchase ended. This gave New Zealand freedom to seek trade agreements with others that would discriminate against British imports.[62] Also, New Zealand had been attempting for more than a decade to develop secondary industry that replaced the need for British imports.[63] Canada and Australia, also,

---

[57] McAloon, 54.

[58] Malcolm McKinnon, *Independence and Foreign Policy: New Zealand in the World since 1935* (Auckland: Auckland University Press, 1993), 55.

[59] Neill, 88; key examples of British failure were the loss of Singapore and the sinking of the battleships the *Prince of Wales* and the *Repulse*.

[60] Henry Brands, From ANZUS to SEATO: United States Strategic Policy towards Australia and New Zealand, 1952-1954, *The International History Review*, Vol. 9, No. 2 (May, 1987), 250-270.

[61] Singleton and Robertson, *Relations*, 1-2.

[62] John Singleton, 'New Zealand, Britain and the survival of the Ottawa agreement, 1945-77', *The Australian Journal of Politics and History*, 43, 2, 1997, 168.

[63] Sinclair, 174-5; Neill, 67.

sought increased trade with countries other than Britain.[64] The preferences given to Britain in the Ottawa Agreements made imports expensive for Canada, Australia and New Zealand and inhibited their trade deals with new customers; unsurprisingly, those countries sought to reduce the preferences.[65]

Attempts by New Zealand, Australia and Canada to reduce preferences for British industrial imports gave Britain concern that priority for Commonwealth trade over European trade might no longer be in Britain's best interests. The British President of the Board of Trade, Peter Thorneycroft, said in 1956 'There was no prospect of our being able to pursue our policies undisturbed' and explained why:

> [I]t had been the aim of... [British] commercial policy to secure the advantages of liberal trade practices in the world at large while retaining the benefit of the preferences [*sic*] system within the Commonwealth. This policy was now under pressure and we could no longer expect to continue to enjoy the best of both worlds. Australia had taken the initiative in seeking a review of the preferences system and New Zealand would follow her lead.... We might soon be confronted in Europe by a powerful discriminatory economic bloc, dominated by Germany and developing into a formidable base for German competition in our markets overseas.[66]

Australia reached agreement with Britain in late 1956 to revise their Ottawa Agreement and the New Zealand government proposed in 1957, as predicted by Thorneycroft, revising its agreement in New Zealand's favour. A major trade mission travelled to Britain in 1957 to press for revising New Zealand's Ottawa Agreement, but the New Zealand government remained unclear on how far revision should be pushed. The Cabinet disliked the phrase 're-negotiating Ottawa'

---

[64] Ward, S., 32.

[65] McAloon, 72. McAloon points out that the disadvantages of preferences for British imports in New Zealand; 'having to pay higher prices for imports' was recognised in the late 1940s, 72; Hiroyuki Ogawa, 'Britain's Commonwealth Dilemma: Discussions with Australia, Canada and New Zealand and Transition of British Trade Policy 1956–59', *Contemporary British History*, 17, 3, 2003, 1–28.

[66] Singleton and Robertson, *Relations*, 1.

because it might open the door for Britain to weaken links with the Commonwealth at a time of moves towards European unification.[67] Holyoake led the New Zealand delegation and felt it necessary to emphasise that the trade mission intended to strengthen ties with Britain.[68] He wanted to avoid the impression that renegotiating the Ottawa Agreement would break ties with Britain. During the trade discussions, there was no agreement on the Ottawa preferences though Britain noted that New Zealand considered that the discussions had been postponed rather than concluded. Singleton points out that 'raising the issue of British preferences had almost backfired on Holyoake, and had only served to emphasise the limitations of New Zealand's bargaining power relative to the UK'.[69]

One success for the 1957 trade mission was that unrestricted access for New Zealand dairy produce up to 1967 was agreed, bringing dairy in line with arrangements already in place for the meat industry. But Holyoake returned from the 1957 trade talks recognising that New Zealand's traditional dependence on Britain could not continue undisturbed. Holyoake expressed pessimism about prospects for the British market after the agreements for unrestricted access ended in 1967.[70] But, new markets could not be found easily. Jack Marshall, Holyoake's Deputy Prime Minister and Overseas Trade Minister, explained the problems facing New Zealand primary producers:

> Many of the developed countries excluded our meat and dairy produce to protect their own inefficient farmers, who in many cases received subsidies to encourage them to produce more. The less developed countries which needed our food exports could not pay for them.[71]

[67] *Salient points of telephone conversation, Holyoake and Watts*, Keith Holyoake papers, MS-1814, 68/04, 14/05/1957, ATL.

[68] 'Minister's Overseas Visit', *Straight Furrow*, 01/04/1957, 3, ATL.

[69] Singleton, 168.

[70] Gustafson, *Holyoake*, 75/6; McAloon, 98, also describes Holyoake as 'ahead of his colleagues' in seeing the need for change.

[71] John Marshall, *Memoirs Vol II; 1960–1988* (Auckland: William Collins Ltd., 1989), 134.

The restrictions imposed by developed countries on imports of livestock products reinforced New Zealand's reliance on Britain. In particular, it was difficult to sell butter and lamb outside Britain. New Zealand needed to hang onto the British market despite the disadvantages and that constrained New Zealand's trade.[72]

In late 1957 Labour won the general election in New Zealand and the new government continued to press Britain to change Imperial Preference arrangements. When Nash, the new Prime Minister, threatened to terminate the Ottawa agreement, Britain finally agreed that New Zealand could 'resort to a limited measure of bilateral trading' provided that caused no 'serious harm' to British exporters.[73] New Zealand could now reduce selectively the Ottawa tariff preferences but not place quota restrictions on British manufactures. The changes in the New Zealand–British trade relationship, accompanied by changes in Australia and Canada, 'accelerated longer term movement in Britain's external trade policy away from the Commonwealth towards Europe' and encouraged Britain's first application to join the EEC in 1961.[74] The New Zealand's Cabinet's fears before the 1957 trade mission proved justified that 'renegotiating Ottawa' would encourage Britain's move towards European unification.

[72] Singleton and Robertson, *Relations*, 2.

[73] Singleton and Robertson, *Relations*, 119–120.

[74] Ogawa, 24.

3

A Brutal Snapping of the Anglo-New Zealand Nexus?

3.1 Introduction

The formation of the EEC in 1955 gave Britain a dilemma; it could join only by reducing or abandoning the Imperial Preference arrangements with the Commonwealth countries. The dilemma was first put to one side by Britain standing aloof from the developments in continental Europe but eventually economic pressures forced Britain to investigate whether a compromise might be possible. Whilst de Gaulle remained President of France no compromise was possible and it was into the 1970s, after de Gaulle had retired, that a compromise was found with special arrangements being agreed for New Zealand. There are multiple interpretations of the economic impact those arrangements had on New Zealand.

3.2 Formation of the EEC and Britain's Dilemma

Continental Europeans realised by the mid-twentieth century that it was time to put an end to the inter-European wars that had culminated in World Wars I and II. Britain took part in discussions of how unification

D. Hall, *Emerging from an Entrenched Colonial Economy*, Palgrave Studies in Economic History, DOI 10.1007/978-3-319-53016-1_3

might be achieved but would not agree to any arrangement that involved giving up sovereignty. But the economic success of the EEC when matched against Britain's own economic struggles made Britain gravitate towards changing its mind.

In the 1950s, six continental European nations (France, the Federal Republic of Germany, Italy, Belgium, Netherlands and Luxembourg) recognised that their economies had suffered terribly through the World Wars and those countries were 'torn and exhausted by internecine wars . . . and were in the mood for cooperation'.[1] The six decided to forgive and forget past conflict and to work together, seeing themselves as partners rather than former enemies, and in 1955 agreed to form a European Economic Community (EEC).[2] Britain took part in the talks and may have joined if the EEC had been solely a customs union. But the continental Europeans wanted a customs union which managed national trade for everyone's benefit; that involved some sacrifice of national sovereignty, something Britain would not accept.[3] Following World War II Britons saw themselves as

> intrinsically superior . . . and were dealing with the vanquished. . . . There was no reason why Britain needed to take part in European unification except to encourage the vanquished to unify.[4]

Britons clung to the view that relationships with the USA and the Commonwealth made themselves distinct from continental Europeans. The British Labour government's National Executive in 1950 rejected participation in European unification by concluding:

---

[1] J. M. Livingstone, *Britain in the World Economy* (Harmondsworth: Penguin Books Ltd., 1971), 110.

[2] Martin Dedman, *The Origins and Development of the European Union: 1945–95* (Abingdon: Routledge, 2000), 57.

[3] J. Young, 'The Parting of the Ways'?: Britain, the Messina Conference and the Spaak Committee, June–December 1955, in M Dockrill and J Young (ed.), *British Foreign Policy, 1945–56* (London: Macmillan Press Ltd., 1989), 197–224. Young shows how British foreign policy had become one of reacting on a day-by-day basis rather than looking ahead strategically, partly reflecting the failings of Eden as a Prime Minister.

[4] Edward Heath, *The Course of my Life: My Autobiography* (London: Hodder and Stoughton, 1999), 122.

> we in Britain are far closer to our kinsmen in Australia and New Zealand on the far side of the world than we are to Europe . . . in language and origins, in social habits and institutions, in political outlook and in economic interest.[5]

In the late 1950s the centrifugal forces tending to separate Britain from the Commonwealth started to be accompanied by gravitational forces drawing Britain into the EEC. Gustafson points out that

> [b]y the 1960s the European markets adjacent to Britain were becoming increasingly large and wealthy. The Commonwealth countries were generally poorer and were diversifying their imports away from Britain.[6]

The EEC's commercial success in its early years, with its productivity and its combined Gross National Product (GNP) increasing far more than Britain, made Britain's need to join urgent.[7] It had excluded itself from a dynamic customs union populated by 170 million people and, in contrast, the undeveloped Commonwealth new nations comprised a poor market for British goods and the relatively rich Dominions had only 30 million people.[8] Whilst outside the EEC Britain faced high tariffs in European major markets, which made British goods uncompetitive.

3.3 Britain's Applications to Join the EEC and Responses in New Zealand

Britain's potential membership of the EEC posed the threat that Britain would no longer allow free and unrestricted entry for New Zealand's meat and dairy produce. Those arrangements could not continue with Britain inside an EEC as originally envisaged by its founder members.

---

[5] Alan Bullock, *Ernest Bevin: Foreign Secretary, 1945–1951* (London: William Heinemann Ltd., 1983), 782.

[6] Barry Gustafson, *Kiwi Keith: A Biography of Keith Holyoake* (Auckland: Auckland University Press, 2007), 291.

[7] Dedman, 112.

[8] Livingstone, 95.

The EEC sought to protect agriculture within the Community through its Common Agricultural Policy (CAP) which included tariffs against those outside. The New Zealand government's Financial Statement in 1961 recorded those fears: 'Our contractual right of duty-free and unrestricted access to the United Kingdom market for our main export products remains the basis of our trading policy' and Britain's entry into the EEC 'could seriously affect our export trade in meat and dairy products'.[9] Britain's first application was in 1961 but it was not until its third application in 1970 that Britain was accepted.

In 1960 it seemed clear to the British government that Britain needed to join the EEC to maintain its role as a major global power. From the start, sentiment made Britain try to join whilst avoiding harm to the Commonwealth. The British Prime Minister, Harold Macmillan, himself remained aware that New Zealand trade needed protection; he considered the New Zealand position to be a 'very special one' that 'must be dealt with in a special way'.[10] Ward describes the British sentiments:

> The enormous weight of British history and tradition imposed a moral obligation on the British Government to consider the welfare of Commonwealth countries as a natural extension of British national interests. . . . The Commonwealth was the object of genuine public sentiment in Great Britain, and abandoning preferential arrangements with the 'British' Dominions and former colonies and replacing these with new preferences in favour of 'foreigners' on the European continent seemed nothing short of preposterous [to public sentiment in Britain].[11]

The New Zealand government demonstrated its first responses to Britain's approach to the EEC at the Commonwealth Finance Ministers' meeting in October 1960. Arnold Nordmeyer, the New Zealand Finance Minister, took an unrelenting attitude in making New Zealand's

[9] 'Financial Statement', *Appendices to the Journal of the House of Representatives (AJHR)*, 1961, Vol. I, B-6, 8/9, Wellington Central Library (WCL).

[10] Harold Macmillan, *At the End of the Day: 1961–1963* (London: Macmillan, 1973), 349.

[11] Stuart Ward, *Australia and the British Embrace: Demise of the Imperial Ideal* (Victoria: Melbourne University Press, 2001), 46.

opposition to British membership clear, warning that any move which threatened New Zealand's traditional market for primary produce 'we could not contemplate with other than very serious concern'.[12] The 1960 election brought National, led by Holyoake, back into power and changed the New Zealand government's approach from Nordmeyer's unrelenting stance. Holyoake viewed Britain's potential EEC membership as regrettable but a necessary evil. As a Prime Minister, Holyoake followed pragmatic rather than doctrinaire policies seeking the feasible and encouraging a consensus to emerge in public and parliamentary minds over a long period.[13] He recognised that, inevitably, Britain would join the massive EEC market on its doorstep and that New Zealand's approach should be to press for special arrangements. Gustafson contends that Holyoake, Prime Minister throughout Britain's attempts to join the EEC,

> came to appreciate that unless Britain joined the Common Market [EEC] she would become a second-rate offshore island and the world would to some extent pass her by and that if she was to remain strong . . . economically and politically . . . she would need to enter upon the European, and that meant Common Market, stage.[14]

Holyoake feared that if Britain became a second-rate offshore island New Zealand might well become second-rate remote islands in the South Pacific that the world passed by. Marshall, in his memoirs, notes that the new government

> had to take a more realistic attitude [than Labour] which recognised that we had no power of veto but which preserved our bargaining position if and when Britain took the plunge. So on 6 February 1961, less than two months after we took office, Cabinet met and decided what its basic policy should be if Britain applied to join the EEC. Briefly summarised, we said

---

[12] Notes of Meeting of Representatives of Producer Boards and Federated Farmers with the Minister of Finance, the Hon. A. H. Nordmeyer, 05/10/1960, T61/3/31 Commonwealth Economic Consultative Council – Finance Ministers Meeting London 1960, 2, Archives New Zealand (ANZ).

[13] Gustafson, *Holyoake,* 119.

[14] Gustafson, *Holyoake,* 4.

> that New Zealand's support for the objectives of political and economic unity in Europe depended on the preservation of our access to the British market, and particularly the right of free and unrestricted entry for our meat and dairy produce, rights which we considered vital to New Zealand's economic well-being.[15]

Marshall's recollections confirm that, amongst Commonwealth countries, New Zealand, 'the country which had most to lose', understood best Britain's problems.[16]

In July 1961, the British Secretary of State for Commonwealth Affairs, Duncan Sandys, visited New Zealand and gave an assurance that

> the British Government would seek to secure special arrangements to protect the vital interests of New Zealand, that Britain would not feel able to join the EEC unless such arrangements were secured.[17]

Britain's determination to retain Commonwealth links became a major contributory factor enabling the French President, de Gaulle, to reject Britain's application in 1963. Politics, economics and long-term suspicions between de Gaulle and Macmillan, all contributed to de Gaulle's actions, but in public de Gaulle based his rejection on Britain being insufficiently 'European'.[18] In doing so he reflected the views of many in Britain and New Zealand that Britain remained not just geographically but also culturally separate from continental Europe. De Gaulle described Britain at a press conference as follows:

[15] John Marshall, *Memoirs Vol II; 1960–1988* (Auckland: William Collins Ltd., 1989), 61.

[16] Livingstone, 128.

[17] Peter Tait, *In the Chair: the Public Life of Sir John Ormond* (Waipukurau: CHB Print, 1989), 99.

[18] Peter Mangold, *The Almost Impossible Ally: Harold Macmillan and Charles de Gaulle* (New York: I.B Taurus, 2006). Mangold shows how Macmillan and de Gaulle had worked together starting during World War II but Macmillan never managed to dispel the resentment by de Gaulle of the neglect shown to him (in his eyes) by the Americans and the British during that War. Into the 1960s the British and Americans worked together, for instance with Britain becoming dependent on the USA for nuclear missile delivery systems. De Gaulle again felt neglected in that relationship.

> Insular, she is maritime, she is linked through her exchanges, her markets, her supply lines to the most diverse and often the most distant countries... the very situation that are England's differ profoundly from those of the continentals.[19]

He had made a fair judgement; Britain wanted to join the EEC whilst retaining its strong connections with 'the most distant countries', such as New Zealand and Australia. Each successive British government, Labour and Conservative, stressed the need to protect New Zealand's interests in subsequent EEC negotiations.

A change in the British government in 1964, when Harold Wilson's Labour party replaced the Conservative party, at first seemed to weaken Britain's resolve to join the EEC. However, Wilson slowly evolved towards realising the advantages that EEC membership would bring, and in 1967 Britain requested membership for a second time. Wilson repeated specifically in Parliament the previous government's commitment that Britain would not enter the EEC without adequate safeguards for New Zealand.[20] De Gaulle again rejected Britain but retired in 1969 enabling Heath, who had become Prime Minister following the Conservative success in Britain's 1970 election, to lead Britain's third and successful bid and Britain became an EEC member on 1 January 1973.[21] Heath noted how he 'placed great emphasis... on the need for an acceptable settlement for New Zealand'.[22] The Labour party still led by Wilson returned to power in 1974 with the party split on Britain's EEC membership. Wilson intended to paper over cracks in his party by renegotiating the terms under which Britain joined, and then holding a

[19] Mangold, 199.

[20] Ben Pimlott, *Harold Wilson* (London: HarperCollins, 1992), 432–439. Pimlott shows how Wilson, himself, was at first strongly in favour of Commonwealth relationships but was gradually persuaded that Britain should at least investigate whether conditions were now ripe for a new bid for membership of the EEC. Marshall, 93, reports the Wilson announcement to the British Parliament in which he mentioned specifically that a satisfactory agreement would have to be found for New Zealand. Marshall notes, also, that the assurance was given by Herbert Bowden, the British Minister who visited New Zealand at that time.

[21] Heath, 372.

[22] Heath, 373.

referendum on the new terms with the government recommending that Britain stayed in the EEC. Wilson's government successfully renegotiated Britain's entry terms, including improving the arrangements for New Zealand, and then, in 1976, sought approval for Britain's continued membership; in the referendum Britons voted 67% in favour.[23]

3.4 The Impact of EEC Enlargement on New Zealand

Marshall led the New Zealand's negotiations on EEC matters, and in parallel New Zealand increased its diplomatic representation in continental Europe. Eventually, the EEC countries accepted that special consideration should be given to New Zealand, and the government and producers welcomed the arrangements agreed between Britain and the EEC. Those historians looking back from the twenty-first century and interpreting British EEC membership as a disaster for New Zealand's economy are not justified by the changes. New Zealand's economy was in difficulties in 1974 because problems in the Middle East made oil prices soar, not because Britain had joined the EEC. The weakening of the trade links with Britain by that time proved to be to New Zealand's benefit.

Through the 1960s Marshall negotiated with both Britain and the EEC countries but had to work through the British during the final negotiations in 1970/1971. Merwyn Norrish explains why we (New Zealand) 'come so well out of the Luxembourg negotiations in 1971, following which Britain joined the Community [EEC]'.[24] In support of Marshall, New Zealand strengthened its impact by increasing representation in the EEC capitals and the EEC Commission, and by inviting key European decision makers to New Zealand to meet the farming community to allay EEC fears of the impact of New Zealand

[23] Pimlott, 659.

[24] Merwyn Norrish, 'Merwyn Norrish' in Malcolm Templeton (ed.) *An Eye, An Ear And A Voice: 50 years in New Zealand's External Relations 1943–1993* (Wellington: Ministry of Foreign Affairs and Trade, 1993), 135.

farming on EEC agriculture.[25] In 1970, with the British/EEC negotiations well underway following Britain's third application for membership, the Opposition Leader in New Zealand, Norman Kirk, wanted New Zealand to embarrass Britain by appealing to EEC opponents in Britain to support New Zealand. Kirk said that New Zealand needed a more aggressive approach than the approach of 'if we were good boys we might get something out of it'.[26] Robertson and Singleton judge that an approach more belligerent than that adopted by Marshall and Holyoake would have jeopardised New Zealand's economic future even more.[27]

Marshall successfully negotiated with the EEC through the British government. His calm, gentlemanly, trusting approach towards Europeans maximised New Zealand's influence far more effectively than hysterical criticism from the touchline telling the British and Europeans how they should organise themselves. In 1970 Marshall said that the negotiations should be seen not as ending New Zealand's relationship with Britain but as New Zealand starting a new relationship with an enlarged EEC. Europe was important for New Zealand. New Zealand was not so important for Europe but he did not believe the Europeans would let New Zealand wither on the vine.[28] New Zealand benefitted from National winning the 1969 general election because that ensured Marshall remained the main contact with the EEC countries. Marshall had come under considerable pressure from the British to accept weaker terms but he demonstrated that under his outward 'gentlemanly' manner he had sufficient strength of character to be successful in 'brinkmanship'.[29] Marshall describes in his memoirs how

[25] Templeton (ed.), 136.

[26] 'Comforting Words About NZ Position "Not Good Enough"', *Straight Furrow*, 09/09/1970, 13, ATL.

[27] Paul Robertson and John Singleton, 'The Old Commonwealth and Britain's First Application to Join the EEC', *Australian Economic History Review*, 40, 2, 2000, 153. In 2014 the author put that question to some of the senior diplomats and politicians who were active in the second half of the twentieth century, all agreed with Robertson and Singleton's judgement.

[28] 'Mr Marshall Sees Start of New Era in NZ Trade', *Straight Furrow*, 09/09/1970, 30, ATL.

[29] McAloon, 142. McAloon reports how Marshall threatened to tell the British media that Britain was letting New Zealand down and, when Rippon doubted that Marshall would go that far, Marshall had responded 'You try me'.

his war service in Italy, together with that of Ian Stewart, New Zealand's Ambassador to Italy, influenced the outcome of the negotiations in New Zealand's favour.[30]

In June 1971, the EEC set out in the Luxembourg Protocol the arrangements agreed for New Zealand. Holyoake described arrangements as 'the best possible deal . . . they [the British] could get for us'.[31] In reporting the arrangements to the House of Representatives, Holyoake looked back with satisfaction on the concentrated efforts of those involved in the negotiations, including the producer boards; the collective effort had served the country well. He said that the British, in the midst of major preoccupations with issues vital for Britain's future, had always kept in mind the undertaking given to New Zealand and the settlement fulfilled those efforts. Holyoake said the arrangements would go a long way to avoid damage to New Zealand's economy; he concluded that disaster had been avoided. Marshall said in his address to the House of Representatives that the profound feelings of kinship and goodwill which the people of Britain had for New Zealand greatly strengthened New Zealand's position. It was deeply moving to find in the House of Commons, the news media and amongst people everywhere a unanimous determination that Britain should not go into Europe unless adequate provision was made to protect New Zealand.[32] Support from British MPs encouraged Marshall to 'remain firm' and enabled him to keep pressure on the British negotiators when they had been willing to accept less.[33] Those who had given that support included Duncan Sandys who told his Prime Minister in 1971 that he would not

[30] Marshall, 112. Both Marshall and Stewart were in the New Zealand Division that secured Trieste for Italy at the end of World War II by 'encouraging' the Yugoslavian occupiers to leave. Neither had used their war service to seek preferment and Stewart reported to the author that he was told, on being puzzled why Italy had negotiated hard on New Zealand's behalf for New Zealand's preferred dairy quota, 'we did it for Trieste' (in conversation with the author on 04/11/2014). Robert Muldoon, New Zealand finance minister at the time of the EEC settlement, was also involved in the Trieste campaign.

[31] Gustafson, *Holyoake*, 308.

[32] Rt. Hon. J.R. Marshall's Opening the Debate in the House of Representatives on the Special Arrangements for New Zealand, 01/07/1971, EEC – The agreement-statements and papers, ABOT W2670 6787 Box 2, 16, ANZ.

[33] Marshall, 107.

vote for British EEC membership in the House of Commons unless there was a fair settlement for New Zealand.[34] Marshall and Muldoon, in their memoirs, agree that the settlement substantially met the guarantee given by Sandys in 1961.[35] Muldoon, New Zealand's Finance Minister at the time of the final EEC negotiations leading to British membership, looking back fifteen years after the negotiations, says that 'Britain steadfastly supported our case . . . even at considerable cost to its own interests'.[36] Another outcome of British membership was that Britain lost the Imperial Preference arrangements for its exports to New Zealand as the 'cost for entry'.[37] That benefitted New Zealand by allowing increased flexibility in negotiating trade agreements with others and reducing inflationary pressures by lowering import costs.

One issue drawing multiple interpretations is the actual impact of British EEC membership on the New Zealand economy. Many in the twenty-first century attribute difficulties for the New Zealand economy in the 1970s and afterwards to Britain joining the EEC, judging the special arrangements agreed for New Zealand pessimistically. Singleton and Robertson say 'the Anglo-New Zealand nexus was finally, and brutally, snapped in 1973'.[38] Belich, based on the halving of the export percentage going to Britain in the decade after Britain became an EEC member, calls the day Britain became an EEC member 'a black-letter day in New Zealand history'. He describes Britain's EEC membership as the 'nemesis of the New Zealand–British recolonial system'.[39] Shane Brownie and Paul Dalziel, after reviewing New Zealand trade relative to world trade, decided that 'the potentially disastrous impact of Britain's entry . . . recognised . . . when it was first mooted . . . was amply justified'.[40]

[34] Heath, 374.

[35] Marshall, 112; Muldoon, 84.

[36] Muldoon, 38.

[37] Meeting with the Minister of Trade in the United Kingdom Government, 24/08/1971, Trade: United Kingdom: Dairy Produce 1971–1972, C 324 075 C1W2358 54 955/UK/1 Part 1, 2, ANZ.

[38] Singleton and Robertson, *Relations*, 6.

[39] Belich, 431.

[40] Shane Brownie and Paul Dalziel, 'Shift-share analyses of New Zealand exports, 1970–1984', *New Zealand Economic Papers*, 27, 2, 1993, 233–249.

In contrast to Belich and Brownie and Dalziel, whose judgements were made on the period after Britain joined the EEC, McAloon points out how the 'British market for New Zealand exports was weakening' from the mid-1950s and that the fall accelerated in the second half of the 1960s.[41] Brian Easton also reports the fall in the export percentage going to Britain in the late 1960s and early 1970s demonstrating that 'ties were already loosening' before Britain joined the EEC.[42] Easton describes Britain's EEC membership as not a 'decisive break, long before 1973 it had been evident that access to the British market was declining'. For Easton, it was a 'political, cultural and even emotional event for New Zealand ... rather than an economic event'.[43] Felicity Barnes has suggested that economic and cultural relationships were inseparable in the first half of the twentieth century during which, in order to sell their commodities in Britain, producer boards fostered the image that British consumers when buying New Zealand produce were buying food produced by Britons, 'Empire and Britishness became integral parts of New Zealand as a farm'.[44] In doing so as we shall see, the attitudes of some producer representatives were influenced by their own imagined England.[45] That cultural element made Britain's applications to join the EEC difficult for many producers to understand and reinforced the fears that there would be a significant economic impact.

Producer fears were reinforced by articles in *Straight Furrow*. Between 1948 and 1971, the period between the first proposals for a European Customs Union and the announcement of the special arrangements agreed for New Zealand, in 275 articles 58% expressed concern and anxiety over the impact of British membership and presented Britain as abandoning Commonwealth trade in favour of trade with Europe. Only

[41] McAloon, 142 – 143.

[42] Brian Easton, *The Nationbuilders* (Auckland: Auckland University Press, 2001), 183.

[43] Brian Easton, *In Stormy Seas: The Post-War New Zealand Economy* (Dunedin: University of Otago Press, 1997), 80.

[44] Felicity Barnes, *New Zealand's London: A Colony and Its Metropolis* (Auckland: Auckland University Press, 2012), 157.

[45] In 2014, the author asked a group of retired New Zealand farmers when they had stopped feeling 'British'. After a long period of musing, they agreed that they have never stopped feeling British.

12% supported British membership as possibly positive for New Zealand, many of those positive articles reporting the views of the British High Commission rather than New Zealanders. The remaining 30% of articles were neutral informing producers on EEC matters. In national and local newspapers more generally at the time of Britain's first application in the period from May 1961 to June 1962 the distribution of articles is similar – 48% negative against 12% positive with the remainder informative.[46] In the immediate years after the special arrangements were known, of 89 articles in *Straight Furrow*, there was still a strong preponderance of articles expressing anxiety (43% against 16% positive) but now accompanied by a higher percentage (41%) of neutral informative articles.

That long period of fear of the consequences of Britain joining European unification established a perception that was not changed by the actual outcome. To Easton, 'the common perception [in New Zealand] of the [negative] impact of Britain joining the EEC is an exaggeration', and there are still (in the twenty-first century) 'those who blame that event for the subsequent difficulties of the New Zealand economy – colonials wringing their hands because Mummy has rushed off with those Continentals'.[47] One example of that common perception is Philippa Mein Smith who stated in 2011 that New Zealanders in 1973 faced the 'prospect of compulsory decolonisation, at speed' and that it is a fair judgement to call Britain's actions a 'betrayal' and that Britain 'announced its decision . . . to abandon its colonial family of food producers for former enemies'.[48] That judgement by historians is reflected also in popular mythology – in March 2016 the journalist, Bill Ralston, in the *New Zealand Listener*, reported that

> [Britain] unceremoniously dumped us in the 1970s to run off with that tarty European Economic Community. That move cost us dearly. Then

[46] Newspaper clippings - Commonwealth and Common Market, June 1961 to February 1962 (European Economic Community - United Kingdom-European Economic Community Negotiations) AAFZ, 7174, W1318, Box 223, ANZ.

[47] Easton, *Nationbuilders*, 183.

[48] Philippa Mein Smith, *A Concise History of New Zealand* (Cambridge: Cambridge University Press, 2011), 207.

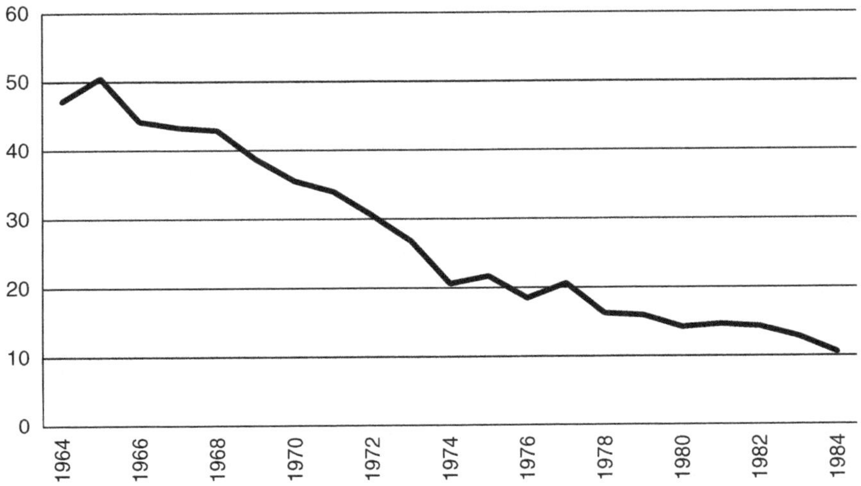

Fig. 3.1 Percentage of earnings from New Zealand exports sold to Britain (NZDYB)

> Prime Minister Rob Muldoon borrowed hugely to make up the loss of income from trade with the UK, poured heaps into some doomed 'Think Big' projects that were eventually mothballed and left the incoming Labour Government to hold a fire sale of our assets so we didn't end up like Greece is today.[49]

The changes in New Zealand's overall economy before and through the period of EEC enlargement are shown in Figs 3.1 and 3.2 and justify the judgements of Easton and McAloon that changes after Britain joined the EEC were simply a continuation of trends obvious in the 1960s. Belich in making his pessimistic judgement based on the halving of the percentage of exports going to Britain in the decade after it joined the EEC misses that during the 1970s the percentage change was less than in the preceding decade: the percentage halved (Fig. 3.1) in the eight years between 1966 (43.0%) and 1974 (20.5%). Also, the description of the changes by Singleton and Robertson – 'The Anglo-New Zealand nexus

[49] Bill Ralston, *New Zealand Listener*, 12 March 2016, 94.

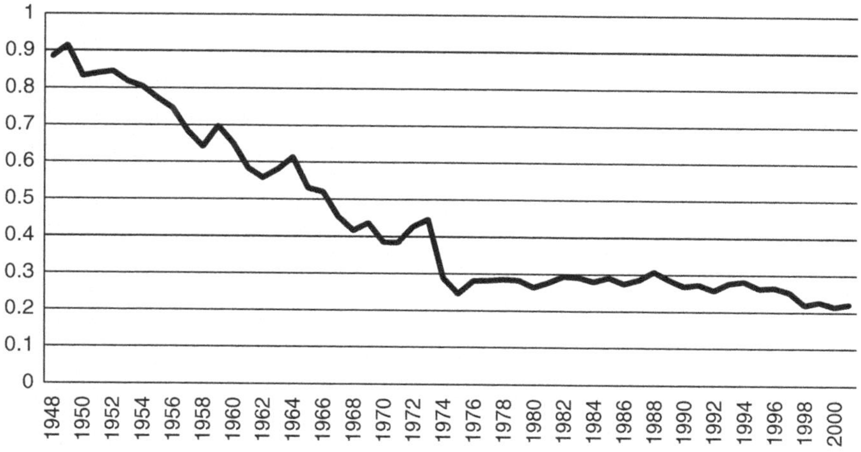

Fig. 3.2 New Zealand's percentage share of world trade (United Nations Conference on Trade and Development (UNCTAD))

was finally, and brutally, snapped in 1973' – is not justified: the decrease in the percentage of exports sold to Britain slowed down after 1973 rather than plummeted. Similarly, Brownie and Dalziel's judgement, based on New Zealand's reduced share of world trade after Britain joined the EEC, misses the point that New Zealand trade decreased relative to world trade far more before Britain joined (Fig. 3.2). The reduction in exports that most strongly influenced Brownie and Dalziel's conclusions took place in the early 1970s when two-thirds of the fall in New Zealand overseas earnings from primary produce was in wool, the export commodity least affected by Britain's membership of the EEC. Between 1950 and 1970 New Zealand's share of world trade decreased because there had been little room for export expansion to Britain, its dominant customer, whilst world trade otherwise increased significantly. After 1973 when New Zealand had diversified sufficiently that Britain took less than 50% of New Zealand exports, New Zealand's trade kept pace with the growth in world trade.

Undoubtedly, the New Zealand economy ran into difficulties coincidentally with 1973, the first year of British EEC membership. McAloon explains why. For the Labour government elected at the end of 1972, the 'biggest problem' during 1973 was managing 'a booming economy' that included 'high export earnings' and 'exporters had money to spend'. But an 'economic crisis of almost unprecedented severity' followed during which 'industrial economies rapidly fell into recession, and New Zealand's pastoral export prices fell precipitously'.[50] The quadrupling of oil prices following Egypt and Syria's invasion of Israel in October 1973 caused the crisis. Gustafson describes the New Zealand economy as 'shattered' by the end of 1974 and agrees that the cause was the 'collapse of economic growth round the world coupled with escalating prices for imported oil and declining prices for agricultural exports'.[51] It was a second oil shock in 1979, accompanying revolution in Iran well after Britain had joined the EEC, that led to Muldoon's 'think big' projects and the 'fire sale of assets' reported by Ralston.

3.5 Conclusion

How New Zealand primary production adapted and reduced its dependence on the British market, putting itself in a better position to cope with difficulties such as the 1973 oil price shock, is analysed in the following chapters. Those chapters demonstrate that the successful breaking away from dependence on Britain encouraged by Britain's engagement with the EEC should be celebrated, not mourned; it put New Zealand in a better position to cope with changes in international trading. It had moved away from over-dependence on a customer whose economy was stagnating to customers whose economies were rapidly developing.

[50] McAloon, 149–152.

[51] Barry Gustafson, *His Way: A Biography of Robert Muldoon* (Auckland: Auckland University Press, 2001), 164.

4

Meat and the British Market

4.1 Introduction

Chapter 4 analyses developments in New Zealand's meat exports to Britain. The British market is described for five specific periods: bulk purchase, from 1945 to 1950; increased belligerence at the perceived unfair treatment of New Zealand by Britain and the end of bulk purchase, from 1951 to 1954; growing doubts about future sales to Britain, from 1955 to 1957; the impact of Britain's growing engagement with European unification from 1956 to 1961; and the ending of duty-free and unrestricted access for New Zealand meat, from 1961 to 1975.

The story is one of an industry dominated by a strong personality, Sir John Ormond. Ormond welcomed the strong links with Britain and reluctantly accepted a weakening of the links. He retained support from producers because he was a strong well-publicised leader who stood up to government in both New Zealand and Britain. But independent exporters and meat producers recognised the changes taking place in Britain and the need for New Zealand to seek markets elsewhere. New Zealand successfully retained the British market whilst increasing

D. Hall, *Emerging from an Entrenched Colonial Economy*, Palgrave Studies in Economic History, DOI 10.1007/978-3-319-53016-1_4

earnings from new markets sufficiently that they overtook the earnings from Britain in the 1970s.

4.2 Continuation of Wartime Bulk Purchase

During World War II and in its immediate aftermath New Zealand meat producers supported Britain, partly through sentiment, and proposed making additional supplies available. Meat Board negotiators with Britain also held back from pressing for higher prices. Bulk purchase by Britain continued after the war and provided New Zealand with a guaranteed, profitable market for its exportable meat surplus, and no significant pressure to sell elsewhere. Britain would take all that New Zealand could produce at remunerative prices. In 1948, Britain's continuing food shortages led the New Zealand government to agree to increase meat supplies to Britain. But New Zealand failed to achieve the increase. By 1950, producers suspected that better prices might be obtained from sales to markets other than Britain and that Britain exploited New Zealand's loyalty. Sentiment began to disappear from the relationship.

Britain wrestled with economic recovery and food shortages after the disruption of World War II and needed additional supplies of meat. New Zealand producers were supportive and even before the war ended the New Zealand Meat Board resolved unanimously to increase meat shipments to Britain.[1] The Board recommended to the government that additional meat be sent by reducing the meat ration in New Zealand and had no doubt that New Zealanders would willingly accept the reduction.[2] Producers avoided exploiting Britain's financial position and food scarcity that made it a sellers' market. The Chairman of the Meat Board, Gilbert Grigg, thought sentiment should override calls to exploit Britain's weak position and seek higher prices, whilst recognising also that future earnings from the British market depended on Britain regaining its economic

[1] Meat Board Minute Book 8, 23/03/1945, 291, ANZ.

[2] Meat Board Minute Book 8, 18/05/1945, 308, ANZ.

strength. Grigg said that every additional gesture that strengthened Britain's financial position guaranteed New Zealand's future security and welfare.[3] Grigg's approach reflected the common view in 1946 that, undoubtedly, New Zealand would continue to depend on the British market.

Britain's long-term policy of free trade meant that it had become dependent on imported food, and in the period 1947–1949 produced, domestically, only 43% of its beef, lamb and mutton, importing the rest mainly from New Zealand (22%), Argentina (21%) and Australia (9%).[4] In the late 1940s, Britain needed additional food imports because political upheaval in Argentina, Britain's main source of imported beef, disrupted supplies to Britain. The new political regime of Juan Peron in Argentina took a more hard-line approach on prices and complicated sales to Britain by dispute over how to treat its sterling balances held in Britain as payment for wartime meat supply. By 1951 Argentinean exports to Britain had fallen to only 25% of the tonnage for the years 1947–1949 (Fig. 4.1).[5] Those political difficulties with Argentina made Britain seek extra food from the Sterling Area, especially, New Zealand and Australia.[6] The British Controller of Meat, Sir Henry Turner, during a visit to New Zealand in 1948, explained Britain's need by telling the Meat Board that Britain could not expand its own meat production quickly and Argentina sought to reduce supplies to the British market. Britain needed meat from the Southern Dominions. Turner supported his plea for increased production by giving an assurance that there would be a market in Britain for New Zealand's exportable surplus 'for a number of years to come'.[7] New Zealand meat producers saw that assurance as granting New Zealand the right to be a prime supplier for the British market, and in the 1940s and 1950s saw no end to that arrangement.

[3] 'Annual Meeting of the Meat Board', *Straight Furrow*, 15/09/1946, 21, ATL.

[4] Ottawa Agreement and Meat Trade with the United Kingdom, MSY-1814 068/1, Holyoake papers, 23/04/1956, Table I, 26, ATL.

[5] 'Two Agreements', *The Times*, 18/09/1946, 5.

[6] 'Argentine Meat Shipments', *The Times*, 17/12/1948, 4.

[7] Meat Board Minute Book 9, 07/04/1948, 528, ANZ.

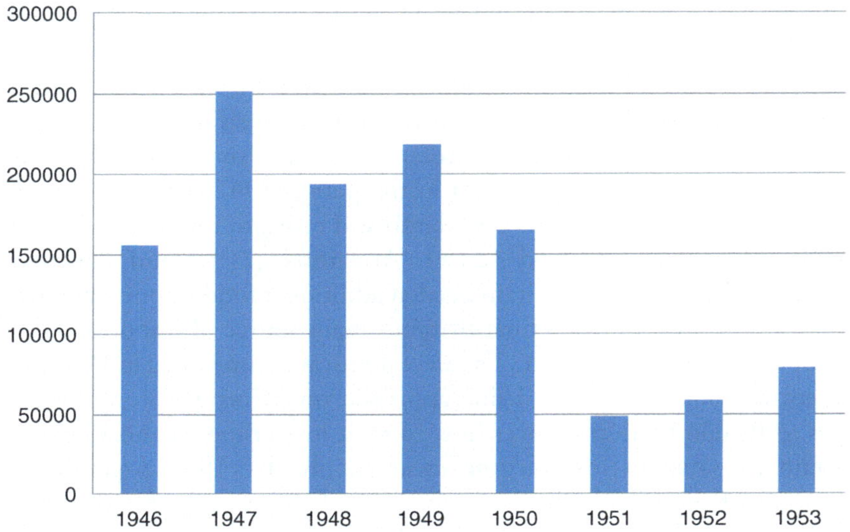

Fig. 4.1 Argentinean beef exports to Britain in tonnes (Source: Report on Argentine Beef, MS1814 – 068/6 Holyoake papers, 30/9/1956, Table II, p. 2, ATL)

In 1948 the New Zealand and British governments agreed that bulk purchase, originally seen as a wartime measure only, would continue until 1955 with annual price reviews and changes restricted to 7.5%.[8] For the bulk contract exports Britain provided and paid for freight, including coastal freight between New Zealand ports, giving New Zealand a major incentive to retain the contract.[9] An editorial in *Straight Furrow* demonstrated the supportive attitude towards Britain amongst producers, agreeing with the approach of 'not twisting England's tail' as it claimed Denmark and Argentina had done to secure even higher prices. The editorial said the New Zealand delegation

[8] Malcolm McKinnon, *The Impact of War: A Diplomatic History of New Zealand's Economic Relations with Britain, 1939–1954*, Doctorate Book, Victoria University Wellington, Wellington, 1981, 313–342, McKinnon describes in full the diplomatic exchanges between New Zealand and Britain over prices during the period of bulk purchase.

[9] 'Shipping Freights', *Straight Furrow*, 15/08/1946, 46, ATL.

'displayed real patriotism' (which it can be inferred translated into responsiveness to British concerns) and appreciated the realities because during World War II Britain had made a disproportionate contribution. In accepting prices lower than might have been the case, New Zealand bore a burden which could 'justly have been undertaken earlier on'.[10] In return for the extension of bulk purchase until 1955 and increased prices it was announced that

> [t]he New Zealand Government has agreed to put into operation a programme for increasing the production of meat with the object of steadily expanding exports to the United Kingdom until by the end of the contract period an increase of the order of 50,000 tons per annum over the present export tonnage will have been achieved.[11]

That would take the tonnage exported to Britain in 1955 to 400,000. The agreement made no provision for a penalty should New Zealand fail to deliver the agreed increase.[12] Including a penalty would have cast doubt on New Zealand's commitment and that would have been out of keeping with the trust between the two countries in 1948.

Meat tonnage exported by New Zealand to Britain in 1955 decreased from that in 1948 by nearly 40,000 tons rather than increasing by more than 50,000 tons as agreed during the 1948 bulk purchase negotiations. The tonnages exceeded that in 1948 in only one year, by 11,000 in 1952 (Table 4.1). The shortfall, taken together with Argentina's unreliability, gave Britain an additional incentive to develop its own agriculture. When the British government questioned the failure to meet the agreement, Grigg and Walter Mulholland, who had been the Meat Board representatives in the New Zealand delegation for the 1948 negotiations, intervened claiming that the Meat Board delegates in 1948 had not

---

[10] 'Produce Prices and Prospects', *Straight Furrow*, 15/04/1948, 1, ATL. Denmark was upset by that criticism and made a formal complaint. Denmark claimed that it too had agreed prices with Britain only on the grounds of increased costs. Denmark was given higher prices because it could demonstrate that its costs were higher.

[11] Bulk Purchase Contract 1948, Keith Holyoake papers, MSY-MS-1814 68/6, ATL.

[12] McKinnon, *Impact*, 279.

Table 4.1 Meat tonnage exported to Britain and earnings from that tonnage (NZDYB)

	1948	1949	1950	1951	1952	1953	1954	1955	1956
Tonnes	347,016	347,053	338,898	271,048	358,311	319,440	347,161	309,278	322,030
£(000)	28,444	26,997	28,208	24,683	37,128	38,093	48,623	49,457	50,252

promised to increase production, only that they would 'endeavour to', thereby passing blame for the commitment to an increase onto the government.[13]

New Zealand farmers worried that in Britain they would be blamed for New Zealand's failure to increase meat exports and would be seen as 'sitting back and refusing to recognise this undertaking'.[14] The Meat Board asked that 'adverse publicity on this matter . . . be kept out of the newspapers'.[15] The New Zealand delegation had upset producers by offering increased production without first engaging producers in discussing the additional resources needed to achieve the increase. Mr Dougherty told the Federated Farmers Meat and Wool Council: 'a great number of farmers got most incensed over being arbitrarily committed to increase their production'.[16] Federated Farmers Meat and Wool Council asked for a public statement by the Meat Board on the actual commitment: 'what commitments had been made . . . by whom . . . and the conditions . . . attached to the commitments'.[17] The Meat Board reported in *Straight Furrow* the actual wording of the 1948 agreement, identical to that quoted above.[18] The Meat and Wool Electoral Committee, concerned at the failure to increase the tonnage, asked the Meat Board to press the New Zealand

[13] Minutes of Meat and Wool Section Council, 07/12/1949, Federated Farmers 90-343 MSY-2730 M&W 123/1950, 3, ATL.

[14] 'Increased production in N.Z.: "No Promise Was Made by Meat Board" says Mr. Grigg', *Straight Furrow*, 16/01/1950, 2, ATL.

[15] Minutes of Meat and Wool Section Council, 07/12/1949, Federated Farmers 90-343 MSY-2730 M&W 123/1950, 3, ATL.

[16] 'Increased production in N.Z.: "No promise was made by the Meat Board" says Mr. Grigg', *Straight Furrow*, 16/01/1950, 2, ATL.

[17] Minutes of Meat and Wool Section Council, 07/12/1949, Federated Farmers 90-343 MSY-2730 M&W 123/1950 3, ATL.

[18] 'Bulk Purchase Contract', *Straight Furrow*, 16/01/1950, 14, ATL.

government 'on behalf of our kinsfolk in Great Britain' for financial incentives to increase production.[19]

The bulk contract enabled farmers to sell all their meat profitably and free of freight charges, but producers wanted additional investment by government to enable increased production. Producers claimed that the increased earnings from Britain covered only costs and were insufficient to allow the investment needed for increased production. When National replaced Labour following the 1949 election, Holyoake, as a former farmer and the new Minister for Agriculture, blamed the previous government for the failure to put into operation a programme to increase production. He reported to Parliament that, although the issues had been explained thoroughly to the Labour government, it chose to do nothing to meet the undertaking to Britain.[20]

A programme for increased production started, at last, when New Zealand itself had a vital need for increased foreign earnings. After National won the 1949 election the pressure for increased production changed from exhortations by the British government to exhortations by Holyoake. Holyoake's first actions as Minister for Agriculture included setting up a Primary Production Advisory Committee to advise him on how to increase production in all primary production sectors.[21] The Committee comprised government representatives, Federated Farmers and the Producer Boards. The new government claimed that increased overseas earnings were made necessary because of the profligate spending of the outgoing Labour government. Bernard Ashwin, the Treasury Secretary, reported to the first meeting that in past years New Zealand had been 'pumping out money' – New Zealand's population had increased but production had not: 'either they had to get down to a lower standard of living all round or get the production up'.[22] But,

[19] Meat Board Minute Book 9, 03/11/1949, 648, ANZ.

[20] The Hon. Mr. Holyoake, *New Zealand Parliamentary Debates (NZPD)*, 1950, Vol. 291, 2376, WCL.

[21] Right Hon. Mr. Holyoake, NZPD, 1950, Vol. 291, 2376, WCL; Dominion Agriculture Produce Section, Circular 122, Federated Farmers 90-343 MSY-2691, 1950, 3/5, ATL.

[22] Minutes of Meeting of Minister with Producer Representatives: Increased Production, 13/04/1950, Keith Holyoake Papers, MS-1814 – 11/1, 7, ATL.

whatever the inheritance from Labour, National's programme called for increased imports thereby making increased exports essential. The Committee needed to identify why increases in production had slowed down since the 1930s.[23] Grigg said at the first meeting that 'the meat industry was vitally interested' in increasing production 'because of the undertaking given to Britain to increase production by 50,000 tons by 1955 . . . small progress had been made'.[24] But increased production was held back also because producers did not want to commit to increases without an assurance that markets would be guaranteed for the additional meat tonnages after bulk purchase ended.[25] Holyoake recognised that the Committee wanted 'to secure the longest term possible of markets that would take New Zealand produce' and undertook to 'work along those lines' in government-to-government negotiations with Britain.[26]

In 1950, the Advisory Committee considered that 'increased fertiliser is probably the most important single factor in increasing grassland production' and that could be achieved in two main ways.[27] First, farmers could exploit more fully the top-dressing using aircraft recently established successfully in New Zealand and, second, government subsidies for superphosphate and lime fertilisers would encourage their increased use. Aerial top-dressing allowed a far more efficient fertiliser application and, following Holyoake's promptings, was expanded using investment from the Meat Board Reserve funds.[28] Evans describes how that technique increased the stock carrying capacity for 'many acres of hill-country previously beyond the scope of traditional

[23] Increased Primary Production, 13/04/1950, Keith Holyoake Papers, MS-1814 – 11/1, 2, ATL.

[24] Minutes of Meeting of Minister with Producer Representatives: Increased Production, 13/04/1950, Keith Holyoake Papers, MS-1814 – 11/1, 2, ATL.

[25] Minutes of Meeting of Minister with Producer Representatives: Increased Production, 04/05/1950, Keith Holyoake Papers, MS-1814 – 11/1, 2, ATL.

[26] Minutes of Meeting of Minister with Producer Representatives: Increased Production, 04/05/1950, Keith Holyoake Papers, MS-1814 – 11/1, 5, ATL.

[27] Working Paper 50/13: Work of the Primary Production Advisory Committee, 08/06/1950, Keith Holyoake Papers, MS-1814 – 11/1, 2, ATL.

[28] 'Meat Board's Part in Aerial Topdressing Industry', *Straight Furrow*, 01/10/1955, 7, ATL; Barry Gustafson, *Kiwi Keith: A Biography of Keith Holyoake* (Auckland: Auckland University Press, 2007), 56.

methods of topdressing . . . to an extent hitherto undreamt of'.[29] But the increased productivity did not work through to increased exports until well past 1955 when Britain's meat shortages had been overcome; the increased exports went elsewhere.

Grigg represented the Board at the 1950 contract discussions with instructions to negotiate a contract for Britain to take New Zealand's exportable surplus for at least another decade. But the Federated Farmers Meat and Wool Section recognised the need for diversification and pressed the Board to negotiate to be allowed increased sales to markets outside Britain.[30] Relations with Britain weakened when producers became disturbed that Britain paid more to its other meat suppliers. Britain based its prices on domestic costs in each country and paid more to Argentina and Australia because their costs were higher than those in New Zealand; irritation grew in New Zealand at being paid less.[31] The Meat Board noted in July 1950 that prices for New Zealand meat had increased by 83% since 1939, for Argentinean meat by 130% and for Australian meat by 100%. The New Zealand delegation now based its argument for increased prices on comparison with those other countries rather than on cost increases in New Zealand alone.[32] Producers thought a significant increase well justified but the changes reflected the differing inflation in each country; New Zealand 'had done better than some other countries' in keeping inflation under control.[33]

The Federated Farmers Research Officer summarised the arguments for price increases and argued that Britain exploited New Zealand's 'loyalty and goodwill'.[34] He pointed out another strong argument for increased prices: prices for British imports into New Zealand had risen

[29] B. L. Evans, *A History of Agricultural Production and Marketing in New Zealand* (Palmerston North: Keeling and Munday, 1969), 20.

[30] Chairman's Address to the Meat and Wool Conference, 27/06/1951, Federated Farmers 90-343 MSY-2732, M&W 37/1951, ATL.

[31] Meat Board Minute Book 9, 3/11/1949, 646, ANZ.

[32] Meat Board Minute Book 9, 20/07/1950, 704, ANZ; Minutes of the Meat and Wool Section Council, 09/08/1950, Federated Farmers 90-343 MSY-2730 M&W163/1950, p6, ATL.

[33] Jim McAloon, *Judgements of All Kinds* (Wellington: Victoria University Press, 2013), 86.

[34] D. L. Martin, 'The Export-Import Relationship: Are We Getting a Fair Deal from Britain?', *Straight Furrow*, 15/12/1950, 7, ATL.

considerably so that lamb exported to Britain in 1950 bought 31% fewer imports from Britain than in 1939.[35] Finally, the Korean War made commodity prices in general rise rapidly. The New Zealand delegation decided to 'withdraw from the talks for a few months to allow Britain to reach agreement with Australia and Argentina'.[36] When talks resumed, Britain agreed to a 5% increase and that New Zealand could sell more to other countries, thereby encouraging a closer look at potential new markets.[37]

4.3 A More Belligerent Approach and the End of Bulk Purchase

The doubts that Britain paid fair prices for New Zealand meat led producers to question the benefits from bulk purchase. Meat Board member John Ormond was soon to become the Board's chairman; his strong attachment to Britain did not prevent him from taking a more belligerent line towards that country. When inflationary pressures in 1952 made the New Zealand Prime Minister, Sidney Holland, reluctant to accept price increases above the contractual limit, Ormond pressurised his own delegation into accepting those increases. The delegation, then, made another commitment to increase supplies to Britain but, again, supplies to Britain did not increase. Markets other than Britain seemed potentially more remunerative and encouraged New Zealand to end bulk purchase in 1954, one year earlier than the original agreement.

In 1950 the Primary Production Advisory Committee at one point considered asking Holyoake to seek a ten-year extension of the bulk contract but producers began to realise that bulk purchase might not be

[35] Chairman's Address to the Meat and Wool Conference, 27/06/1950, Federated Farmers 90-343 MSY-2730 M&W 152/1950, 5/6, ATL.

[36] Minutes of the Meat and Wool Section Council, 09/08/1950, Federated Farmers 90-343 MSY-2730 M&W163/1950, 6, ATL.

[37] McKinnon, *Impact*, 324–326 gives the full details of the British negotiations with all three countries.

to their advantage.[38] The 1951 Federated Farmers Meat and Wool Conference called for an end to bulk purchase because it prevented New Zealand investigating more comprehensively other markets which seemed more profitable than selling to Britain.[39] The Federated Farmers Meat and Wool Chairman said New Zealand farmers would be 'staggered' with the price Britain had agreed to pay Argentina.[40] Meat producers in 1950 were very aware that during the Korean War wool prices increased threefold because wool sold on the open market following the end of wool bulk purchase in 1945. Grigg, in presenting his last annual report as Meat Board Chairman in September 1951, reported that 'the next four years will be used to explore the potentialities of markets other than the United Kingdom' and hoped that when meat bulk purchase ended New Zealand would have 'established permanent markets . . . at least in North America'.[41] Grigg said that New Zealand would be faced in 1953 with the major decision on whether to extend bulk purchase or revert to normal trading on an open market.

Producers concerned over the prices paid by Britain found in John Ormond a loud voice to make Britain aware of their concerns. Ormond represented the Meat Board at the 1951/2 price negotiations and had first taken part in the negotiations in 1949 when the delegation secured a 7.5% increase in prices; the Meat Board, at that time, recorded its appreciation of the excellent work 'during the recent Meat Contract Discussions by . . . J.D. Ormond'.[42] Ormond's brusque, outspoken manner and determination made him effective with both the media and politicians. He was not skilled at reasoned debate but was an early example of politicians who push their argument through the media

[38] Working Paper 50/13: Work of the Primary Production Advisory Committee, 08/06/1950, Keith Holyoake Papers, MS-1814 – 11/1, 2, ATL.

[39] Chairman's Address to the Meat and Wool Section Conference, 27/06/1951, Federated Farmers 90-343 MSY-2732, M&W39/151, ATL.

[40] Minutes of the Meat and Wool Section Council, 09/05/1951, Federated Farmers 90-343 MSY-2732 M&W28/1951, 2, ATL. The disparity was in the sale of beef, Argentina received 40% more than New Zealand; for lamb the prices were the same – 'Price Discrimination by Britain for Meat', *Straight Furrow*, 01/02/1953, 15, ATL.

[41] 'Bright Year Ahead for N.Z. Meat Industry', *Straight Furrow*, 15/09/1951, 13, ATL.

[42] Meat Board Minute Book 9, 15/09/1949, 631, ANZ.

rather than statutory bodies.[43] Gustafson's comments on Robert Muldoon were appropriate for Ormond; he 'asserted rather than explained the positions he took' and 'he speaks in newspaper headlines'.[44] Peter Tait, in his biography of Ormond, reports that Ormond 'fully realised the value as a farmer politician of keeping his name to the fore' and he 'did his best to ensure that he was not only available to the press, but that he was good copy'.[45] Ormond became by far the dominant force in New Zealand meat activities until his retirement in 1972. He had become a member of the Meat Board in 1933–1934 whilst a leading proponent of the New Zealand Legion, a radical, extreme right-wing party.[46] When it became clear that the Legion would not grow into a significant party Ormond stood, unsuccessfully, as a National candidate for election to Parliament in 1935. His approach at the time demonstrated his self-opinionated manner and determination. His election posters told voters that 'he is convinced that efficient government necessitates more independent expression of opinion by members'. He supported National but 'will not necessarily vote with the party but with discretion'.[47] Throughout his years in primary producer politics he often took an independent approach and inevitably at times conflicted with other producers. His role as a Meat Board Chairman gave him far more influence over New Zealand governments than he would have had as a Member of Parliament.

In 1951 Ormond decided that negotiations with Britain needed a new approach. In an interview with *Associated Press*, he 'vigorously attacked the United Kingdom's attitude to prices for New Zealand

[43] Geoffrey Palmer, *Reform,* (Wellington: Victoria University Press, 2013), 711, Former Prime Minister, Sir Geoffrey Palmer claims that politicians deploying the media dominate New Zealand politics in the twenty-first century.

[44] Barry Gustafson, *His Way: A Biography of Robert Muldoon* (Auckland: Auckland University Press, 2001), 190 and 359.

[45] Peter Tait, *In the Chair: the Public Life of Sir John Ormond* (Waipukurau: CHB Print, 1989), 57.

[46] Tait, 17–21.

[47] Election Poster John Ormond, Independent Nationalist, System Id 23466, Museum, Theatre, Gallery (MTG) Hawke's Bay.

meat' saying 'it's time we twisted the lion's tail'.[48] The publicity given to Ormond's remark led to a debate amongst producers on future relations with Britain. Some agreed that New Zealand should seek higher prices for her produce rather than being treated as 'one of the underpaid sons' of Britain.[49] But concern remained at the Federated Farmers meat and wool annual conference over breaking too far from Britain and typical comments were 'twisting of the Lion's tail could be overdone . . . we don't want our main market to collapse'; 'we have been prepared in the past to hang on to the Lion's tail'; 'we've relied on Britain to take over a large share of Empire defence and if we get full value for our produce we should also shoulder a larger share of the defence of the Empire'.[50]

An Electoral College elected Meat Board members, with farmers electing College members. In September 1951, two months after Ormond's remarks on twisting the lion's tail, the Electoral College Chairman, John Graham, approached Ormond wanting him to take on the Meat Board chairmanship. Phillip Herman claims that the Electoral College arrangement led to 'accountability . . . far removed from . . . those whose interests that system had been designed to serve'.[51] The relative lack of accountability would have appealed to Ormond with his impatience with having to consult widely before making decisions; he preferred to settle issues over informal drinks rather than at formal meetings.[52]

Apart from Grigg's and Ormond's differing approaches to Britain – both with a traditional respect, but Ormond less prepared to accept a subservient trade relationship – in appointing Ormond as chairman the

[48] 'Should N.Z. Find New Markets?', *Evening Post*, 19/07/1951, 1. The *Evening Post* article reports that Ormond said 'shook' rather than 'twisted', but all other sources including Ormond himself point to 'twisted' being the word used. The phrase was not coined by Ormond; it had been in common usage amongst Primary Producers for several years, for instance, in references to Argentina and Denmark's pressure for increased prices from Britain in the 1940s.

[49] 'New Deal for N.Z. Produce', *Straight Furrow*, 15/08/1951, 47, ATL.

[50] 'Twisting the Lion's Tail', *Straight Furrow*, 15/08/1951, 12, ATL.

[51] Phillip Herman, 'The Electoral Committee of the New Zealand Meat and Wool Boards', *Political Science*, June 1974, 26, 1, 56. During its task in voting for Board members the organisation was called the 'Electoral College', at all other times it was called the Electoral Committee.

[52] Tait, 54.

Electoral College opted for continuity rather than change. Ormond's background as a member of New Zealand's equivalent of Britain's landed gentry mirrored Grigg's. One reason given by Graham for asking Ormond to be Chairman was because he was 'the offspring of one of the most honoured families in New Zealand'.[53] Both Grigg and Ormond had been active in the New Zealand Legion; both families had established major roles in New Zealand farming starting in the mid-nineteenth century; both had a strong interest in horse racing and played polo.[54] Graham nonetheless urged Ormond to show more respect and be more cautious in his public statements:

> [Y]ou must not let the Board, the College and the producers down by wild tactless statements such as twisting the lion's tail. The matter of what you were saying was indisputably correct, but your manner of saying it hurt.[55]

Ormond became chairman but never moderated his independent nature. He recognised that colourful statements to the press, rather than doing harm, strengthened his support amongst farmers; he appeared as one of them rather than, as frequently the case for Board members, a bureaucrat out of touch with the community. Ormond's 'penchant for headline grabbing remained with him in his later years as chairman'.[56]

Ashwin told the Meat Board in September 1951 that an increase above the 7.5% maximum stipulated in the bulk purchase agreement could be secured if Australia managed to secure a higher increase, and in October Australia secured a 17.5% increase.[57] A Meat Board member,

---

[53] Tait, 58.

[54] Ormond's background is described by Tait; the Hawke's Bay Museum has a photograph of Ormond as a polo player (Photograph of Polo Players in New Zealand including Ormond, System ID 66706, MTG Hawke's Bay). There is no biography of Grigg but his background is clear from newspaper reports: '*New Zealand Legion*', Auckland Star LXIV Issue 247, 19 October 1933, 8; '*N. Z. Polo Team to play in Melbourne*', Auckland Star, Vol. LXV, Issue 159, 7 July 1934, 18; *Obituary*, Evening Post, Vol. CXII, Issue 57, 4 September 1926, 7.

[55] Reported in Tait, 58.

[56] Tait, 57.

[57] Meat Board Minute Book 10, 12/09/1951, 799, ANZ.

F Johnstone, in London at that time, announced that New Zealand expected its prices to be brought into line with those received in other countries.[58] Ormond rebutted claims that New Zealand should sell its meat at a cheaper rate through loyalty to Britain and said that loyalty to Britain no longer had anything to do with price and trade agreements.[59] Typically, Ormond wanted a free hand in negotiations with Britain and he tried to persuade Holyoake that the Meat Board should be given 'full responsibility for the negotiations concerning the sale of our meat to Britain'.[60] But Holyoake would agree only that 'the Government will be pleased to have a member of the Board take full part in the negotiations'.[61]

Ormond made a nuisance of himself during the 1951/1952 negotiations. He later told the Meat Board that he had left Wellington for the talks believing that New Zealand would ask for the same percentage increase as Australia, but it emerged that the Cabinet had not agreed that Britain should be pressed for an increase above the 7.5% contractual limit.[62] The difficulty seemed not to be with Holyoake, who led the New Zealand delegation, but the Prime Minister, Sidney Holland, because the Cabinet wanted to avoid significant increases in income for meat and dairy producers whilst it struggled to control inflationary pressures from the high wool prices stimulated by the Korean War.[63] The Prime Minister wanted to accept no more than the 7.5% contractual limit. Ormond put pressure on the government by threatening to stay in New Zealand and not take part in the price negotiations but eventually he agreed to continue his journey. According to Ormond, at one point in the talks an increase between 12% and 13% seemed possible but the lack of clear pressure by the New Zealand government threatened to have the offer reduced to 7.5%. Ormond at that point

---

[58] 'Demand for Price Increase', *Straight Furrow*, 15/10/1951, 43, ATL.

[59] 'Demand for Price Increase', *Straight Furrow*, 15/10/1951, 43, ATL.

[60] Ormond to Holyoake, 11/12/1951, Keith Holyoake papers, MS-1814 – 22/3 Meat, ATL.

[61] Holyoake to Ormond, 21/12/1951, Keith Holyoake papers, MS-1814 – 22/3 Meat, ATL.

[62] Meat Board Minute Book 10, 03/10/1952, 891, ANZ; 'He Can Take It! Criticism Leaves John Ormond Unruffled', *Straight Furrow*, 01/02/1955, 3, ATL.

[63] Cabinet Papers, 52(4), 4/02/1952, ANZ.

briefly withdrew from the talks ('retired to the pavilion' in Ormond's words) apparently to put pressure on his own delegation to press for the higher price. Ormond eventually returned and New Zealand secured a 12.5% increase.[64] Britain agreed, also, that there would be unrestricted and duty-free access for New Zealand meat for fifteen years up to 1967 because it would 'greatly encourage' the increases in exports to Britain agreed in 1948 'if there were an assurance of a market for all meat produced in future years'.[65]

Producers remembered Ormond going to London to twist the lion's tail, and he received sole credit for achieving the price increase. Malcolm McKinnon suggests that Britain's urgent need for increased production of New Zealand meat eased Ormond's task.[66] The outcome of the negotiations confirmed Ormond's image as someone who would stand up to Britain. Producers now saw 'standing up to Britain' as the appropriate way to conduct trade negotiations. Ormond later issued a statement praising Holyoake's role to correct any impression that Holyoake had caused difficulties. Probably in private he told the full story, and a Mr Fleming told Marlborough Federated Farmers that 'The Prime Minister should be rapped on the knuckles for telling the UK Food Ministry that we don't want more than 7.5% increase in our meat price'; Fleming 'urged support' for Ormond who had been 'chided by the Prime Minister'.[67] Ormond, in his first year as Meat Board Chairman, firmly established himself as someone who spoke for producers, and his frequent resort to colourful language helped to keep him unopposed in that position for two decades.

Ormond said farmers should 'put their shoulders to the wheel . . . for this increased production', first agreed in 1948 and reconfirmed in 1952.[68] Once again the agreement anticipated up to 400,000 tons

[64] 'Meat Price Increase', *Straight Furrow*, 15/02/1952, 3, ATL.

[65] Joint Declaration by the United Kingdom and New Zealand Governments, Keith Holyoake papers, MS-1814 – 68/6 Meat, ATL.

[66] McKinnon, *Impact*, 328.

[67] 'What Provincial Members Have to Say', *Straight Furrow*, 01/11/1952, 10, ATL.

[68] 'Immediate Need for More Production Says Board Chairman', *Straight Furrow*, 15/01/1952, 15, ATL.

exported to Britain annually.[69] But, in the following years, exports to Britain decreased with the highest tonnage being 347,000. Production increased eventually but, rather than to Britain, the meat export increases went to countries that paid more, for instance, the countries that became the first members of the European Economic Community (EEC). Producers had put their shoulders to the wheel for EEC countries rather than Britain. Later, in 1957 the New Zealand delegation in trade talks with Britain explained that the increased production had not been sent to Britain to 'endeavour not to over-supply the British market' thereby admitting that seeking higher prices had become more important than helping Britain with its food shortages.[70]

In anticipation of the annual negotiations in 1953, the Federated Farmers President took up the theme that business and not sentiment should now rule New Zealand's dealings with Britain on meat prices.[71] But when to end bulk purchase became the prime topic. The British Food Ministry proposed that the agreement should be terminated as planned in 1955 but the Meat Board recommended that the contract be terminated on 30 September 1954. Federated Farmers and the Minister agreed because the strong global demand for meat opened opportunities in markets other than Britain.[72] Following the end of bulk purchase, New Zealand could, if it wished, still send its exportable surplus to Britain, but Britain would no longer pay guaranteed prices.

In retrospect, the bulk purchase agreement had led to Britain buying as much meat as New Zealand could produce under a cost-plus arrangement through which prices had increased as New Zealand costs increased. In addition to paying farmers sufficient to cover their costs, the Meat Board, prudently, built a substantial reserve by withholding

---

[69] 'A Challenge to Farming Ability', *Straight Furrow*, 01/06/1952, 32, ATL.

[70] Memorandum on Production, Consumption and Marketing Problems Relating to Meat, November 1957, United Kingdom/New Zealand Agricultural Discussions, 2, ANZ.

[71] 'Taranaki: Federation's Value', *Straight Furrow*, 01/06/1953, 19, ATL.

[72] Meat Board Minute Book 11, 06/05/1954, 1022/1023, ANZ.

some income. The Board built up more than £27 M assets by 1949 from prices paid by Britain during the war years.[73] Even into the 1970s, when lamb prices fell, the '$100 million . . . legacy of the wartime UK Bulk Purchase agreement' allowed the Meat Board to 'bolster returns'.[74] It is doubtful whether during the bulk contract period New Zealand could have sold the same tonnage at the same prices to markets other than Britain. Even well after the war New Zealand never found a significant market for the main contract item, lamb, outside Britain. The difficulties of operating in a free market soon became clear when bulk purchase ended; retaining sales to Britain remained important.

4.4 Growing Doubts About Reliance on the British Market

Prices in the British market fell following the end of bulk purchase because Argentina once again began selling significant meat exports to Britain. Ormond reintroduced sentiment and adopted shaming Britain into maintaining remunerative prices by emphasising past New Zealand loyalty to Britain. Ormond prompted Holyoake to initiate major trade discussions with Britain in 1957, mainly to persuade Britain to restrict meat imports from Argentina. But those discussions demonstrated a hardening of Britain's preparedness to help New Zealand. Federated Farmers grasped that Britain could no longer take increased meat exports from New Zealand and the time had come for a closer look at new markets. Eventually, the Meat Board agreed.

Early in 1956, recovery of beef exports to Britain from Argentina caused falls in the prices of all meats. New Zealand officials described

[73] Dai Hayward, editor: *Golden Jubilee: the Story of the First Fifty Years of the New Zealand Meat Producers Board 1922–1972* (Wellington: Universal Printers, 1972), 84.

[74] Mick Calder and Janet Tyson, *Meat Acts: The New Zealand Meat Industry 1972–1997* (Wellington: Meat New Zealand, 1999), 17.

the cause as 'a sudden surge in imports from foreign sources' into the British market.[75] Ormond wanted Britain to restrict Argentinean imports but instead Britain eased restrictions by replacing quotas for Argentinean beef with a tariff.[76] The Federated Farmers Auckland President, Mr J Scott Davidson, expressed his concern that Britain would not help New Zealand by restricting beef imports from Argentina and complained that Argentina had in the past

> commercially blackmailed Britain, consistently breached agreements . . . laid siege to a meat-starved Britain in the style of a merciless brigand. New Zealand on the other hand, through sentiment, patriotism and family suffering, gave Britain all the meat we could at a price she could afford.

Scott Davidson concluded that 'The time has come for a showdown'.[77] Meanwhile, Ormond became even more concerned when he realised Britain's actions were in line with the GATT Agreement of the 1940s that included in Annex A of Article 1 the provision that quota restrictions placed by Britain on non-Commonwealth suppliers 'in respect of . . . frozen beef and veal, frozen mutton and lamb . . . shall be eliminated and replaced by tariff preferences . . . as soon as practicable'.[78] The GATT provision would have breached the Ottawa Agreement of 1932 but a waiver had been agreed by participants, including the New Zealand government.[79] New Zealand officials investigated and concluded that the

[75] Trade Discussions between the Government of New Zealand and the Government of the United Kingdom of Great Britain and Northern Ireland, London, T61/3/25/1, 8 April to 29 May 1957, ANZ.

[76] Notes Re: Entry of Commonwealth Meat to the United Kingdom Market, 24/08/1955, Keith Holyoake papers, MS-1814 068/1, ATL; 'Sheer Madness: Mr Ormond's View If Imperial Preference Shelved', *The Daily Telegraph*, Keith Holyoake papers, 27/06/1956, MS-1814 068/6, ATL.

[77] 'Some Straight Speaking on U.K. Trade Agreements by Auckland Prov. President', *Straight Furrow*, 01/07/1956, 14, ATL.

[78] http://www.wto.org/english/docs_e/legal_e/gatt47_e.pdf, accessed 14/11/2013.

[79] Secretary of State for Commonwealth Relations, London, to Prime Minister, Wellington, 12 February 1957, T1, 61/3/21, Pt I, ANZ.

Ottawa Agreement no longer justified British quota restrictions on Argentinean beef.[80]

Ormond gave his usual good copy to the media in calling for the government, in June 1956, to 'combat the influence of people in London trying to write off imperial preference'. Ormond said 'these people are hardly less dangerous than those who were trying to break down the Commonwealth by more violent means'.[81] Ormond's statement embarrassed Holland, in London at the time for the Commonwealth Prime Ministers' Conference. He rebutted Ormond, denying knowledge that plans existed to write off Imperial Preferences: 'the preferences played an important part in maintaining closest possible economic ties' within the Commonwealth.[82] Ormond complained that New Zealand negotiators had agreed to a clause during the GATT discussions that 'sought to write a death warrant for the Ottawa system', and he claimed that that 'had not been published' in New Zealand until he had raised the issue in 1955. The Meat Board complained to the Cabinet Committee on Economic Policy that 'the farmers of New Zealand were not parties to this arrangement'.[83] The Comptroller of Customs warned Holyoake that Ormond had made 'misleading' statements.[84] The Comptroller explained that the phrase in the GATT agreement, that quota restrictions should be replaced by tariffs, had been added, reluctantly, at New Zealand's request to avoid the other countries giving up both quota restrictions and tariffs. The Comptroller added that the clause

> far from being the one which 'sought to write a death warrant', for meat preferences, was therefore the maximum obtainable safeguard for them.

[80] New Zealand's Rights Under the Ottawa Agreement and Possible Courses of Action, 23/04/1956, Keith Holyoake Papers, MS-1814, 068/1, 2, ATL.

[81] 'Mr. J. D. Ormond Calls for Prompt Govt. Action Over Imperial Preference', *Straight Furrow*, 01/07/1956, 4, ATL. Likely a reference to violent rebellions in colonies such as Kenya and Cyprus at the time.

[82] 'Effect of G.A.T.T. on N.Z. Meat Exports', *Evening Post*, 28/06/1956, in Keith Holyoake papers, MS-1814 068/6, ATL.

[83] Submission of New Zealand Meat Producers Board, 1956, T/1/61/3/21 PtII, ANZ.

[84] Comptroller of Customs to Minister for Agriculture, 28/06/1956, Keith Holyoake papers, MS-1814 068/1, ATL.

Finally, the agreement had been published in full in New Zealand in White Papers on GATT in 1948 and 1949.

The Chairman of the Cabinet Committee on Economic Policy reported that 'the United Kingdom . . . appears incapable of absorbing the full increase in our exportable surpluses in future years at remunerative prices'.[85] But the Treasury noted that 'meat farmers . . . are building almost all their hopes on the UK market' in contrast with wool and dairy producers who realised the need to pursue alternative markets to absorb the intended increased production.[86] Ormond's claim to a favoured place as of right to the British market remained for more than a decade a key strand in his arguments. Ormond thought his claim justified partly because at Ottawa it had been agreed that the British policy for meat imports would be to ensure 'progressively increasing the share of the Dominions in the United Kingdom market'.[87] Ormond and the Meat Board argued that New Zealand had increased meat supplies to compensate for

> Argentina's defection [from the UK market] during the last fifteen years. . . . Is Argentina to be now permitted to wreck the UK meat market for New Zealand simply because it now suits Argentina to resume greater supplies to the UK?[88]

Ormond wanted pressure on Britain to be increased by replacing producer discussions due in Britain in 1957 with discussions at a higher level. He proposed to Holyoake in December 1956 that 'a delegation proceed to the United Kingdom in the first week in March 1957 for discussions with the United Kingdom at Ministerial level'.[89] The government discussed the possibilities with other producers and decided

---

[85] Review of New Zealand's trade policy – Cabinet Committee on Economic Policy, 30/11/1956, T/1/61/3/21, Pt II, ANZ.

[86] Note from Treasury to H G Lang, London, 08/01/1957, T1 424 61/3/21, ANZ.

[87] Trade Discussions between the Government of New Zealand and the Government of the United Kingdom of Great Britain and Northern Ireland, London, ABHS, 37/1/1E Part 1, 8 April–29 May 1957, 11, ANZ.

[88] New Zealand Meat Producers Board Report to Government, 10/12/1956, T/1/61/3/21 Pt II, ANZ.

[89] Ormond to Holyoake, 20/12/1957, T1 61/3/21, ANZ.

that there should be Ministerial trade talks with Britain covering all commodities. New Zealand government officials saw increases in meat and dairy exports as necessary 'to support a growing population and to maintain living standards' but fears that Britain could not absorb the increases were growing rapidly.[90] The trade mission had the problem that the Meat Board wanted Britain to introduce quantitative restrictions but the Dairy Board feared that, if Britain changed its policy in favour of quantitative restrictions, over-supply of dairy exports to the British market might justify restrictions being imposed on other exporters, including New Zealand.[91] Ormond told New Zealand ministers in preparation for the trade talks that

> New Zealand had a right to the British market and, in fact, should claim a greater percentage than was talked of in the old days . . . they should have it out with the British Government as to where they stood.[92]

In contrast, *Straight Furrow* demonstrated growing confidence in New Zealand's possibilities for selling to markets other than Britain. In a leader, it noted that if the trade mission's efforts were not 'crowned with complete success' New Zealand will know where it stands and 'a glance at the Pacific Basin should reassure many of us about that future'.[93] Producers realised that eventually New Zealand would no longer be Britain's farm with an absentee landlord, but New Zealand's farm with a far broader range of local customers.

At the trade talks in early 1957, the British delegation comprised the Minister for Agriculture and officials from the Board of Trade, Ministry of Agriculture and Commonwealth Relations Office. The New Zealand delegation, led by Holyoake, included, in addition to Ormond, representatives of the Dairy Board, the President of Federated Farmers and

---

[90] New Zealand – United Kingdom Trade Discussions: note of meeting of Officials and Producers' Representatives, 8/02/1957, T1 61/3/21, ANZ.

[91] Notes of Deputation of Producer Organizations which waited on members of the Cabinet Committee on Economic Policy, 5/2/1957, T1 424 61/3/21, ANZ.

[92] McAloon, 99.

[93] 'The Trade Delegation', *Straight Furrow*, 01/03/1957, 3, ATL.

officials from the Departments of Agriculture, and Industries and Commerce. The British Board of Trade President chaired the discussions. Holyoake opened the talks by pointing out New Zealand's disadvantages in a free market. He said 'it is only recently with the resumption of a free market for food that the long-term character of the market has become clear'.[94] He wanted Britain to allow free and unrestricted entry at remunerative prices for all New Zealand primary produce but also to impose quotas against Argentinean beef. Britain responded that 'in practice' New Zealand enjoyed free, unrestricted entry for all her produce but Britain would look into whether to increase her formal commitments.[95] Britain considered it 'highly questionable whether present market conditions warrant . . . such drastic action' as introducing quota restrictions on beef from Argentina; Britain noted that New Zealand's market share had increased since the 1930s, as anticipated at Ottawa.[96] Britain thought also that control over one supplier would lead to a need for control over all suppliers, including those from the Commonwealth. Britain pointed out also the commitments under GATT to eliminate quotas on beef from Argentina.

Ormond's main objective had been to increase New Zealand's share of the British meat market by persuading Britain to restrict Argentinean beef imports. In addition, 'racial affinity between the United Kingdom and New Zealand' encouraged the Meat Board to anticipate Britain remaining 'our principal market' for 'all the foreseeable future'.[97] Ormond clearly felt a strong affinity with Britons to the extent that during trade talks a New Zealand Official reported Ormond as 'enjoying every moment'.[98] He had a broad range of social contacts and his letters home are mainly reporting to

[94] Holyoake's opening statement, 08/04/1957, New Zealand Trade – United Kingdom Discussions 1957, ABHS W4628 7148 Box 12 LONB 37/1/1E Part 1, 3, ATL.

[95] Statement by President, Board of Trade, 10/04/1957, New Zealand Trade – United Kingdom Discussions 1957, ABHS W4628 7148 Box 12 LONB 37/1/1E Part 1, ATL. The rest of the paragraph is a summary of that statement.

[96] Trade Agreements Affecting the UK Market, 30/04/1956, Keith Holyoake papers, MS-1814 68/6, ATL.

[97] Review of New Zealand's Trade Policy 1956/7: Outline of Present Position, 05/02/1957, T1 424 61/3/21, 1, ANZ.

[98] To Dorothy and Kevin by unnamed official, 25/04/1957, Keith Holyoake Papers, MS-1814 70/04, ATL. The letter is a 'gossipy' letter sent back to New Zealand by a member of the delegation who is commenting mainly on social activities and other members of the delegation.

his wife the people he met socially.[99] Ormond's polo playing would have set him apart from other New Zealanders in British eyes. He regretted that an 'official luncheon' had stopped him 'going to Newmarket [racecourse] for the Guineas [one of Britain's classic horse races]'.[100] Ormond's affinity with Britain encouraged him to retain strong links with Britain and he showed no inclination to glance at the Pacific Basin.

The 1957 trade negotiations continued for six weeks but Britain would not change its position and refused to introduce quantitative restrictions on meat imports from Argentina. Holland reported to Holyoake that the Cabinet was 'intensely disappointed' and had hoped that

> membership of, and loyalty to the Empire and Commonwealth would have meant more . . . but apparently foreign countries such as Argentina, which confiscated British-owned railways and performed other anti-British acts, count as much when it comes to buying produce.[101]

Ormond's insistence had pushed the government to ask Britain to make the change despite the doubts within New Zealand, doubts that increased and led to Holyoake, according to Ormond, 'getting windy [a 1950's phrase for becoming frightened]' during the discussions.[102] But Ormond did not 'retire to the pavilion' as he had in 1952 to put pressure on his own delegation. The meetings' minutes show no forceful contribution from Ormond; perhaps he made forceful contributions over drinks outside meetings.

In July 1957, following the trade mission's return, the Federated Farmers President succinctly summarised the conclusions for producers.[103] He stressed that Britain would continue to be New Zealand's

---

[99] John Ormond to Judith Ormond, 26 April 1957, System ID, 73944, 1, MTG Hawke's Bay.

[100] John Ormond to Judith Ormond, 26 April 1957, System ID, 73944, 2, MTG Hawke's Bay.

[101] Cablegram Personal from Prime Minister to Holyoake, 08/05/1957, Keith Holyoake Papers, MS-1814 68/04, ATL.

[102] John Ormond to Judith Ormond, 26 April 1957, System ID 73944, 1, MTG Hawke's Bay.

[103] 'President's Conclusions: Trade Mission Talks with British Govt.', *Straight Furrow*, 01/07/1957, 1, ATL.

main market for the foreseeable future but would not give New Zealand priority by restricting meat imports from foreign sources. New Zealand would need to compete on equal terms with all other meat suppliers to the British market. *Straight Furrow* considered that, most importantly, the mission had cleared the air.[104] New Zealand could no longer anticipate that Britain would absorb expanded production and it had become essential to explore and develop supplementary markets. Britain might continue to take present tonnages but there was little hope that Britain would take the increased tonnages. A Federated Farmers Provincial President summarised that now New Zealand should break away from the Mother Country's 'apron strings': New Zealand had 'come of age'.[105] Federated Farmers were always in advance of the Meat Board in recognising the need for diversification away from Britain; Ormond faced up to that need more reluctantly and seemed to welcome being tied to the Mother Country's apron strings.

Ormond was disappointed by the outcome of the trade mission and for once gave no good copy on his return. According to its minutes the Meat Board did not discuss the trade talks' outcome until twelve months later. Perhaps Ormond did not want to publicise the failure to achieve what for him had been the main objective – convincing Britain to restrict Argentinean meat imports. He returned to New Zealand having been unsuccessful in 'standing up to Britain' unlike his triumphant return from the 1952 price discussions. But he knew also that he could return to the issue: the trade mission had secured agreement for annual discussions with Britain on agricultural matters, the first scheduled for November 1957. Ormond again tried to persuade Britain to give increased protection for New Zealand meat by restricting imports from Argentina.[106] He suggested using a foot-and-mouth outbreak in Argentina as an excuse, but the British refused, pointing out how earnings for New Zealand meat in Britain had increased by 5% per annum

[104] 'President's Conclusions: Trade Mission Talks with British Govt.', *Straight Furrow*, 01/07/1957, 3, ATL.

[105] 'Away from Apron Strings', *Straight Furrow*, 01/08/1957, 31, ATL.

[106] United Kingdom – New Zealand Consultations on Agriculture and Food Policies, November/December 1957, ANZ.

since 1946 in real terms and that prices in 1957 exceeded those in 1956. Britain did not fear over-supply because further increases in meat consumption in Britain remained possible.[107]

The trade delegation's visit to Britain in April 1957 represented a watershed for the New Zealand meat trade. The agreement for free and unrestricted entry for New Zealand meat would continue until 1967 but, following the talks, and echoing Nash's concern in 1934 on British market saturation, Holyoake broadcast his apprehension that the British market could not absorb increased production by New Zealand.[108] The possibility remained that from 1967 New Zealand would no longer have guaranteed free and unrestricted access for the first time for nearly three decades. The 1957 discussions demonstrated Britain's clear reluctance to increase priority for Commonwealth countries; New Zealand's failure to meet the agreements in 1948 and 1952 to increase meat supplies cannot have helped. The calls that had been made in New Zealand for commercial considerations to override sentiment, including calls by Ormond, now echoed back from Britain. Britain would not interfere in the free market or change its agricultural policies because of a temporary price decrease for New Zealand meat. Britain's dependence on Commonwealth food supplies had weakened: 'Wellington found it much more difficult to obtain a sympathetic hearing in London' because Britain's food shortages had ended.[109]

Following the November 1957 talks, the Meat Board at last realised that it needed a major effort to build markets outside Britain. A significant start had been made by private exporters such as Borthwick's in selling beef to Japan in 1957 and to the USA in April 1958. In July 1958 Ormond reviewed for the Meat Board the problems in marketing the additional tonnages from increased production; the Board arranged

107 Note on Meeting of the Meat Group, 29/11/1957, United Kingdom/New Zealand Consultations on Agricultural and Food Policies, ANZ.

108 '"Apprehension Justified" Says Mr Holyoake', *New Zealand Herald*, 30/05/1957, Keith Holyoake Papers, MS-1814 70/05, ATL.

109 John Singleton, 'New Zealand, Britain and the survival of the Ottawa agreement, 1945–77', *The Australian Journal of Politics and History*, 43, 2, 1997, 170.

increased overseas visits by members to seek new markets.[110] Ormond agreed that more should be spent on overseas promotion and less on domestic problems. New Zealand already had well-established contacts in the USA and, also, in continental Europe through the Board's representation in London. In addition, the Board arranged visits to Canada, Japan and the West Indies. Meat Board members spoke publicly about the changed strategy, but, unlike other occasions, Ormond did not take the lead in announcing the changes.

4.5 The Threat from British Membership of the EEC

Between 1956 and 1961 European unification threatened eventual loss of New Zealand meat's free and unrestricted access to the British market. Ormond emphasised the threats especially when the National government led by Holyoake took a more moderate approach in 1961 than its Labour predecessor. Other producers, including meat producers, also took a more moderate approach than Ormond. Producers recognised Britain's dilemma in being forced to choose between giving preference to the Commonwealth and becoming more integrated with continental Europe. Ormond strove to prevent change; other producers accepted the need for change.

Federated Farmers expressed, in October 1956, its concern about Britain's possible involvement in a European Customs Union because such a union might have a single external tariff for exports to it from outside.[111] In preparation for the 1957 trade talks the New Zealand External Affairs Minister told the British government that New Zealand's interests in a European Customs Union 'were directed principally to obtaining expanded opportunities for our exports to important markets in Europe'.[112] The trade talks included discussion of the issues

[110] Meat Board Minute Book 12, 03/07/1953, 1505, ANZ.

[111] 'U.K. May Become Member of European Customs Union', *Straight Furrow*, 01/10/1956, 32, ATL.

[112] Telegram Minister of External Affairs to UK Government, 20/03/1957, T/1/61/3/21 Pt 1, ANZ.

and the British Board of Trade official, Mr Golt, told the New Zealand delegation that

> it had always been realised that the UK would not be able to join a customs union with its single tariff against the outside world because this would mean the end of Imperial Preference.

Britain wanted a European free trade area that would apply only to industrial products 'thereby safeguarding Commonwealth markets in the UK for food'. Ormond told Golt that he 'doubted whether the UK could hold the line on agriculture'.[113] Ormond doubted already that Britain could persuade Europeans to grant concessions for Britain's Commonwealth partners, and that doubt contributed to his vehement objection four years later to Britain's proposal to join the EEC. Holyoake did not share concerns over Britain's involvement in European unification. In reply to a question from Federated Farmers, he said that the New Zealand government knew that such discussions had been taking place since the late 1940s and had kept a close watch on developments.[114]

In 1961, as Britain moved towards applying for EEC membership, the reactions in New Zealand and Australia included the extreme negative reaction that, by joining the EEC, Britain would be rejecting Commonwealth countries that had helped it through its most difficult periods, and that its potential EEC membership should be opposed vigorously. Ormond played a key role in that opposition in New Zealand.[115] Paul Robertson and John Singleton suggest that one influence prompting Ormond to conduct a 'lurid' campaign against Britain's attempt to join the EEC was that Britain proposed that priority would be given to butter as the commodity most at risk, a strategy that angered meat farmers.[116] Ormond's strident opposition

---

[113] European Common Market, 1st Meeting, 12/4/1957, T/1/61/3/21 Pt 1, United Kingdom/NZ Trade Discussions, ANZ.

[114] 'UK May Become Member of European Customs Union', *Straight Furrow*, 1/10/1956, 32, ATL.

[115] Tait, 93.

[116] Paul Robertson and John Singleton, 'The Old Commonwealth and Britain's First Application to join the EEC: 1961–3', *Australian Economic History Review*, Vol. 40, No.2, 2000, 159.

to British EEC membership can be seen also as another strand in his long-term preference for holding on to the British market at all costs. Stuart Ward describes the outrage in Australia in response to Britain's actions and quotes the Australian Ambassador in the USA:

> Although Australia had traditionally seen itself in a European rather than an Asian context, this viewpoint was increasingly being challenged by the course of events. In particular, the prospective entry of the United Kingdom into the European Common Market had created ferment in Australian thinking and a search to identify the country's future role.[117]

Ormond led the 'ferment' in New Zealand but to maintain rather than change New Zealand's future role.

During what Robert McLuskie calls the 'Great Debate' over potential British EEC membership, media exposure represented Ormond's opposition as a campaign on the whole country's behalf and not just for the meat industry.[118] Some have suggested that Ormond supported fully the approach taken by the New Zealand government, and, perhaps, his tirades against British EEC membership expressed in public what the circumspect government could not say.[119] In September 1960, Ormond gave his first warning that if Britain's alliance with any European grouping undermined Commonwealth preferences it would be the 'hardest economic blow ever struck at New Zealand'. He welcomed Britain and the Commonwealth becoming associated closely with the EEC but not if it damaged 'the lifeline between Britain and ourselves'.[120] Ormond and the Meat Board had been investigating possible markets outside Britain since 1958 and already realised in 1960 the difficulty in selling New Zealand's main meat product, lamb, outside Britain. The Meat Board recognised Britain's exceptional consumption of imported

---

[117] Stuart Ward, *Australia and the British Embrace: Demise of the Imperial Ideal* (Victoria: Melbourne University Press, 2001), 58.

[118] Robert McLuskie, *The Great Debate: New Zealand, Britain and the EEC: The Shaping of Attitudes, 1960–63*, (Wellington: Decision Research Centre, Victoria University of Wellington, 1963), 11.

[119] A former senior diplomat in conversation with the author, 22/10/2014.

[120] 'Loss of Preference Could Be Hardest Blow Ever Struck', *Straight Furrow*, 07/09/1960, 13, ATL.

sheepmeat: 'unlike many countries – there is no national meat eating prejudice against mutton and lamb'.[121] The British lamb market remained essential for New Zealand's exports 'lifeline'.

The Meat Board thought the 'attitude' (reported in Chapter 2), adopted by Holyoake's government elected at the end of 1960, to be too sympathetic towards Britain's potential engagement with the EEC.[122] Ormond continued his 'lurid' campaign through 1961 using his strong media contacts. He appealed to sentiment and nostalgia despite having vociferously maintained, since the early 1950s, that sentiment should no longer have a place in business dealings with Britain. He said that Britain would be 'divorcing the Commonwealth to marry into Europe'; 'if you chopped my arms off to the butt I would still fight for the Commonwealth'; 'Britain should not forsake its past and its British friends to join with the foreigners of Europe'; 'France was always letting us down and could not fight its way out of a paper bag'; '[French President] de Gaulle was a dictator who was trying to dictate our agricultural policy to us'.[123]

When Duncan Sandys, the British Secretary of State for Commonwealth Affairs, visited New Zealand in mid-1961 to survey potential Commonwealth reaction to a British application to join the EEC, his visit prompted New Zealand government officials to review more specifically the consequences should Britain join.[124] For meat exports, the officials noted that New Zealand's production had been developed to supply the British market but pointed out that the agreement for free and unrestricted access lasted only until October 1967 and could be ended at six months' notice by either side. After bulk purchase had ended in 1954 it had become increasingly realised that Britain could

[121] New Zealand Meat Producers Board Report to Government, 10/12/1956, T/1/61/3/21, Pt II, ANZ.

[122] Meat Board Minute Book 12, 24/01/1961, 1728, ANZ.

[123] Newspaper clippings – Commonwealth and Common Market, June 1961 to February 1962 (European Economic Community – United Kingdom – European Economic Community Negotiations) AAFZ, 7174, W1318, Box 223, ANZ.

[124] Visit of Mr Sandys to discuss the United Kingdom and Europe, 26 June 1961, Cabinet Committee on Economic and Financial Questions, 03/07/1961, Cabinet Minutes 61(30), AAFD, W3738, 807, Box 8, ANZ.

no longer be relied upon in the long term to take all New Zealand's meat at acceptable prices. Officials noted that by mid-1961 New Zealand had been successful in developing a new market for beef in the USA, but protectionism in developed countries and limited financial resources in Africa, Asia and Latin America stymied possibilities for other markets. Potential trade openings in Asia were possible should living standards rise sufficiently that Asians could afford to buy New Zealand produce, but New Zealand should not delude itself that it could gain a place in a purely Asian group. Officials no longer saw any real prospect that the Commonwealth would form an effective political and economic union. Britain had reached that conclusion, and it influenced its decision to apply for EEC membership in 1961. New Zealand officials concluded that if Britain joined the EEC, and accepted fully the proposed Common Agricultural Policy (CAP), New Zealand beef exports would lose preferential treatment. A 20% tariff would be imposed on imports into Britain together with other possible restrictions. The CAP had, however, no reference to sheepmeat and the only barrier seemed to be a tariff, but the threat remained that, if sheepmeat imports had a significant impact on other meat sales within the EEC, it would be restricted in the same way as beef.

Producer organisations met Sandys, following which Ormond reported to the Meat Board that producers had stated positive views, but the drafting of the final communiqué excluded Ormond and he feared it would be too sympathetic towards Britain.[125] Egged on by a journalist from the *Dominion*, Ormond made one last effort to prevent a too sympathetic response and issued 'a blunt contradictory statement which . . . received headline treatment'.[126] Ormond said:

> If Mr Sandys is honest in what he said when the Producer Boards met him he will not sell out the Commonwealth and he will not ask us to consent to Britain's entry into negotiations with the European Economic Community. Mr Sandys told us a very good story which we received at

[125] Meat Board Minute Book 12, 05/07/1961, 1767, ANZ.

[126] Hayward, 179.

> its face value but I consider that New Zealand should now reserve its position on the whole question.[127]

Ormond's statement damaged his future influence outside the meat industry in that he seemed unable to act as a team member and instead continually sought individual publicity. The British High Commissioner judged that Ormond had taken the lead in public discussion through his 'strident tones' in an effort to

> gain the maximum publicity for himself as a tough protector of the farmer and he has stuck to the exaggerated line that Britain is betraying the Commonwealth and that utter ruin stares New Zealand in the face.[128]

The High Commissioner said that Sandys had reassured the Producer Boards but not Ormond who remained 'truculent'. The other Producer Board representatives and Federated Farmers were 'so annoyed by the tone of Ormond' that 'they went out of their way' to express recognition of Britain's difficulties 'and appreciated Sandys assurances'. But the High Commissioner remained concerned that public opinion would be 'misled by repeated jeremiads from Mr Ormond'.

Ormond's statement clearly represented his own rather than all producer views. The Chairman of the Dairy Board, Andrew Linton, had been chosen to make a statement for the producer boards and he expressed his satisfaction with 'the explanations and assurances given by Mr Sandys'.[129] Linton called for Ormond's resignation, but Ormond covered his rear immediately by persuading the Meat Board, retrospectively, to support him.[130] Britain's decision at the end of August 1961 to apply for EEC membership took the wind out of Ormond's campaign, not because its goal was achieved but because it had been by-passed by

---

[127] Tait, 98.

[128] New Zealand: Visit of the Secretary of State for discussions about possible United Kingdom Association with EEC, 23/08/1961, FO371/158322 XC21689, Public Records Office (PRO). The following two paragraphs are a summary of the main points with regard to primary producers.

[129] McLuskie, 59.

[130] Tait, 98.

events. McLuskie notes that during the late 1960s, though Ormond 'continued to make known his opposition to entry, and in particular his dislike of the French, he was no longer a focal point of opposition'.[131]

As reported by the British High Commissioner, Federated Farmers reacted more moderately than Ormond to the Sandys assurance. The General Secretary, Alec O'Shea, had written on behalf of the Federation for *The Times* in December 1960 that New Zealand producers recognised the need for a prosperous Britain and that Britain could not divorce herself from Europe, politically or economically. Continental Europeans endeavoured to solve social as well as economic problems, and that led to complications in agricultural trade. Producers in New Zealand viewed sympathetically efforts to widen trade in Europe and would like to see a way by which Britain could join the EEC without destroying Britain's trade with New Zealand. O'Shea concluded that 'Britain has always been and is likely to remain New Zealand's main market'.[132]

Straight Furrow reflected Federated Farmers more moderate approach and an editorial said 'it would be unrealistic, as well as impossible, to forbid Britain to start negotiations'. *Straight Furrow* recognised New Zealand's weakness in wanting unrestricted meat entry into Britain whilst New Zealand obstructed manufactured imports from Britain.[133] The Federated Farmers President saw Britain's need for change as partly caused by industrialisation in countries such as New Zealand. The Federation had first warned in 1956 that New Zealand seemed not to be keeping to the Ottawa Agreement, causing difficulties for British exports to New Zealand.[134]

Not all meat producers supported Ormond's opposition to British EEC membership. The Federated Farmers Meat and Wool Chairman, Alec Begg, sympathised with Britain's position and adopted a line when addressing the section at its annual conference that went against

[131] McLuskie, 116.

[132] A. P. O'Shea, 'A Dominion View of the Problems', *The Times Supplement on Agriculture*, 5/12/1960, ii.

[133] 'At Crossroads Says Dominion President: Must Choose the Path to Follow', *Straight Furrow*, 19/07/1961, 5, ATL.

[134] 'Where Do We Go from Here?', *Straight Furrow*, 19/07/1961, 5, ATL; Annual Address by the Chairman to the Meat and Wool Section Conference, 20/06/1956, Federated Farmers 90-343 MSY 2732 M&W19/1956, ATL.

Ormond's strident opposition to British entry.[135] Begg said that rights in the British market came from the Ottawa agreement that gave New Zealand unrestricted entry for exports to Britain; Britain gained preferential tariffs for her manufacturers and an 'assurance that they would be permitted to compete for the consumers' favour' in New Zealand. He quoted from the Ottawa agreement and pointed out that Britain had 'scrupulously observed her obligations'; New Zealand, through its import restrictions had, though,

> deliberately broken the agreement, not just once or twice but systematically. . . . Many classes of British manufacture have been completely excluded from the New Zealand market.

Begg continued that if New Zealand

> sincerely believed that her interest would be better served by developing increased trade within the Commonwealth then New Zealand should offer to increase opportunities for British and inter-Commonwealth trade within New Zealand.

That strategy would be better than the 'most vociferous protests prompted by mere self-interest'. Begg warned that the prospects for New Zealand meat sales to Britain remained the same whether or not Britain joined the EEC.[136] He thought it 'unwise' to believe that New Zealand would be able to retain the free entry rights to the British market. When Britain had set a time limit (1967) on the agreement for free and unrestricted access, New Zealand should have taken that limitation as 'a serious warning'. He noted that there had been, for some years, strong sentiment in Britain favouring meat import controls.

Ormond seemed to have personal motives rather than representing those of primary producers. Others saw his objections as personal

[135] Annual Address by the Chairman to the Meat and Wool Section Conference, 20/06/1962, Federated Farmers 90-343 MSY2738, M&W64/1962, 2-8, ATL.

[136] Address by Chairman of the Meat and Wool Section to the Annual Conference, 20/06/1962, Federated Farmers 90-343 MSY2738 M&W64/1962, 3/4, ATL.

'truculence' rather than the result of a thorough understanding of the issues. Perhaps his closest allies against British EEC membership were the right-wing nationalists in Britain who pressed that Britain should cling to Commonwealth links rather than join the EEC. McLuskie points out that in 1961 newspapers marshalled and shaped public opinion in the debate that took place in the New Zealand media during Britain's first application to join the EEC.[137] The sensitive negotiations with Britain and the EEC made the government circumspect, and Ormond's contributions captured the headlines and fixed in the public's mind the image of Britain treacherously deserting its friends. In the long-term it is Ormond's strident opposition ('jeremiads') in the early 1960s that has been remembered rather than the moderate responses from the government, Dairy Board, Wool Board and Federated Farmers. To the public, Ormond's lurid opposition created the fear that British EEC membership would be a disaster for New Zealand. As always, the disaster threats raised far more interest than telling newspaper readers that not much would change or that change had been taking place gradually. The common perception in New Zealand in the twenty-first century noted by Easton reflects the image that Ormond tried to project: an ungrateful Britain rejecting the friends that had helped it through difficult times.[138] Holyoake and Marshall remained unmoved by Ormond's pleas for a more belligerent approach. Robertson and Singleton agree that an approach more belligerent than that adopted by Marshall and Holyoake would have put New Zealand's economic future in even more jeopardy.[139]

4.6 Losing Privileged Access to the British Market

Ormond remained adamant from 1961 onwards that continued free access would give substantial opportunities for expanding meat exports to Britain. He continued that approach through de Gaulle's rejections in

[137] McLuskie, 119.

[138] Brian Easton, *The Nationbuilders* (Auckland: Auckland University Press, 2001), 183.

[139] Robertson and Singleton, 153.

1963 and 1967 of Britain's applications for EEC membership. Ormond tried to persuade Britain to place restrictions on its own primary production to favour New Zealand producers but, more realistically, Federated Farmers recognised from 1964 the inevitable restrictions on New Zealand exports. Meat Board members other than Ormond, also, recognised the inevitability of restrictions. Britain extended the long-term agreement for New Zealand's access from 1967 but now with qualifications that allowed Britain in 1969 to impose a levy on lamb imports and end, finally, duty-free and unrestricted access. The EEC tariff replaced the British levy in 1973 but war in the Middle East, and the consequent oil price shock proved to be the most damaging event for New Zealand's meat exports in 1973. When, in 1980, the EEC agreed sheepmeat regulations, they were seen as a substantial success for the New Zealand negotiators.

In 1961 Ormond rebutted the 'new found experts' who had been saying that consumption limits for New Zealand meat in Britain had been reached.[140] He claimed that 'this is the sort of thing we have heard throughout the history of our trade'.[141] De Gaulle's rejection in January 1963 of Britain's application to join the EEC did not ease Ormond's concerns about possible restrictions on New Zealand meat exports to Britain. He told his Electoral Committee in April 1963 that, even after the EEC negotiations had broken down, some in Britain thought in terms of trade restraint and reducing imports from New Zealand. Ormond countered that New Zealand had tailored its meat products for the British housewife and that Britain should not restrict entry. But, 'tailoring' for the British market had been essential to make sure that lamb sold to consumers in Britain at affordable prices. Ormond said that the British market remained the best able to give an economic return.[142]

[140] Meat Board Chairman's Address to the Electoral Committee, 22/08/1961, Federated Farmers 90-343 MSY-2738 M&W40/1961, 4, ATL.

[141] Meat Board Chairman's Address to the Electoral Committee, 22/08/1961, Federated Farmers 90-343 MSY-2738 M&W40/1961, 3, ATL.

[142] Meat Board Chairman's Address to the Electoral Committee, 03/04/1963, Federated Farmers 90-343 MSY2739 M&W19/1963, 1/2, ATL.

Tonnage for lamb markets outside Britain measured in ten-thousands and not the hundred-thousands exported to Britain.[143] Lamb could not be sold easily outside Britain because, in most other countries, domestic production satisfied lamb consumption; only 4% of New Zealand's lamb exports shipped to countries other than Britain in 1963. Meat Board members other than Ormond stated vociferously the need for change. One member, John Andrew, told Federated Farmers Southland Provincial Executive that the British government had asked the Meat Board to develop new markets because the British market could not accept increased sales from New Zealand. Unlike Ormond, who claimed room for expansion existed in the British market, another Meat Board member, P. J. Scott, said that New Zealand could not continue increasing production, and hoping to find a market for the extra in Britain.[144] Ormond's views seemed to be out of step with those of other Meat Board members.

At the start of 1964 the British Minister for Agriculture, Christopher Soames, began a policy of managing food imports, first, for cereals but with the eventual intention that meat imports would also be managed.[145] Ormond responded that it would be a 'bold Cabinet Minister who took action to raise the price of food' through import restrictions, perhaps forgetting (ignoring?) that he had sought exactly that in 1957 in wanting restrictions on Argentinean produce.[146] Formal discussions on restricting New Zealand meat imports took place early in 1964 but agreement could not be reached.[147] A quota for New Zealand of 303,000 tonnes for lamb and mutton, close to the average for the previous five years, had been suggested with no increase in subsequent years.[148] The Federated Farmers Vice-President, P. S. Plummer, took a more realistic line than Ormond and told a provincial annual conference

143 'Report on Farming', *Straight Furrow*, 17/04/1963, 1, ATL.

144 'U.K. Can't Take All', *Straight Furrow*, 03/04/1963, 7, ATL.

145 'Mr Soames Wants a Managed Market', *Straight Furrow*, 22/01/1964, 22, ATL.

146 Meat Board Chairman's Address to the Electoral Committee, 09/04/1964, Federated Farmers 90-343 MSY2739 M&W54/1964, 3, ATL.

147 Meat Board Chairman's Address to the Electoral Committee, 09/04/1964, Federated Farmers 90-343 MSY2739 M&W54/1964, 2.

148 Market Promotion for Export Meat, Meat Export Development Company (New Zealand) Limited – General, AAFZ W1318 7174 Box 228 April 1965, p6, ANZ.

that, inevitably, at some future time the British would impose a quota on New Zealand meat. Plummer noted the marked trend towards managed markets because countries such as Britain pursued 'policies designed to boost and protect their own agriculture'.[149] He warned New Zealand meat producers to note the changing trade patterns.

Britain's balance of payments problems led, in 1964, to a short-term surcharge on most imports, though exempting nearly all imports from New Zealand.[150] Early in 1965 the British Minister for Agriculture, now Fred Peart, Labour having been elected in October 1964, made it clear that both the Labour government and the Conservative Opposition agreed that food imports into Britain should be phased and integrated with home production, though the means of achieving that remained unclear.[151] Britain told the New Zealand government that it could not accept the increased production being planned in New Zealand.[152] Another Meat Board member, Charles Hilgendorf, saw that change would be needed, noting that both political parties in Britain were committed to a managed market in meat and to 'featherbedding' their agriculture. But New Zealand could 'scarcely complain' because it had a managed market and included featherbedding for products such as bicycles. New Zealand would need to accept a quota on the British market in the 'quite near future'.[153]

Ormond continued his line that 'It is our New Zealand's producers' chief mission in life to produce meat for the British housewife' and continued to fight against quotas imposed by Britain. He thought it surprising that 'there should be so much thinking among Government officials today based on the arguments of theorists who propose to restrict . . . the kind of food the people shall eat'.[154] In July 1964, one

[149] 'Co-operation to Avoid Controls?', *Straight Furrow*, 03/06/1964, 7, ATL.

[150] Alec Cairncross, *The British Economy Since 1945* (Oxford: Blackwell, 1992), 152; 'Financial Statement', *AJHR*, Vol. I, B-6, 1965, 24, WCL.

[151] W. D. Thomas, 'Wither the UK Meat Industry?', *Straight Furrow*, 06/01/1965, 12, ATL.

[152] Market Promotion for Export Meat, Meat Export Development Company (New Zealand) Limited – General, AAFZ W1318 7174 Box 228 April 1965, p6, ANZ.

[153] 'Managed Market for UK Meat', *Straight Furrow*, 15/07/1964, 27, ATL.

[154] Meat Board Chairman's Address to the Electoral Committee, 27/08/1964, Federated Farmers 90-343 MSY2739 M&W74/1964, 4, ATL.

such 'theorist', M. G. Hollard, an academic from Lincoln College, told a farmers' conference in Blenheim:

> the halcyon days of meat marketing in the United Kingdom . . . appeared to be over . . . due mainly to the renaissance of British farming efficiency . . . the British market is no longer a 'bottomless pit into which . . . New Zealand could tip as much pastoral produce as they could muster and receive an acceptable price for it.[155]

In early 1965 the end approached for the arrangement agreed in 1952 that Britain would take unrestricted tonnages of duty-free meat. Ormond told his Electoral Committee in August 1965 that 'the most vital thing in our meat trading future . . . is still the right-of-entry agreement that we have for our meat into Britain'. He considered it to be vital to New Zealand's economic welfare and to 'the future of everyone in New Zealand'.[156] Ormond had feared the right of entry would be lost if Britain joined the EEC; he now feared Britain would be reluctant to renew the agreement despite being outside the EEC. Following the 1957 trade talks with Britain, Holyoake had recognised that Britain would be reluctant to renew the agreement from 1967. Ormond probably also recognised that but tried to persuade Britain to continue the agreement, using his bluster to embarrass Britain with his claims of Britain letting down those that had helped it during difficult times.[157] Such bluster had built Ormond's reputation in his early days as a farmer–politician when Britain faced food shortages but by 1965 his bluster had become far less effective.

The British Agriculture Minister, Fred Peart, questioned in September 1965 on the British attitude to extending the long-term agreement, answered the question 'cautiously' saying that no formal approach had been made by New Zealand and 'we have the best part

[155] 'Halcyon Days Over for NZ?', *Straight Furrow*, 15/07/1964, 21, ATL.

[156] Meat Board Chairman's Address to the Electoral Committee, 24/08/1965, Federated Farmers 90-343 MSY2741 M&W30/1965, 3, ATL.

[157] Meat Board Chairman's Address to the Electoral Committee, 24/08/1965, Federated Farmers 90-343 MSY2741 M&W30/1965, 4, ATL.

of two years' for discussions.[158] Following a visit by Peart to New Zealand, *Straight Furrow* interpreted that he left a 'vague . . . disquietude' with those who spoke with him. New Zealand should be concerned with the final implication – New Zealand would need to face up to losing free and unrestricted access to the British market.[159] The future rights-of-entry discussions started early in 1966 soon after Peart's visit. Peart, when interviewed by the *New Zealand Herald* editor about the discussions, said that Britain recognised the value attached to rights-of-access undertakings, but noted the complex issues associated with the wider trading relations between New Zealand and Britain.[160] He implied that the agreement would depend on arrangements made for British exports into New Zealand. The recently concluded trade agreement between New Zealand and Australia irked Britain because British exports into New Zealand might be displaced by Australian.

In 1967, Britain agreed that rights-of-entry would continue but with the qualification that Britain retained the right to 'regulate imports if there were intergovernmental commodity agreements among all suppliers' and 'to prevent market disruption or the threat thereof'.[161] In April 1967 the British government announced increased support for its domestic agriculture with a view to reducing imports, and for the first time in over twenty years New Zealand could no longer be sure that it could dictate how much meat it sent to Britain.[162]

When the British Prime Minister, Harold Wilson, announced in May 1967 a new application to join the EEC and de Gaulle again rejected Britain's application, the threat to New Zealand sales remained because the British farming community continued to press for import controls on meat. In 1968, Ormond finally recognised that changes were needed, but continued to regret the weakening links with Britain, resembling one of Easton's 'colonials wringing their hands' at the weakening ties of

158 'Visit of Mr. T. F. Peart', *Straight Furrow*, 15/09/1965, 7, ATL.

159 'Was His Journey Really Necessary?', *Straight Furrow*, 06/10/1965, 3, ATL.

160 'NZ-UK Market Has Uncertain Future', *Straight Furrow*, 19/01/1966, 11, ATL.

161 'Still Some Doubt on Right of Entry for Meat', *Straight Furrow*, 03/08/1966, 1, ATL.

162 '£40m Boost to British Farming: Emphasis on Import Saving', *Straight Furrow*, 05/04/1967, 5, ATL.

Empire.[163] Touchingly, Ormond still hankered after the past relationship with Britain, and did not want to 'pass too hurriedly over the partnership we have with the United Kingdom ... too many New Zealanders ... think of Britain as a has-been' and think 'we would best to forget her and find ... trading partners elsewhere'. But to Ormond that would be 'folly'; he still saw Britain as 'pulsating in life and energy ... reflected in its commerce'.[164] Calder and Tyson report 'apocryphal stories about indulgence in the trappings of UK visits ... like Ascot and Wimbledon ... going back to Sir John Ormond'.[165] Perhaps Ormond's clinging to the British market partly reflected the muted appeal of the trappings of Asian visits.

The British All-Party House of Commons Select Committee on Agriculture increased the pressure for import restrictions, proposing in March 1969 that Britain should substitute home-grown food for temperate foodstuffs' imports. Even more worrying for New Zealand, the Committee recommended that the domestic agricultural expansion should no longer be inhibited by rigid provisions in international agreements which offered British market sections to overseas suppliers.[166] The British Opposition spokesman on agriculture, Joseph Godber, reinforced that by saying that conditions had changed since Britain had adopted free trade in the nineteenth century. Godber added:

> if we were still the richest country in the world ... we might be able to continue our present policy of allowing food to come without hindrance. ... Conditions have changed ... it is time for us to change our thinking.[167]

---

[163] Easton, *Nationbuilders*, 183.

[164] Meat Board Chairman's Report to the Electoral Committee, 22/08/1968, Federated Farmers 90 - 343 MSY2746 M&W57/1968, 8/9, ATL.

[165] Calder and Tyson, 57.

[166] 'Time We Stated Our Case', *Straight Furrow*, 19/03/1969, 3, ATL.

[167] 'UK Conservatives Favour Restrictions on Food Imports', *Straight Furrow*, 19/03/1969, 15, ATL.

The Federated Farmers Meat and Wool Chairman warned New Zealand meat producers that their British equivalents 'make no secret of their wish to see quota limitations placed on imported meat'.[168] In addition the Federated Farmers General Secretary warned that New Zealand could no longer take for granted assumptions regarding duty-free and quota-free access.[169] By February 1970 the British Labour government had moved towards introducing levies on lamb imports, and Edward Heath, now leader of the British Conservative party, made it clear during a visit to New Zealand that, if his party won the forthcoming general election, it would introduce levies.[170] In June 1970 the Conservative party won the election, and Ormond soon expressed his concern that the new government intended to introduce a levy on imported foodstuffs:

> [W]hat the British Government is proposing is a tax on imported foodstuffs – a tax on lamb after a trading partnership [in frozen meat between New Zealand and Britain] of 88 years.[171]

He warned that New Zealand lamb marketing could be faced by a major change in the years ahead. Ormond's good copy reinforced the impression that he wanted to carry on for the next eighty-eight years in the same way as the previous.

Britain introduced the expected levy on lamb imports in October 1970 and, despite warnings since 1969, the Federated Farmers Meat and Wool Chairman called the introduction 'abrupt and cold blooded'.[172] He described it as a 'cruel blow' that signalled the end of the 'long-established era of duty-free entry of New Zealand meat products',

[168] Chairman's Address to the Meat and Wool Council, 19/06/1968, Federated Farmers 90-343 MSY2746 M&W36/1968, 3, ATL.

[169] 'UK Market Access Must Not Be Presumed', *Straight Furrow*, 02/04/1969, 3, ATL.

[170] Chairman's Address to the Meat and Wool Section Council, 18/06/1969, Federated Farmers 90-343 MSY2745, M&W31/1969, 5, ATL; 'Proposed UK Levy on Beef Imports Has Very Serious Implications', *Straight Furrow*, 04/02/1970, 16, ATL.

[171] 'UK Promise on NZ Lamb', *Straight Furrow*, 09/09/1970, 8, ATL.

[172] Bruce Dryden, 'UK Levy – Major Threat', *Straight Furrow*, 04/11/1970, 2, ATL.

and called for reprisals against British manufacturing imports into New Zealand.[173] He said the levy cost would be borne, either by the British housewife in higher prices, or by the New Zealand producer. Ormond called it a 'slap in the face' with Britain treating New Zealand 'as a foreigner' showing that Ormond still saw New Zealand as British in 1970.[174] Ormond still seemed unable to grasp how the New Zealand/ British relationship had changed from the days of an entrenched colonial relationship. The British Farmers Union President welcomed the levy: 'when overseas producers [New Zealand?] talk of their "traditional right" to the British market they must be reminded that if anyone has first claim . . . it is British farmers'; implying that, to him, New Zealand farmers were no longer 'British' farmers.[175] Britain no longer saw itself in a colonial relationship with New Zealand; Ormond had yet to reach that conclusion. New Zealand meat sales to Britain started to fall but sales to other countries more than compensated. In contrast to Ormond's bluster, Meat Board officials reviewed 'prospects for Europe' in 1969 and saw 'optimism rather than pessimism' if Britain 'ever gets into the EEC'. Consumers paid much higher prices for sheepmeat in continental Europe than in Britain, even the EEC tariff of 20% 'could no doubt be borne competitively'.[176]

In 1969 Ormond accepted publicly the need to 'build bridges' between New Zealand and the EEC whether or not Britain became a member. Ormond had continued to make derogatory statements about continental Europeans through the 1960s, but Marshall's quiet diplomacy in his dealings with the EEC countries eventually convinced Ormond that many European countries had definite goodwill for New Zealand.[177] Ormond at last recognised that Europeans tried to help New Zealand – he told the Meat Board in 1970 – 'The markets are there, let's get into

[173] 'A Cruel Blow – Dryden', *Straight Furrow*, 04/11/1970, 3, ATL.

[174] 'A Slap in the Face – Ormond', *Straight Furrow*, 04/11/1970, 3, ATL.

[175] 'UK Farm Leader Welcomes Levies', *Straight Furrow*, 19/11/1970, 8, ATL.

[176] Lamb Prospects in Europe: Meat Board Note, 16/06/1969, Federated Farmers 90-343 MSY2745, 2, ATL.

[177] 'A Friendly Hand to Europe', *Straight Furrow*, 03/09/1969, 3, ATL.

them – EEC or no EEC'; extra effort went into meeting with EEC countries.[178] The Meat Board's 'prospects for Europe' saw New Zealand meat exports to Europe 'blossoming . . . with a growing number of enquiries for our lamb . . . obstacles are wearing down'.[179]

When the EEC accepted Britain as a member in 1971 and agreed special arrangements for New Zealand, the main issue for meat, export of lamb, remained in abeyance. The special arrangements included that sale of beef to Britain would be restricted but that represented only 3% of New Zealand's meat exports. For sheepmeat sales, which represented more than 30%, there had been no EEC system, and sheepmeat had not been part of the formal discussions but 'a common regulation was to be instituted at some future date'.[180] Meanwhile, the EEC 20% Common External Tariff would replace the British levy but only reaching 20% over a five-year transition period. Holyoake told Parliament that both the British and New Zealand governments considered that an acceptable trade volume in New Zealand lamb would continue to flow over such a tariff.[181] The Meat Board Deputy Chairman said that an eventual EEC common policy on lamb may not be so bad because it would give New Zealand access to possible new EEC markets.[182]

After Britain had been accepted into the EEC without the disastrous restrictions on New Zealand exports that he had feared, Ormond responded by being conciliatory and reflective. He noted that strong bonds of sentiment and sympathy remained between New Zealand and the people of Britain, but he, at last, recognised the growing gap in trading interests. He thought that New Zealand had always had the feeling of being protected, but now that had changed. New Zealand had become 'an independent nation depending more than ever on our own

[178] Meat Board Minute Book 15, 02/12/1970, 803, ANZ.

[179] Lamb Prospects in Europe: Meat Board Note, 16/06/1969, Federated Farmers 90–343 MSY2745, 2–4, ATL.

[180] New Zealand and the European Economic Community, paper presented to the House of Representatives by Leave, Government Printer, Wellington, 1971, 20, ANZ.

[181] New Zealand and the European Economic Community, paper presented to the House of Representatives by Leave, Government Printer, Wellington, 1971, 23, ANZ.

[182] 'EEC Lamb Consideration', *Straight Furrow*, 07/07/1971, 11, ATL.

resources'.[183] Ormond accepted that mother's apron strings had become untied and no longer used his bluster in attempts to re-tie them.

The impact on New Zealand meat exports from the global economic changes during the late 1960s/early 1970s reduced the impact of the EEC levy. Those changes started with President Nixon, following difficulties in the American economy, announcing that 'the United States could no longer afford the luxury of supporting the Western economic system as a whole'.[184] Later, the recession following the 1973 oil price shock impacted severely on New Zealand meat exports; exports to all markets fell by more than 20%. New Zealand's long-term worry over import restrictions in the British market became insignificant in comparison with the consequences when Egypt and Syria attacked Israel in October 1973. The Meat Board's chief economist gave reasons for the fall in New Zealand's meat earnings in 1973/1974:

> the effect of Watergate on US politics and the President's price freeze in 1971, the oil crisis with its effect on . . . Europe and . . . the Japanese balance of payments . . . industrial problems in the UK and the snap election, and the decline in supplies of animal feedstuffs.[185]

He did not include Britain's entry into the EEC. Gustafson agrees that the New Zealand's economy had been 'shattered' by the end of 1974, not because Britain had joined the EEC but because of the 'collapse of economic growth round the world coupled with escalating prices for imported oil and declining prices for agricultural exports'.[186]

Years later, Ormond's prophecies of doom remained unfulfilled. The EEC finally agreed sheepmeat regulations in 1980, inviting importing countries to restrict their sales to EEC countries through a Voluntary Restraint Agreement (VRA) in return for a reduction in the EEC external tariff. New Zealand negotiated a VRA that guaranteed rights-of-entry for 240,000 tonnes a year, 10% above its average annual exports

[183] 'We Are Now More Alone', *Straight Furrow*, 20/10/1971, 19, ATL.

[184] McAloon, 145.

[185] Calder and Tyson, 63.

[186] Gustafson, *Muldoon*, 164.

to EEC countries including Britain, for the previous three years. Muldoon describes the quota as 'adequate and, indeed, sometimes in the early years not filled'.[187] The external tariff reduced to 10%. Calder and Tyson call the agreement 'a substantial success for the [New Zealand] negotiators'; New Zealand had 'achieved most where there was most to lose'.[188] In 1994 that EEC quota for New Zealand changed to 226,700 tonnes, 75% of sheepmeat imports to the EEC from all countries; further, the external tariff became zero.[189] Britain remained New Zealand's best customer for sheepmeat up to 2012.[190]

4.7 Conclusion

Food shortages in Britain in the late 1940s led Britain to exhort New Zealand to increase meat production, but specific measures did not start until the early 1950s when New Zealand recognised its own need to increase export earnings. Meat Board investment in aerial top-dressing that benefitted all primary production sectors increased productivity, but the extra meat did not go to commitments made to Britain but to new markets where better prices might be obtained. After the bulk purchase agreement with Britain ended in 1954, New Zealand retained unrestricted and duty-free access to the British market up to 1967 but from 1957 fears grew that the situation would eventually change. Britain, since the late 1940s, had started to expand its own agriculture to reduce its dependence on food imports. Britain's first application to join the EEC in 1961 strengthened fears that the British market would eventually have a tariff against New Zealand imports, and, perhaps, even quota restrictions.

Ormond, in his long-term role as Chairman of the Meat Board, welcomed the colonial relationship between Britain and New Zealand

---

[187] Muldoon, 101.

[188] Calder and Tyson, 114; Calder and Tyson, 109.

[189] www.archive.defra.gov.uk/evidence/economics/foodfarm/ . . . /chapter1.pdf accessed 18/07/2013.

[190] http://portal.beeflambnz.com/tools/export-tool/ accessed 05/07/2016.

and fought against change in that relationship. He shared with many in Britain a reluctance to recognise how Britain's position in world trade had changed and that Britain could no longer afford to allow duty-free and unrestricted access for meat imports. Between 1945 and 1975, farmers made successful contributions to change by increasing meat available for export through increased productivity in the case of lamb and mutton, and also by changing their farming, with sheep farmers introducing more cattle, and dairy farmers turning to beef production as a supplement to dairying. Ormond's bluster and public front gave an impression that he resisted change and, undoubtedly, he regretted the weakening links with Britain. But it would be unfair to describe the meat industry overall as a constraint on New Zealand's trade. By the late 1960s meat exports had become New Zealand's best export earner and earned nearly twice as much as the next best. Ormond publicly blustered to prevent change and fought hard to increase exports to British market, partly because no one else would buy lamb in significant quantities. That remained the case through the period up to EEC sheepmeat regulations coming into force in 1980, and beyond. The fears of losing the British market proved to be groundless; not only did the Anglo-New Zealand nexus for sheepmeat remain unsnapped, but complementary meat markets had been developed. It is to that diversification that we now turn.

5

Diversification of Meat Exports

5.1 Introduction

Diversification of meat markets was a continuous development with the most significant new markets being the USA and Japan. New Zealand's meat sector between 1945 and 1975 faced the dilemma of how much effort should be put into retaining the British market and how much should be put into developing new markets. New markets easily compensated for the failure to increase meat exports to Britain. Producers, particularly within Federated Farmers, had discussed the need for new markets as early as 1945.[1] In 1947, the Meat Board discussed how it would use reserve funds accumulated during wartime and devised a new long-term policy that included setting aside significant resources for seeking and establishing new markets.[2] Six years later, anticipating the end of bulk purchase, the Meat Board invited all

[1] On average through 1945 and 1946, there were two articles each month in *Straight Furrow* mentioning the need for new markets.

[2] Meat Board Minute Book 9, 07/03/1947, 454, ANZ.

D. Hall, *Emerging from an Entrenched Colonial Economy*, Palgrave Studies in Economic History, DOI 10.1007/978-3-319-53016-1_5

export companies to assist the Board in exploring new markets. The Westfield Freezing Works Manager illustrated the response, saying: 'now the bulk purchase agreement is ending the meat firms will be seeking markets for meat . . . throughout the world'.[3] But success, in terms of tonnage sales anywhere near comparable with those to Britain, came only in the late 1950s and 1960s when it had been accepted by the Meat Board that Britain could no longer absorb increases in exports and eventually there would be restrictions.

New Zealand successfully diversified meat exports through mutton sales to Japan and beef sales to the USA, and by the end of the 1960s more than 75% of New Zealand's meat exports outside Britain shipped to those two countries. There was successful diversification to many other countries, for instance, Greece and in the Middle East, but, in total, the tonnages sold to those others rarely reached more than 15% of combined sales to Britain, the USA and Japan. Nonetheless, by mid-1968 Ormond could proudly describe to his Electoral College how the meat industry had achieved high earnings through the 'fruit of past efforts by the producer, the board and the trade to develop, supply and maintain old and new markets'.[4] Meat export earnings reached record levels because the pattern of the export trade had changed in relatively few years. In 1955, for meat exports, only 13% shipped outside Britain; fifteen years later the meat sales to Britain remained unchanged but in addition New Zealand sold the same amount to markets outside Britain (Fig. 5.1). Meat became New Zealand's most successful export sector in 1970, earning 41.3% of total earnings with the next highest being wool at 21.7%.[5] In 1970 meat earned (at 1971 prices) three times the revenue earned in 1950 (Fig. 5.2) and the tonnage exported had doubled during those twenty years (Fig. 5.3).

[3] Meat Board Minute Book, 10, 28/04/1953, 934, ANZ; 'Farmers Forum: In the Market', *Straight Furrow*, 01/08/1954, 19, ATL.

[4] '"Hard Sell" Is Succeeding', *Straight Furrow*, 04/09/1968, 16, ATL.

[5] 'Graph Prepared by the Meat Board', *Straight Furrow*, 08/04/1970, 17, ATL.

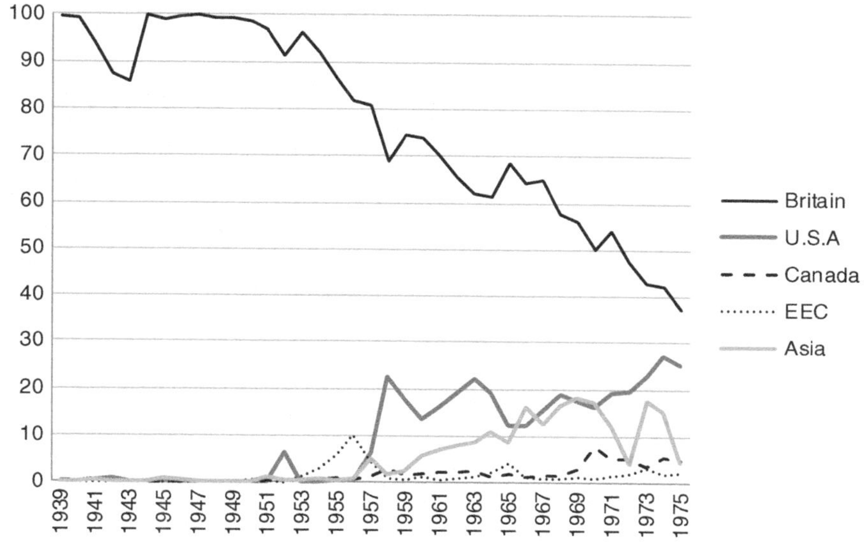

Fig. 5.1 Percentages of New Zealand meat tonnages for various destinations (NZDYB)

5.2 The First Tentative Steps in Exporting to the US Market

The tonnages New Zealand sold to Britain stabilised through the 1950s and 1960s, and additional tonnages as a result of increased productivity sold mainly as beef to the USA. The Meat Board formed a company to develop the lamb market in the USA but that proved unsuccessful. As early as 1945 proposals were made that New Zealand should put more effort into selling beef rather than lamb, and that proved to be correct in the long term with beef sales to the USA eventually becoming a successful diversification. Demand grew for New Zealand beef but the sales, though significant for New Zealand, remained small in comparison with the overall American beef trade. In contrast, the far smaller American domestic lamb trade made New Zealand sales a significant threat for US lamb producers.

Links with the USA had been built by New Zealand providing food for the American South Pacific Armed Forces during World War II but, in

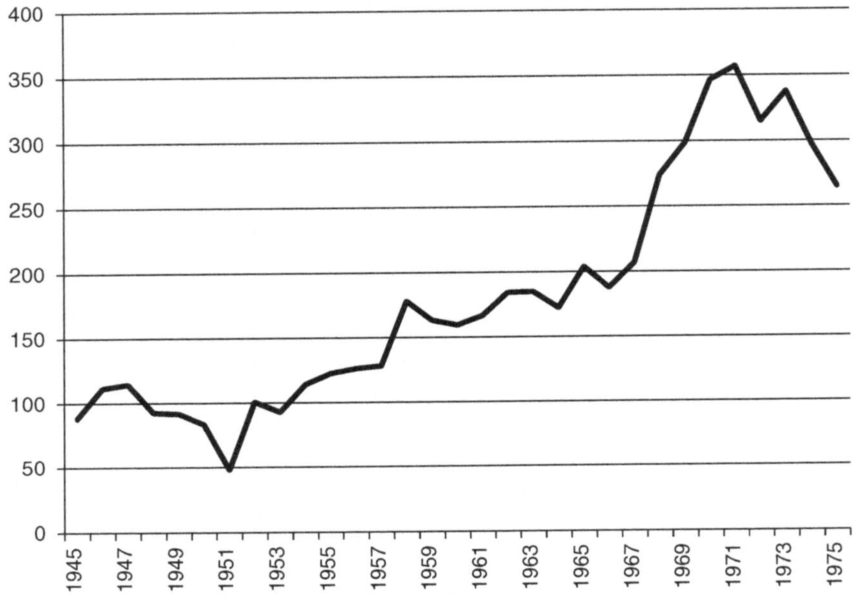

Fig. 5.2 New Zealand meat exports in $ million at 1971 prices (NZDYB)

the late 1940s, heavy tariff protection prevented the USA from being a significant market for New Zealand meat. That protectionism caused resentment amongst New Zealand producers particularly because an American company had been allowed to buy the Wellington Meat Export Company.[6] But it did not stop proposals being made that, because the British preferred lamb, there would be mutton available to start a market in the USA. Mr Leov of the French Pass Branch of Federated Farmers advocated selling meat to the USA 'at a loss for years on end in order to get established'.[7] Federated Farmers recognised that, to break into the American lamb market, links needed to be established with the powerful farming organisations that strongly influenced Congress.[8] Also,

[6] 'London or Washington?', *Straight Furrow*, 15/04/1946, 1, ATL.

[7] Harold Leov, 'Ewe Mutton', *Straight Furrow*, 15/06/1946, 27, ATL.

[8] 'Meat and Wool Section', *Straight Furrow*, 15/07/1950, 15, ATL.

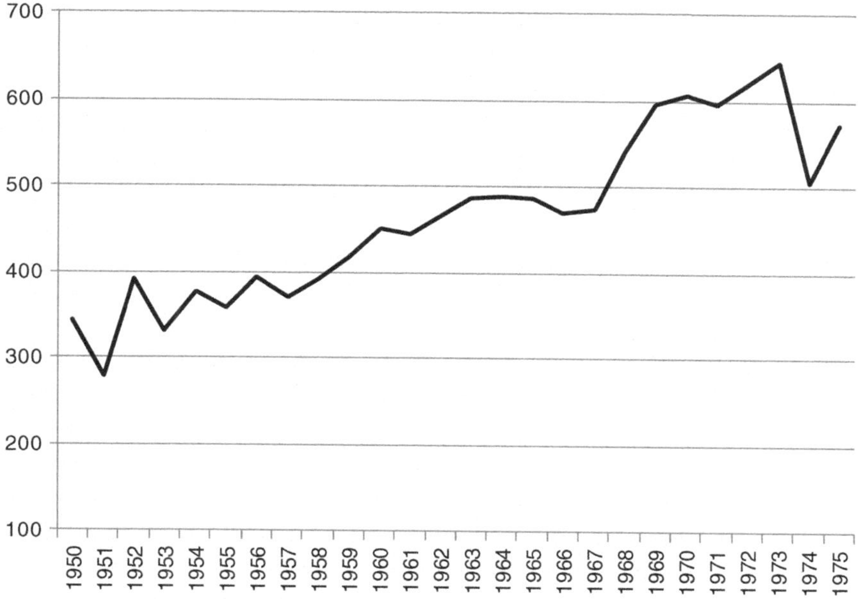

Fig. 5.3 New Zealand meat exports in tonnes (000) (NZDYB)

producers should not try to sell to the USA without first ensuring support from American producers, for instance, by proposing to phase sales to avoid interference with peak selling seasons.[9] Roger Buchanan, who had marketed wool to the USA for the Wool Board, calls the USA 'the Great Seducer' – it always held out promise of accepting increased exports from New Zealand but turned out to be a 'big tease'; that also proved to be the case for lamb exports, but not for beef.[10]

An American farmer writing in the magazine *The National Woolgrower* in 1950 illustrated the potential problems, noting that the 'persistent rumours of importation of lamb from Australia and New Zealand are

[9] 'Trade with the United States Must Be Handled Carefully', *Straight Furrow*, 15/11/1950, 3, ATL.

[10] Roger Buchanan, *The Last Shepherd: Anecdotes and Observations from Five Decades in the Wool Industry* (Wellington: Ngaio Press, 2012), 161.

soon to become a reality' with the first 'token' shipment due to arrive in November 1950. The writer feared lamb imports but recognised that legally they could not be prevented. He felt that if brokers with little interest in the meat market sold the lamb the outcome could be serious for the entire lamb industry. But, if American processors handled it under the present short-supply conditions, there might be an advantage putting lamb in the market to supply orders that could not be met by domestic production. The writer did not want to advocate increased lamb importation but tried to 'see a bright side to a problem over which we have little control'.[11]

Late in 1951 the Federated Farmers General Secretary, Alec O'Shea, advocated working jointly with American suppliers. He said it would be important to have a real understanding with the American farmers because, traditionally, they opposed primary produce imports; nothing could be done unless the American farmers approved.[12] O'Shea had family connections in the USA and advocated strongly that New Zealand should look towards developing the American market by selling lamb surplus to Britain's needs. He thought increases in the American market seemed far more likely in comparison with other markets; the population would increase and the USA might face domestic shortfalls. Also, rarely for a country in the early 1950s, the USA could afford food imports. Finally, developing a market in the USA would be important because New Zealand, inevitably, would become tied in the Pacific politically with the USA.

It remained uncertain which meat product would be sold most successfully in the USA. In April 1952 a former trade commissioner told the Federated Farmers Meat and Wool Council that the large and growing populations of recent European heritage in the USA made lamb sales a possibility.[13] In 1954 an agricultural attaché in the American Embassy in Wellington encouraged beef sales rather than lamb because

[11] 'Here's What Americans Think of N.Z. Meat Imports: Acceptance in Many Quarters', *Straight Furrow*, 15/12/1950, 3, ATL.

[12] 'America Must Be Our New Market', *Straight Furrow*, 15/11/1951, 5, ATL.

[13] 'Trade with the USA: Many Factors Need Careful Handling', *Straight Furrow*, 01/04/1952, 7, ATL.

Americans consumed far more beef and changing that preference from beef to lamb would be difficult.[14] He reported that developing a significant market for lamb remained a more distant prospect; American and New Zealand producers needed to work together to develop such a market.[15]

New Zealand quickly learnt the difficulties of selling to the USA when an opportunity arose in 1953 because Canada encountered problems in trying to sell its meat to the USA. New Zealand agreed to divert its exports from Britain to the USA so that Canada could send its meat to Britain instead. However, New Zealand made no additional effort to make its shipment suitable for the USA, and the meat did not meet the required cleanliness and packaging standards.[16] The well-publicised failure to meet the standards damaged New Zealand's reputation. But the experience forced New Zealand to be wary about future approaches to the American market and made New Zealand better able to meet American requirements. The Federated Farmers Meat and Wool Council passed a resolution expressing its deep concern over shipments to the USA being 'below the standard expected in the United States', asking that the

> Meat Board should take immediate action to ensure that the standard and reputation which New Zealand meat has earned in the past should be maintained in the future.[17]

The Federated Farmers Dominion President called for a meeting of all who handled New Zealand meat to discuss how to make sure that proper processing and handling took place now that opportunities had opened up in the American market.[18]

---

[14] Robert D. Hopkirk, 'There's a Market in the USA. For Good Quality Lamb', *Straight Furrow*, 01/01/1954, 7, ATL.

[15] 'Otago Executive Discussions', *Straight Furrow*, 03/12/1958, 21, ATL.

[16] 'Beef Shipment to America: Board Chairman's Statement', *Straight Furrow*, 01/05/1953, 16.

[17] Minutes of the Meat and Wool Section Council, 04/02/1953, Federated Farmers 90 – 343 MSY-2732, M&W168/1953, 3, ATL.

[18] 'Meat Handling Conference Proposed', *Straight Furrow*, 16/04/1958, 20, ATL.

Early in 1954 the Meat Board had approved a schedule of exporters permitted to sell lamb to the USA together with distributors in the USA, but Robert Hopkirk, soon to be appointed the 'Washington representative' for *Straight Furrow* in growing recognition of the importance of the American market, repeated the warnings given by others. He explained that downward pressure on prices in the USA had led to pressures against imports from low cost areas, which in American eyes included New Zealand.[19] American lamb producers exerted pressure on their government to ensure a fair return for lamb, either, by higher tariffs, or, a price support programme. Hopkirk recommended that New Zealand producers should base their marketing on quality rather than low prices: 'price cutting will only arouse emotions and bring anti-dumping protests'.[20] He said that New Zealand should export to the USA only top-quality lamb. By expert handling of preparation, cutting, dressing, packaging, grading and publicity there would be no insurmountable problems in the American lamb market. Hopkirk reported also that self-service retailing had led to innovative methods and tools in the USA to reduce the extra costs in cutting, boning and trimming in processing factories; those innovations would be needed in New Zealand.[21]

In the first season after bulk purchase ended, New Zealand exported well below 1% of its meat exports to the USA. The Meat Board remained optimistic that lamb exports to the USA would be considerable but recognised that there was prejudice against frozen meat that would have to be overcome.[22] Efforts to break into the American market intensified when New Zealand's 1957 trade talks with Britain cast doubts on Britain's capability to take increases in meat exports. The Meat Board introduced a new policy in mid-1958, and the Board

[19] 'Meat Exports to Other Than U.K.', *Straight Furrow*, 01/01/1954, 14, ATL.

[20] Robert D. Hopkirk, 'Unrealistic Approach to Opportunities in American Market', *Straight Furrow*, 01/02/1954, 16, ATL.

[21] Robert D. Hopkirk, 'Meat Handling Methods in USA.', *Straight Furrow*, 01/04/1954, 10, ATL.

[22] 'What Are the Prospects for Increased Lamb Exports to USA.?', *Straight Furrow*, 01/01/1956, 24, ATL.

member Mr A. B. Baker summarised that policy two weeks after the July 1958 Board meeting.[23] Baker said Britain's own increases in production had made the British market 'overtaxed'. It had become 'of utmost importance to develop new markets.... The meat industry was doing just that'. Increased beef production in New Zealand would be needed because beef would sell well in 'numerous markets'. Britain would remain the main market for New Zealand lamb, but sheepmeats had to be introduced to new customers in other countries. Baker continued that the Board had negotiated already the improved shipping services 'vital to the growth of the meat trade with North America', and the Board arranged permanent representation in America. Cutting had begun for South Island lamb to the 'particular specifications of the [American] supermarkets handling it'. Baker concluded that 'nothing and no one could be permitted to stand in the way of the revolution in ideas and methods that had got to take place'. The North American market became a permanent item on the Meat Board meeting agendas, and, in the third season after bulk purchase, sales to the USA had increased ten times, but the market remained insignificant compared with sales to Britain.

Early in 1958, O'Shea, still Federated Farmers General Secretary, repeated his 1951 plea for New Zealand to establish good relations with the American farm organisations.[24] O'Shea claimed that the lamb market could be developed by helping to arrest the decline in the sheep-breeding industry in the USA, and thereby improve the supply continuity for the American housewife; discontinuity in supplies discouraged sales.[25] Federated Farmers invited the main American farming organisation leaders to make a goodwill visit to New Zealand early in 1959.[26] The visit established valuable links between producers in both countries, and the American National Farmers Union President gave encouragement for New Zealand to increase exports to the USA. In

[23] 'Great Future for Meat Exports: Too Much Pessimism', *Straight Furrow*, 16/07/1958, 3, ATL.
[24] 'U.S. as New Primary Exports Market for N.Z.', *Straight Furrow*, 19/03/1958, 3, ATL.
[25] 'Potential of USA. Market for Lamb', *Straight Furrow*, 06/08/1958, 34, ATL.
[26] 'Invitation to U.S. Farm Leaders', *Straight Furrow*, 07/05/1958, 4, ATL.

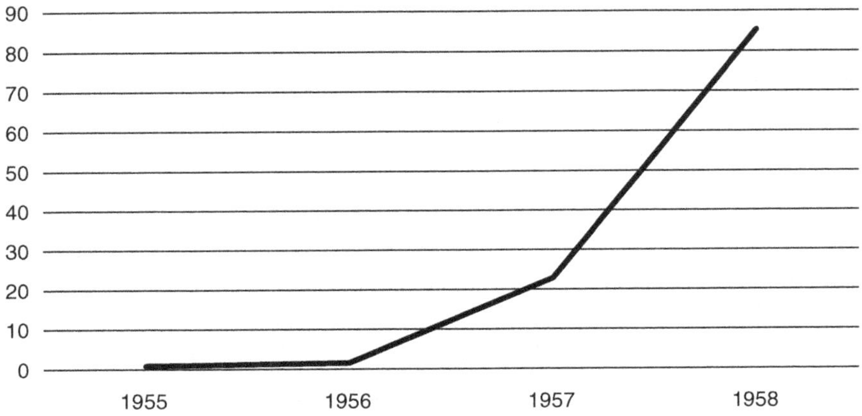

Fig. 5.4 Growing sales of beef, in tonnes (000), to the USA in the 1950s (NZDYB)

particular, 'a proper appreciation was gained [by the Americans] of the limitations of New Zealand meat production' relative to the 'meat consumption of the 175 million population of the United States'.[27]

Beef sales to the USA were increasingly successful (Fig. 5.4); New Zealand had established a niche selling beef suitable for hamburgers, avoiding competition in the prime steak market.[28] The New Zealand manager of the mercantile firm Dalgety's, M. G. Laird, saw beef as the better prospect than selling lamb, pointing out that a beef shortage had been caused by decline in American herds.[29] The New Zealand Agriculture Department, at the Meat Board's request, introduced rigorous inspection for all meat exported to the USA and announced in April 1958 with clear satisfaction that a New Zealand beef shipment to New York had nearly all passed without blemish at close inspection.[30]

[27] 'Meat and Wool Chairman's Annual Address', *Straight Furrow*, 01/07/1959, 8, ATL.

[28] 'Meat Industry Review', Reserve Bank, October 1981, 458, gives the best description of the differences between American and New Zealand grown beef and why that made New Zealand beef suitable for the processed food industry in the USA, ANZ.

[29] 'Beef Markets in USA and Japan Opening for N.Z.', *Straight Furrow*, 06/01/1958, 13, ATL.

[30] 'Cleanliness of Export Meat', *Straight Furrow*, 05/03/1958, 12, ATL.

The shipment demonstrated how New Zealand's meat trade could adjust itself to meet the specific presentation requirements for the American market.[31] Borthwick's Chairman, A. M. Borthwick, later pointed out that private enterprise had developed the trade in beef in the USA, and the Meat Board left the beef market to private initiative.[32] For the 1957/58 season New Zealand exported most of its beef to the USA, with only 12.5% exported to Britain, making the USA the second largest customer for New Zealand meat after Britain.[33] The W and R Fletcher general manager reported that 'a complete revolution' had taken place in New Zealand meat handling and production methods; that included a move to meat packed in polythene liners and cartons.[34] But occasional objections from within the USA against New Zealand's meat exports, both beef and lamb, continued.

5.3 Attempts to Overcome the Resistance from US Producers

Between 1960 and 1975 New Zealand gradually moved towards export levels acceptable to American producers. Because beef sales were small compared to domestic American beef production, New Zealand sold beef more successfully than lamb. For lamb, special steps were needed to overcome American sensitivities, for instance, forming a lamb exporting company with a monopoly for New Zealand lamb sold to the USA. Eventually sale of New Zealand lamb to the American market stabilised but only through considerable subsidies within New Zealand.

In March 1960, a major threat to sheepmeat sales arose when the American Tariff Commission investigated whether sheepmeat imports threatened 'serious injury to the home industry'. The American

[31] 'Boneless Beef Processing Meat Shipped to USA.', *Straight Furrow*, 02/04/1958, 4, ATL.

[32] 'A Mistake in Lamb Exports?', *Straight Furrow*, 21/12/1960, 6, ATL.

[33] 'Meat and Wool Section Chairman's Address', *Straight Furrow*, 01/07/1959, 7, ATL; 'Mr D. J. Ormond's Address to Electoral Committee', *Straight Furrow*, 02/09/1959, 5, ATL.

[34] 'Revolution with Selling Drive', *Straight Furrow*, 15/05/1963, 32, ATL.

Woolgrowers' Association feared that New Zealand exports to the USA would 'ruin our domestic sheep industry'.[35] The Association claimed that New Zealand Meat Board representatives were already in the USA seeking outlets for one million lamb carcasses. The American Tariff Commission refused to recommend import restrictions but the American woolgrowers' concerns led the Federated Farmers Gisborne President to propose that New Zealand should take those concerns into account by self-regulation.[36]

The Meat Board and Freezing Companies first discussed a lamb export development company in March 1960.[37] O'Shea, following a visit to the USA in mid-1960, proposed that the company should take into account the political atmosphere in the USA by careful timing, pricing and geography of sales.[38] In October 1960 the Meat Board approved the arrangements for such a company and the Board announced that from January 1961 'no New Zealand lamb could be exported from New Zealand to North America except by or through the Meat Export Development Company (NZ) Limited'.[39] The company, which quickly became known as DEVCO, intended to bring more order to New Zealand lamb marketing in North America taking into account American sensitivities. The Meat Board 'firmly held the view that orderly development and expansion of new markets . . . is beyond the efforts that can fairly be expected of meat export companies'.[40] That upset the meat export companies. Their Association wrote to Marshall, the Overseas Trade Minister, pointing out, justifiably, that their members 'had proved their usefulness in developing export trade not only in the USA but also throughout the world'.[41] They had willingly taken part

[35] 'U.S. Tariff Commission to Consider Lamb and Mutton Imports', *Straight Furrow*, 20/01/1960, 1, ATL.

[36] 'N.Z. Must Watch How the Wind Blows Overseas', *Straight Furrow*, 20/07/1960, 5, ATL.

[37] Meat Board Minute 12, 03/03/1960, 1644, ANZ.

[38] 'Need to Get Alongside USA Farmers', *Straight Furrow*, 07/09/1960, 1, ATL.

[39] Meat Board Minute Book 12, 04/08/1960, 1680/81, ANZ.

[40] Meat Board Chairman to Minister for Agriculture, 05/05/1960, Meat Export Development Company (New Zealand) Limited – General, AAFZ W1318 7174 Box228 1, ANZ.

[41] Meat Exporters Association to Minister for Overseas Development, 20/06/1961, Meat Export Development Company (New Zealand) Limited – General, AAFZ W1318 7174 Box228 2, ANZ.

in discussions of a New Zealand consortium for lamb export to the USA but the Meat Board 'had dropped the consortium proposal without further consultation'; that decision carried the hallmark of Ormond in wanting full control even if that meant rejecting advice from those perhaps better informed.[42]

DEVCO began as a cooperative effort between the Board and New Zealand-owned freezing companies but set up as a private company with freezing industry members as shareholders. The Board, however, maintained the right to appoint half the directors. In setting up DEVCO there was an expectation that losses would be made at first, and 'as is often the case with new ventures, the operation of DEVCO proved a difficult undertaking'.[43] Only support from the Meat Board Reserve funds saved DEVCO from bankruptcy. Borthwick's Chairman thought DEVCO to be a mistake and unnecessary; lamb had not been sold to the USA privately because lamb sold at higher prices in Britain than in the USA. But he did not want 'to criticise the project until it had been given a chance to see how it will do'.[44]

The networking with the American farming community that O'Shea had been advocating seemed to be paying off in 1961 when two American newspaper editors encouraged New Zealand lamb exports to the USA. One, the *Western Livestock Journal* editor, suggested that rather than 'adverse criticism' perhaps American sheep farmers should listen to those from a country more 'scientific and exact' in breed and flock management, and who marketed 'uniform and carefully sorted products'. With close control over shipments it might be possible to supplement the American domestic supply and give a more uniform flow to consumers.[45] The other editor, of *The Shepherd*, who had previously been hostile to New Zealand shipments, said that perhaps New Zealand could be encouraged to sell lamb 'in areas of the country

[42] Meat Exporters Association to Minister for Overseas Development, 20/06/1961, Meat Export Development Company (New Zealand) Limited – General, AAFZ W1318 7174 Box228 1, ANZ.

[43] Hayward, 116.

[44] 'A Mistake in Lamb Exports?', *Straight Furrow*, 21/12/1960, 6, ATL.

[45] 'More Understanding Wanted by U.S. Farm Editor', *Straight Furrow*, 01/02/1961, 11, ATL.

where the per capita consumption is practically nil'; such markets could be developed until 'our own lamb industry could increase lamb numbers and compete on a favourable basis'.[46] In June 1962, the largest farm organisation in the USA, the American Farm Bureau Federation, claimed that 'imported lamb . . . will increase the overall demand for lamb instead of disrupting the domestic market'.[47] The Federation encouraged New Zealand to sell lamb in the central states and the Deep South, no one produced lamb there and New Zealand would not need to compete with fresh, locally grown, meat; but there would need to be a promotion campaign persuading people to switch to eating lamb.[48]

Every year except 1969 DEVCO reported losses, which reached $2.2 million in 1971.[49] DEVCO asked the Meat Board for financial support and the Board approached the Cabinet which agreed, reluctantly, that Meat Board Reserve funds should be used. Despite the Cabinet in 1964 expressing concern about the 'continuing commitment of the Reserve Account for these losses', every year use of the Meat Reserve funds was approved.[50] Producers recognised the need to open the American market but began to worry how DEVCO losses would be financed. Southland producers noted that lamb sales to Greece, a country with no Meat Board promotion, exceeded those to the USA: 'Can the investment in the US be justified?'[51] Doubts about selling lamb to the USA forced Holyoake to step in to say that the US lamb market would not be abandoned despite New Zealand losing 3 million pounds in the previous five years, 'the need to develop

[46] 'Change of Front', *Straight Furrow*, 18/01/1961, 5, ATL.

[47] 'The Great Breakthrough?', *Straight Furrow*, 08/08/1962, 14, ATL.

[48] 'USA Market for NZ Lamb', *Straight Furrow*, 18/09/1963, 5, ATL.

[49] Meat Board Minute Book 13, 04/12/1963, 2044, ANZ; Treasury Note: Meat Export Development Company (NZ) Ltd., 02/11/1971, AAFZ W1710 7174 Box 120 Meat Export Development Company (New Zealand) Limited - General, 1, ANZ.

[50] Minister of Agriculture to Deputy Chairman of the Meat Board, 03/09/1964, AAFZ W1318, 7174 Box 228 Meat Export Development Company (New Zealand) Limited - General, ANZ.

[51] 'Meat Export Problems', *Straight Furrow*, 21/10/1964, 8, ATL; 'Development Company Activities', *Straight Furrow*, 07/07/1965, 15, ATL.

new markets for our meat requires a continuing market development programme'.[52]

DEVCO sales proved Borthwick's chairman correct when he had pointed out that lamb sold at higher prices in Britain than in the USA. Producers and exporters clearly needed a financial incentive to sell to the USA. Early in 1966, when the Meat Board accepted that tonnages from increased production could not be sold to Britain, the Board devised a diversification scheme to encourage lamb exports mainly to the USA through DEVCO.[53] The diversification scheme involved the Meat Board, the government and the freezing works' owners, and would determine the lamb weight percentage which should be sold outside Britain, with any loss in revenue paid to exporters from the Meat Industry Reserve Account. [54] The payment was called a 'Market Development Cost' to mask the fact that lamb producers now received subsidies. If exporters still chose to sell all their lamb to Britain they would make a payment to the government based on the percentage identified as appropriate for selling outside Britain.[55]

In 1968 producers still accepted the need for DEVCO but patience lessened with unease that 'the long-awaited breakthrough so often said to be almost at hand still seems some way off'.[56] The Federated Farmers Meat and Wool Chairman pulled no punches. He said in 1968 that

> a large question mark still lies over that organisation . . . policies which some years ago were confidently expected to give us a growing share of the

---

[52] 'Big Losses on Meat Drive', *The Dominion*, 15/12/1965, Meat Export Development Company (New Zealand) Limited – General, AAFZ W1318 7174 Box 228, ANZ.

[53] Diversification of Markets for Lamb, 22/12/1965, Federated Farmers 90 - 343 MSY2741 M&W53/1965, 1-6, ATL.

[54] Diversification of Markets for Lamb, 05/01/1966, Federated Farmers 90-343 MSY2742 M&W60/196, 1, ATL.

[55] Diversification of Markets for Lamb, 05/01/1966, Federated Farmers 90 - 343 MSY2742 M&W60/1966, 1, ATL.

[56] 'DEVCO Sound but Too Slow', *Straight Furrow*, 04/09/1968, 4, ATL.

> North American markets are under scrutiny . . . operations have cost the meat producers . . . $8.2 million . . . the benefits . . . are difficult to assess.[57]

The Council passed a resolution insisting that the Meat Board employ a 'capable' consultant to review DEVCO administration and management.[58]

New Zealand beef continued to sell well in the USA but not without occasional threats of import restrictions. In 1963 the impact on local prices led to the USA Department of Agriculture being asked to restrict beef imports, but the Department found no legal justification and refused.[59] President Johnson asked New Zealand to voluntarily restrict its beef imports to present levels and New Zealand agreed.[60] Pressure for a more formal beef import restriction continued on the grounds that overseas suppliers forced down prices; eventually American legislation in the mid-1960s provided for mandatory import quotas to be imposed if beef imports increased above 900 million lbs.[61] By September 1968 New Zealand and Australia held back sales to prevent the limit for mandatory quotas being reached.[62]

New Zealand gradually persuaded American consumers to eat lamb. The American magazine *The Shepherd* in 1970 eulogised the 'successful onslaught' by New Zealand that had led to a significant increase in lamb consumption on the American eastern seaboard. The article chastised American sheep producers for being too timid in their attempts to sell their product: 'USA growers can no longer hide behind a rock and say "The public just doesn't go for lamb, all they want is beef"'.[63] The article

---

[57] Chairman's Address to the Meat and Wool Council Section, 19/06/1968, Federated Farmers 90 – 343 MSY2746, M&W36/1968, 3, ATL.

[58] Minutes of Meat and Wool Section Council Meeting, 19/06/1968, Federated Farmers 90 – 343 MSY2746, M&W38/1968, 7, ATL.

[59] 'Imports Restricted', *Straight Furrow*, 04/09/1963, 15, ATL.

[60] Meat Board Minute Book 13, 04/02/1964, 2050, ANZ.

[61] Importation of New Zealand Meat in to USA, 1 April 1967, AAFZ W5705 7174 Box 204, ANZ.

[62] 'Beef Exports Held Back from US Market', *Straight Furrow*, 18/09/1968, 3, ATL.

[63] 'U.S. Reaction to N.Z. Success in Lamb Market', *Straight Furrow*, 08/04/1970, 26, ATL.

concluded that the time had come to work with these 'bright foreigners... in lifting the whole framework of lamb consumption in the United States'. Talks started between New Zealand, American and Australian sheep farmers on lamb market development in the USA. American authorities believed that the sheep industry would find the rising New Zealand lamb sales acceptable. But a Trade Bill being considered by the USA Senate contained provisions limiting imports to 15% of the American market; New Zealand needed to encourage increases in the American domestic supply if it wished to increase its own lamb sales to the USA.[64] In December 1970 American lamb producers joined with those from New Zealand and Australia in an 'Education, Compatible Lamb Program' to co-ordinate the promotion and marketing for lamb in the USA.[65]

Despite the effort and expenditure put into developing the market for lamb in the USA the tonnages remained no more than 10% compared with tonnages sold in Britain and often well below that level. In 1971, the *Otago Daily Times* repeated the point made by Southland Producers six years earlier: sales to Greece equalled those to the USA but did not need the 'lavish promotional spending' of DEVCO; 'DEVCO's operations cannot be regarded as successful'.[66] Significant increases in lamb sales to the USA remained unlikely because even at those low levels New Zealand's market share remained about 15%, the maximum percentage set by the USA for lamb imports. In 1970, the USA encountered financial difficulties partly because of overseas commitments and, much to Ormond's disgust, discussed legislation for quotas on lamb imports.[67] By mid-1969 the measures to protect the American economy included a 10% surcharge

[64] 'Talks on USA Lamb Market to Resume', *Straight Furrow*, 09/09/1970, 3, ATL.

[65] Education, Compatible Lamb Programs Goal of Joint Committee, 11/12/1970, Meat Export Development Company (New Zealand) Limited – General, AAFZ W1710 7174 Box120, 1-3, ANZ.

[66] *Otago Daily Times*, 25/03/1971, Meat Export Development Company (New Zealand) Limited – General, Lamb in America, AAFZ W1710 7174 Box120, ANZ.

[67] 'U.S. Lamb Quotas Would Be Bitter Blow', *Straight Furrow*, 04/06/1969, 5, ATL.

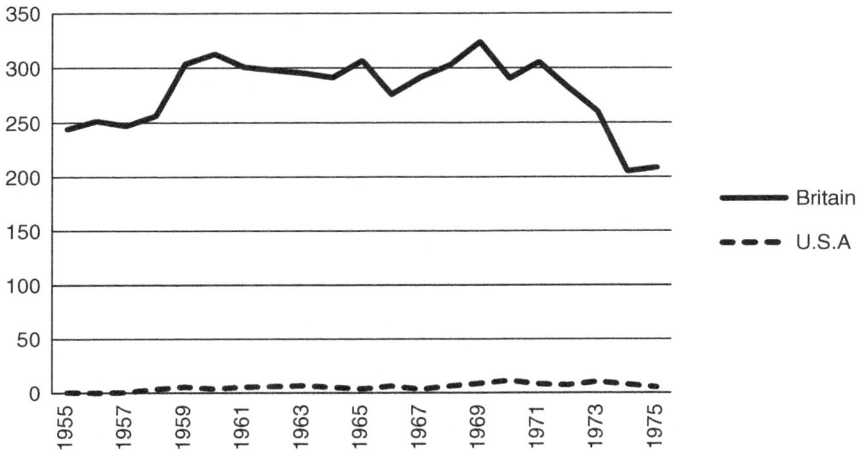

Fig. 5.5 Sheepmeat sales to Britain and the USA in tonnes (000) (NZDYB)

on imports.[68] If New Zealand increased its lamb sales to the USA restrictions on those imports would be strengthened. Despite the lamb tonnage being significant at 10%–20% of the market in the USA, sales to Britain remained ten- to twenty-fold more (Fig. 5.5).

Ormond claimed in 1979 that his 'greatest achievement during his time with the Meat Board' was the setting up of DEVCO and 'sales of lamb into America through DEVCO are today proving it was the right move to make'.[69] But in 1979 tonnages to the USA were still only 2% of New Zealand's total meat exports, only 7% of the lamb exports sold to Britain, and barely more than the tonnages sold to Greece (14,466 to 14,294). DEVCO continued until 1986 when its deteriorating financial position led to it becoming the New Zealand Lamb Company.[70] Calder and Tyson say by that time 'despite the odds' DEVCO had been 'a modest success' but, to paraphrase Winston Churchill's description of his political rival, Clement

[68] McAloon, 145; 'Govt Concern at USA Surcharge', *Straight Furrow*, 08/09/1971, 14, ATL.
[69] Tait, 89.
[70] Calder and Tyson, 255.

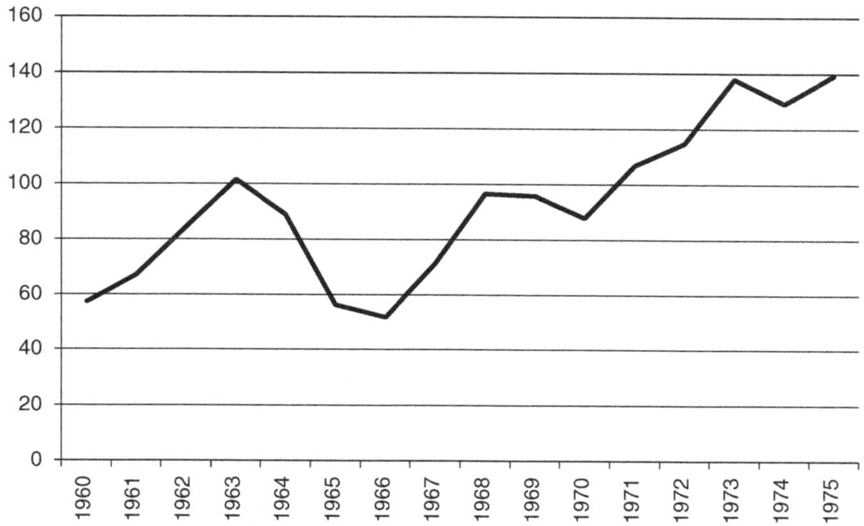

Fig. 5.6 Beef exports to the USA in tonnes (000) (NZDYB)

Attlee, 'it was a modest success with much to be modest about'.[71] The prime reason for DEVCO had been to compensate for any decrease in sales to Britain by increased sales in the USA and DEVCO did not achieve that goal. When lamb sales to Britain began to fall in the 1970s lamb sales to the USA did not take up the slack but fell also, halving between 1973 and 1975. Investment in DEVCO had become a method for supporting lamb producers using Reserve Account funds, and for avoiding running down the sheep industry, or, providing more overt subsidies. Even the modest sales would have been less without the 'market development cost' paid to farmers.

In contrast, New Zealand sold beef to the USA successfully (Fig. 5.6), but not through a Meat Board-supported development company but by private export companies adapting to the US market. Beef cattle had always been part of sheep farming; land for sheep farming improved with cattle grazing on it and beef production provided an additional outlet for sheep

[71] Calder and Tyson, 226.

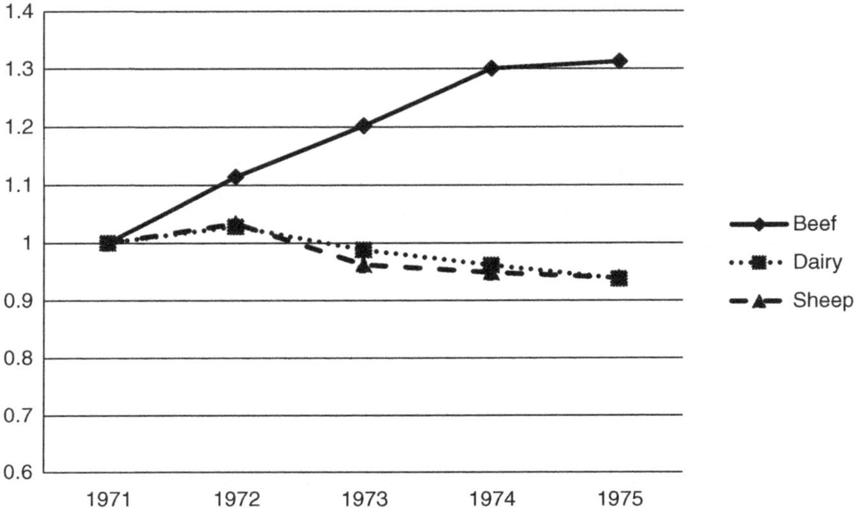

Fig. 5.7 Relative changes in livestock numbers ('Meat Industry Review', Reserve Bank, October 1981, Table 1, p. 350.)

farmers. Also, beef had always been one dairy farming by-product through slaughtering dairy cattle, and in the 1960s an increasing supply of 'beef fattening animals' came from 'the national dairy herd'.[72] In 1969 the government introduced a Dairy Beef Diversification Scheme which subsidised dairy producers to increase their beef production.[73] In 1970 the Agricultural Economic Research Unit at Lincoln College remained optimistic that beef sales to the USA would encourage an increase in farming cattle for beef. Beef cattle herds would expand more than dairy herds and sheep farmers who were able to increase the carrying capacity of their farms turned to cattle rather than increasing their sheep flocks.[74] That proved to be the case through the 1970s with sheep and dairy cattle numbers falling, compensated by an increase in beef cattle (Fig. 5.7).

[72] Agricultural Policy in New Zealand, OECD Report, February 1974, 28, ANZ.
[73] Agricultural Policy in New Zealand, OECD Report, February 1974, 69, ANZ.
[74] 'Changes Likely in Beef Exports Soon', *Straight Furrow*, 08/04/1970, 16, ATL.

5.4 Diversification to the Japanese Market

Producers were aware of meat trade possibilities with Asia as early as 1947. Because of its large population and relative proximity compared with Europe, Japan became a prime target especially when the Japanese preference for mutton became clear. Efforts continued to increase sales of lamb and beef to Japan but unsuccessfully.

In the 1940s New Zealanders called Asia 'the East' or 'Far East' reflecting that New Zealand saw itself as Britain's distinct hinterland (Belich's 'town-supply district of London') rather than an independent island group in the Pacific. In 1947 a remit to the Federated Farmers Dominion Council proposed that the Council should investigate additional trade with 'the East'.[75] The Meat Board claimed to be fully aware and ready to move at the appropriate time but thought sale to 'the East' to be impracticable; Britain still needed all that New Zealand could produce.[76] In 1951 Holyoake, as Minister for Agriculture, described the 'Far East' as a 'giant awakening hungry for food'.[77] New Zealand's trading with Japan had rebuilt quickly after World War II by, in 1947, returning to the wool trading that had been in place before the war, and New Zealand already had a trade commissioner in Japan by the mid-1950s. The New Zealand public remained 'virulently anti-Japanese' following World War II but the government wanted to 'forestall an American monopoly' in trade with Japan.[78] In addition, US diplomacy encouraged links between New Zealand, Australia and Japan to cement Japan's relations with the non-communist world.[79]

A prominent Taranaki dairy farmer reported, following a private visit to Japan in 1957, that Taranaki could build a reciprocal trade with

---

[75] Minutes of the Meat and Wool Council, 16/09/1947, Federated Farmers MSY2730, M&WM30/1947, 5, ATL.

[76] 'Meat Board Replies to Resolutions', *Straight Furrow*, 15/11/1947, 35, ATL; Meat Board Minute Book, 9, 03/10/1947, 491, ANZ.

[77] 'An Awakening Giant – The Far East', *Straight Furrow*, 15/08/1951, 17, ATL.

[78] John Singleton and Paul Robertson, *Economic Relations Between Britain and Australasia 1945–1970* (Basingstoke: Palgrave, 2002), 126.

[79] Singleton and Robertson, 124.

Japan. He noted the Japanese gradually changing to a diet including meat and butter, and, in contrast to the 'shoddy' goods Japan produced before World War II, Japanese factories now turned out high-quality cameras, binoculars and electrical equipment.[80] The economist, Bryan Philpott, pointed out the complementarity between New Zealand and Japan now that, whilst Japan wanted cheap food and a market for its manufactures, New Zealand wanted cheap manufactures and a market for its food.[81]

The Meat Board gradually realised the need to promote New Zealand in Asian markets, and in October 1957 the New Zealand Chambers of Commerce encouraged the Board to support a trade fair in Japan.[82] The Meat Board also developed the Japanese market by arranging suitable shipping and for the General Manager and a Board member to visit Japan.[83] Japan had never been a market for New Zealand meat but, as in the USA, exports started in the mid-1950s through private initiative with Borthwick's actively seeking new markets. In 1957 Borthwick's reported to the Meat Board the first meat (beef) sale to Japan.[84] An American trading company's Japanese representative told an audience in Auckland that 'the marked trend of the Japanese people toward a Western way of life was largely responsible for the development in Japan of a demand for beef'; he saw Japan as 'a promising avenue for marketing . . . New Zealand meat'.[85] In March 1959, following prompting once again by Federated Farmers, the Meat Board decided that Ormond should visit Japan and he did so within the next two months.[86]

Trade Commissioners from the Ministry for Industries and Commerce introduced Meat Board members to important Japanese contacts and the Board considered Trade Commissioners to be 'one of

[80] 'Reciprocal Trade with Japan', *Straight Furrow*, 15/11/1957, 28, ATL.

[81] 'New Markets: An Age Old Problem' *Straight Furrow*, 01/11/1961, 14, ATL.

[82] Meat Board Minute Book 11, 05/12/1957, 1438, ANZ.

[83] Meat Board Minute Book 11, 13/06/1957, 1374, ANZ.

[84] Meat Board Minute Book 11, 06/03/1957, 1354, ANZ.

[85] 'Japan Develops Taste for Beef', *New Zealand Herald*, 15/04/1957, Keith Holyoake Papers MS-1814 70/05, ATL.

[86] Meat Board Minute Book 12, 19/03/1959, 1562, ANZ.

New Zealand's most essential services'.[87] But private exporters, in this case C S Stevens and Dalgety's, started the sheepmeat sales to Japan.[88] Such exporters, with their overseas networks, were prime catalysts that enabled New Zealand to diversify into the American beef and the Japanese mutton markets, the main markets that expanded through the 1950s and 1960s. In 1968, Borthwick's General Manager summarised the role of independent exporters in the diversification into Asian markets.[89] He said that independent exporters such as Borthwick's

> appoint agents overseas, make frequent visits to their markets, encourage buyers to come to New Zealand and at all times accept that full blast of competition from domestic suppliers in overseas markets and from imported meat from other supplying nations.

Former Meat Board employees Calder and Tyson agree,

> independent exporters . . . led the way in almost all of the newer markets for New Zealand meat . . . they boldly went where few had been before . . . and usually went alone . . . they were supreme risk takers.[90]

The New Zealand and Japanese governments began discussing a trade agreement as early as 1953 but New Zealand moved cautiously, partly, because Britain feared that its exports to New Zealand might be replaced by Japanese. Also, Japan would not relax its agricultural protectionism thereby inhibiting New Zealand's main interest in increasing primary produce exports.[91] In parallel, New Zealand refused to relax its industrial protectionism, preventing increased imports of manufactures from Japan. Late in 1957, when the Japanese Prime Minister visited New Zealand to encourage imports of Japanese goods, Holyoake, who had just become New Zealand's Prime Minister, avoided encouraging expansion of Japanese

[87] Meat Board Minute Book 12, 07/05/1959, 1565, ANZ.
[88] Calder and Tyson, 128.
[89] 'Marketing New Zealand Meat', *Straight Furrow*, 16/10/1968, 22, ATL.
[90] Calder and Tyson, 125.
[91] Singleton and Robertson, 130–135.

exports to New Zealand. He told the Japanese Prime Minister that whilst he understood that Japan 'wanted to rebuild her trade . . . New Zealand is obliged to give protection to our own manufacturers'.[92] But Australia had signed an agreement with Japan earlier in 1957 and eventually that gave impetus for New Zealand to reach agreement; Australia exported to Japan produce that otherwise might be sourced from New Zealand. New Zealand and Japan signed an agreement in September 1958 that specifically included expanding New Zealand's meat exports.[93]

In 1960 a market survey confirmed the fortunate coincidence for New Zealand that the Japanese preferred ewe mutton, a product with no great demand in Britain.[94] The Meat Board Deputy Chairman said 'a few years ago people had laughed at a suggestion that ewe mutton should be marketed in Japan' and he spoke optimistically about the future Japanese market saying that Japan had started increasing protein intake as living standards increased. He 'foresaw a very great future in trading relationships with Japan though there was still some ill-feeling against the country left over from World War II and that should be forgotten'.[95] In 1962, the investment in meat advertising in Japan became second only to that in Britain and the Meat Board could claim justifiably that New Zealand had become Japan's principal overseas meat supplier, supplying 90% of meat imports.[96]

By 1960 Japan had become the second largest market for New Zealand sheepmeat after Britain and by far the largest market for mutton (Fig. 5.8). At its peak, in 1969, the percentage of New Zealand meat exports sold to Japan reached 15%. Hope remained that lamb could be sold as well as mutton, and even into the 1970s New Zealand made attempts to encourage lamb sales in Japan.[97] But market research demonstrated the difficulties, in particular a 'widespread prejudice

[92] State Luncheon in Honour of the Japanese Prime Minister, 02/12/1957, Keith Holyoake Papers MS-1814 – 071/4, Visit of the Japanese Prime Minister, 1–5, ATL.

[93] Singleton and Robertson, 134.

[94] Lamb Research in Japan, August 1972, Importation of Meat Into Japan, AAFZ W1714 7174 Box 36 Part 2, 1-3, ANZ.

[95] 'Orderly Marketing in U.S. Advocated', *Straight Furrow*, 21/12/1960, 25, ATL.

[96] Meat Board Minute Book, 06/06/1962, 1870, ANZ.

[97] Meat Board Minute Book 16, 03/06/1971, 880, ANZ.

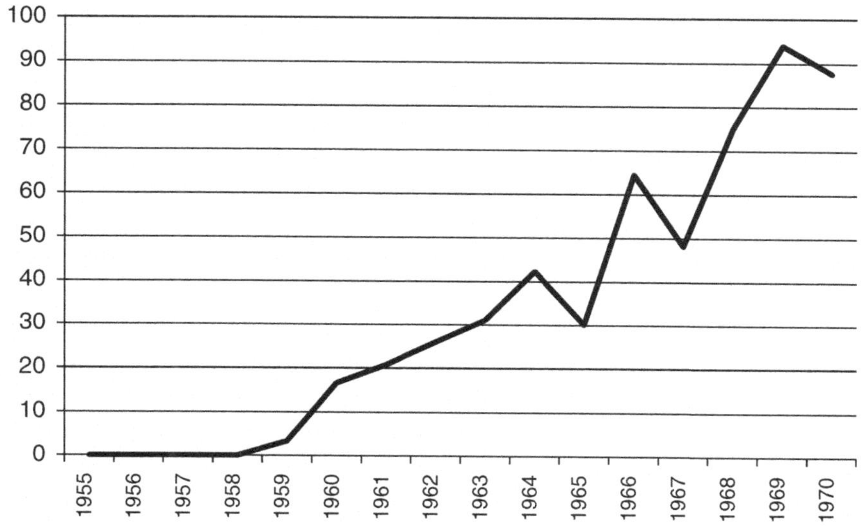

Fig. 5.8 Growth in sheepmeat exports to Japan in tonnes (000) (NZDYB)

against the odour of lamb' and housewives' reluctance to change to an 'unknown' meat.[98] A significant lamb market never grew and mutton sales remained ten times higher.[99]

Ormond continued to have doubts about diversification and, in 1962, said that despite successfully selling mutton to Japan

> the Far Eastern countries cannot provide a substitute for the United Kingdom market for lamb . . . the substance of our trade must continue to lie with the highly developed countries of the northern hemisphere.[100]

---

[98] Lamb Research in Japan, August 1972, Importation of Meat Into Japan, AAFZ W1714 7174 Box 36 Part 2, 2, ANZ. Partly, the problem seemed to be that lamb was not kept in good condition in butchers' shops.

[99] Meat Board Chairman's Report to the Electoral Committee, 03/04/1963, Federated Farmers MSY2739 M&W19/1963, 9, ATL; Japan's Potential Market for Meat, 22/01/1973, Importation of Meat Into Japan, AAFZ W1714 7174 Box 36 Part 2, 2, ANZ.

[100] 'Healthy Demand for N.Z. Lamb', *Straight Furrow*, 05/09/1962, 9, ATL. Evidently, at the time Japan was not regarded as one of the 'highly developed countries'.

Ormond worried at that time that Britain had been considering whether to introduce managed markets for meat imports through quotas; success for New Zealand in selling meat elsewhere made that British move easier to justify. New Zealand tried to increase beef sales to Japan, and an 'Agreed Minute' between Japan and New Zealand in 1968 set a target of 20,000 tonnes per annum. But sales never rose above one third of that tonnage.[101] Japan satisfied its requirements by buying beef from China, and New Zealand exporters preferred to send their beef to the USA rather than Japan.[102]

New Zealand never managed to achieve its prime target of significant exports of lamb to Japan but managed to find a niche market, ewe mutton. Three factors helped New Zealand successfully sell meat to Japan: New Zealand already had trade commissioners in Japan through the sale of wool; the USA sought to tie Japan to the Western Hemisphere and anti-communism by encouraging Australasian contact with Japan; and, dietary changes occurred in Japan. The initiative of independent exporters provided the final catalyst that led to the growth of the Japanese market.

5.5 Conclusion

Ormond continued to place emphasis on expanding sales to Britain but, fortunately, other meat board members, independent exporters, farmers and Federated Farmers recognised the need for market diversification from the 1940s and encouraged change. Meat processors changed to meet the needs of new customers especially by adapting to the more demanding hygiene requirements and by producing a more diverse

[101] Beef and Veal – Kennedy Round, 15/02/1968, NZ – Japan Relations – Exports to Japan – Meat, 1965–1974, ABHS W5330 6956 Box 29 TKY 26/3/10, 1, ANZ.

[102] Meat from Mainland China, Embassy Tokyo to Wellington, 14/02/1969, NZ – Japan Relations – Exports to Japan – Meat, 1965–1974, ABHS W5330 6956 Box 29 TKY 26/3/10, ANZ; Trade with Japan, Embassy Tokyo to Foreign Affairs Wellington: Trade with Japan, 16/10/1970, NZ – Japan Relations – Exports to Japan – Meat, 1965–1974, ABHS W5330 6956 Box 29 TKY 26/3/10, 3, ANZ.

range of products, including cuts for supermarkets rather than complete carcasses. Change first started in the 1950s, mainly with beef being sold to the USA and mutton to Japan. The USA eventually became a stable and, for New Zealand, sizeable market for beef exports. Those exports were initiated by private enterprise rather than the Meat Board. In the American beef market New Zealand sales accounted for 15% of the overall sales, and that 15% gave a very significant income for New Zealand.

Britain's applications to join the European Economic Community (EEC) provided the stimulus for the Meat Board to put additional effort into diversification of markets for lamb, for instance, in creating DEVCO and the 1960s lamb diversification scheme to encourage sales in the USA, but neither created significant new sales. Tonnages remained less than 7% of those sold to Britain and far less significant than beef sales to the USA. To increase lamb exports to the USA New Zealand had to help American lamb suppliers in developing the market, and had to subsidise New Zealand farmers. The investment in DEVCO may well have given more assistance to the USA lamb industry than to New Zealand. Lamb exports to the USA never reached anywhere near the levels needed in case sales to Britain fell significantly - that had been DEVCO's prime, original objective and it failed to achieve that objective.

The meat industry recognised that it would eventually need to turn to Asian markets, and in the mid-twentieth century Japan proved the most promising market with its large population, and with its culture, encouraged by the USA, changing to American/European. The New Zealand trade agreement with Japan in 1958 helped meat sales to Japan grow; mutton sales, in particular, developed successfully through private enterprise assisted by the Department for Industries and Commerce Trade Commissioners. Fortunately, the Japanese palate preferred mutton, a product difficult to sell to Britain.

6

Dairy and the British Market

6.1 Introduction

Chapter 6, after reviewing the distinctive domestic organisation of dairying in New Zealand, analyses the long battle by primary producers to hold onto the British market for butter and cheese and to prevent price collapses in that market. Between 1945 and 1975 international dairy markets changed significantly, moving from shortages caused by the dislocation of markets in World War II to over-supply by the 1960s. Many European countries and the USA developed their own dairy industries through price support schemes and that led to surplus produce that could not be sold domestically. Surpluses were dumped overseas by selling at less than the cost of production thereby depressing prices for the exports from other countries. In 1958, dairy produce dumping onto the British market led to Britain restricting dairy imports using quotas, partly for New Zealand's benefit. By 1961, New Zealand, reluctantly at first, accepted a quota being placed on its exports and eventually welcomed the quota arrangements even though they ended New Zealand's right of unrestricted access to the British market. The dairy quotas for New Zealand introduced when Britain joined the

D. Hall, *Emerging from an Entrenched Colonial Economy*, Palgrave Studies in Economic History, DOI 10.1007/978-3-319-53016-1_6

European Economic Community (EEC) in 1973 continued the annual British quotas in place through the 1960s. Clinging to the British market for selling butter and cheese suggested that the New Zealand dairy industry suffered an endemic conservatism but that ignores four difficulties in diversification: protectionism in many countries; surplus dairy product dumping by the USA; Asian countries unable to afford high-fat dairy produce; and, finally, Asian diets rarely including milk-based products.

6.2 Domestic Organisation

A distinctive feature for the New Zealand dairy industry, that set it apart from the meat and wool industries, was introduced by the first Labour government in 1936 – that was payment at the start of each season of a 'guaranteed price'. The government sought to 'ensure for Producers an Adequate Remuneration for the Services rendered by them to the Community' and to protect them from 'the effect of fluctuations in the market-prices'.[1] Guaranteed prices took into account 'The general standard of living of persons engaged in the dairy industry in comparison with the general standard of living throughout New Zealand'.[2] At first, the government set the guaranteed price but in 1947 marketing was transferred from government to a more independent body, the New Zealand Dairy Products Marketing Commission, which had three government and three industry representatives under an independent chairman appointed by the government. The overall objective of the Commission was to export dairy produce 'to the best advantage'.[3] The Commission purchased all butter and cheese for export and conducted the annual negotiations with Britain. It determined the guaranteed price to be paid to farmers taking into account the proviso that the 'general economic stability in New Zealand' needed to be considered

[1] Primary Products Marketing Act, 1936, p. 60.
[2] Primary Products Marketing Act, 1936, p. 68.
[3] 'Commission Control of NZ Dairy Industry', *Straight Furrow*, 15/05/1947, 6, ATL.

and the Commission needed to comply with the 'general trade policy of the Government and with any general or special directions issued by the Minister'.[4]

The Commission operated in parallel with the Dairy Board whose functions were to

> promote and organize the orderly development of the dairy industries in New Zealand . . . expanding production . . . and adoption of measures and practices designed to promote greater efficiency.[5]

Inevitably, relations between the Dairy Commission and the Dairy Board were tense, especially when the Commission sought to reduce the guaranteed price for the 1955/1956 season. Dairy farmers declared that the guaranteed price should be reduced only in harmony with reductions in income for other sections of the community and claimed there were increases rather than reductions for others.[6] Holyoake suggested that there should be more consultation with the Dairy Board but the Commission chairman, William Marshall, refused on the grounds that legislation intended the commission to set the price acting as an independent tribunal in a 'judicial capacity'.[7] The furore caused by the Commission's actions led in 1956 to an inquiry into the industry administration and eventually the price-fixing powers were transferred from the Dairy Commission to a separate price authority with the guaranteed price now taking into account how much 'produce is realising on the overseas market' and also taking into account Dairy Board recommendations.[8]

Andrew (later Sir Andrew) Linton became Chairman of the Dairy Board in 1956. Unlike the chairmen of the Meat and Wool Boards

---

[4] 'Commission Control of NZ Dairy Industry', *Straight Furrow*, 15/05/1947, 6, ATL.

[5] Dairy Board Act, 26/11/1953, Section 12.

[6] 'Farmers Unable to Reconcile Contradictory Statements of Dairy Board Leaders', *Straight Furrow*, 01/09/1955, 3, ATL.

[7] Notes on the Deputation which waited on the Minister of Agriculture and the Minister of Finance, 12/08/1955, Keith Holyoake papers MS-1814 46/1 Dairy Produce, 16, ATL; Marshall to Holyoake, 06/10/1955, Keith Holyoake papers MS-1814 46/2 Dairy Produce, ATL.

[8] Guaranteed Price of Dairy Produce, 16/08/1957, Keith Holyoake papers MS-1814 56/3 Dairy Produce, 1-3, ATL.

through the 1960s and early 1970s, John Ormond and Ormond's brother-in-law, Jack Acland, respectively, Linton did not belong to the New Zealand landed gentry. He had worked in cheese-making factories before first buying a dairy farm when established as a factory manager.[9] He was a 'friendly man' with a 'warm personality and ability to listen and negotiate with farmers, Ministers of the Crown and business people'.[10] He was non-confrontational, unlike Marshall, Chairman of the Dairy Commission at the time of the 1956 controversy. It was high praise when Marshall remarked on Linton's appointment as Dairy Board Chairman – 'Looking to the future, I could say that Mr Linton was cut out for bringing harmony and goodwill among the people in the industry.'[11] Led by Linton, moves began for amalgamating the Board and the Commission and those came to fruition in 1961 with creation of the single Dairy Production and Marketing Board.[12] In 1965, once sensitivities over the Commission's disappearance had eased, the title changed to the Dairy Board. Linton's non-confrontational approach successfully, through the 1950s and 1960s, maintained good relations with Britain in dairy industry matters despite the potential disharmony that changes in both countries threatened.

6.3 The British Market

New Zealand's dairy exports to Britain fell 20% by 60,000 tonnes between 1950 and 1972 whilst dairy exports overall increased by more than 200,000 tonnes (Fig. 6.1). Two major influences restricted New Zealand's dairy export to Britain: Britain's investment in its own agriculture to save expenditure on food imports, and Britain's free trade that led to several other

[9] 'Sir Andrew Linton - The Dairy Industry's Man for the Times', *The New Zealand Dairy Exporter*, Vol. XLIV, No.6, December 1968, 18, ATL.

[10] Tony Nightingale, 'Linton, Andrew', from the Dictionary of National Biography, Te Ara – The Encyclopedia of New Zealand, updated 5-Nov-2013.

[11] Arthur Ward, *A Command of Co-operatives* (Wellington: New Zealand Dairy Board, 1975), 172.

[12] Cabinet paper CM(60)29 Dairy Industry, 18/07/1960, Dairy Industry and General, T1 274 40/648/8, ANZ.

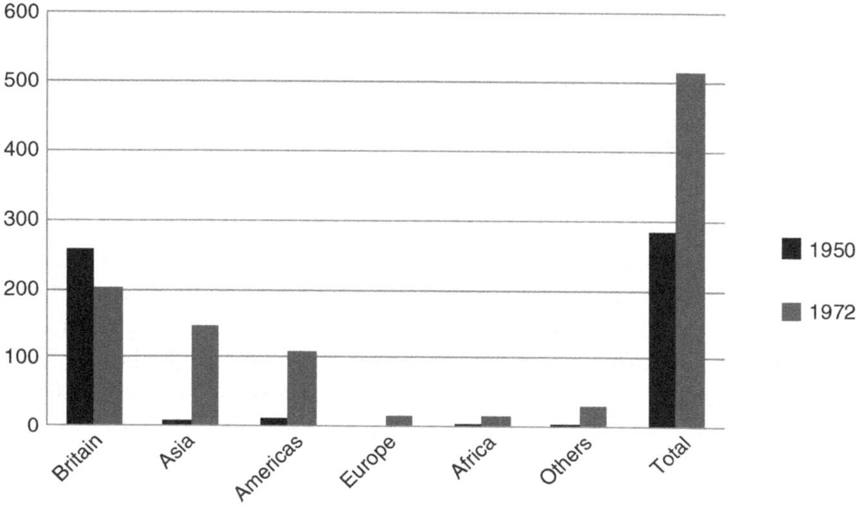

Fig. 6.1 Dairy tonnages (000) exported in 1950 and 1972 (NZDYB)

countries dumping their dairy surpluses on the British market. Between 1945 and 1975, the New Zealand dairy industry went from the relative security of bulk purchase by Britain through a period of uncertainty as the industry engaged with the free market. A return to protection by Britain followed, to mitigate the impact of dumping, with New Zealand accepting a quota imposed on its dairy exports to Britain. When Britain became a member of the EEC in 1973 the arrangements agreed between Britain and the EEC for the New Zealand dairy industry were mainly welcomed in New Zealand.

There were warnings in 1945 that in the long-term Britain might restrict import of New Zealand dairy produce but the security of bulk purchase and year-on-year price increases masked any potential long-term difficulties. As early as 1950, Britain refused to increase prices because over-production in many countries made the global dairy market a buyers' market. New Zealand producers saw Britain's approach as exploiting New Zealand's loyalty and goodwill rather than a response to dairy over-production. Ill feeling strengthened because Britain paid higher prices to other suppliers. Eventually, Britain agreed to a price increase, but Britain would not agree to unrestricted access for dairy produce and the Dairy

Commission recognised the need to change to selling in a free market. New Zealand agreed to end bulk purchase one year early.

New Zealand dairy producers benefitted from the years of wartime bulk purchase but in 1945 they were warned by a delegation from the British National Farmers Union (NFU) that eventually import restrictions would be needed in Britain. The NFU claimed that Britain's cheap food policy with unregulated food imports had failed to protect British farmers – Britain's market could become saturated; it had only a limited volume.[13] New Zealand producers argued that free trade should be maintained but the New Zealand Farmers Union President warned them that the British market within a decade or two might not be able to absorb increases in New Zealand dairy production.[14] He called for a levy on dairy exports to fund investigating markets other than Britain. In March 1946, partial reassurance came from the former permanent Under-Secretary to the British Ministry of Food that New Zealand should not be anxious about future exports to Britain but it had to be realised that the British farmer must have first call on the British home market.[15]

Those warnings hardly seemed urgent whilst prices for New Zealand's dairy exports to Britain increased through the late 1940s. But in 1950 Britain at first refused to increase prices over the previous year.[16] The high butterfat yields in many dairy-producing countries had made the global market a buyers' market with supply exceeding demand.[17] In particular, the USA threatened the market by dumping surplus dairy produce at prices half those paid by Britain.[18] The Managing Director of the New Zealand exporter, Amalgamated Dairies, who had just visited London, wrote to Holyoake that he thought the British offer to pay the same prices

[13] 'British Delegation: Leader's Reply', *Straight Furrow*, 15/01/1945, 65, ATL.

[14] 'Mr Mulholland's Statement to Conference', *Straight Furrow*, 15/01/1945, 17, ATL; 'Post War Marketing', *Straight Furrow*, 16/07/1945, 12, ATL.

[15] 'Britain's Market for N.Z. Food', *Straight Furrow*, 15/03/1946, 9, ATL.

[16] Minister for Food to Chairman of the Dairy Commission, 07/07/1950, Keith Holyoake papers, MS-1814 – 4/2 Dairy Produce, ATL.

[17] Prices for Dairy Produce, Keith Holyoake papers, MS-1814 – 4/2 Dairy Produce, 24/09/1950, 6, ATL.

[18] Secretary External Affairs to New Zealand Counsellor Washington, 20/08/1950, Keith Holyoake papers, MS-1814 – 3/6 Dairy Produce, 1, ATL.

as the previous year 'was a very good offer' in view of the 'radical change for the better' in food supplies in Europe – 'if there were a free market all dairy produce prices would come down rapidly'.[19] The Federated Farmers Dairy Section Chairman warned the section's annual conference that steps needed to be taken to increase efficiency with the 'passing of a sellers' market'.[20] Following the British refusal to consider price increases, Marshall wrote to Holyoake that New Zealand faced the choice: 'accept . . . a United Kingdom dictated price or renounce the contract'.[21] For the first time dairy producers questioned the value of bulk purchase.

The Federated Farmers Research Officer, D L Martin, thought Britain treated New Zealand unfairly. He pointed out that, whilst New Zealand received £252 a ton for butter, Denmark received £271.[22] The British Minister for Food explained that in Denmark the 'whole economy' differed from New Zealand; for instance, cattle had to be fed on imported feedstuffs during the winter and that increased costs. Also, 'New Zealand has been able consistently to put into a reserve fund part of the price' that Britain paid.[23] Marshall said that it was a 'cold shock to many of our farmers, who had tried to do the fair thing by the British people to be told . . . that they have all along been making good profits'. If New Zealand had been more 'spendthrift . . . we would today be given a higher price'.[24] Martin compared the change in the prices paid for New Zealand exports with changes in prices paid for British

[19] Managing Director Amalgamated Dairies to Holyoake, 27/07/1950, Keith Holyoake papers, MS-1814 – 3/4 Dairy Produce, ATL.

[20] Minutes of Dairy Section Annual Conference, 20/06/1950, Federated Farmers 90-343 MSY 2708 Dairy Produce Section, 1, ATL.

[21] Chairman of the Dairy Commission to Holyoake, 19/07/1950, Keith Holyoake papers, MS -1814 – 3/4 Dairy Produce, 3, ATL.

[22] United Kingdom Bulk Purchasing Contracts: Butter and Cheese Prices, 20/04/1950, Keith Holyoake papers, MS-1814 – 4/2 Dairy Produce, 3, ATL.

[23] Prices for Dairy Produce, 24/09/1950, Keith Holyoake papers, MS-1814 – 4/2 Dairy Produce, 4, ATL; Willis, Richard, 'Farming in New Zealand and the EEC - the case of the Dairy Industry', *New Zealand Geographer*, 40, 1, 1984, 2-11. Willis explains the natural advantages that made New Zealand a more efficient and cheaper dairy producer than countries such as Denmark. He concludes that God and not man was responsible for New Zealand's advantages.

[24] Prices for Dairy Produce, 24/09/1950, Keith Holyoake papers, MS-1814 – 4/2 Dairy Produce, 7, ATL.

exports to New Zealand. Prices for New Zealand dairy produce had increased by 122% since 1949 whilst British export prices had increased by 153%.[25] Martin concluded that Britain refused to pay fair prices; Britain unjustly exploited New Zealand's loyalty and goodwill.

The Korean War outbreak made commodity prices surge and, in December 1950, Marshall reported to Holyoake that increases in the British wholesale price index justified a new approach seeking both increased prices and increases in the tonnage that could be sold outside Britain.[26] Britain accepted immediately that up to 10% could be sold outside Britain but still refused to raise prices. Federated Farmers decided that British public opinion should be mobilised in support of higher prices. The federation cabled Holland, attending the Commonwealth Prime Ministers' Conference in London in January 1951, urging him to 'tell the British public New Zealand very dissatisfied dairy and meat prices under bulk contracts . . . suggest you make strong public statement'. Martin wrote to Holyoake to explain the background.[27] He said the issue had been discussed thoroughly amongst farming organisations and 'can be taken as representing the general opinion of farmers'. Farmers had decided that the only way to obtain fair prices was to 'tell the British public the full facts through the British Press'; without a means of fixing fair prices 'the goodwill that exists between the two countries must eventually be impaired'.

Holland, through Holyoake, dismissed the proposal; he thought it would not benefit New Zealand.[28] Holland said that the British public already thought prices too high and rations too low; by asking for higher prices New Zealand was asking for the ration to be cut further. New Zealand, also, would be seen as 'pretty greedy' whilst it was 'receiving such high prices for wool [as a result of the Korean War]'. The proposed public statement would widen the gap between British and New

[25] 'The Export-Import Relationship: Are We Getting a Fair Deal from Britain?', *Straight Furrow*, 15/12/1950, 6/7, ATL.

[26] Marshall to Holyoake, 18/12/1950, Keith Holyoake papers, MS-1814 – 4/2 Dairy Produce, ATL.

[27] Martin to Holyoake, 18/01/1951, Keith Holyoake papers MS-1814 – 16/3 Dairy Produce, ATL.

[28] Holyoake to Martin, 23/01/1951, Keith Holyoake papers, MS-1814 – 16/3, ATL.

Zealand ministers rather than closing it, taking away 'whatever small chance there is for an increase'. The Federated Farmers Dairy Section Council 'deplored' that 'Ministers of the Crown did not take to opportunity to inform the British public'.[29]

Three months later Britain agreed a 7.5% increase in price retrospectively for dairy produce for the 1950/1951 season on the grounds that the Korean War preparations 'in recent months have led . . . to increases in the cost of production'.[30] Marshall was sceptical; in his view, the expected increases were known to be inevitable during the original negotiations. Two months later Britain agreed another 7.5% increase, this time for the 1951/1952 season.[31]

In 1952 Britain agreed free and unrestricted entry up to 1967 for New Zealand meat but not for dairy produce. Marshall, from London, cabled the negotiations to Holyoake: 'No chance whatever of securing unrestricted entry for 15 years . . . attitudes have hardened since the meat agreement'.[32] Failure to agree unrestricted entry for dairy produce caused strong resentment in New Zealand, and the Under-Secretary to the Minister of Agriculture pointed out that New Zealand had done everything possible during the war years to provide food for Britain and did not quibble over price. New Zealand had done that not only to help Britain but also to build goodwill that would help Dominion producers following the war.[33] The Federated Farmers Dairy Section Chairman said the decision should

> dispel any lingering doubts that there is any sentiment . . . between our Government and the Government of the United Kingdom. . . . This development is a warning to the Marketing Commission to renew its efforts to establish alternative markets . . . on the Continent, in the East [Asia], and elsewhere.[34]

[29] Minutes of the Meeting of the Federated Farmers Dairy Section Council, 07/02/1957, Federated Farmers 90-343 MSY-2709, 3/4, ATL.

[30] Statement by Mr Marshall, 03/04/1951, Keith Holyoake papers, MS-1814 – 16/5, ATL.

[31] Contract for Dairy Products for 1951-52 season, Keith Holyoake papers, MS-1814 – 16/6, 16/06/1951, ATL.

[32] Cable to members (of the Commission), Minister and W.E.Hale, 07/07/1952, Keith Holyoake papers, MS-1814 – 26/3 Dairy Produce, ATL.

[33] 'Dairy Industry and Government: Under-Secty Explains', *Straight Furrow*, 01/11/1953, 35, ATL.

[34] Chairman's Address to the Dairy Section Annual Conference, 16/06/1953, Federated Farmers 90-343 MSY-2709, D131/1953, 1/2, ATL.

To the British Ministry of Food it was becoming clear that dairy produce supply exceeded demand; taking unrestricted supplies would risk price collapse. In New Zealand eyes the British Ministry of Food officials had become hard-headed businessmen with price negotiations based on prices expected in a free market; that was not welcomed by New Zealand and increased doubts over the value of bulk purchase. Despite the increases, prices paid by Britain remained low compared to payments to others, but the Minister for Industries and Commerce pointed out the lack of alternative markets for New Zealand, warning that few countries other than Britain would buy significant dairy produce tonnages.[35] The Dairy Board and the Commission agreed that a two-year extension of the bulk contract should be sought and at the start of 1953 Federated Farmers still preferred extending the contract.[36]

Unlike Ormond, Marshall, the Dairy Commission Chairman, recognised that in the long term New Zealand could not rely on secure access to the British market. In 1953, Marshall warned about possible drops in dairy prices; the food supply in Britain had changed with no more dairy produce shortages. He said Britain had moved away from rationing, and people could now buy whatever they chose in quantities they themselves determined.[37] Also, cheese and butter production within Britain continued to increase. Holyoake added to Marshall's warnings, pointing out that, with Britain ending rationing and price controls, prices would be determined by supply and demand; production in New Zealand would need to be directed at what the consumer wanted and could afford.[38] Global dairy markets weakened again and New Zealand accepted in 1953 a 7.5% price reduction for milk powder exports to Britain and only a 4% increase for butter and cheese. Holyoake said that the Dairy Commission

[35] 'Bulk Buying Favours Government Trading', *Straight Furrow*, 01/07/1952, 5, ATL; 'Our Farming Industry Stands on the Threshold of a New Era', *Straight Furrow*, 01/06/1953, 1, ATL.

[36] Holyoake to Marshall and Hale, 18/04/1952 and 21/04/1952, Keith Holyoake papers, MS-1814 – 26/1, Dairy Produce, ATL; Minutes of the Dairy Section Council, 04/02/1953, Federated Farmers 90-343 MSY-2709 D117/1953, 3, ATL.

[37] 'Lower Prices Predicted for Dairy Exports', *Straight Furrow*, 01/08/1953, 18, ATL.

[38] 'What Mr Holyoake Told the Dominion Conference: A Note of Optimism Throughout', *Straight Furrow*, 01/08/1953, 3, ATL.

negotiators had done well taking into account price trends in other markets.[39] The Dairy Board monthly review reported in February 1954 'a downward movement in butter and cheese [prices] in most countries' and Holyoake warned that New Zealand could not expect the high prices of recent years to continue; the period when primary produce sold easily, at prices which had been increasing yearly, had ended.[40]

In mid-1954 Britain offered to end dairy bulk purchase early and New Zealand considered it to be 'in the best interests of producers' to terminate the purchase one year early.[41] The frequent complaints that Britain paid unfair prices led New Zealand to decide it would earn more on a free market than the best prices that might be negotiated with the British Ministry of Food; in 1954 Britain had been proposing reduced prices. The Dairy Board and the Commission were 'unanimously of the opinion . . . that the contract should be cancelled this year'.[42] They recognised that the change would need to be made at some time and 'the sooner the change was made the better'.[43] Producers had convinced themselves that British obstinacy restricted their income and they would benefit by freeing themselves from dependence on Britain.

6.4 The Difficulties of a Free Market

During bulk purchase producers knew there was a market for as much as they could produce under a cost-plus system in which payment more than met costs despite the impressions that Britain treated New Zealand unfairly. But after bulk purchase ended the dairy industry seemed out of

[39] 'New Prices for Dairy Exports', *Straight Furrow*, 01/07/1953, 11, ATL.

[40] Dairy Board Monthly Review, 01/02/1954, Keith Holyoake papers, MS-1814 – 39/3 Dairy Produce, 2, ATL; 'Production Costs Must Be Watched', *Straight Furrow*, 01/07/1953, 12, ATL.

[41] 'Economic Survey', *AJHR*, Vol. I, B-5, 1954, 24, WCL.

[42] Memorandum for the Rt.Hon. Minister of Agriculture, 03/06/1954, Keith Holyoake papers, MS-1814 – 40/1 Dairy Produce, 1, ATL.

[43] Memorandum for the Rt.Hon. Minister of Agriculture, 03/06/1954, Keith Holyoake papers, MS-1814- 40/1 Dairy Produce, 1, ATL.

line with world conditions, and for the first time selling exports at prices sufficient to cover costs became difficult. Dairy prices in the British market slumped partly because countries with surplus dairy produce were dumping their surpluses at prices less than the cost of production. Also, New Zealand producers were unprepared for a change from a protected market. In 1957 the New Zealand government again sought duty-free and unrestricted access to the British market and this time Britain agreed. Britain was asked, also, to restrict imports from other dairy-exporting countries to protect New Zealand prices and in 1958 Britain persuaded the dumping countries to restrict supplies. But those agreements were short term and New Zealand, repeatedly, had to renew its requests for anti-dumping measures whilst gradually realising that it too would have to restrict its exports to Britain.

Soon after bulk purchase ended the price for wholesale butter in Britain fell by 20% without warning.[44] Holyoake warned that the British guaranteed price for milk from its own farmers had fallen for the first time in fourteen years.[45] Producers gradually accepted the need to cope with lower prices.[46] Holyoake called a meeting of dairy producers at short notice after their leaders had taken 'the first steps in this economic wind that is blowing . . . coldly in their quarter' by approaching the government for help.[47] The South Taranaki Federated Farmers Provincial President suggested that bulk purchase had made producers 'lose touch with the modern market and its requirements'.[48]

In mid-1956 dairy prices slumped again on the British market. Denmark's traditional markets such as France and Germany had been satisfied by low-price American surplus dairy produce and Denmark sent more produce than usual to Britain causing a glut on the market.

[44] 'Bank of New Zealand Market Summary', *Straight Furrow*, 01/10/1954, 45, ATL.

[45] 'There Is No Room for Complacency', *Straight Furrow*, 01/09/1954, 29, ATL.

[46] 'Farmers Forum', *Straight Furrow*, 01/10/1954, 16, ATL.

[47] Opening Remarks of Minister of Agriculture to Meeting re. Rural Economy, 09/06/1955, Keith Holyoake papers MS-1814 45/5 Dairy Produce, 2, ATL.

[48] 'Provincial President Sounds Note of Warning', *Straight Furrow* 01/07/1955, 22, ATL; 'Our Economy Is Getting out of Line with World Conditions', *Straight Furrow* 01/07/1955, 23, ATL.

Sweden, Finland and Ireland also began to send more to Britain to relieve their own surpluses.[49] Fears surfaced that Britain's own guaranteed price scheme might be leading to surpluses that could not be sold.[50] Prices in Britain recovered before the season end, but, clearly, oversupply in dairy produce had become established and the problem could not be ignored. The low prices during the 1956–1957 season led the New Zealand Reserve Bank to estimate that losses would be £10 M for the dairy industry and the reserves would be reduced to £18–£19 M.[51] If the low prices for butter and cheese persisted the Dairy Reserve would be fully spent early in 1958.

At first in 1957 when Ormond prompted comprehensive trade talks with Britain, the dairy industry doubted whether clear objectives could be identified for itself.[52] The Dairy Commission had already started plans for pursuing alternative markets through bilateral arrangements; those were put on hold until after the discussions with Britain.[53] In particular the industry worried that if Ormond and the meat industry pressed Britain to introduce quota restrictions on beef from Argentina, Britain's response might be to ask New Zealand to fix permanently existing preferences for British goods imported into New Zealand. That would make new bilateral deals for dairy produce more difficult to negotiate. Also, the dairy industry feared that if Britain started a policy of imposing quotas, a quota might be introduced for New Zealand dairy exports to Britain.[54] Eventually the dairy industry decided to take part in the talks and agreed on two key points that should be raised with Britain. First, Britain should be asked to put dairy exports on the same footing as meat exports with a long-term agreement for duty-free and unrestricted entry. Second, Britain should be encouraged to

[49] Jim McAloon, *Judgements of All Kinds* (Wellington: Victoria University Press, 2013), 120.

[50] 'Eight Billion Dollars Worth of Surplus Food', *Straight Furrow*, 01/10/1956, 17, ATL.

[51] 'Reserve Bank Comment on Dairy Industry', *Straight Furrow*, 01/11/1957, 11, ATL.

[52] Meeting of Producer Organizations and Members of the Cabinet Committee on Economic Policy, 05/02/1957, T1 454 61/3/21, ANZ.

[53] Note from Treasury to H G Lang, London, 08/01/1957, T1 424 61/3/21, ANZ.

[54] Supplementary Notes Re: Ten Year Free Entry of Dairy Produce, July 1957, Keith Holyoake papers MS-1814 – 56/2, 1, ATL.

take action against countries depressing dairy produce prices by dumping their produce onto the British market.

At the start of the trade talks in April 1957, E. J. Fawcett, the New Zealand Director-General of Agriculture, made a strong, apparently sentimental, case on behalf of the dairy industry for protection by Britain.[55] He reminded Britain that New Zealand had increased supplies during shortages in post-war Britain and had made changes between butter and cheese to suit Britain during wartime. The British negotiators agreed that there should be free and unrestricted access for New Zealand dairy produce for ten years up to 1967. But the British refused to take action against dumping, pointing out a more formal procedure that might be followed if New Zealand's concerns increased.[56]

The Federated Farmers President, who had been a trade delegation member, said it remained clear that Britain for the foreseeable future would be the main customer for New Zealand dairy produce. But Britain would not limit imports from foreign sources in order to accommodate New Zealand's expanding exports.[57] Federated Farmers felt that the position had become clear; New Zealand could not rely on Britain to absorb its expanded production. The New Zealand economy now had to take into account that increased production would mean that extra New Zealand produce needed to be sold outside Britain.[58] The Dairy Board shared the view with Federated Farmers that 'it had to be accepted that the UK could not absorb all New Zealand's butter'.[59] Unrestricted access had been agreed but market reality made that a hollow right.

[55] Trade Discussions Between the Government of New Zealand and the Government of the United Kingdom, April/May 1957, ABHS W4628 7148 Box 12, Minutes of the Milk Products Group meeting 16/04/1957, 1, ANZ.

[56] Trade Discussions Between the Government of New Zealand and the Government of the United Kingdom, April/May 1957, ABHS W4628 7148 Box 12, Report to the House of Representatives, 29/05/1957, 7, ANZ.

[57] Re: The Trade Mission, 17/06/1957, Federated Farmers 90-343 MSY-2713, D74/1957, 1/2, ATL.

[58] Re: The Trade Mission, 17/06/1957, Federated Farmers 90-343 MSY-2713, D74/1957, 3, ATL.

[59] Working Party on Economic Policy, meeting with representatives of the Dairy Industry, 12/12/1956, T/1/61/3/21 Pt II, ATL.

The hope that a free market would see New Zealand produce sold at the same price as Denmark proved wrong; Denmark butter prices remained 14% higher.[60] Marshall rather than Britain now had to explain why. He told the Dominion Dairy Conference that Denmark produced butter differently to New Zealand. Denmark used a 'starter' that induced lactic acid development whilst New Zealand producers sought to prevent lactic acid development because butter needed to survive during the long sea voyage to Britain. Some consumers preferred Danish butter and were prepared to pay more. In addition, far more New Zealand butter than Danish sold in Britain, and sometimes in the year heavy New Zealand supply accompanied Danish short supply enabling Danish butter to command a substantial premium.[61] In the opinion of the British delegation at the 1957 trade talks in London, Danish butter commanded a premium partly as 'the result of sustained salesmanship over many years', implying that New Zealand lacked that sustained salesmanship.[62]

In October 1957 butter and cheese prices again fell on the British market; for butter, caused by imports from Ireland, Argentina, the Netherlands, Finland, Sweden and South Africa; for cheese by increased production in Britain.[63] That third major price fall in the mid-1950s emphasised the growing difficulties for New Zealand in the free market. Prices remained low as 1958 started with no sign that butter imports from non-traditional suppliers to the British market would decrease. In his annual address the New Zealand Co-operative Dairy Company Chairman painted a gloomy picture.[64] He reported that

> every country with the exception of ourself and Denmark has embarked on ... subsidised agriculture ... with the dual aim of self-sufficiency in time of war and the saving of external currency. In addition, most

[60] 'Bank of New Zealand: Our Primary Produce Markets in U.K.', *Straight Furrow* 01/04/1955, 17, ATL; 'New Zealand Dairy Board's Monthly Review', *Straight Furrow* 01/05/1955, 18, ATL.

[61] 'Danish Butter Preference', *Straight Furrow* 01/09/1955, 22, ATL.

[62] Meeting of Milk Products Group, 17/04/1957, LONB, 37/1/1E Part 1, ANZ.

[63] 'Dairy Commission's Review: London Market Report', *Straight Furrow*, 15/10/1957, 5, ATL.

[64] Address by Chairman of the New Zealand Dairy Co-operative Company, 21/08/1957, Keith Holyoake papers, MSY1814 – 56/3 Dairy Produce, 1–18, ATL.

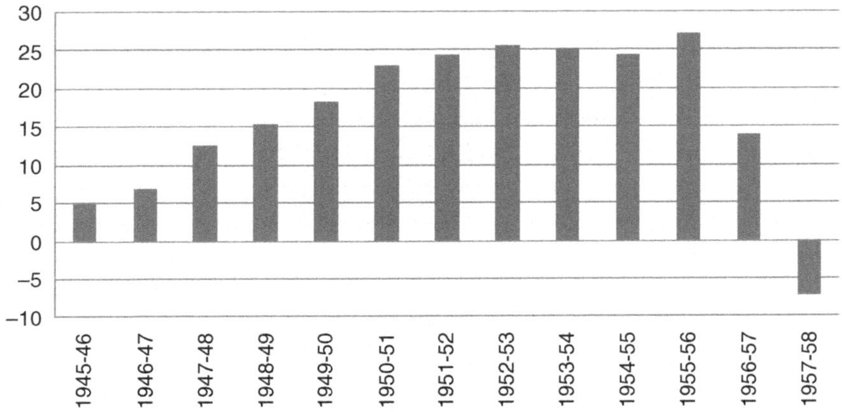

Fig. 6.2 Dairy Reserve balance in £ million (NZDYB)

> countries except the United Kingdom have imposed almost complete embargoes or high tariffs. . . . Great Britain is thus acting as a sponge. . . . If losses were to continue at this staggering rate . . . dairy farmers hard won savings will have run dry.

The Chairman concluded that 'the industry must intensify its efforts to find alternative markets. . . . Overseas advertising of our dairy produce must be intensified'. Losses continued and, as the Reserve Bank had predicted, the Dairy Reserve Account went into deficit (Fig. 6.2) forcing the Dairy Board borrow from the Reserve Bank.

The New Zealand government made a formal request asking the British government to introduce anti-dumping measures.[65] That followed a recent precedent in which Britain had introduced measures to protect its domestic industries.[66] Before agreeing to anti-dumping measures the

[65] Statement by the Prime Minister of New Zealand, the Right Hon. Walter Nash, Dumping of Dairy Produce in United Kingdom May 1958–February 1959, AAFZ W5705 7174 Box 64 3288 Part 2, 1, ANZ; Statement by the Prime Minister of New Zealand, 21/05/1958, Dumping of Dairy Produce in United Kingdom May 1958–February 1959, AAFZ W5705 7174 Box 64 3288 Part 2 1, ANZ. McAloon, 120, reports that Macmillan was criticised 'for denying the British consumer cheap European butter'.

[66] 'Govt. Asks U.K. to Use Anti-Dumping Act', *Straight Furrow*, 19/02/1958, 3, ATL.

legislation required the British to consider three main issues, whether: dumping took place; it injured the complainant; and, anti-dumping measures would be in Britain's national interest. The first two issues seemed not in doubt; the third entirely a political matter and less clear. The British Minister for Agriculture welcomed the lower food prices resulting from dumping as a contribution to checking inflation.[67] The retail trade in Britain objected to the government artificially raising the price through import barriers; retailers said perhaps New Zealand should find new markets or make less butter and earn a living by making something people would pay for.[68] Britain worried also that anti-dumping measures might trigger retaliatory measures against British exports, for instance, by Sweden. Britain's hesitation led Phillip Holloway, the New Zealand Minister of Industries and Commerce, to make a speech that was interpreted in Britain as 'bitter'. Holloway asked if the British government 'were turning their back on a loyal Dominion such as New Zealand'.[69] But sympathy for New Zealand remained strong in Britain and, in the House of Commons, the British Minister was reminded how 'all sides' of the House remembered 'with gratitude how New Zealand stood by us in a very difficult period'.[70] A British farmer recalled New Zealand's gesture in supplying Britain during the war.[71]

The increased supplies to the British market that caused the low prices were obvious. Between 1955 and 1957 butter imports had increased by 59,000 tons including 24,000 from New Zealand and 35,000 from the countries named as dumpers by New Zealand. In addition, British production increased by 19,000 tons. But even if Britain embargoed

[67] 'How the Dairy Crisis Came About', *Straight Furrow*, 19/03/1958, p. 6, ATL.

[68] 'Grocers' Viewpoint', *Straight Furrow*, 19/03/1958, 16, ATL.

[69] Extract from Hansard, 24/03/1958, Dumping of Dairy Produce in United Kingdom January–April 1958, AAFZ W5705 7174 Box 64 3288 Part 1, 1, ANZ. From here onwards the discussion up to mid-1962 of dumping and the introduction of quotas has benefitted from access to Archive NZ papers gathered together by John Singleton for his work with Paul Robertson on *Britain, Butter and European Integration, 1957–1964* in Economic History Review, L. 2 (1997), 327–347.

[70] Extract from Parliamentary Debate on Trade and Commerce, 17/04/1958, Dumping of Dairy Produce in United Kingdom May 1958–February 1959, AAFZ W5705 7174 Box 64 3288 Part 2, 2, ANZ.

[71] 'Initiations of Price Reductions (Butter) by New Zealand', *Straight Furrow*, 02/04/1958, 1, ATL.

supplies from the dumping countries New Zealand could no longer continue to increase its exports to Britain without risking a collapse in prices; New Zealand could no longer send unrestricted tonnages.[72]

Butter prices dropped further in early 1958 though with the advantage that butter consumption increased and demand again began to equal supply. But that added to New Zealand's dilemma; if Britain raised duties against dumping countries would the higher prices reduce butter consumption? C. F. Skinner, Deputy Prime Minister and Minister of Agriculture in the Labour government elected in 1957, visited Britain in April 1958 to discuss dumping; another catastrophic drop in prices took place during his visit. Skinner acknowledged that change would be essential in New Zealand, possibly with some dairy farmers turning to beef production; a one-eighth reduction in New Zealand production would stop too much butter being exported to the British market.[73] But he hoped that Britain would restrict other suppliers rather than New Zealand.

New Zealand had seen itself as the strongest advocate for free trade in agriculture but in requesting anti-dumping measures wanted Britain to abandon free trade and introduce import restrictions to protect New Zealand dairy farmers. In May 1958 the British government accepted New Zealand's request for action against dumping countries and announced that 'material injury has been caused to the New Zealand Dairy Industry' and it was in Britain's 'national interest to take action'. Britain asked the dumping countries to voluntarily 'keep their exports within agreed limits', backing that up with the threat to impose countervailing duties if the countries refused the agreed limits. Britain expected voluntary restraint to reduce imports by 10% thereby strengthening the market and giving New Zealand substantial assistance.[74] By July 1958, the dumping countries had agreed to restrict their exports to Britain voluntarily.[75] Eventually the reduced supply made butter prices rise

[72] 'What Our New Zealand Negotiators Are up Against', *Straight Furrow*, 16/04/1958, 1, ATL.

[73] 'Harrop's Impressions of Prospects: Interview with Mr Skinner', *Straight Furrow*, 07/05/1958, 1, ATL.

[74] Cable from London dated 19 May 1958 No 26, 19/05/1958, Dumping of Dairy Produce in United Kingdom May 1958–February 1959, AAFZ W5705 7174 Box 64 3288 Part 2, ANZ.

[75] 'Dairy Commission's Review: Latest Market Report', *Straight Furrow*, 02/07/1958, 5, ATL.

reaching the level anticipated by Britain in setting the voluntary levels.[76] The year 1958 ended with better prospects for New Zealand's dairy produce exports; the price for butter had risen by 40% from the low point earlier in the year with cheese prices also high.[77] The Dairy Board repaid borrowing from the Reserve Bank. Dumping countries had lowered domestic prices to increase domestic consumption and reduce the need for exports.[78]

At the start of 1959 Britain decided that it could remove the restrictions and assured New Zealand that it would again review the situation sympathetically if New Zealand had to lodge another anti-dumping application.[79] For the first time since free marketing resumed in 1954, the butter price did not fall between December and March.[80] In mid-1959 Europe experienced a much drier summer than usual and that depressed dairy supply to the British market strengthening the price paid to New Zealand even more.[81] Continental Europeans also started to buy New Zealand butter.[82] Demand began to exceed supply.[83]

Eventually the British market again started to weaken and the first change in New Zealand's butter price for more than a year took place in January 1960 with a 7% fall.[84] European suppliers looked to sell to

---

[76] External Affairs, Wellington, to High Commission, London, 20/11/1958, Dumping of Dairy Produce in United Kingdom May 1958–February 1959, AAFZ W5705 7174 Box 64 3288 Part 2, 1, ANZ; 'Dairy Commission's Market Report', *Straight Furrow*, 05/11/1958, 5, ATL.

[77] Trends and Prospects in the Market for Dairy Produce, February 1960, Federated Farmers 90-343 MSY-2715 Dairy Section, D55/1960, 3, ATL.

[78] 'Dairy Commission's Market Report', *Straight Furrow*, 21/01/1959, 5, ATL.

[79] Trends and Prospects in the Market for Dairy Produce, February 1960, Federated Farmers 90-343 MSY-2715 Dairy Section, D55/1960, 7, ATL; 'Dairy Commission's Market Report', *Straight Furrow*, 21/01/1959, 5, ATL.

[80] 'Dairy Commission's Market Report', *Straight Furrow*, 18/03/1959, 5, ATL.

[81] Trends and Prospects in the Market for Dairy Produce, February 1960, Federated Farmers 90-343 MSY-2715 Dairy Section, D55/1960, 3, ATL.

[82] Trends and Prospects in the Market for Dairy Produce, February 1960, Federated Farmers 90-343 MSY-2715 Dairy Section, D55/1960, 6, ATL.

[83] 'Dairy Commission's Market Report', *Straight Furrow*, 19/08/1959, 7, ATL.

[84] 'Dairy Commission's Marketing Report', *Straight Furrow*, 03/02/1960, 4, ATL; 'Dairy Commission's Marketing Report, *Straight Furrow*, 16/03/1960, 5, ATL.

the British market now that production had increased above 1959's low levels.[85] Stocks built up and efforts increased to promote butter consumption but, clearly, supply once again threatened to overtake demand.[86] New concerns over dumping surfaced in August 1960 with worries that Poland sold butter to Britain at prices far below those paid by Polish consumers.[87] In New Zealand again the Dairy Reserve Account went into deficit and the Board borrowed from the Reserve Bank.

The Agriculture Ministers of the Organisation for European Economic Cooperation (OEEC) set up a working party to investigate butter markets in Europe and it recommended changes.[88] All butter suppliers should 'maintain discipline amongst themselves'. For the British market, OEEC countries who were not traditional suppliers 'should avoid exporting . . . to that market'; OEEC countries who were traditional 'marginal' suppliers should export 'only normal supplies'; OEEC countries who were 'important' traditional suppliers 'should endeavour not to exceed the quantities normally exported'. So that the efforts of OEEC countries 'were not nullified' by actions of non-members, such as New Zealand, Britain was asked to discuss the measures with countries which were not OEEC members with the clear intention being that those countries should show the same 'discipline'. The OEEC invited New Zealand to future working party meetings.

For New Zealand the OEEC proposals implied that, as an important traditional supplier, it, too, 'should endeavour not to exceed the quantities normally exported'. In 1961 the International Federation of Agricultural Producers (IFAP) which included New Zealand as a member, recommended that 'all butter producing countries should . . . implement these [OEEC] recommendations'.[89] New Zealand could no longer send to

---

[85] 'Dairy Marketing Commission Report', *Straight Furrow*, 30/03/1960, 7, ATL.

[86] 'Butter Prices Unchanged', *Straight Furrow*, 04/05/1960, 3, ATL.

[87] 'Dairy Labour Saving', *Straight Furrow*, 03/08/1960, 23, ATL.

[88] New Zealand Embassy, Paris, to External Affairs, Wellington: Butter, 30/09/1960, Dumping of Dairy Produce on United Kingdom Market 1958–1961, AAFZ W5705 7174 Box 64 3288 Part 3, 1–3, ANZ.

[89] IFAP Special Meeting on Dairy Products, 13/10/1961, Federated Farmers 90-343 MSY-2716 Dairy Section, 1, ATL.

Britain 'unrestricted' supplies and was now expected to show restraint in not exceeding traditional supplies. The OEEC Ministers recommended also that farmers should be encouraged to shift from dairying to other commodities. Skinner welcomed the proposals as lifting 'a very heavy cloud' because, if OEEC countries followed the recommendations, New Zealand dairying would be 'freed from the constant fear of dumping by European countries' and 'it could be a milestone on the highway to a saner policy on agricultural protectionism'.[90]

Through late 1960 and early 1961 Britain made several moves to ensure that OEEC countries stuck to the recommendations to prevent dumping. But, once discussions started on whether to apply to join the EEC, Britain put on hold any further action. Linton and the Dairy Board became uneasy that nothing would happen if New Zealand made a new anti-dumping application, and instead the Board wanted Britain to compensate New Zealand financially. Linton wrote to the Cabinet Committee on Economic and Financial Questions (CCEFQ) in February 1961 proposing that Britain should be asked to agree that New Zealand suffered damage from dumping. [91] Linton pointed out that despite the 'repeated and continuous efforts . . . made to persuade New Zealand to join international groups . . . to consider measures leading to stability' those had been strongly resisted by New Zealand's dairy industry because those measures 'will inevitably lead to quotas'. New Zealand turned down the invitation to join the OEEC Working Party. Linton argued that if Britain decided not to take anti-dumping action because of 'her overriding desire to keep food costs to a minimum' then New Zealand should be compensated financially. The Board expected Britain to support the New Zealand dairy industry, either, through British butter consumers paying more, or, the British government paying a subsidy to New Zealand.

The CCEFQ met in March 1961 with its considerations influenced by concern that the government might be 'subjected to strong criticism

---

[90] Press Statement released by C.F.Skinner, 18/10/1961, Dumping of Dairy Produce on United Kingdom Market 1958 -1961, AAFZ W5705 7174 Box 64 3288 Part 3, 1/2, ANZ.

[91] Memorandum on Behalf of the Dairy Industry, 28/02/1961, Dumping of Dairy Produce on United Kingdom Market 1958–1961, AAFZ W5705 7174 Box 64 3288 Part 3, 1–4, ANZ.

by the Dairy Industry'.[92] Linton attended part of the meeting and all those present agreed that New Zealand should not make a formal request for Britain to take measures against dumping at that time. New Zealand would need to name all countries considered to be dumping and that included Australia and Denmark. That naming would cause difficulties in 'New Zealand's trading relationship with Australia'; also, Britain would not want to take action against a Commonwealth country. Moreover, for Denmark, New Zealand considered that 'the Danes had been our firmest supporter . . . where trading problems have been discussed'.[93] The CCEFQ decided also that a request for compensation 'would not be desirable'.[94] Holyoake visited Britain at that time and 'that provided an opportunity for making strong representations'. If, after those representations, 'no improvement was forthcoming' the CCEFQ agreed that New Zealand would have 'no alternative' to invoking formal anti-dumping measures. [95] Holyoake's representations failed to improve the situation.

6.5 The Acceptance of a Quota for New Zealand

The Dairy Board forced the National government elected at the end of 1960 to once again ask Britain to introduce measures against dumping. Britain proposed that the GATT Secretariat should resolve the problems. Linton was furious because he could see that the outcome would be a market sharing agreement that would include New Zealand. That proved to be the outcome and was accepted, reluctantly,

[92] Butter Dumping, 22/03/1961, Minutes of Cabinet Committee on Economic and Financial Questions, T1/40/645/13, 1, ANZ.

[93] Butter Dumping, 22/03/1961, Minutes of Cabinet Committee on Economic and Financial Questions: T1/40/645/13, 1, ANZ.

[94] Butter Dumping, 22/03/1961, Minutes of Cabinet Committee on Economic and Financial Questions: T1/40/645/13, 4, ANZ.

[95] Butter Dumping, 22/03/1961, Minutes of Cabinet Committee on Economic and Financial Questions: T1/40/645/13, 3, ANZ.

by Linton and the New Zealand government. Producers had mixed feelings about market sharing but eventually accepted it as necessary and that New Zealand needed to take part. Britain next proposed a more formal quota system and New Zealand accepted that it would no longer have unrestricted access to the British market. The discussions on dumping ran parallel with Britain's first application to join the EEC. Linton decided that the dairy industry would be in a better position with Britain inside the EEC; preventing dumping had become more of a concern than the protectionism that might be introduced should Britain become an EEC member.

In May 1961, the Dairy Board asked the government to make a formal application for Britain to take steps against dumping.[96] No response had been received by mid-June and Linton became more Ormond-like in directly approaching Holyoake, Prime Minister since the general election at the end of 1960. Linton reported that the industry had become 'extremely restive', and action should be taken immediately with 'all the vigour' at the government's command.[97] Support by farmers had contributed to Holyoake's success in the election and pressure from Linton clearly had a significant impact on government thinking; by mid-July the government decided that 'pressure on the Government . . . cannot be withstood any further'.[98] In early August New Zealand requested that Britain introduce anti-dumping measures. Britain responded by proposing that a meeting should be arranged by the GATT Secretariat and attended by all butter suppliers to Britain. New Zealand, as a member of GATT, would be expected to attend. Britain anticipated that 'restraint by the appropriate exporting countries would be the appropriate solution' as in 1958.[99]

[96] Linton to Holyoake, 2 May 1961, Dumping of Dairy Produce on United Kingdom Market 1 March 1961–31 July 1961, AAFZ W5705 7174 Box 64 3288 Part 4, ANZ.

[97] Linton to Holyoake, 20 June 1961, Dumping of Dairy Produce on United Kingdom Market 1 March 1961–31 July 1961, AAFZ W5705 7174 Box 64 3288 Part 4, ANZ.

[98] External Affairs, Wellington, to High Commission, London, 19/07/1961, Dumping of Dairy Produce on United Kingdom Market 1 March 1961–31 July 1961, AAFZ W5705 7174 Box 64 3288 Part 4, ANZ.

[99] High Commission, London, to External Affairs, Wellington, 17/08/1961, T1/40/645/13, 2, ANZ.

Britain could claim that concerns of New Zealand and Denmark made the GATT meeting necessary. Britain did not need to accuse others of dumping, such as Australia, a fellow Commonwealth country. Linton and the Dairy Board saw that an obvious outcome would be an agreement on market sharing. The Board did not want to be party to any such agreement and reacted furiously to Britain asking the GATT Secretariat to arrange a meeting, with New Zealand expected to attend. Linton called the meeting 'a direct approach to weakening our right of free and unrestricted entry' and inevitably such a meeting would lead to pressure for New Zealand to accept a 'market sharing' arrangement.[100] Linton wanted the government to protest and refuse the British proposal. New Zealand officials advised that such a refusal carried the danger that countries at present voluntarily restraining supplies might abandon restraint. Also, refusal would 'not create a favourable atmosphere' amongst Europeans, especially the French, for the 'United Kingdom/EEC negotiations on commodities of interest to us'.[101] The dairy industry wanted Britain to impose countervailing duties but the officials pointed out that that would still need a GATT meeting for Britain to obtain a waiver to allow imposition of duties; the meeting outcome might be no different to that from the meeting as presently proposed by Britain.

The New Zealand government agreed to send a delegation to the GATT meeting under the condition that Britain 'understood' that New Zealand 'should not be asked to offer any reduction in its own supplies'.[102] The High Commission in London led the New Zealand delegation, with Linton and the Dairy Board General Manager, Dai Ward, only as advisers, thereby allowing the Board to keep its distance from the any agreement reached at the meeting. As expected the meeting discussed market sharing, and the New Zealand delegation refused to

[100] Statement by Mr Linton: Comments on United Kingdom Proposal Re. Anti-Dumping Case, 21/08/1961, T1/40/645/13, 1/2, ANZ.

[101] Butter Dumping: Chairman of Officials Committee to Chairman of Cabinet Committee on Economic and Financial Questions, 28/08/1961, T1/40/645/13, 1/3, ANZ.

[102] Report of the New Zealand Delegation to the GATT Consultation on the Marketing of Butter in the United Kingdom, 21/09/1961, T1/40/645/13, 2, ANZ.

agree to participate in any such arrangement. The delegation sought 'a scheme by which others would refrain from causing injury by dumping and subsidisation' and not one that involved New Zealand accepting 'reductions to enable others to continue these practices'.[103] Despite its stance, the delegation considered that the 'goodwill and understanding of the United Kingdom was maintained' and Britain thought the New Zealand approach to be reasonable.[104] No doubt the New Zealand High Commission succeeded in softening Linton's distaste for the meeting and in smoothing the relations between Britain and New Zealand.

The meeting agreed that the Executive Secretary of GATT should continue to communicate with the relevant countries to try to find a compromise, and, one week after the meeting, Britain asked New Zealand whether it would accept a reduction or 'some presentational device' that made it appear that New Zealand had accepted a reduction. The response was that the latter 'might have some value in Geneva' where the GATT meeting had been held but 'would be impossible to explain to the New Zealand industry and public'.[105] But New Zealand agreed that, if all others accepted the GATT Executive Secretary's proposal, Britain could tell those others that New Zealand 'would confine shipments' to its 'existing programme of 91,000 tons'.[106]

In early November 1961 agreement had been reached that 'all except one [Ireland] of the butter suppliers . . . have voluntarily agreed on the level of their supplies' for the six-month period to the end of March 1962.[107] The Dairy Commission and Dairy Board saw no alternative solution and welcomed the agreement because dumping had threatened to wreck the British market. The Dairy Commission called the

---

[103] Report of the New Zealand Delegation to the GATT Consultation on the Marketing of Butter in the United Kingdom, 21/09/1961, T1/40/645/13, 12, ANZ.

[104] Report of the New Zealand Delegation to the GATT Consultation on the Marketing of Butter in the United Kingdom, 21/09/1961, T1/40/645/13, 15, ANZ.

[105] Note for File, External Affairs, T1/40/645/13, 27/09/1961, ANZ.

[106] External Affairs, Wellington, to High Commission, London: Butter, 20/10/1961, Dumping of Dairy Produce in United Kingdom 1961, AAFZ W5705 7174 Box 65 3288, ANZ.

[107] 'What GATT Did', *Straight Furrow*, 24/01/1962, 19, ATL.

agreement the 'news of the year', demonstrating that at that time dumping carried more importance for the industry than Britain's formal application to join the EEC which had been submitted two months earlier.[108] Britain imposed countervailing duties on Irish butter; Britain did not need GATT approval for a waiver to impose the duties because Ireland was not a GATT member. Despite the earlier resistance to market sharing, Linton welcomed the agreement but needed to defend himself against accusations that he had been 'jockeyed' into it. He called New Zealand's market share a 'quota', and claimed that New Zealand was the only country 'not to have our quota reduced' and had willingly accepted the agreement. [109] Linton also said that 'there is no doubt whatever that the action taken by the United Kingdom Government was of great benefit to this country'.[110] By late 1961 the butter price in Britain had increased. Another benefit from the meeting was that, in addition to the main butter-supplying countries, officials from the Commission of the EEC attended. The meeting left Linton feeling confident that Britain's negotiations with the EEC would give New Zealand 'some measure of protection against unfair trading'.[111]

Britain intended to review the quotas after six months. Linton reported that he would be happy with the same quota in future to avoid dumping threatening to wreck the British market; something needed to be done. Perhaps Linton spoke in relief that a solution seemed to have been found and New Zealand could continue sending the same volume to Britain. Producers at the June 1961 Federated Farmers Dairy Council's annual conference had 'greeted with loud applause' and agreed unanimously a resolution that included 'our export right of free and unrestricted entry . . . to the United Kingdom must be preserved in full', but in December 1961, Ralph Woolerton, President of the Council,

[108] NZ Dairy Production and Marketing Board: Radio Report, 03/11/1961, Press Statements – 4/11/58–10/10/63, ABBU W4244 Box 33, ANZ.

[109] 'NZ Not "Jockeyed Into Agreement"', *Straight Furrow*, 10/01/1962, 14, ATL.

[110] 'Address by Mr A. Linton on Butter-Dumping History', *Waikato Times*, April 1962, Dumping of Dairy Produce on the United Kingdom Market 1962, AAFZ W1318 7174 Box 189 3288 Part 6, ANZ.

[111] 'Mr Linton Is Confident: We Will Not Be Sold Out', *Straight Furrow*, 18/10/1961, 15, ATL.

accepted that Britain's actions would strengthen the market.[112] But the quota now made the reality more formal; New Zealand no longer had unrestricted access to the British market, and had given up one of the 'vital rights' that in 1961 the government had sought to retain should Britain join the EEC. Jack Marshall, as Minister for Overseas Trade, saw the agreement as setting a pattern for both short-term and long-term action leading to fairer marketing. The action was 'appreciated by New Zealand' as a 'first step to more stable and profitable marketing of butter'.[113] The Minister for Agriculture told the House of Representatives that the agreement was 'most welcome to the Government . . . to the industry and to the country was a whole'.[114] He stressed that New Zealand had not agreed to reduce supplies.[115]

The New Zealand government and Dairy Board thought that continuation 'of the short-term arrangements beyond the present six-month period will be essential'.[116] In February 1962 Britain proposed a more formal quota system for the next twelve months and asked New Zealand to grant Britain a waiver 'from their obligation to allow' unrestricted entry of New Zealand butter into Britain.[117] The CCEFQ now accepted market sharing as long as Britain introduced measures that raised the butter price to an 'economic return' for New Zealand. The CCEFQ recognised that New Zealand exports would be restricted to the average for the 1956/1960 period but had no difficulty in accepting because dairy production would not reach that tonnage. The CCEFQ thought it 'was an ingenious way of avoiding a formal quota' but no one

[112] Chairman's Address to the Dairy Section Annual Conference, 13/06/1962, Federated Farmers 90–343, MSY-2716 D64/1962, 4, ATL; 'A "Dumping" Breathing Space', *Straight Furrow*, 06/12/1961, 15, ATL.

[113] 'What GATT Did', *Straight Furrow*, 24/01/1962, 19, ATL.

[114] Hon. T. L. Hayman, *NZPD*, 1961, Vol. 329, 3290–91, WCL.

[115] Careful thought was given to what should be announced; the typescript for the Minister said 'restricted' but that was crossed out and 'reduced' handwritten alongside.

[116] External Affairs, Wellington, to High Commission, London, 24/11/1961, Dumping of Dairy Produce in United Kingdom 1961, AAFZ W5705 7174 Box 65 3288, ANZ.

[117] Draft Reply to British Aide-Memoire, 08/03/1962, Industry and Commerce - Primary Industries - Dairy Industries 1960–1969 - E(62)M.14, AAFD W3738 811 Box 1032 CAB 123/10/1, ANZ.

doubted that it was a formal quota and 'quota' was the word used in subsequent discussion. The CCEFQ recognised that if production exceeded that average New Zealand would have accepted a reduction. But there seemed 'no practical alternative'.[118]

Edward Greensmith, Chairman of the Cabinet Committee on Economic and Financial Policy (CCEFP) and Secretary to the Treasury, demonstrated New Zealand's dilemma by noting that Britain's proposal breached the agreement that New Zealand should be allowed unrestricted access. He worried that that right had become the 'keynote' for New Zealand's attitude towards Britain's EEC negotiations and that losing that right would set a precedent for those negotiations. He recognised that New Zealand 'cannot hope to retain' that right if Britain did join but 'as far as the public are aware' New Zealand based its policy on retaining the right.[119] But he recommended that the British proposal be accepted 'with reluctance' because New Zealand's balance of payments could not withstand 'a serious price fall' that might follow if there were no agreement on restraint for the period after March 1962. Trying to retain unrestricted access seemed more likely to lead to disaster than losing it.

The Prime Minister and the CCEFQ agreed that Linton should publicly welcome the British proposals whilst noting New Zealand's regret.[120] New Zealand could now export 156,000 tons of dairy produce and agreed, for twelve months, to waive its right for unrestricted entry. Linton pointed out that that right would have little value without restrictions placed on other countries and he hoped that the quotas would prevent the butter market collapsing.[121] The quotas successfully prevented collapse and caused the butter price to rise significantly. As in 1960, butter consumption did not fall as the price rose.[122]

[118] Minutes of Committee on Economic and Financial Questions, 27/02/1962, T1/61/1/8 E.62. M14 2, ANZ.

[119] Butter, Industry and Commerce – Primary Industries – Dairy Industries 1960–1969, T/1/61/1/8, AAFD W3738 811 Box 1032 CAB 123/10/1, 08/03/1962, ANZ.

[120] Minutes of the Cabinet Committee on Economic and Financial Questions, T/1/61/1/8, 08/03/1962, ANZ.

[121] 'No Alternative to Butter Deal', *Straight Furrow*, 18/04/1962, 13, ATL.

[122] 'Market Survey: Dairy Produce', *Straight Furrow*, 20/06/1962, 3, ATL.

Producers remained unconvinced that quotas were a benefit and Woolerton, at the 1962 Dairy Council meeting, now complained about the imposition of a quota on New Zealand dairy produce, reminding producers of the resolution passed at the 1961 meeting.[123] Linton explained to the Dominion Dairy Conference in 1963 why quotas had become essential. He said that quotas permitted New Zealand butter to be sold in large quantities at reasonable prices in a stable market. New Zealand would have preferred anti-dumping duties but Britain had decided on quotas. Producers needed to face up to the tremendous changes in British thinking including moving away from its historic open door policy. Whether New Zealand liked it or not it had to live with the changes.[124]

The discussions on dumping and the introduction of quotas ran parallel with Britain's first application to join the EEC. At first, dairy producers saw Britain's EEC membership as important for Britain to maintain economic strength, and hoped that Britain could come to an arrangement with the EEC that enabled Britain to remain New Zealand's best customer. Woolerton believed that New Zealand could not ignore the disadvantages to Britain and ultimately New Zealand if Britain did not have the substantial benefits from EEC membership.[125] The immediate threat from dumping gave far more concern than the more remote threat that Britain might join the EEC. That possibly shaped Linton's rather mild reaction, compared with John Ormond's reaction as the Meat Board Chairman, to Britain's application to join the EEC in 1961. The dairy industry had worked through 1959 and 1960 to build goodwill with Britain to encourage protection against dumping. When Ormond seemed to criticise Duncan Sandys' honesty in mid-1961, Linton would have seen Ormond as placing New Zealand's goodwill at risk; unsurprisingly he reacted to Ormond's negative statement following the Sandys meeting with a call for Ormond's resignation.

---

[123] Chairman's Address to the Dairy Section Annual Conference, 13/06/1962, Federated Farmers 90–343, MSY-2716 D64/1962, 4, ATL.

[124] 'Butter Quotas in Best Interests of Dairy Industry', *Straight Furrow*, 07/08/1963, 27, ATL.

[125] 'Mr Woolerton: Review of Dairy Situation', *Straight Furrow*, 07/12/1960, 16, ATL.

After Britain's application for EEC membership had been submitted in August 1961, the uncertainties raised doubts amongst dairy producers, and Woolerton now reacted as strongly as Ormond to the prospect of Britain joining. He feared that New Zealand would be 'tossed out into the snow'. He told the annual Dairy Council Conference in 1962 that if suitable arrangements were not made for New Zealand then New Zealand would have to 'plead' with Iron Curtain countries 'to take more from us'. He quoted the President of the British Chambers of Commerce who said that 'unless Britain reached agreement with the EEC on compensation for Commonwealth countries we might present Khrushchev [the USSR leader] with a heaven-sent opportunity of bringing down the West without going to war'.[126] Woolerton said 'we must put forward our position clearly and strongly.... Countless New Zealanders will be affected by what happens in Europe'. He concluded by appealing to the Dairy Council to 'persuade rank and file dairy farmers to interest themselves in the industry's problems beyond their farm-gate'.[127]

Linton remained positive, believing that the British Cabinet 'had a first-class appreciation of the problems New Zealand faced' and Britain knew that protection would be needed for New Zealand to continue to sell its traditional quantities. He pointed out dairy products 'presented a more difficult problem than any other' because if Denmark and Ireland joined the EEC at the same time as Britain, as was their intention, that would bring into one common market all the major dairy exporters except for Australia and New Zealand. Britain, Ireland and Denmark would need to raise their butter prices to harmonise with the rest of the EEC; raising the price too high might limit sales.[128] The British High Commission believed that if Denmark joined the EEC that would ease pressure on the British market because, whilst outside the

[126] Chairman's Address to the Annual Conference of the Dairy Council, 13/06/1962, Federated Farmers 90 - 343, MSY-2716, D64/1962, 2, ATL.

[127] Chairman's Address to the Annual Conference of the Dairy Council, 13/06/1962, Federated Farmers 90 - 343, MSY-2716, D64/1962, 8, ATL.

[128] 'Welfare of the Dairy Industry', *Straight Furrow*, 18/07/1962, 8, ATL.

EEC, Denmark diverted produce increasingly to the British market to New Zealand's detriment, produce that otherwise would have gone to Germany.[129]

The producer board chairmen, including Linton, accompanied Holyoake to the Commonwealth Prime Ministers' meeting in September 1962 that reviewed EEC negotiations.[130] At the meeting Holyoake remained hopeful that New Zealand's export income would not be placed in danger.[131] During the discussions in London, in addition to discussing the scenario for Britain being inside the EEC, Macmillan described British policy should Britain remain outside. At a meeting of producer representatives and Jack Marshall back in New Zealand, producers

> recognised also that trade in dairy products would present considerable difficulties if the British were in the Common Market or not. Mr Linton confirmed that in London he had expressed the view that the position would be better with the British in. Mr Ormond expressed agreement with this view also. There was no formal dissent in any way from other members of the meeting . . . if the United Kingdom did not join the community, the meeting recognised that probably the principal threat would derive from increased production of British producers.[132]

However, de Gaulle's rejection of British membership in January 1963 delayed for another eight years testing how British EEC membership would impact on New Zealand dairying. During that period producers and the New Zealand government accepted that quotas were beneficial and encouraged Britain to maintain the arrangements.

---

[129] 'Mr Eaton Says It Mightn't Be So Bad', *Straight Furrow*, 07/06/1961, 3, ATL.

[130] 'All Eyes on PM's Meeting', *Straight Furrow*, 05/09/1962, 3, ATL.

[131] Barry Gustafson, *Kiwi Keith: A Biography of Keith Holyoake* (Auckland: Auckland University Press, 2007), 300.

[132] Producer Consultations, Note of meeting, 24/10/1962, T61.5.4.2.3, EEC negotiations: Consultations with Producers February 1962–September 1966, ANZ.

6.6 Living with British Quotas in the Shadow of the EEC

From 1963, quotas governed New Zealand dairy exports to Britain, accompanied by uncertainty over how EEC enlargement would affect those exports. Linton remained positive that a satisfactory outcome would be achieved but those closer to farmers remained less certain. The New Zealand Dairy Board and government eventually lost any doubts about the need for quotas but it took longer for those closer to farmers to accept that quotas were to New Zealand's advantage.

In 1963 Linton succinctly summarised the status of dairy markets. He said that since World War II and especially in the late 1950s and early 1960s the economic considerations that once dominated dairy produce marketing had been replaced by political considerations, for instance, the price support policies in the USA and European countries.[133] Linton saw the Dairy Board's first job as supplying the British market with butter and cheese exports of which 90% and 88%, respectively, went to Britain. Britain remained the most important market because other major countries, the USA and in continental Europe, prohibited or restricted tightly New Zealand's dairy exports whilst seeking to dump their own surpluses. Linton said those countries had forced Britain to introduce quotas to assist New Zealand.[134]

After de Gaulle rejected British membership of the EEC in 1963, Woolerton summarised for the Dairy Council that New Zealand could breathe more freely but it would be foolish to believe that New Zealand had no more troubles. Britain's expanded butter production could not be ignored, nor could the heavy butter subsidies in other exporting countries.[135] Those threats to New Zealand's butter exports had not been changed by de Gaulle's actions. Woolerton said 'it was up to the Commonwealth to do all it could to assist the United Kingdom' but

[133] 'Marketing Objectives of Dairy Board', *Straight Furrow*, 04/09/1963, 37, ATL.

[134] 'Dairy Marketing Policy Put to the Test', *Straight Furrow*, 17/04/1963, 15, ATL.

[135] 'Increased U.K. Butter Quota Would Affect Returns to N.Z.', *Straight Furrow*, 20/02/1963, 25, ATL.

later in 1963 Woolerton demonstrated the underlying anxieties amongst producers. He stressed the importance of the dairy industry for every man, woman and child in New Zealand and continued, rhetorically:

> [W]ho would have thought... Britain would have quotas on New Zealand produce? Who would have conceived Britain trying desperately to enter a Community of European Nations whose rules forbid the entry of but small amounts of our produce? Who would have thought that after all the New Zealand dairy industry had done to help the British economy, its place in the British market was to be handed to the French dairy exporters?[136]

Woolerton disagreed with Linton who accepted that British quotas had restored butter prices to remunerative levels and protected New Zealand. Also, Linton understood the EEC situation far better than Woolerton because he attended the 1962 talks in London, following which he had said that the industry would be better with Britain inside the EEC. Woolerton demonstrated that producers one or two steps removed from the actual negotiations tended not to share Linton's confidence and put a worse interpretation on British actions, representing the strand in New Zealand public response, fostered by Ormond jeremiads, that Britain was betraying New Zealand. Woolerton's rhetoric would have grabbed the headlines and carried more weight in the public's eyes than Linton's quiet confidence.

Despite Woolerton's concerns, the quota arrangements ensured that butter and cheese prices continued to rise through 1962/1963 and reduced the deficit in the Reserve Account.[137] Linton recognised that, unusually for an agricultural country, New Zealand did not have dairy produce surpluses because New Zealand had an 'immensely valuable connection with the world's largest dairy market – the United Kingdom'.[138] When prices rose in the early 1960s, New Zealand

[136] Chairman's Address to the Annual Dairy Council Conference, 12/06/1963, Federated Farmers 90 - 343, MSY-2717, 2, ATL.

[137] 'Dairy Produce Account', *Straight Furrow*, 17/07/1963, 3, ATL.

[138] 'UK Must Continue as Most Important', *Straight Furrow*, 07/08/1963, 13, ATL.

avoided forcing prices even higher and spread supplies evenly throughout the year to give buyers a first-class sales service. Federated Farmers Dominion Dairy Council asked the Dairy Board to explain the low New Zealand prices whilst other suppliers exploited the market.[139] The Board responded that it aimed at maintaining stable prices at reasonable levels and an outlet for the maximum tonnage. Forcing prices higher might encourage Britain to relax quotas to increase the supply into Britain thereby letting others into the market. Also, there might well be a significant decrease in butter consumption if prices rose higher.[140]

In May 1964 Linton reported the outcome of the annual dairy quota negotiations.[141] He had no doubt that the agreed quota arrangements would be the best ever and would give the stability that allowed the New Zealand dairy industry to face the future with confidence. He said that the quota system benefitted New Zealand as a long-term, traditional supplier. He paid tribute to Britain's fair-minded attitude, and thought Britain appreciated New Zealand not forcing higher prices in 1963 but maintaining an even supply.[142] The Dairy Board General Manager, Stan Murphy, stressed the importance for New Zealand that Britain continued its quota system: that 'much valued arrangement' gave a 40% market share for New Zealand butter exports to Britain. Even Woolerton said the quota was 'satisfactory and . . . our negotiators are to be congratulated'.[143] The more confident spirit in the dairy industry was noted by the Department of Agriculture in its Annual Report and put down to unexpected benefits from Britain's approach to the EEC. The threats from that approach had prompted review and improvements for dairy production, manufacture and marketing.[144]

[139] Minutes of the Dairy Section Conference, 04/09/1963, Federated Farmers 90 - 343, D36/1963, 3, ATL.

[140] 'Too High a Price – Other Butter In', *Straight Furrow*, 04/12/1963, 13, ATL.

[141] Linton was now Sir Andrew - John Ormond had to wait another year before becoming Sir John.

[142] 'Butter Quota Arrangements the "Best Yet"', *Straight Furrow*, 20/05/1964, 16, ATL.

[143] Chairman's Annual Report to the Dairy Council, 15/06/1964, Federated Farmers 90 - 343, MSY-2717, 1/2, ATL.

[144] 'Dairying's "More Confident" Spirit', *Straight Furrow*, 01/07/1964, 12, ATL.

Early in 1965, in a further demonstration that any remaining qualms the New Zealand government suffered over quotas had disappeared, Holyoake visited Britain arguing for quotas to be retained.[145] Labour had replaced the Conservatives in Britain and the new government wanted to cut living costs by, for instance, reducing butter prices. The new British government 'wished to ensure that the interests of the British consumer and the British balance of payments were given greater weight'.[146] The New Zealand Cabinet Economic Committee (CEC) was warned 'that informal discussions have indicated some disposition at official level to suspend the quota arrangements' in Britain.[147] Quotas might be revised to allow increased imports, but New Zealand feared that the quota system would become unworkable and the market would collapse. Holyoake insisted that British quotas remained with little change.[148] New Zealand could justifiably claim that it had never dumped produce; that strengthened its case. But, as the British High Commission had pointed out in 1961, with Denmark outside the EEC, Denmark sent increased supplies to Britain because Danish sales to Germany were threatened.[149] Denmark could claim, like New Zealand, to have been a good and faithful supplier for Britain and could expect a sympathetic hearing. Eventually, Britain kept the quota system but with increased quantities because Britain's 'economy was in a perilous state' and the government needed to stop prices 'rising steeply'.[150]

[145] Minutes of Cabinet Economic Committee, 01/02/1965, Dumping of Dairy Produce on the United Kingdom Market 1963–1965, AAFZ W1318 7174 Box 189 3288 Part 8, 2, ANZ.

[146] United Kingdom Butter Quotas, 21/12/1964, Foreign Trade - Dairy Produce – General, AAFD W3738 811 Box1141 CAB130/2/1, 1, ANZ.

[147] United Kingdom Butter Quotas, 21/12/1964, Foreign Trade - Dairy Produce – General, AAFD W3738 811 Box1141 CAB130/2/1, 1, ANZ.

[148] Butter Discussions with Secretary of State for Commonwealth Relations, 01/02/1965, Dumping of Dairy Produce on the United Kingdom Market 1963–1965, AAFZ W1318 7174 Box 189 3288 Part 8, 2, ANZ.

[149] High Commission, London to External Affairs, Wellington, 08/01/1965, Dumping of Dairy Produce on the United Kingdom Market 1963–1965, AAFZ W1318 7174 Box 189 3288 Part 8, 2, ANZ.

[150] Butter Discussions with Secretary of State for Commonwealth Relations, 01/02/1965, Dumping of Dairy Produce on the United Kingdom Market 1963–1965, AAFZ W1318 7174 Box 189 3288 Part 8, 3, ANZ.

In 1965, once again Woolerton remained unconvinced by the benefits of the quota system but *Straight Furrow* carried out a survey of other producers in New Zealand and found that most favoured retaining quotas.[151] Fred Peart, the Minister of Agriculture in the British Labour government, responded to New Zealand concern over butter quotas, by giving the British view. Peart said that those quotas had been introduced to protect New Zealand from unduly low prices; they had not been introduced to protect the British consumer.[152]

In 1965 the Labour government in Britain released its National Plan for the five years up to 1970 and included targets for expanding dairy produce production to enable reduction of food imports to save foreign exchange. Production in Britain threatened to exceed any increase in consumption and, clearly, New Zealand could not expand dairy exports to the British market; exports might even be reduced if British agriculture achieved the optimistic targets that had been set in the Plan.[153] The New Zealand Director-General of Agriculture, D N R Webb, gave a realistic view when he told the Fertiliser Manufacturers' Research Association that it had been in New Zealand's interests to stand by Britain during World War II; Britain did not owe New Zealand a living. Britain had a responsibility to its own farmers that could not be thrown aside. Webb concluded that New Zealand had to move with the times in line with changes throughout the world.[154]

In Britain the Labour government had come to power opposing British EEC membership but by 1966 began to be persuaded that membership had become essential. J J Parsons, who had taken over from Woolerton as Federated Farmers Dairy Council Chairman, reminded his annual conference that potential British EEC membership remained as vital as it had been before de Gaulle's rejection. New Zealand must not allow time to induce apathy towards this vital issue;

[151] 'Butter Quota: "Manipulation" Says Chairman', *Straight Furrow*, 17/03/1965, 6, ATL. In addition to reporting Woolerton's views, the article reports a 'cross section' of opinion from eight New Zealand newspapers.

[152] 'NZ–UK Market Has Uncertain Future', *Straight Furrow*, 16/01/1966, 11, ATL.

[153] 'U.K.'s "National Plan" and Its Affect', *Straight Furrow*, 17/11/1965, 1, ATL.

[154] 'Britain Doesn't Owe NZ a Living. . . . ', *Straight Furrow*, 01/12/1965, 31, ATL.

the EEC was a ruthless protectionist union designed solely to benefit its members. The New Zealand government should remind Britain that assurances given in 1963 allowed no compromise on trade barriers against traditional dairy supplies into Britain.[155]

6.7 Quotas Are Welcomed and Sales Continue to Increase

In 1966 Britain extended New Zealand's right of duty-free and unrestricted entry for dairy produce from 1967 to 1972 but under conditions that kept temporary restrictions in place. The New Zealand quota increased in 1967 taking up a shortfall in supplies from Australia. When, in 1967, Britain tried, for a second time, to join the EEC, New Zealand producers were far more preoccupied with the annual quota arrangements and gave less attention to prospective British EEC membership. Despite a quota reduction in 1969, New Zealand managed, partly by taking up shortfalls in the quotas of others, to sell more than its original butter quota. High earnings continued into the 1970s.

Jack Marshall reminded the House of Representatives in 1966 that New Zealand had 'waived the right of unrestricted entry' for butter since 1962 to enable Britain to operate quotas 'for the benefit of New Zealand'. Butter quotas had now become 'an integral part of the trading relationship' and Britain 'reaffirmed that they have no intention of removing quota restrictions'.[156] Marshall addressed the 1966 Federated Farmers Dominion Conference with cautious optimism saying that the new agreement should give New Zealand a secure base to plan for the future.[157]

[155] Chairman's Address to Dairy Section Conference, 08/6/1966, Federated Farmers 90-343, MSY-2719, D/1966, 2/3, ATL.

[156] Statement by Right Hon. J. R. Marshall to the House of Representatives, 12/07/1966, United Kingdom – New Zealand Trade Agreements, 1966–1967, AAFZ W1318 7174 Box 96 2339 Part 27, 1-6, ANZ.

[157] 'Cautious Optimism on Butter', *Straight Furrow*, 03/08/1966, 4, ATL.

On 2 May 1967 the British Prime Minister, Harold Wilson, announced Britain's second attempt to join the EEC.[158] In reporting to the British Parliament, Wilson identified specifically that

> [t]here are also highly important Commonwealth interests . . . for which it is our duty to seek safeguards in the negotiations. These include, in particular, the special problems of New Zealand.[159]

But Parsons doubted whether New Zealand could rely on the 'good intentions of others'; he saw the British market as New Zealand's economy's 'sheet anchor' and 'there is no other market that can absorb 176,000 tons of butter from New Zealand'.[160] Linton remained optimistic that Britain would honour its assurances that in joining the EEC it would secure safeguards for New Zealand.[161] Linton based his confidence on his close contacts with the British government and other Europeans through the annual discussions on dairy quotas, and on the way that Britain had honoured assurances that it would protect New Zealand against dumping; the quota system had been arranged to achieve that and had been successful. However, de Gaulle once again rejected the British approach and Linton's confidence was not tested for another four years.[162]

In 1967 the New Zealand quota of 170,000 tons was increased by 8,000 tons taking up a shortfall in supplies from Australia. The CEC considered that price had become more important than the quota volume; a higher quota but lower price was not in New Zealand's

158 Ben Pimlott, *Harold Wilson* (London: HarperCollins, 1992), 432–439. Pimlott shows how Wilson, himself, was at first strongly in favour of Commonwealth relationships but was gradually persuaded that Britain should at least investigate whether conditions were now ripe for a new bid for membership of the EEC.

159 http://hansard.millbanksystems.com/commons/1967/may/02/european-economic-community-application, accessed 25 September 2014.

160 Chairman's Address to the Dairy Section Council, 13/06/1967, Federated Farmers 90–343, MSY-2720 D27/1967, 2, ANZ.

161 '"Have Confidence in Your Industry": Dairy Board Chairman Sees No Real Cause for Gloom', *Straight Furrow*, 19/04/1967, 14, ATL.

162 Linton's confidence was justified by the outcome in 1971 but, unfortunately, he did not live to see it.

interest. The CEC advised the New Zealand delegation 'to seek a settlement which could reasonably be expected to lead to a modest increase in price of New Zealand butter'.[163] In 1968 Britain agreed that the quota for New Zealand would be kept the same as 1967 whilst the overall quota for imports into Britain reduced, thereby implying an increased price. New Zealand would also have first refusal if there were again shortfalls in the quotas allocated to others.[164] Linton reported a real understanding of New Zealand's position by Britain and intent to foster the best possible trade relations. Britain had appreciated how New Zealand had maintained supplies even during wharf strikes.[165] Parsons seemed satisfied and congratulated Marshall who had led the New Zealand team in the negotiations and his advisers such as Linton. Parsons said that the agreement provided an assured outlet at a time when surpluses elsewhere threatened to disrupt completely international trade.[166] In mid-1968 the butter price on the British market remained firm despite a major deterioration in world prices for milk products. That demonstrated well the protection given to New Zealand by Britain managing the butter market through quotas.[167]

In 1969 'exceptionally high and rising' British butter stocks led to a reduction in import quotas. That included, for the first time since the imposition of a quota, a reduction (5%) in the New Zealand quota whilst the overall quota to all countries reduced by more than 10%.[168] Parsons accepted the benefits of the quota system calling the settlement 'realistic', saying 'we cannot be happy at a 6000-ton reduction' but

[163] Minutes of the Cabinet Economic Committee, 20/12/1966, Foreign Trade - Dairy Produce – General, AAFD W3738 811 Box1141 CAB130/2/1, 2, ANZ.

[164] Butter Import Arrangements 1968/1969, 15/03/1968, New Zealand Trade - United Kingdom - Dairy Produce: Butter 1968, ABHS W4268 7148 Box 13 LONB 37/1/2 Part 16, 1–3, ANZ.

[165] 'Britain wants to help NZ', *Straight Furrow*, 17/04/1968, 24, ATL.

[166] 'Butter Quota "Satisfactory" but Stock Build-Up "Ominous"', *Straight Furrow*, 03/04/1968, 9, ATL.

[167] 'Lactic Butter Price Falls on UK Market', *Straight Furrow*, 05/06/1968, 11, ATL.

[168] Board of Trade to High Commission, 20/03/1969, New Zealand Trade – United Kingdom – Dairy Produce: Butter, ABHS W4268 7148 Box 13 LONB 37/1/2 Part 17, ANZ.

'it is better for New Zealand to maintain reasonably stable prices'.[169] Frank Onion had replaced Linton as Dairy Board Chairman, and now attended the talks in Britain. His praise for British efforts matched that of Linton's in previous years, demonstrating that Linton's praise had not simply been Linton succumbing to a British embrace. Onion reported that the talks had taken place in a friendly atmosphere with Britain appreciating New Zealand's problems. The British decision ensured firm corrective action to bring about a stable market, and New Zealand again would have first call if other quota countries reported shortfalls. Onion concluded that the decisions were in the best interests of Britain and New Zealand.[170] He restated that the quota system prevented material injury to New Zealand producers and remained vital for New Zealand's economy.

Despite the quota reduction in 1969, New Zealand managed, by taking up shortfalls in the quotas of others, to sell a record 196,000 tons of butter to Britain in the 1969/1970 season and also 86,000 tons of cheese. There were also record casein sales to Britain and Europe.[171] Casein, made from the proteins in milk, had a chemical structure that made it valuable for various industrial uses in the 1950s such as glues, paper coating and synthetic fibres. Onion attributed the record sales partly to surpluses being eliminated within the EEC to the extent that 'even French traders have been seeking to buy from New Zealand'.[172] In Britain the butter price increased for the first time in four years, by 5% in mid-1970, and by the same amount two or three months later, accompanied by price rises for milk powder.[173] Onion predicted that the Reserve Account would have a comfortable balance at the season's end.[174] New Zealand also dominated the international market for casein sufficiently that the price increased by 11% over six months without

[169] 'Quota Cut Will Help Keep Prices Stable', *Straight Furrow*, 02/04/1969, 8, ATL.

[170] 'Dairy Board Satisfied by Quota Decisions', *Straight Furrow*, 02/04/1969, 9, ATL.

[171] '106,000 Tons of Butter Sold in UK Last Year', *Straight Furrow*, 10/06/1970, 19, ATL.

[172] Dairy Markets at High Level, 05/04/1971, Dairy Industry – Export of Dairy Products New Zealand Policy, AAQW WS3379 Box 11 4/1/4, ANZ.

[173] 'NZ Dairy Prices Rise Overseas', *Straight Furrow*, 04/11/1970, 14, ATL.

[174] 'Butterfat Boost Brings Warm Response', *Straight Furrow*, 08/07/1970, 7, ATL.

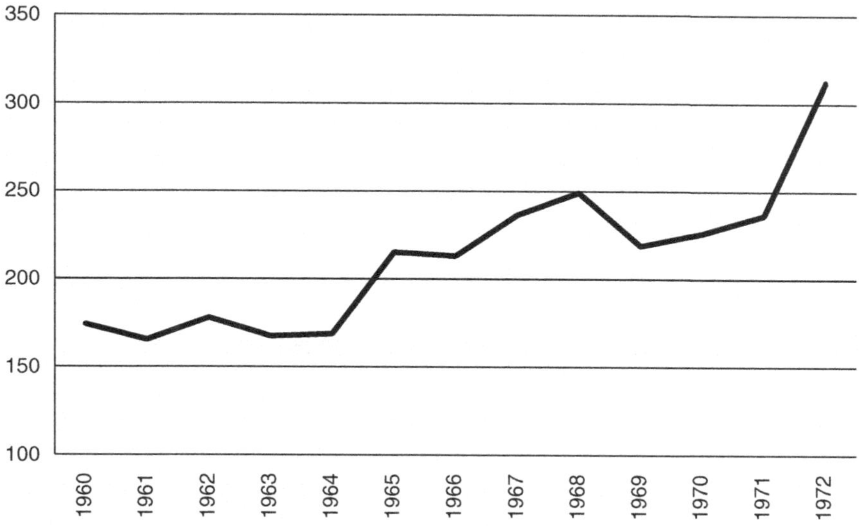

Fig. 6.3 New Zealand dairy exports in $ million at 1971 prices (NZDYB)

endangering casein use compared with similar commodities.[175] The changes between 1965 and 1970 had encouraged reducing the dependence on the British market; dairy export earnings increased in real terms during that period (Fig. 6.3) with only a 5% increase accounted for by sales to Britain. But dairy exports to Britain still accounted for more than 60% of the overall total; 89% of butter and 76% of cheese shipped to Britain.[176]

Satisfactory quotas for the British market were agreed for New Zealand for the 1971/1972 season with the butter quota the same as the previous season and the largest quota for cheese being given to New Zealand.[177] Because there was no longer surplus milk, New Zealand suspended the Dairy Beef Diversification Scheme introduced in 1969 to

[175] 'NZ Dominates Casein Trade', *Straight Furrow*, 20/01/1971, 21, ATL.

[176] 'Dairying Growth Rate 4c. Yearly', *Straight Furrow*, 03/02/1971, 7, ATL; 'Primary Products – Sales Outside United Kingdom', *Straight Furrow*, 19/11/1970, 22, ATL.

[177] Annual Butter Negotiations with the United Kingdom, 14/02/1972, Trade: United Kingdom: Dairy Produce 1971–1972, C 324 075 C1W2358 54 955/UK/1 Part 1, 1, ANZ.

encourage the change from dairy to beef production. Also, a cull to eradicate the disease brucellosis reduced milk output.[178] However, drought in Australia and New Zealand reduced supplies to the British market and Britain suspended the quota system.[179] There was now a shortage and the butter price on the British market increased by 30% reaching 'the highest price ever paid for butter on the United Kingdom Market'.[180]

6.8 The Shadow of the EEC Passes

British EEC membership became a near-certainty following the resignation of de Gaulle in 1969. New Zealand's (initially reluctant) acceptance of quotas for the British market meant that the threat from Britain joining the EEC was no longer whether free and unrestricted access would be lost but the level of quota that would be agreed.[181] High dairy prices in the British market made dairy producers nervous, not wanting to be seen to be doing too well economically with the EEC negotiations within a few weeks of being concluded. The Luxembourg Protocol of 1971 defined the special arrangements for New Zealand on Britain being accepted as an EEC member. Both the government and most dairy producers welcomed the agreement, despite the agreement anticipating the phasing out cheese exports to Britain and causing consternation amongst New Zealand's cheese producers. New Zealand's successful diversification of dairy sales to other markets meant that the EEC quotas were not taken up fully, embarrassing the government and producers. New Zealand dairy production now struggled to keep pace with the growing markets.

---

[178] 'Dairy Beef Scheme Suspended', *Straight Furrow*, 07/04/1971, 10, ATL.

[179] 'Economic Review', *Straight Furrow*, 19/05/1971, 3, ATL.

[180] 'Dairy Industry Had Its Best Season for Long Time', *Evening Post*, 07/12/1971, Dairy Industry – Export of Dairy Products New Zealand Policy, AAQW WS3379 Box 11 4/1/4, ANZ.

[181] Prospects for the Industry, 27/03/1969, Dairy Industry – Export of Dairy Products New Zealand Policy, AAQW /WS3379 Box 11 4/1/4, p5, ANZ. The paper assumed that should Britain join the EEC the British quotas would continue at 1969 levels.

Murphy had warned the Agricultural Production Council after the record exports of 1968/1969 that the Dairy Board was 'not saying more publicly about the favourable features of the trading situation' because the Board did not want to give the 'Common Marketeers' of the EEC the impression that New Zealand does 'not rely as heavily upon the British market as we have been claiming'.[182] The Waikato Dairy Section Chairman tried to play down the gains from the increased butter price – it might be a short-term peak and increased costs threatened to reduce the gain from the price increases.[183] Onion emphasised recent cost increases rather than record earnings, which were expected to be exceeded in 1971.[184] The present demand exceeded New Zealand's supplies and markets needed to be chosen carefully. Onion said that, whatever the present market prospects, the EEC negotiations remained critical. Accommodating New Zealand remained important for the British public and Parliament but marginal for the EEC countries.

The Luxembourg Protocol of 1971 included that the first five years of British Membership would start with the existing New Zealand quotas for butter and cheese until 1973, then the quota for butter would reduce by 4% p.a. and, for cheese, by 20% p.a.[185] Comprehensive and specific criteria would govern a review after the third year on how to maintain the special arrangements after 1977, with the review formula a major concession to New Zealand. Prices would be based on the average for the years 1969–1972. Once again New Zealand would receive guaranteed prices rather than the uncertainty of market forces. In another important provision the EEC agreed to 'strive to pursue a commercial policy which does not run counter to' New Zealand's diversification into other markets. The arrangements included that sales of casein to Britain would not be threatened. Milk powder exports to Britain would continue to run down

[182] Notes of Market Report to the Agricultural Production Council, 10/09/1970, Marketing of New Zealand Dairy Produce in United Kingdom and Elsewhere 1959–1972, AAFZ W1710 7174 Box 15 Part 10, 2, ANZ.

[183] 'Note of Caution on Butter Price Rises', *Straight Furrow*, 05/05/1971, 3, ATL.

[184] Frank Onion, 'Dairy Demand Never Stronger', *Straight Furrow*, 19/05/1971, 4/5, ATL.

[185] Text of the EEC Protocol on Dairy Products, 21/01/1972, Federated Farmers, 90–343 03/5, 2, ATL.

but that simply continued the Dairy Board's policy of diverting sales to other markets; by mid-1972 the Board had phased out milk powder exports to Britain.[186]

In New Zealand the Luxembourg Protocol on dairy exports received favourable responses. Federated Farmers, in a major article in *Straight Furrow*, responded that the Agreement held out the prospects for developing an orderly international dairy market, something that only the most idealistic had hoped for. [187] The article continued that in the long term the EEC may have crystallised advances that would otherwise have been impossible. The dairy industry could become an even stronger force contributing to New Zealand's well-being. At Luxembourg new doors to international dairying were unlatched. The New Zealand Trade Promotion Council, one month after the Luxembourg agreement, assessed the impact of the EEC special arrangements and the consequences for trade diversification. Onion told the Council that 'he had warned the British Authorities that New Zealand may not fulfil the dairy quota' for 1971 because Britain had advised New Zealand to diversify.[188] He said that diversification had been taking place for many years and the industry had recognised that sales to Britain would no longer grow. The EEC had pledged it would not frustrate New Zealand's efforts to sell its produce elsewhere. If the EEC withdrew from potential markets for New Zealand there were markets for 35,000 tons of butter in the Pacific Basin and 100,000 tons in markets elsewhere. Britain's Prime Minister Edward Heath confirmed in a letter to the Opposition that there would be access in Britain for New Zealand butter after 1977.[189]

Phasing out cheese exports to Britain caused 'consternation' in New Zealand's main cheese-producing region, Taranaki. Finance Minister

---

[186] Prospects for New Zealand Dairy Produce in World Trade in the 1970s, 05/07/1972, Dairy Industry – Export of Dairy Products New Zealand Policy, AAQW WS3379 Box 11 4/1/4, 16, ANZ.

[187] 'The End Is . . . Only the Beginning', *Straight Furrow*, 07/07/1971, 3, ATL.

[188] Extract from Trade Promotion Council Meeting, 27/07/1971, Dairy Industry – Export of Dairy Products New Zealand Policy, ANZ AAQW WS3379 Box 11 4/1/4, 1, ANZ.

[189] 'Butter Market Assured After 1977 – Mr Heath', *The Press*, 08/08/1973, New Zealand Trade – United Kingdom – Dairy Produce: Butter 1973–1988, ABHS W5503 7148 Box 42 LONB 37/1/2 Part 20, ANZ.

Robert Muldoon found that consternation 'understandable' but he had 'no doubt' in the Dairy Board's judgement that the necessary 'change-over could be made'.[190] The Dairy Board Marketing Executive Officer J. B. Parker noted 'Consumption [of cheese] throughout the world was rising spectacularly' and that the resumption of fair trading by the EEC would increase world demand and ensure a very good future for this cheese: 'Now is the time to buy a Dairy Farm', he remarked in September 1971, three months after the Luxembourg Protocol had been agreed.[191] *Straight Furrow* pointed out that cheese 'to be placed in new markets by the end of the transition represented only 1.5% of New Zealand's cheese production annually'.[192] The Dairy Board told the CEC that the Board 'was not disturbed by the cheese situation ... it was a passing phase which the industry would cope with given time', though the Board agreed that there would be 'problems for some companies in the Taranaki region'.[193]

In July 1972 a paper for the CEC reviewed prospects for New Zealand's dairy trade outside Britain. The review maintained that the dairy industry had

> the capacity to remain profitable ... given the present healthy state of the industry, and the significant guarantees N.Z. has obtained in regard to its most important market [Britain] under the Luxembourg Arrangement.[194]

The Officials Committee on Economic and Financial Policy judged the arrangements to be

[190] 'Let the Dust Settle', *Straight Furrow*, 11/08/1971, 5, ATL.

[191] 'Optimism in Dairy Industry Questioned' *Straight Furrow*, 08/09/1971, 19, ATL.

[192] 'The End Is ... Only the Beginning', *Straight Furrow*, 07/07/1961, 3, ATL.

[193] Minutes of the Cabinet Economic Committee, 17/05/1977, Industry and Commerce – Primary Industries – Dairy Industries, AAFD W3738 811 Box 1033 CAB 123/10/1, 2, ANZ.

[194] Prospects for New Zealand Dairy Products in World Trade in the 1970s, 05/07/1972, Dairy Industry – Export of Dairy Products New Zealand Policy, AAQW WS3379 Box 11 4/1/4, 1, ANZ.

> broadly satisfactory subject to our objection to the pricing formula which includes two years of low prices and makes no provision for the effects of inflation.[195]

In 1972 that fine print of the Luxembourg Protocol came under scrutiny. How was the average price for 1969–1972 to be agreed?[196] The 1970s started with considerable inflation in both Britain and New Zealand. Also, Britain abandoned maintaining sterling's value and let it depreciate; the depreciation 'punched a $1m hole' in New Zealand's 'Dairy coffers' in 1972.[197] The prices agreed in Luxembourg did not allow for inflation or currency changes; how would sterling's depreciation and inflation be taken into account?[198] The Chairman of the Officials Committee warned the CEC that New Zealand might need to hold direct discussions with the EEC.[199] But that might mean revealing to the EEC that, because of the strength of its sales to markets other than Britain, New Zealand had over-estimated the quota needed for the British market; that over-estimate had been downplayed during the EEC negotiations. Murphy, the Dairy Board General Manager, said 'it would seem that we should come clean with the [EEC] Commission before they find out the true situation'.[200] The Federated Farmers Dairy Section Chairman remained optimistic about the positive state of markets, and, in his address to the annual conference, his prime concern was the potential 'shortage of dairy products with which to take advantage of market opportunities'.[201]

---

[195] Visit of German Minister of Agriculture, November 1971, European Economic Community (EEC) – General, T1 W2666 41 75/4 Part 3, ANZ.

[196] Clarification of the EEC Protocol, 14/06/1972, Federated Farmers 90–343 03/5, 1, ATL.

[197] 'Floating Pound Punches $1m Hole in Dairy Coffers', 03/07/1972, Dairy Industry – Export of Dairy Products New Zealand Policy, AAQW /WS3379 Box 11 4/1/4, ANZ.

[198] Inflation, 29/07/1972, Federated Farmers 90–343 03/5, 1, ATL.

[199] Marketing of New Zealand Dairy Products, 01/06/1972, Trade: United Kingdom: Dairy Produce 1971–1972, C 324 075 C1W2358 54 955/UK/1 Part 1, 5, ANZ.

[200] Meeting of the Economic Working Party with the New Zealand Dairy Board, 12/06/1972, Trade: United Kingdom: Dairy Produce 1971–1972, C 324 075 C1W2358 54 955/UK/1 Part 1, 3, ANZ.

[201] Dairy Section Chairman's Address to the Annual Conference, 20/06/1972, Federated Farmers 90–343 03/5, 1, ATL.

In 1972 the Federated Farmers Dominion President and General Secretary visited Britain partly to make sure that New Zealand's issues over the Protocol fine print were not forgotten. An EEC butter surplus was growing and how that was traded would test the 'non-frustration' clause through which the EEC undertook not to inhibit New Zealand markets. The visit successfully solicited the response from the Vice-President of the EEC that the EEC would avoid the 1960s policies that led it to substantially upset world markets. Also, in integrating agriculture into the EEC there would be room for food imports, and access for New Zealand would continue after the five-year period.[202] Moves by the Commission to reduce surplus butter demonstrated that it honoured the non-frustration clause in the Luxembourg Protocol.[203]

The Federated Farmers delegation pointed out to Britain and the EEC Commission that New Zealand viewed the price agreement in the Protocol as a minimum, and provision for inflation and other cost increases should be taken into account.[204] The actual average price for 1969–1972, £383 per ton, exceeded the level quoted in Parliament by Marshall which farmers in 1970 would have 'accepted with alacrity even if it did not start until 1973'.[205] But that price did not take into account inflation during 1972; fortunately for New Zealand the EEC Monetary Compensatory Amounts deemed that the payment to New Zealand should be in real terms, taking into account also sterling's depreciation.[206] Britain accepted those regulations with, according to Federated Farmers, little complaint and no real effort to contest the New Zealand case.[207]

[202] 'EEC Declares Prudent Policy on Restitution Prices', *Straight Furrow*, 29/11/1972, p. 6, ATL.

[203] 'EEC Protocol Being Honoured', *Straight Furrow*, 13/12/1972, 17, ATL.

[204] 'No One Owes Us a Living', *Straight Furrow*, 15/11/1972, 1, ATL.

[205] Rt. Hon. J.R.Marshall's Opening the Debate in the House of Representatives on the Special Arrangements for New Zealand, 01/07/1971, EEC – The agreement-statements and papers, ABOT W2670 6787 Box 2,11, ANZ.

[206] '$20m Compensation for Butter, Cheese, Eases Strain with UK', *Evening Post*, 18/07/1973, New Zealand Trade – United Kingdom – Dairy Produce: Butter 1973–1988, ABHS W5503 7148 Box 42 LONB 37/1/2 Part 20, ANZ.

[207] 'Dairy Drive Needed', *Straight Furrow*, 08/08/1973, 3, ATL.

Britain agreed to compensate New Zealand with a $20 million payment.[208] Selling butter to Britain remained lucrative. Federated Farmers commented also that the Dairy Board and New Zealand had cause to be satisfied with the co-operation it had been receiving from the EEC more generally.[209]

After Britain became an EEC member on 1 January 1973, New Zealand could export 163,000 tons of butter to Britain and the other EEC countries, 10% more than the previous year's tonnage. An annual pricing review had been agreed and welcomed by the Dairy Board. The Federated Farmers Senior Vice-President, John Kneebone, after visiting Britain in mid-1973 said Britain would continue to be the most significant market for NZ produce for the foreseeable future.[210] Kneebone proved to be correct as three years later New Zealand's earnings from its butter, at 1971 prices, were the highest since 1959, an exceptional year.

In 1973 New Zealand fell 30,000 tons (about 15%) short of filling the quota agreed by the EEC (Fig. 6.4). That must have raised a few European eyebrows after all the time and effort that had gone into securing continuing access for New Zealand on the grounds that it

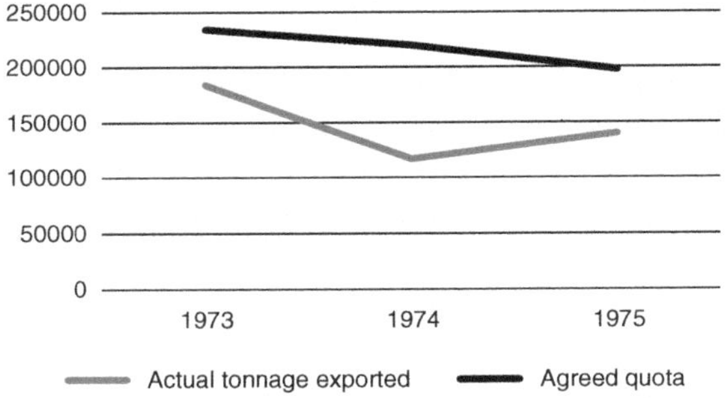

Fig. 6.4 Agreed dairy quota and actual tonnage exported to the EEC (NZDYB)

[208] 'A Just Reward', *Straight Furrow*, 26/07/1973, 3, ATL.

[209] 'Dairy Drive Needed', *Straight Furrow*, 08/08/1973, 3, ATL.

[210] 'Confident of NZ place in UK market', *Straight Furrow*, 26/07/1973, 8, ATL; John Singleton and Paul Robertson, *Economic Relations Between Britain and Australasia 1945–1970* (Basingstoke: Palgrave, 2002), 6.

would be disastrous if New Zealand could no longer send its traditional volumes to Britain.[211] The High Commission in London had warned the New Zealand Foreign Affairs Ministry in 1971 that if New Zealand failed to fill the quota the EEC might conclude that 'there are no longer special circumstances justifying guaranteeing' New Zealand quotas in the long term, and the 'credibility of our original case could be questioned'.[212] Marshall had made the point when presenting the Luxembourg Protocol to the House of Representatives that if New Zealand wanted to secure 'satisfactory levels after 1977 . . . every effort' needed to be made to meet the EEC dairy quotas from 1973.[213] But in 1972 the CEC had recognised that judgement would have to be made on political grounds whether to 'ship to the UK up to the guaranteed quantities of milkfat or to divert a proportion of these to third markets'.[214]

The Dairy Board faced the dilemma that to fill the EEC quotas the Board must 'break contractual obligations elsewhere' and that would 'adversely affect long term market prospects elsewhere'.[215] The Ministry of Foreign Affairs reported in a paper to officials that 'it would be nice to be able to re-open the [EEC] negotiation and say that we would after all like to have double the price and half the quantity!'. The exclamation mark (a symbol extremely rare in government papers) demonstrated that officials recognised the irony.[216] Federated Farmers saw three reasons

[211] 'Dairy Drive Needed Now', *Straight Furrow*, 08/08/1973, 1, ATL.

[212] High Commission, London, to Wellington – UK Dairy Market, 02/09/1971, United Kingdom - Export - Dairy Products - Policy and Information 1971–1985, AATJ W4838 7428 Box 284 162/3/1 Part 2, 2, ANZ.

[213] Rt. Hon. J.R.Marshall's Opening the Debate in the House of Representatives on the Special Arrangements for New Zealand, 01/07/1971, EEC – The agreement-statements and papers, ABOT W2670 6787 Box 2, 13, ANZ.

[214] Prospects for New Zealand Dairy Products in World Trade in the 1970s, 05/07/1972, Dairy Industry - Export of Dairy Products New Zealand Policy, AAQW WS3379 Box 11 4/1/4, 5, ANZ.

[215] Ministry of Foreign Affairs to High Commissioner London, 05/10/1971, United Kingdom - Export - Dairy Products - Policy and Information 1971–1985, AATJ W4838 7428 Box 284 162/3/1 Part 2, 2, ANZ.

[216] Discussion Paper for Officials Meeting, 26/05/1972, Marketing of New Zealand Dairy Produce in United Kingdom and Elsewhere 1959–1972, AAFZ W1710 7174 Box 15 Part 10, 1, ANZ.

why New Zealand had to increase its dairy production: to fill the EEC quota; to take advantage of improved prospects in South and Central America and Japan; and in response to the request by the American Administration that the Tariff Commission consider allowing skim-milk power sales to the USA. The USA agreed also that New Zealand could export 14,000 tons of butter to the USA in 1973 and the allowable quota of cheese imports would be increased.[217] Again 1973 seemed not to be a disastrous year for New Zealand dairy produce following Britain's entry into the EEC.[218]

Increases in butter and cheese sales to the USA compensated for the reduced income from the British market but those proved to be short term as the US Administration would not agree to a long-term arrangement.[219] The fall in earnings from Britain did not alarm the Board and it decided not to make up the 30,000 tons deficiency in the EEC quota. No doubt New Zealand's increased possibilities for dairy produce sales in developing Asian countries made the Board less concerned about filling its EEC quota. The oil-price shock of late 1973 had inhibited the trading of developed countries and their share of world trade fell significantly for the first time since World War II. Developing Asian countries suffered less and their share of world trade increased significantly.[220] Dairy prices increased globally above those due to New Zealand under the Luxembourg Protocol and left New Zealand in a quandary. Britain remained its largest customer for butter but prices were higher outside the British market; New Zealand sold butter to Britain only if it could not be sold elsewhere.[221]

[217] 'Big Lift Likely in NZ Cheese to USA', *Straight Furrow*, 12/12/1973, 16, ATL.

[218] 'Dairy Drive Needed Now', *Straight Furrow*, 08/08/1973, 1–3, ATL.

[219] 'Little Chance of Long-term Dairy Deal with USA', *Straight Furrow*, 17/04/1974, 16, ATL.

[220] These comments on world trade are based on statistics provided by the United Nations Conference on Trade and Development at http://unctadstat.unctad.org/TableViewer/tableView.aspx. The Conference databases include percentage shares of world trade for both individual countries and groups of countries.

[221] 'British Price Increases Won't Improve Our Return Levels', *Straight Furrow*, 20/03/1974, 16, ATL.

6.9 Renegotiation in Dublin

Early in 1974 Harold Wilson returned to power in Britain with his Labour party still split on EEC membership. Wilson intended to keep Britain in the EEC whilst papering over the cracks in his party by renegotiating the terms under which Britain had joined, and then holding a referendum on membership under the new terms.

Marshall, now New Zealand's Opposition Leader after National lost the 1972 election, met Wilson, soon after Wilson's successful election in 1974. Wilson told him that review of prices paid to New Zealand would be separate from the full renegotiation of Britain's EEC terms. Wilson reported 'great sympathy and affection at all levels in Britain for New Zealand' and 'he himself always bought New Zealand butter'.[222] Britain agreed that the EEC Commission should assess increases in production and transportation costs for New Zealand butter and consider whether the prices set through the Luxembourg Protocol remained appropriate.[223] The dramatic changes in global economics following the oil-price shock had made some Protocol features outdated. The British Minister of Agriculture said that in future there should be an annual price review. A group of New Zealand MPs visiting Britain in May 1974 'found many British people apologetic about the adverse effect of membership of the EEC may have had on New Zealand'. The leader of the group 'told them not to worry and that we are doing all right'.[224]

Britain regarded as essential re-negotiating New Zealand's dairy agreement with the EEC for the period after 1977. In July 1974, the British Minister of Agriculture asked the EEC to consider the future arrangements for New Zealand butter immediately rather than waiting until 1975 as originally anticipated. He suggested that the quotas for New Zealand butter for the five years 1978–1982 should remain at the 1977

[222] High Commissioner, London, to Treasury, Wellington, 30/04/1974, Agricultural Commodities UK EEC (European Economic Community) Discussions - Dairy Products, AALR W3158 873 Box100 T61/7/1/15, 1–4, ANZ.

[223] 'EEC Study of NZ Butter', *Straight Furrow*, 05/06/1974, 5, ATL.

[224] Extract from Air Mail Bulletin, 17/05/1974, New Zealand Trade – United Kingdom – Dairy Produce: Butter 1973–1988, ABHS W5503 7148 Box 42 LONB 37/1/2 Part 20, ANZ.

level of 140,000 tons and there should be provision to continue that quota after those five years. There should also be a review of arrangements for cheese.[225] Norman Kirk, during his last days as New Zealand's Prime Minister in July 1974, believed that a satisfactory arrangement for dairy exports to Britain would be agreed after 1977.[226] In November 1974, Britain and the other EEC countries agreed that prices set in 1971 were no longer appropriate because of the changed global economy. The prices paid by Britain to New Zealand were increased by 18%.[227]

The British Secretary of State for Trade, Peter Shore, visited New Zealand in 1974 convinced that Britain's traditional relationship with New Zealand would continue. He said that the Labour government considered that Britain's EEC entry terms negotiated by the Heath government were not in Britain's best interests; the terms would be renegotiated. Shore said Britain wanted New Zealand dairy products to continue to find a large and stable market in Britain long after 1977; New Zealand need no longer worry about trade diminution with Britain let alone a cut-off.[228] The Dairy Board general manager, Stan Murphy, expressed his confidence that butter and cheese sales to Britain would continue long after 1977; the challenge for New Zealand had become finding sufficient milk for the markets rather than finding markets for milk.[229]

In early 1975 an EEC Heads of State meeting in Dublin finalised the agreed re-negotiation of Britain's entry terms. Bill Rowling had become New Zealand's Prime Minister on the death of Norman Kirk, and he visited Britain to agree on future arrangements for New Zealand to be sought during the Dublin talks. The year 1975 had started with the announcement that Britain and New Zealand had agreed to seek protection for cheese imports into Britain after 1977 and to a 'milk equivalent' programme within which New Zealand and Britain could

[225] 'Britain's Policy on NZ Butter', *Straight Furrow*, 25/07/1974, 6, ATL.
[226] 'Government's Vote of Confidence in Farming', *Straight Furrow*, 25/07/1974, 10, ATL.
[227] 'New Zealand Win in EEC Dairy Price', *Straight Furrow*, 27/11/1974, 3, ATL.
[228] 'UK–NZ Trade Ties to Stay', *Straight Furrow*, 21/08/1974, 6, ATL.
[229] 'Dairy Outlook Changing Rapidly', *Straight Furrow*, 18/09/1974, 13, ATL.

decide the balance between butter and cheese. That would mark a major change from the Luxembourg Protocol principles and Britain argued for those changes within the EEC.[230] Wilson began the Dublin talks with 'a strong appeal on New Zealand's behalf for greater access for their dairy products'.[231]

The Dublin meeting agreed that access for New Zealand butter should continue until 1980 at prices better than those secured by the Luxembourg Protocol.[232] In addition, Rowling announced that meeting had 'opened up the possibility of continued access to the British market for New Zealand cheese' thereby revoking the Luxembourg Protocol that had envisaged cheese export finishing in 1977.[233] Access for those products after 1980 would depend on whether New Zealand filled whatever quotas were agreed.[234] The European Commission proposed quotas starting higher than New Zealand had sent to Britain in 1974 reducing to 3% below it in 1980.[235] The New Zealand Minister of Agriculture reported assured access to the British market until 1980 with highly satisfactory pricing arrangements.[236] Rowling said 'Britain has been a very good friend to New Zealand'.[237]

When, in November 1975, the EEC agreed that prices for New Zealand produce after 1975 should be increased by 18%, the Federated Farmers President, then in London, said New Zealand farmers had reason to be grateful for the way the British government guarded New Zealand's interests in Europe. It showed Britain's obvious loyalty to New Zealand. The Dairy Section Chairman also congratulated the British government

[230] 'British NZ Trade Safeguards', *Straight Furrow*, 05/03/1975, 9, ATL.

[231] James Callaghan, *Time and Chance* (London: Collins, 1987), 322.

[232] 'EEC Allows NZ Concessions', *Straight Furrow*, 19/03/1975, 9, ATL.

[233] 'Rowling Discloses Trade Developments', *Dominion*, 13/06/1975, New Zealand Trade – United Kingdom – Dairy Produce: Butter, 1973–1988 ABHS W5503 7148 Box 42 LONB 37/1/2 Part 20, ANZ.

[234] 'EEC Dairy Door Open to NZ', *Straight Furrow*, 04/06/1975, 10, ATL.

[235] 'Short Term Expedients and Doom and Gloom', *Straight Furrow*, 06/08/1975, 9, ATL.

[236] '"Export, Diversify" – Moyle's Call to the Milk Industry', *Straight Furrow*, 20/08/1975, 10, ATL.

[237] 'Rowling Discloses Trade Development', *Dominion*, 13/06/1975, New Zealand Trade – United Kingdom – Dairy Produce: Butter 1973–1988, ABHS W5503 7148 Box 42, LONB 37/1/2 Part 20, ANZ.

for arguing on New Zealand's behalf.[238] The Anglo-New Zealand nexus in dairy trading continued well beyond 1973. In 1976 the Federated Farmers Dairy Section Chairman reported that Britain remained 'a very important market for New Zealand dairy products' and there had been a 'further significant rise in returns from the United Kingdom market'.[239]

For the dairy industry, Belich's conclusion that Britain's entry into the EEC was a black letter day for New Zealand, together with Singleton's and Robertson's conclusion that there was a brutal snapping of the Anglo-New Zealand nexus, seems to have been based on the fears of what might have happened rather than what actually happened. Opinions seemed to have formed based on the 1960s fears rather than the 1970s satisfaction. Another example is that Lind calls the EEC negotiations 'machinations' ['malicious intrigue' according to the OED]; he does not describe how or why the negotiations were malicious; he simply assumes that they were. McAloon calls Britain's EEC entry 'almost an anti-climax' and Easton and McAloon give the reason – the impact was 'symbolic' rather than economic. Britain's EEC membership felt like a personal betrayal to many but was not a betrayal for New Zealand's dairy industry.

The New Zealand dairy industry emerged from the 1960s shadow of Britain's impending EEC membership not tossed out into the snow as Woolerton had feared in 1962 but with confidence in continuing access to the British and rest of the EEC markets. That was demonstrated in 1982 when New Zealand opened, in Swindon in Britain, a butter and cheese packing plant for which '[t]he technology and knowledge of the 1980s has been used to create the most advanced and hygienic packing plant in Europe' for distribution of New Zealand dairy produce.[240] Even two decades after Britain had joined the EEC, Britain remained New Zealand's top single buyer of dairy products according to the *New*

[238] 'Politicians Praised on EEC Price', *Straight Furrow*, 26/11/1975, 3, ATL.

[239] Dairy Section Chairman's Address to Conference, 08/06/1976, Federated Farmers, 90-343 03/6, 4, ATL.

[240] The Story of the Anchor Brand, 14/04/1982, United Kingdom - Export - Dairy Products - Policy and Information 1971–1985, AATJ W4838 7428 Box 284 162/3/1 Part 2, ATL.

Zealand Digital Yearbook.[241] Even more positive for the dairy industry was that, by the mid-1970s, sales to other countries had overtaken dairy sales to Britain.

6.10 Conclusion

New Zealand never managed to find another significant buyer for its butter in the period up to 1975 and, except for a brief period between 1954 and 1958 when New Zealand experienced fully free market realities, remained dependent on British protection. The view had developed that Britain treated New Zealand unfairly over the prices it paid during bulk purchase but New Zealand encountered lower prices in a free market, and, for the first time, domestic payments to dairy farmers decreased. The balance in the Dairy Reserve Account built up to a surplus of more than £20 million during bulk purchase, but went into deficit within three years after bulk purchase ended. Eventually New Zealand appealed to Britain to again give New Zealand favourable treatment by restricting imports from others and Britain gave that protection.

Britain agreed in 1957 to accept unrestricted exports of dairy produce from New Zealand, but within two years market realities demanded that New Zealand should limit its exports to Britain to prevent price collapses. From 1962 the Dairy Board accepted that quotas set by Britain, even for New Zealand dairy exports, benefitted New Zealand. The protection provided New Zealand with a sheet anchor and breathing space to diversify into new markets. Sales to Britain were not falling through the 1950s and 1960s but New Zealand dairy producers faced the problem that Britain could not take increased sales. Through those decades New Zealand needed to increase exports to maintain growth and standards of living. New markets needed to be found for those increases.

The disaster that had been predicted for the New Zealand dairy industry as a result of the enlargement of the EEC failed to materialise.

---

[241] http://www3.stats.govt.nz/New_Zealand_Official_Yearbooks/1994/NZOYB_1994.html#idsect1_1_127188, accessed 6 September 2014, Table 23.6.

The main problems from the enlargement, at first, were the declining cheese exports and that the EEC quota could be filled only by damaging the new markets outside Britain and the EEC. The EEC continued the quotas set by Britain to protect New Zealand through the 1960s, and New Zealand benefitted because prices became guaranteed. For instance, EEC regulations made Britain pay compensation for sterling's depreciation. The agreement that the EEC would not frustrate New Zealand's efforts to build new markets gave another major advantage for New Zealand. The government and producers accepted that the special arrangements agreed in 1971 were satisfactory, and Britain renegotiated those successfully in 1975 to improve the arrangements, including abandoning the intention to run the cheese quota down to zero. By late 1975 farmers' leaders expressed gratitude for Britain's loyalty to New Zealand and the way it guarded New Zealand's exports of dairy produce, as Britain had done for most of the period 1945–1975. Even without British EEC membership New Zealand exports of dairy produce to Britain would not have differed much. By the 1970s the New Zealand dairy industry remained dependent on the British market and Britain remained the main buyer for New Zealand dairy produce for at least two more decades. But the relative importance of that market declined rapidly as sales to others overtook sales to Britain; that achievement amidst many difficulties is analysed next.

7

Diversification of Dairy Exports

7.1 Introduction

Chapter 7 reviews the development of dairy exports to countries other than Britain, noting the diversification of both products and marketing, together with the many obstacles to that diversification. Those obstacles rather than endemic conservatism hindered development of new markets. Exports of the traditional products sold to Britain, butter and cheese, stopped growing in the 1960s and the realisation that the British market would not grow gave a prime incentive for diversification. Up to the 1960s even for milk powder Britain remained the prime customer buying more than the combined total sold to others. But milk powder earnings from Britain declined from the mid-1960s because sales to Asia/Pacific customers increased significantly.[1] The increased sale of milk powder and by-products to Asia and the Americas made New Zealand's earnings from dairy produce export, at 1971 prices, 60% higher in 1975 than in 1945. The New Zealand dairy

[1] Joyce Bewley, 'A Survey of Changes in Production, Manufacturing and Marketing in the New Zealand Dairy Industry, 1947–48 to 1967 – 68', *New Zealand Geographer*, 26, 1, 1970, 47.

D. Hall, *Emerging from an Entrenched Colonial Economy*, Palgrave Studies in Economic History, DOI 10.1007/978-3-319-53016-1_7

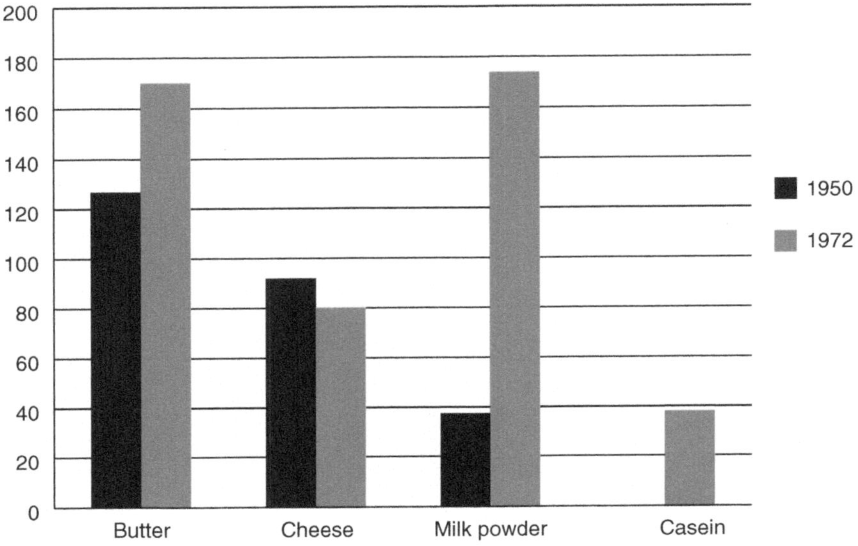

Fig. 7.1 Dairy produce tonnages (000) exported in 1950 and 1972 (NZDYB)

industry achieved the necessary change despite American restrictions on dairy imports and sales of domestic surpluses in competition with New Zealand, especially in Asia. Because New Zealand had diversified both markets and products (Figs. 7.1 and 7.2), the imposition of quotas by the EEC at the time Britain joined in 1973 proved to be far less a concern than expected when Britain first applied in 1961.

7.2 The Difficulties Accompanying the Growing Pressure for Diversification

As early as 1950 Federated Farmers pressed the government to encourage dairy exports to countries other than Britain. Diversification needed producers and government to work closely together to overcome the many difficulties that included the USA dumping dairy surpluses. New Zealand's growing political relations with the USA also inhibited a start in selling dairy exports to Communist China. The move from bulk

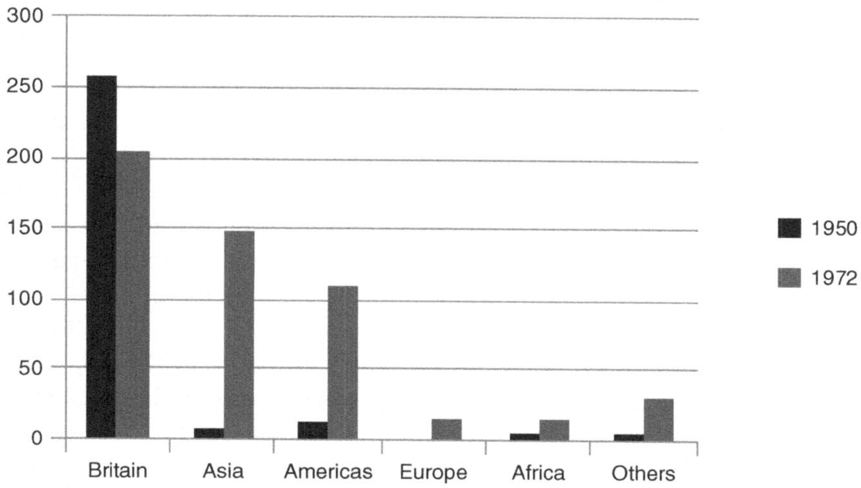

Fig. 7.2 Destinations for dairy tonnages (000) exported in 1950 and 1972 (NZDYB)

purchase to a free market in 1954 brought home to producers that they now experienced a harsher world that called for new approaches. The need to develop new markets had been realised and the difficulties foreseen, but preparations had not been made to overcome those difficulties.

In the early 1950s, Britain wanted to decrease prices under the bulk contract because global dairy trading had become a buyers' market, and that forced the New Zealand dairy industry to review the need for change. There were fears that five prosperous years after 1945, together with Britain's extended commitment to buy all New Zealand's dairy produce until 1955, had lulled New Zealand into a false sense of security. Producers became increasingly aware that in the long-term Britain might be unable to absorb increasing shipments of butter, cheese and dried milk, and might want New Zealand to find other markets.[2] That point had been made by Nash in the 1930s but the disruption of

[2] 'The Future of the Dairy Industry', *Straight Furrow*, 16/01/1950, 3, ATL.

war delayed the changes in Britain by more than two decades. In 1950, Federated Farmers pressed the government to establish Trade Commissioners in Malaya, Indonesia, India and Pakistan, countries identified as potential outlets for New Zealand produce even before World War II. *Straight Furrow* noted that Australia traded in dairy products with Asia and New Zealand should follow that lead.[3] The government responded that it would add more commissioners in addition to those already operating in Bombay and Tokyo. Holyoake likened the 'Far East [Asia]' to a giant awakening, hungry for food.[4]

As early as 1950, the Dairy Commission Chairman, William Marshall, could point to sales to 37 countries other than Britain.[5] But he identified four problems in extending markets still further: securing sufficient refrigerated transport; import restrictions that protected domestic production and overseas exchange; trade arrangements that needed discussions at governmental level; and diverse quality standards.[6] In 1951, Marshall reported to the Dominion Dairy Conference that sales to countries other than Britain were seven times higher in 1950/1951 compared with 1947/1948 with some sales at prices higher than those paid by Britain.[7] He announced that for the following season New Zealand would be allowed to sell up to 15% of its exportable surplus outside Britain, but he warned that it was unclear whether it would be possible to sell the whole 15%. Five years later, when New Zealand had become entirely free to choose its markets, still New Zealand could sell no more than 10% of its butter and cheese to countries other than Britain, demonstrating the difficulties of breaking into new markets.

Norman Kirk, when leader of the New Zealand Opposition, summarised in 1969 that 'there is a conflict of interest between our own farmers . . . and the farming community of . . . the USA'. That is most

[3] 'Trade with Malaysia and Indonesia Urged', *Straight Furrow*, 15/08/1950, 10, ATL; 'There's a Market for NZ Produce in the East', *Straight Furrow*, 16/10/1950, 2, ATL.

[4] 'An Awakening Giant – The Far East', *Straight Furrow*, 15/08/1951, 17, ATL.

[5] 'Marketing of Dairy Produce', *Straight Furrow*, 15/03/1950, 21, ATL.

[6] 'Probing Potential Markets', *Straight Furrow*, 15/04/1950, 51, ATL.

[7] 'Dairy Commission Is in Touch with the Situation', *Straight Furrow*, 16/07/1951, 27, ATL.

appropriate for the dairy industry.[8] The conflict of interest extended back to at least the early 1950s when America's production exceeded domestic consumption by far. The USA sought to sell the surplus on world markets threatening global dairy sales. The American price support scheme, introduced originally to stem the numbers leaving farming in the 1930s, generated that surplus.[9] In August 1950, Alister McIntosh, the New Zealand Secretary of External Affairs, wrote to the Director-General of the United Nations Food and Agriculture Organisation (FAO) to protest that 'sale of surpluses at prices well below normal trade parity is prejudicial to smooth-working international trade'.[10] He asked the FAO to intervene pointing out the damage that dumping by the USA caused for countries such as New Zealand, whose standard of living depended on exporting dairy produce.[11] Officials from the Treasury and the Departments of External Affairs, Agriculture, and Industries and Commerce recommended that the letter should be followed up by a direct approach to the American government.[12] That approach should point out also the adverse impact of American restrictions imposed on butter exports from New Zealand.

New Zealand again protested formally to the USA against restrictions imposed on dried milk and butterfat in 1952.[13] A 'butter mountain' had grown in the USA and the incoming Administration of President Eisenhower needed to sell the butter. The whole British ration for six weeks could be satisfied by sale of the 'mountain', and its release onto world markets would deflate prices for countries such as New Zealand.[14] The USA, also, sold its surplus milk powder cheaply to Japan as part of its relief programme; that sale damaged a small but growing trade in milk powder between New Zealand and Japan.[15] Finally, New Zealand

[8] Reported in Brian Easton, *The Nationbuilders* (Auckland, Auckland University Press, 2001), 180.

[9] 'USA Farm Leader Addresses Dairy Section Council', *Straight Furrow*, 01/03/1955, 17, ATL.

[10] McIntosh to FAO, 20/08/1950, Keith Holyoake papers, MS-1814 – 3/6 Dairy Produce, 1, ATL.

[11] McIntosh to FAO, 20/08/1950, Keith Holyoake papers, MS-1814 – 3/6 Dairy Produce, 2, ATL.

[12] Fawcett to Holyoake, 28/08/1950, Keith Holyoake papers, MS-1814 – 3/6 Dairy Produce, ATL.

[13] 'USA Import Restrictions on Dairy Products', *Straight Furrow*, 01/02/1953, 23, ATL.

[14] 'World Conditions Threaten Stability of Dairy Industry', *Straight Furrow*, 01/05/1953, 1, ATL.

[15] United States Disposal of Surplus Dairy Products, 05/08/1954, Keith Holyoake papers, MS-1814 – 40/1, Dairy Produce, 3, ATL.

had established a significant market for butter in Panama and other Latin America countries but disposal of American surpluses in that region 'seriously prejudiced New Zealand's prospects of continuing and expanding exports to them'.[16]

The Federated Farmers Dairy Section Chairman warned in 1953 that building markets in other countries had become essential because, first, the British refused to agree, unlike for meat, unrestricted entry for New Zealand dairy produce for fifteen years, and, second, the USA continued butter and cheese import restrictions and prohibited milk powder imports. Those actions by Britain and the USA confirmed the transition to a buyers' market.[17] In May 1954 the New Zealand ambassador in the USA protested again that selling American surplus cheese, butter and milk powder would be a clear danger to market stability.[18] The surplus stocks in the USA equalled 40% of the world's annual butter trade, 50% of the cheese trade and 250% of the milk powder trade. The USA claimed that it would avoid disturbing global markets and would not sell other than at world prices. New Zealand hoped that goodwill recently developed through the ANZUS defence collaboration between the USA, Australia and New Zealand would keep the USA well aware of the danger for New Zealand agriculture, but early in 1955 the USA dumping of surplus butter forced yet another New Zealand protest with Prime Minister, Sidney Holland, complaining directly to the American Secretaries of State and Agriculture.[19] The USA claimed 'to understand' New Zealand's problem but did not cease selling surpluses; New Zealand could do nothing but 'continue to protest at appropriate times'.[20] In March 1955 the USA persuaded the GATT countries that an open-ended waiver should be granted to allow the USA to impose

[16] Dairy Commission Marketing Bulletin, United States Disposal of Surplus Dairy Products, 25/07/1957, Keith Holyoake papers, MS-1814 – 40/1, Dairy Produce, 6, ATL.

[17] 'Need for Alternative Export Markets', *Straight Furrow*, 01/07/1953, 9, ATL.

[18] United States Disposal of Dairy Products, 05/08/1954, Keith Holyoake papers, MS-1814 – 40/1, ATL.

[19] Memorandum from New Zealand Embassy Washington to Minister of External Affairs, 18/02/1955, Keith Holyoake papers, MS-1814 – 45/4, 1, ATL.

[20] Memorandum from New Zealand Embassy Washington to Minister of External Affairs, 18/02/1955, Keith Holyoake papers, MS-1814 – 45/4, 3, ATL.

import restrictions on butter, cheese and milk powders, and for more than a decade New Zealand pressed for abolition of the waiver or 'progressive relaxation' of the restrictions.[21] But Federated Farmers pointed out that New Zealand's own import restrictions made it inappropriate to criticise the USA. In May 1955 once again New Zealand had to protest, this time because the USA exported milk powder surpluses.[22]

New Zealand's growing dependence on the USA for security caused further difficulties for dairy diversification. In particular, it restricted New Zealand from building trade with the People's Republic of China – 'Communist China' to New Zealanders and Europeans in the 1950s. When Britain recognised Communist China in 1950, New Zealand did not; in 1951, New Zealand 'inclined in its Far Eastern [Asian] policy much more closely to the American than British point of view'.[23] But New Zealand kept itself informed on developments in China via the British Embassy in Peking.[24] China had been a customer for New Zealand wool before World War II and sales recommenced in 1954, but opposition within New Zealand to building links with the Communist government hindered other trade. Warren Freer reports the opposition within his own [Labour] party when he intended to visit Communist China in 1955; Nash, the party leader, tried to stop Freer's visit.[25] That opposition reflected the intense opposition to Communism in the USA at that time, illustrated by McCarthyism that 'destroyed' careers overnight for those with the merest hint of communist sympathies. Freer says that 'mood . . . was prevalent throughout the Western world including New Zealand where the Catholic

[21] Cabinet Economic Committee – International Dairy Situation, 29/09/1967, Foreign Trade – Dairy Produce – General, AAFD W3738 811 Box1141 CAB130/2/1, 3, ANZ.

[22] Secretary of External Affairs to Minister of Agriculture, May 1955, Keith Holyoake papers, MS-1814 – 45/5, ATL.

[23] 'New Zealand's Choice', *The Observer*, 10/06/1951, Keith Holyoake papers, MS-1814 – 16/6, ATL.

[24] London to Embassy of New Zealand Japan, 26/04/1965, NZ – Japan Relations – Exports to Japan – Meat, 1965–1974, ABHS W5330 6956 Box 29, TKY 26/3/10, ANZ.

[25] Warren Freer, *A Life in Politics: The Memoirs of Warren Freer* (Wellington: Victoria University Press, 2004), 71.

Church in particular actively engaged in an anti-communist type of purge'.[26]

Freer's visit encouraged growing links between Communist China and New Zealand. An agriculturalist who had spent time in China recommended selling milk powder because he thought many Chinese were becoming interested in milk powder for their children. He said that if the Communist government would liberalise trading conditions, China would take milk powder immediately and other dairy produce later.[27] The Waikato representative told the Federated Farmers Dairy Section that trading with Communist China should be encouraged. He claimed that the USA traded with China 'through the back door' by selling milk powder to Japan who then sold it on to China.[28]

At the end of 1955, the New Zealand government wanted to see primary industries, including dairy, increase exports by 2.5% each year to prevent New Zealand living standards falling. Director-General of Agriculture E. J. Fawcett suggested that dairy increases would be possible by spreading techniques learnt from the most efficient farms to marginal dairy farms in hill country. But he warned that growth in the British market would be limited and New Zealand would either have to displace other countries in the British market or change consumer choice.[29] A fall in cheese prices in Britain at the start of 1955 increased fears that the British cheese market had become saturated and encouraged change from cheese to other products.[30] The Dairy Commission encouraged change by paying producers who turned to casein production the same as they would have been paid if their milk had been used to make cheese.[31] The Ruawai Dairy Company invested in a new factory for producing milk powder despite its concerns about the market strength.

---

[26] Freer, 72.

[27] 'Dairy Products to China?', *Straight Furrow*, 01/02/1956, 23, ATL.

[28] 'Trade Bureau Advocated', *Straight Furrow*, 01/11/1957, 27, ATL.

[29] 'Expansion Potential of Primary Industry', *Straight Furrow*, 01/11/1955, 36, ATL.

[30] 'British Prices for Dominion's Butter and Cheese Decline', *The Dominion*, 17/02/1955, 9.

[31] Director General, Department of Agriculture to Minister, 18/03/1955, Keith Holyoake papers, MS-1814 – 40/1 Dairy Produce, 1, ATL.

The Chairman visited Holyoake to seek government support saying that the Colombo Plan countries (Ceylon, India and Pakistan) could take all the milk powder that New Zealand produced but could not pay for it. He suggested that New Zealand loan money to those countries; Holyoake suggested that 'in connection with the Colombo plan' a 'gift' rather than a loan should be investigated.[32] Co-operative international action amongst dairy exporting countries built commercial demand over a long period, and rising standards of living created new demands in Asia and the Middle East.[33] An international group representing milk powder producers looked into how best to devise a 'cooperative international approach'. That approach might entail 'provision of special plant, technical assistance facilities, and in the early stages perhaps supply of milk powder at concessional prices'. New Zealand appointed William Marshall, recognising the importance of making a strong contribution to such a group.[34]

By early 1956 markets outside Britain had grown, butter sold to 50 countries whilst cheese went to 41. The 30 most important markets for New Zealand dairy exports in 1955 are shown in Table 7.1. The demand for milk powder illustrated the demands of the diversified markets; eight different types packaged in 30 different ways met the market requirements in over 40 countries.[35] Irregular shipping hindered the considerable scope for the trade expansion with countries such as Malaya and Ceylon.[36] The Dairy Board told the Cabinet Committee on Economic Policy that 'the question of... developing trade... may also call for consideration of shipping difficulties'.[37] New Zealand had appointed a Trade Commissioner in Singapore

[32] Deputation on Skim Milk Powder, 06/07/1954, Keith Holyoake papers, MS-1814 – 40/1 Dairy Produce, 1–3, ATL.

[33] 'Dairy Commission Chairman's Address', *Straight Furrow*, 01/09/1955, 13, ATL.

[34] Note on Dried Skim Milk, undated, Keith Holyoake papers MS-1814 46/2 Dairy Produce, ATL.

[35] 'Dairy Commission's Monthly Review: Milk Powders', *Straight Furrow*, 01/04/1956, 5, ATL.

[36] 'Dairy Commission's Monthly Review: Shipping Services To The East', *Straight Furrow*, 01/06/1956, 5, ATL.

[37] Trade Policy Review: Supplement to Dairy Produce Statement, undated, T/1/61/3/21 Pt II, ANZ.

Table 7.1 New Zealand dairy exports in 1955

Country	Tonnes	%
United Kingdom	249,798	85.29
German Federal Republic	8,293	2.83
India	8,094	2.76
Small countries not identified	5,955	2.03
Malaya and Singapore	5,363	1.83
Czechoslovakia	3,061	1.05
British West Indies	2,979	1.02
France	1,016	0.35
Switzerland	1,016	0.35
Italy	924	0.32
United States of America	906	0.31
Philippines	734	0.25
Fiji	707	0.24
Panama Republic	700	0.24
Rhodesia–Nyasaland	587	0.2
Bermuda	426	0.15
Belgian Congo	317	0.11
Denmark	305	0.1
Netherlands	295	0.1
Society Islands	231	0.08
British Guiana	183	0.06
Netherlands Antilles	180	0.06
Western Samoa	178	0.06
Hong Kong	176	0.06
Hawaii	149	0.05
Ceylon	86	0.03
Australia	83	0.03
British West Africa	68	0.02
Tonga	43	0.01
Portuguese East Africa	30	0.01
Japan	2	0
Total	292,886	100

but the opportunities for trade expansion there remained threatened by unsuitable shipping arrangements.[38]

New Zealand producers doubted whether the dairy industry organisation set up for bulk purchase was appropriate for competition in a free market.

[38] 'Dairy Commission's Monthly Review: Shipping Services to the East', *Straight Furrow*, 01/06/1956, 5, ATL.

Federated Farmers had noted the need for change as soon as the end of the contract approached in 1954. A resolution at the Dairy Section Council expressed every confidence in the Dairy Commission but asked what 'research is being made into marketing conditions having regard to the availability, demand, and packaging requirements . . . for different parts of the world'.[39] A year later doubts remained on whether there had been essential changes and a farmer, David Randall, in a major article in *Straight Furrow*, did some 'plain speaking' criticising Marshall.[40] Randall thought Marshall was excellent in administration and negotiations with the British government, but lacked the additional skills now needed within the Commission. Randall said the Commission needed a streamlined sales organisation led by someone with drive and experience in dairy produce marketing. Marshall needed support in technical aspects for selling in heightened competition. Those technical aspects included: attractive packaging; research into preferred flavours, and how to improve flavour if necessary; diversifying flavours rather than keeping with just one standard variety: and, selling butter in smaller packs to suit the consumers who preferred to buy in small quantities. Randall continued that consumers needed to be convinced that the New Zealand butter's bright yellow colour came not artificially but from a bountiful climate which allowed cattle to be fed outdoors all year round.[41] Those considerations needed to be investigated by a highly qualified sales executive trained in selling at international level.

7.3 Increased Prominence Given to Finding New Markets

Following the 1957 trade talks with Britain, Holyoake and the Dairy Commission had no doubt that prominence should be given to finding new markets. Free and unrestricted access for dairy produce had been

[39] Minutes of Dairy Section Council, 22/06/1954, Federated Farmers 90-343 MSY-2709, D22/1946, 3, ATL.

[40] David Randall, 'Some Blunt Truths About Marketing and Packaging of N.Z. Butter, Cheese', *Straight Furrow* 01/04/1955, 3, ATL.

[41] 'Struggle for Purse of British Housewife', *Straight Furrow* 01/04/1955, 9, ATL.

agreed with Britain, but over-supply depressed prices paid by Britain and that took away any advantage. New markets required new products and that demanded a greater flexibility with dairy factories amalgamating into bigger units. Asian markets increased in importance, and it became clear that selling a product such as milk powder would be more successful than trying to sell butter and cheese to Asians at prices appropriate for European markets. The Dairy Board wanted to investigate possible sales to Communist China but the Department of External Affairs feared upsetting the USA and dissuaded the Board. India became a promising customer for milk powder sales and the 1958 trade agreement with Japan raised hopes that dairy trade with Japan might grow.

When Holyoake spoke to the Federated Farmers Dominion Conference after the 1957 trade talks with Britain, he said that the talks brought home the need to find new markets. Neither Britain's population increased nor its per capita consumption. New Zealand produce had free access to the British market but with no assurance that prices would be remunerative.[42] Fawcett warned that New Zealand now had the problem of disposal and not production; the lack of increased sales made increased production meaningless.[43] Marshall told the Dominion Dairy Conference: 'There appears to be a need to develop new markets if we are to avoid periods of low prices'.[44] Holyoake had been warned by Marshall that

> experience since the termination of our bulk contracts . . . has clearly shown that there is a growing need to find outlets in other markets . . . especially butter . . . it would be dangerous to assume that the United Kingdom will be able to absorb an ever increasing exportable surplus from New Zealand at economic prices.[45]

[42] 'Agriculture Minister Addresses Conference', *Straight Furrow*, 01/08/1957, 3, ATL.

[43] 'Next Congress Vital for U.S. Dairy Farmers', *Straight Furrow*, 01/11/1957, 1, ATL.

[44] Dairy Market Bulletin from the New Zealand Dairy Commission, 27/06/1957, Keith Holyoake papers, MS-1814 – 56/2 Dairy Produce, 4, ATL.

[45] Marshall to Holyoake, 24/06/1957, Keith Holyoake papers, MS-1814 – 45/6 Dairy Produce, ATL.

Marshall's warnings were his last before he retired at the start of August 1957 when his second term ended as Commission Chairman. An independent review of dairy produce export to Britain made Holyoake encourage producers to seek new markets. The review told him that for butter 'there seemed no immediate danger of the United Kingdom market being over-supplied because production seemed stable in all major butter-producing countries'.[46] But for cheese 'the future of cheese does not appear as bright as for our other export commodities' because production had increased in all producer countries. For milk powder, low prices in the United Kingdom and other markets made 'substantial productive capacity . . . idle' in New Zealand. Further, the milk powder market remained threatened because the USA dumped surpluses.[47] Holyoake said, 'our problems are staring us in the face'; national thinking had to be conditioned to the need for new markets. Holyoake said that the government had inaugurated more diplomatic offices in Southeast Asia, and would open up trade posts to prepare the way for market exploitation.[48] In addition, trial shipments went to the Pacific Rim countries Chile and Peru.[49]

Diversifying markets required not just finding new customers but also diversifying products to suit those new customers. By 1957 new products already under development included animal feed made from milk whey as a cheap substitute for milk powder, and, for an American customer, exylone, an ice-cream base containing butterfat.[50] The Chairman of the Cardiff Co-operative Dairy Company in Taranaki suggested that diversification of products would be encouraged by dairy company amalgamation. He suggested that in Taranaki 56 small companies amalgamating into four would ease changes between dairy

[46] Memorandum for Rt. Hon. Minister, 05/07/1957, Keith Holyoake papers, MS-1814 – 45/6 Dairy Produce, 1, ATL.

[47] Memorandum for Rt. Hon. Minister, 05/07/1957, Keith Holyoake papers, MS-1814 – 45/6 Dairy Produce, 2, ATL.

[48] 'Mr. Holyoake Confident: Alternative Market Solutions', *Straight Furrow*, 01/10/1957, 7, ATL.

[49] 'Trial Shipments of Butter to South America', *Straight Furrow*, 15/10/1957, 10, ATL.

[50] 'Spray Process Whey Powder', *Straight Furrow*, 01/05/1957, 5, ATL; 'Exylone Exports to U.S.', *Straight Furrow*, 01/06/1957, 5, ATL.

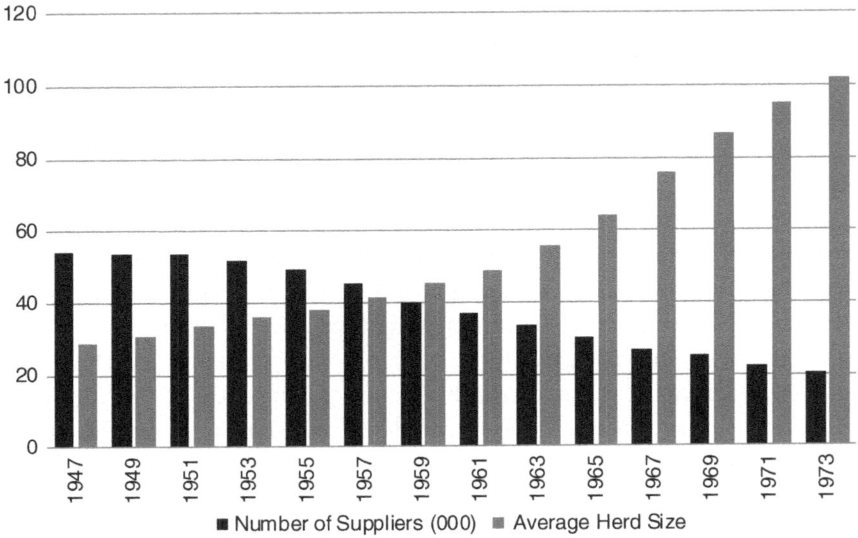

Fig. 7.3 Number of dairy suppliers (000) and their average herd sizes (Ward, A., *A Command of Cooperatives* (Wellington: New Zealand Dairy Board, 1975), Table 1, p. 244)

products in line with changed consumer demand. In addition, improved transport made amalgamation more appropriate: the transport limitations of horse-drawn vehicles and poor roads that had restricted company sizes originally had been overcome by motorised tankers operating on better roads.[51] Amalgamation of farms leading to fewer farms but bigger herd sizes accompanied amalgamation of dairy companies (Fig. 7.3). In addition to giving increased flexibility in products, the changes in transport, dairy companies and farms through the 1950s and early 1960s increased significantly dairy production efficiency.[52]

Meanwhile, Asian markets received more attention. The Commission had little doubt that Asia would become important as a market for milk powder but the market growth would be dictated by the American

[51] 'Merger of 56 Dairy Companies Suggested', *Straight Furrow*, 01/10/1956, 50, ATL.

[52] Bewley, 36 – 49.

policies on disposal of surpluses.[53] Marshall complained that the USA was 'playing havoc with our milk powder markets in India and other places'. New Zealand's milk powder exports to India continued to grow despite the import restrictions introduced by India on other countries. Japan again bought significant volumes and markets continued to develop in Malaya and Singapore. But it became clear in 1957 that butter and cheese remained unaffordable in Asian countries despite the increased dairy production efficiency in New Zealand.[54]

In 1957 the Dairy Commission wanted to send its General Manager, Stan Murphy, to Communist China to discuss potential trade. But New Zealand's Department of External Affairs worried about the impact on relations with the USA:

> [A]ny advantages which the development of trade . . . with Communist China may present should be weighed carefully against the consequent harm which could be done to New Zealand's relations with the United States.[55]

The Secretary of External Affairs agreed that Murphy's visit should go ahead but it had to be made clear that it was not an 'official' visit and Murphy should not invite the Chinese to visit New Zealand. It was also 'desirable to restrict any publicity with regard to the visit to the minimum'. Murphy visited Hong Kong, the Philippines and Singapore but seems not to have visited Communist China.[56] In the mid-1960s Murphy said China's purchasing power was considerable and the Chinese were short of food. He noted the growth in Chinese trade with the West in industrial products.[57] He thought it now reasonable to start trading but significant New Zealand dairy trade with China did not start until the 1970s, following the USA finally breaking the ice with President Nixon's visit to China in 1972.

---

[53] Dairy Commission Marketing Bulletin, 19/08/1957, Keith Holyoake papers, MS-1814 – 45/6 Dairy Produce, 7, ATL.

[54] 'Far East Trade Prospects', *Straight Furrow*, 01/09/1957, 5, ATL.

[55] Secretary for External Affairs to Acting Minister of External Affairs, 28/06/1957, Keith Holyoake papers, MS-1814 – 56/2 Dairy Produce, 1-2, ATL.

[56] Dairy Commission Marketing Bulletin, 21/07/1957, Keith Holyoake papers, MS-1814 – 45/6 Dairy Produce, 5, ATL.

[57] 'Trade With Communist China?', *Straight Furrow*, 20/10/1965, 31, ATL.

Despite American dairy farmers still pressing for retention of barriers against foreign imports, prospects for casein and pure butterfat sale to the USA improved in 1957.[58] The USA suspended its tariff on casein to ensure that substitutes did not replace it, anticipating that casein production in the USA might be rejuvenated.[59] In 1957 the USA set a quota for pure butterfat, a product pioneered by New Zealand, and New Zealand imports took up nearly the entire quota.[60]

Sales of new products and to new markets continued to increase. Casein had become the dairy product sold most freely outside Britain; other major buyers in addition to the USA were Japan, Italy, Germany and the Netherlands.[61] Against world competition in 1958, New Zealand supplied 73% of skim milk powder bought by India's largest buyer.[62] The USA's sale of surpluses had stimulated milk powder consumption in India but increased domestic demand within the USA took up the surpluses leaving the Indian market open to New Zealand.[63] Also, in September 1959, the Dairy Commission announced that New Zealand had secured the entire global quota for pure butterfat allowed into the USA.[64] Through the late 1950s steps taken to develop markets outside Britain included shipping lines starting a direct service between New Zealand and Peru, taking away transhipment via New York or Panama.[65] In Northland another new casein factory opened, and visiting Indian and Japanese trade delegations encouraged hope that there would be further expansion in milk by-product exports.[66] The 1958 trade agreement with Japan led to a visit to Japan by New Zealand Dairy Commission's General

[58] 'Next Congress Vital for U.S. Dairy Farmers', *Straight Furrow*, 01/11/1957, 4, ATL.

[59] 'Casein Prospects', *Straight Furrow*, 01/10/1957, 5, ATL.

[60] 'N.Z. Butter Oil for U.S.', *Straight Furrow*, 01/11/1957, 1, ATL.

[61] '2000 Tons Casein for Japan', *Straight Furrow*, 15/11/1957, 6, ATL.

[62] 'Tribute to N.Z. Milk Powder', *Straight Furrow*, 17/12/1958, 5, ATL.

[63] 'USA. As Exporter of Dairy Products', *Straight Furrow*, 17/12/1958, 8, ATL.

[64] Press Statement, 15/09/1959, Dairy Products Marketing Commission Press Statements 04/11/1958 – 10/10/1963, ABBU W4244 Box 33 7/2/2 Part 2, ANZ.

[65] 'Dairy Commission's Market Report', *Straight Furrow*, 18/02/1959, 13, ATL.

[66] 'New Casein Factory Opened in North', *Straight Furrow*, 04/03/1959, 13, ATL.

Manager, and he announced on his return that Japan would accept increased casein imports. He said that the milk powder market in Japan would be valuable also for New Zealand but for the market distortion caused by dumping of American surpluses.[67]

7.4 Diversifying Both Products and Marketing Techniques

Diversification increased through the 1960s by changing not just products but also marketing methods. Milk powder became a major export to Asian countries because New Zealand invested in processing plants in those countries that turned that milk powder into the specific products best suited for Asian, domestic, consumption. Marketing became a technical exercise informing prospective customers of the possibilities and working with them to introduce the necessary facilities. Emphasis changed from trying to break into the American market to breaking into Asian markets. Many improvements to domestic productivity and many new specialist dairy factories demonstrated long-term confidence in the industry's prospects.

In 1960 New Zealand sold, outside Britain, six times the volume of dairy exports sold outside before World War II, amounting to 18.5% of all sales.[68] The greatest expansion occurred in non-fat products such as casein and milk powder. Three-quarters of casein exports went to countries other than Britain, mainly to the United States, Japan, Germany, Italy and other industrialised countries, accounting for 10% of New Zealand dairy exports.[69] But producers now recognised that Asia offered the greatest chance for dairy export expansion; living standards steadily improved and new eating habits developed. Markets for milk powder grew in the Philippines, Malaya, Singapore and Burma; tropical

[67] Press Statement, 05/07/1959, Dairy Products Marketing Commission Press Statements 04/11/1958 – 10/10/1963, ABBU W4244 Box 33 7/2/2 Part 2, 2, ANZ.

[68] 'Record Sales Outside UK', *Straight Furrow*, 06/07/1960, 7, ATL.

[69] 'Good Results with Powder and Casein', *Straight Furrow*, 06/07/1960, 7, ATL.

countries found that milk production from powder supplied by New Zealand preferable to producing their own fresh milk.[70]

When the Dairy Board and the Dairy Commission amalgamated to become the Dairy Production and Marketing Board in 1961, Murphy became the general manager. He spoke positively about the outlets opening up in Asia for dairy products at remunerative prices, especially in milk powder.[71] In 1962, a milk processing plant in Singapore operated at a profit and Linton could announce, proudly (and possibly patronisingly), that it had now been proven that milk processing could be undertaken successfully in a Chinese community. Chinese businessmen in Singapore helped build a similar plant in Malaya, and the Dairy Board joined with local interests for one to be set up in the Philippines.[72] Dairy produce consumption in Japan remained low compared with Europe but rising fast. In the previous five years Japanese butter and cheese consumption had doubled and ice cream consumption increased eightfold. But high tariffs still hampered trade with Japan.

The quota restrictions placed on dairy imports into Britain from the early 1960s led to European countries with surplus dairy produce now directing their surpluses to other markets and that threatened the new, Asian, markets that New Zealand had painstakingly developed over many years.[73] Also, in the West Indies the USA was undercutting New Zealand's established markets. Linton, usually mild in his comments, thought it 'nonsense' that a great and wealthy country such as the USA followed a policy that priced its produce off its domestic market, then dumped the surplus in the established markets of a small friendly country, such as New Zealand, which depended on those markets for a livelihood.[74]

In 1963, Linton outlined the Dairy Board's approach to building new markets. A potential market had to be remunerative, or show clear signs

[70] Milk Markets in Asia, 17/05/1960, Dairy Industry and General, T1 274 40/648/8, ANZ.
[71] 'Asian Markets As Likely Outlet for N.Z.', *Straight Furrow*, 18/10/1961, 34, ATL.
[72] 'N.Z. Help for Malaya And Philippines', *Straight Furrow*, 18/04/1962, 19, ATL.
[73] 'Competition for Export Outlets', *Straight Furrow*, 18/04/1962, 12, ATL.
[74] 'Dairy Board Looks to the Future', *Straight Furrow*, 01/05/1963, 17, ATL.

that it would become remunerative. Milk processing operations had been underway for some time in Singapore, Hong Kong and Mauritius, and, now, the Board planned operations in Barbados and Thailand. Linton hoped that in the long run those operations would become important outlets for milk solids, but local people still needed persuasion to buy milk products regularly. By setting up the operations, New Zealand helped those countries industrialise and took some of the financial risk. Linton concluded that it would be wrong for New Zealand to delude itself that sales would rapidly and substantially increase. There were not millions of Asians eagerly waiting for fresh milk. New Zealand supplied milk to Asian schools to encourage the taste for milk.[75] The government recognised the importance of building new markets and provided support by guaranteeing an overdraft for the Dairy Board.[76]

The Targets Committee of the 1964 Agricultural Development Conference set a target for dairy exports at 4% per annum increase as part of the national effort to maintain New Zealand's standard of living.[77] An economist pointed out the question of what could be exported to world markets at economic prices needed to be answered before deciding where priority should be given to encourage further growth.[78] Linton demonstrated areas where priority might be given, pointing out that the manufacturing industry based on skim milk had shown the most remarkable growth of any industry in New Zealand. The continued growth through the 1960s justified his judgement (Fig. 7.4) and prospects were excellent because New Zealand, more than any other country, had the capacity to expand the manufacturing facilities. Half the exports now shipped to countries other than Britain through advances made in Asia, Africa, South America, Central America and the Caribbean.[79] But Linton repeated his earlier warning: those markets carried no guarantee of a developed

[75] '"UK Must Continue As Most Important"', *Straight Furrow*, 07/08/1963, 13, ATL.

[76] Overseas Dairy Projects, 08/05/1964, Foreign Trade – Dairy Produce – General, AAFD W3738 811 Box1141 CAB130/2/1 1-3, ANZ.

[77] *The Agricultural Development Conference 1963–64*, Government Printer, Wellington, 1966, 14.

[78] 'Marketing Production Policies "Inconsistent"', *Straight Furrow*, 01/07/1964, 20, ATL.

[79] '"Most Remarkable Growth"', *Straight Furrow*, 01/07/1964, 4, ATL.

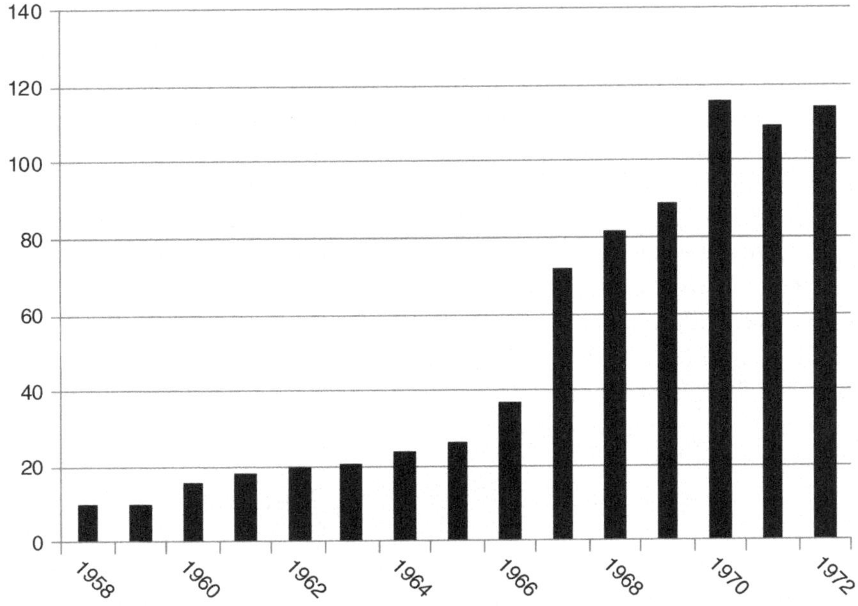

Fig. 7.4 Milk Powder Exports to Asia, tonnes (000) (NZDYB)

market. Low per capita income, political instability and a diet that did not yet include dairy products made some new markets questionable.[80]

Towards the end of 1965, Murphy reported how the Dairy Board had established trade in new products and new places. The Board had radically changed marketing methods with the commercial traveller with an order book giving way to a sales engineering approach. Technical officers now accompanied sales representatives and visited every major marketing area outside Europe, for instance, Asia, the Middle East, the Caribbean and South America. Milk, recombined in its many forms, interested many buyers who wanted to carry out the processing operations themselves.[81] Joyce Bewley notes that marketing in the mid-1960s 'when virtually every order is to a precise specification, is the work of specialists – chemists and engineers who

[80] 'Far East Dairy Markets', *Straight Furrow*, 16/09/1964, 3, ATL.

[81] 'Dairymen Get Out and Sell', *Straight Furrow*, 20/10/1965, 34, ATL.

know milk and its products'.[82] Murphy said it had to be faced that any increased production in New Zealand would need to be sold in markets other than Britain, but a 'strait-jacket' of import restrictions to protect local agriculture inhibited the world's trade in butter and cheese.[83] Murphy continued that New Zealand had anticipated since World War II that the USA would be the obvious alternative to the British market, but, as Asian living standards rose, trade with Asia might well be better than trying to break into the over-protected USA market. In mid-1965, the growing success in market diversification made producers concerned that produce should not be taken away from 'developing markets . . . to make up the United Kingdom quota'.[84] Filling British dairy quotas had become far less important.

Eventually the Dairy Board showed its disillusion with the USA and Japan because the Board could see no end to dairy produce import restrictions in those countries. Federated Farmers asked the government to intervene when the USA imposed 'drastic restrictions' on New Zealand dairy exports that threatened 'recent achievements in market diversification'.[85] Jack Marshall made a 'bold and forthright statement' criticising the USA but that had no effect on the restrictions.[86] Also, New Zealand thought the 1958 trade agreement with Japan had a 'promising understanding' but exports were 'languishing' because Japan restricted imports. New Zealand raised the matter on 'numerous occasions' but, at first, without success.[87] New Zealand sought 'complete liberalisation of Japanese dairy product imports' but expected improvements to be 'many years distant'.[88] That expectation proved to be wrong and the situation 'dramatically changed' at the end of 1966 when Japan accepted that it could not meet domestic needs for milk

---

[82] Bewley, 48.

[83] 'Dairy Export Prospects Bright', *Straight Furrow*, 20/10/1965, 36, ATL.

[84] Minutes of Dairy Section Council, 05/05/1965, Federated Farmers 90-343, MSY-2718 Dairy Section, D17/1965, 3, ATL.

[85] United States Dairy Imports, 31/07/1967, Federated Farmers 90-343, MSY-2720 Dairy Section, D44/1967, 1, ATL.

[86] World Dairy Surpluses, 15/09/1967, Federated Farmers, 90-343 MSY-2720 Dairy Section, D56/1967, 1, ATL.

[87] Visit of Japanese Officials, 25/11/1965, IC1 114/1/1, ANZ.

[88] Trade with Japan, July 1967, IC1 114/1/1, ANZ.

products. In early 1967 the Dairy Board obtained significant new contracts for the supply of butter and milk powder to Japan.[89]

The three main efforts for the dairy industry in the mid-1960s remained to hold its place in the British market, break the barriers in developed and developing countries, and concentrate on promoting new products and dairy product uses.[90] Milk powder production facilities continued to grow in New Zealand in the first half of 1966, with five established factories installing new production plants and six entirely new factories.[91] The New Zealand dairy industry justifiably claimed it had become an innovator and no longer used the manufacturing methods and approaches that had been adopted from older countries during the industry's original creation.[92] Increases in efficiency were demonstrated through 1966 when dairy suppliers in New Zealand declined by 6% but the overall production for the remaining suppliers increased.[93] There had been considerable increases in productivity in both dairy factories and by dairy farmers.[94] Over the previous decade milk transported to factories had increased by 20% whilst the number of suppliers had decreased by 41%. The increase in productivity had been achieved by several new developments such as electric fences, herringbone milking sheds, the tank vat, circular yards and motorised backing gates, pressure hoses and circulation cleaning of milking machines. There had been increases in herd sizes and increased production per cow; better management and breeding, especially through the increased use of artificial insemination, had led to a 20% increase in butterfat per cow.[95]

[89] New Zealand/Japan Trading Relations: New Zealand Embassy in Japan to Prime Minister, 2/3/1967, IC 26/2/1, ANZ.

[90] 'UK Still Most Important', *Straight Furrow*, 15/06/1966, 5, ATL.

[91] 'Six New Milk Powder Factories', *Straight Furrow*, 20/07/1966, 26, ATL.

[92] 'Phenomenal Growth of Dairy Industry', *Straight Furrow*, 19/10/1966, 16, ATL.

[93] 'Fewer Factory-Supply Dairy Farmers, *Straight Furrow*, 10/01/1968, 15, ATL.

[94] Bewley, 43–46. Bewley gives details of specific changes in manufacturing that enabled increased production in response to the needs of market diversification.

[95] 'Dairy Industry Revolution: On the Farm as well as In the Factory', *Straight Furrow*, 05/06/1968, 5, ATL; Bewley, 38–9, gives more detail on the techniques used to improve herds and productivity.

7.5 Finally Overcoming Inhibitions and Achieving Successful Diversification

By the early 1970s, successful adaptation had reduced the New Zealand dairy industry's dependence on the British market. Britain still provided a sheet anchor for butter and cheese sales but dairying had emerged from an entrenched colonial economy. The industry could claim that extensive reconstruction and new market diversification programmes had started well before Britain became an EEC member. There had been a significant increase in skim-milk products and casein production, and sales to markets outside Britain included a broad range of dairy products. Also, New Zealand finally lost its reservations over trade with China and found the country that would take over from Britain as New Zealand's main customer for dairy produce in the twenty-first century.

In 1968, Parsons reflected on how he saw the future for New Zealand.[96] After World War II, New Zealand had begun to widen her horizons and look to the Pacific region, where in time she would take her full place as a nation with her own culture, trade, ideas and industry. Present ties with Britain would continue to loosen as each generation emerged. Parsons saw New Zealand as part of the Pacific Basin but it had made little effort to know that region. Among the Pacific Basin developed countries, too much self-sufficiency constricted trade and threatened to create prosperity without a sound foundation. New Zealand could not be an exception; it should give up undue protectionism to promote freer trade across the Pacific Basin. Parsons said that Britain would remain New Zealand's sheet anchor in trade for many years, but New Zealand had now matured from colonial dependence; the relationship with Britain was now one of equal partnership.

Linton remained confident that the dairy industry would continue to expand. It would export 170,000 tons of butter to Britain annually up to 1972 and good outlets would be found elsewhere for increased

[96] Chairman's Address to the Annual Dairy Council Conference, 12/06/1968, Federated Farmers, 90-343, MSY-2721 Dairy Section, D40/1968, 2-3, ANZ.

production above that tonnage.[97] The aggressive marketing policy by the Dairy Board as a sole marketing organisation achieved continuing export expansion. The British market gave a secure base that enabled the Board to concentrate efforts on finding new and expanding markets. But in April 1967 the *Economic and Social Review's Quarterly Predictions* contradicted Linton's confidence by estimating that New Zealand's primary produce exports would grow by only 1 or 2% in the five years up to 1972, mainly because the British market would grow slowly. The conclusions drawn by the editor reinforced that New Zealand needed to diversify products and markets. Also, the predictions called into question New Zealand's long-term wisdom in expanding production of traditional export products such as butter and cheese.[98] Difficulties for New Zealand in exporting to the USA were emphasised once again; the dairy industry in the USA was declining annually by 5% and American dairymen were pouring milk down drains in protest against low prices and imports of dairy produce.[99]

In 1970 Under-Secretary for Agriculture, A D Dick, summarised how the New Zealand dairy industry had changed. Through selective breeding, production had been increased with Friesians, which gave a better solids-not-fat ratio, gaining ground at the expense of Jerseys.[100] The trend would continue if solids rather than butterfat products continued to become important. Amalgamation of companies formed originally at the time of horse transport had led to larger companies, manufacturing a much wider product range. The greater financial resources from amalgamation had allowed investment in mechanisation of butter and cheese production. There had been a significant increase in skim-milk products and casein production, and sale of such products to South-East Asia had increased thirty-fold in the 1960s.[101] As Bewley notes: 'Major

[97] 'Have Confidence In Your Industry: Dairy Board Chairman Sees No Real Cause for Gloom', *Straight Furrow*, 19/04/1967, 14, ATL.

[98] 'NZ Exports: Slow Growth in World Demand Forecast', *Straight Furrow*, 19/04/1967, 7, ATL.

[99] 'U.S. Farmers Fight to Limit Dairy Imports: Consequences Serious for New Zealand', *Straight Furrow*, 19/04/1967, 13, ATL.

[100] *Agricultural Policy in New Zealand*, OECD Report, February 1974, 30; Bewley, 40, discusses the relative merits of Jerseys and Friesians in terms of milk, milk-fat and beef production.

[101] Some Aspects of New Zealand Dairy Produce Export Trade, 23/04/1969, Dairy Industry – Export of Dairy Products New Zealand Policy, AAQW /WS3379 Box 11 4/1/4, 5, ANZ.

technology advances on the farm and in the factory, backed by research and advisory services over the entire dairy industry', enabled tonnages of dairy produce exports to double between the 1940s and the 1960s.[102] Charles Patrick, the Dairy Board's Assistant General Manager, wrote optimistically about the future market in Asia. The population was two billion and in thirty years would be three billion; there should be a fruitful and constructive future for everyone in international dairying.[103]

Murphy told the Auckland Dairy Factory Managers' Association in 1970 that there would be continuing growth in manufacturing new dairy products. The Dairy Research Institute carried out intensive research into 32 specific products suitable for the Middle East, South American and other markets, including milk powder that gave 'instant milk' when stirred in water.[104] The concept of dairying as just a primary and not a secondary industry had to go 'out of the window'.[105] The industry's response to technological change had been fourfold: become more competitive, extend the range of products, develop new uses, and open up new markets with products tailored to meet the markets' special needs.[106]

As 1972 started, the Dairy Board rebutted concerns that with Britain an EEC member, the industry would need extensive reconstruction and new market diversification programmes to accommodate reduced butter and cheese exports to Britain.[107] The Board claimed, justifiably, that such programmes had been in place for many years. The Board claimed that diversification had started when bulk purchase ended in 1954, and milk product sales outside Britain had increased in value by five times since 1961. Exports based on mainly butter and cheese had been replaced by the widest possible range of wholemilk products. Sales to

[102] Bewley, 36 – 49.

[103] 'Dairy Prospects in the Far East'. *Straight Furrow*, 02/12/1970, 2, ATL.

[104] 'Instant Milk', *Straight Furrow*, 07/10/1970, 19, ATL.

[105] '"Concept of Dairy Production As a Primary Industry Must Go"', *Straight Furrow*, 23/09/1970, 14, ATL.

[106] 'Mr Dick Says Dairy NZ Industry Has Ability to Face Crises', *Straight Furrow*, 25/06/1970, 19, ATL.

[107] 'Board Is Prepared for Development', *Straight Furrow*, 19/01/1972, 16, ATL.

90 markets outside Britain included several varieties of cheese, infant milk foods, milk powders of various compositions, casein and products of increasing sophistication such as caseinates. The industry had increased its product and market research considerably and now had 150 research projects in hand. For market research the Board operated through 150 agents in the 90 markets. The Board could claim, justifiably, that it had begun preparing for reduction in the British market even before British first sought EEC membership in 1961. For the 1972/1973 season, the Dairy Board could announce 'the significant stage was reached where more than half the dairy industry's export earnings came from markets other than the United Kingdom'.[108]

Freer describes the reluctance to build links with Communist China even as late as 1969 when the Labour party leader, Norman Kirk, 'was adamantly opposed to anything to do with communism'. Freer worried that New Zealand would 'find ourselves alongside the United States as the last to accept the inevitable' thereby 'losing the opportunity of getting a foot inside the most promising market in the world'.[109] Murphy told the Dairy Board in 1969 that 'Mainland China . . . is showing signs of stirring . . . a representative of the Board's interests is at present in China'.[110] When Labour won the 1972 election, Kirk finally agreed to recognise China, partly because the American President, Richard Nixon, had decided to break the ice and visit China.[111] Diplomatic relations were established at the end of 1972 followed by a New Zealand–China Trade Agreement, with Trade Commissions and Embassies established in Wellington and Beijing. In 1975, Charles Patrick of the Dairy Board, following a trade mission to China, reported that increased economic well-being had led to more variety in diet and to foods that were not customary. There were growing prospects that import of milk solids would be needed.[112] That proved to be correct,

[108] Clive Lind, *Till the Cows Came Home* (Wellington: Steele Roberts, 2013), 61.

[109] Freer, 157.

[110] Some Aspects of New Zealand Dairy Produce Export Trade, 23/04/1969, Dairy Industry – Export of Dairy Products New Zealand Policy, AAQW /WS3379 Box 11 4/1/4, 5, ANZ.

[111] Freer, 158.

[112] 'Chinese Milk Imports Possible', *Straight Furrow*, 12/12/1973, 16, ATL.

and New Zealand had at last overcome its inhibitions and found the country that eventually would overtake Britain as New Zealand's main trading partner in dairy products in the twenty-first century.[113]

7.6 Conclusion

The many attempts to build significant dairy sales to the USA foundered on protectionism. In addition, American actions in disposal of domestic surpluses threatened New Zealand's diversification into new markets, for instance, in Asia and Latin America. The ambition to build significant sales to the USA also hindered New Zealand's exploitation of the Chinese market; until 1972 it feared retribution by the USA if New Zealand recognised China diplomatically. At first in the early 1960s the new markets that would become permanent and significant were not obvious, but by 1973 New Zealand had found sufficient new markets in Asia that sales to others overtook sales to Britain. Those new markets were established by putting emphasis on selling products such as milk powder, and helping Asian buyers to set up the processing facilities that turned the powder into other dairy produce. New Zealand adapted by diversifying both products and the marketing techniques necessary to sell those products. By 1975, following the USA's change in attitude towards Communist China, New Zealand had established a dairy trading relationship with China, the country that would eventually take over from Britain as New Zealand's main customer for dairy produce.

[113] 'China: A trade burst after a shut-off era', *Straight Furrow*, 17/09/1975, 3, ATL.

8

Wool Marketing and Reform

8.1 Introduction

New Zealand wool exports were far less dependent on sales to Britain than meat and dairy exports. Unlike the meat and dairy sectors, the wool story is not a story of clinging to the British market whilst seeking to diversify into new markets. In 1949 only half of New Zealand's wool exports went to Britain and sales to Britain declined through the next two decades to about 20% in 1972 (Fig. 8.1). Sales to markets other than Britain easily made up for the reduction in sales to Britain. Chapter 8 tells the story of marketing and attempts at reform for the wool industry in three periods between 1945 and 1977. The importance of key policymakers and their motives are emphasised, together with the responses from woolgrowers' representatives and the woolgrowers themselves.

During 1945–1957, wool sales were generally profitable as marketing returned to normal after World War II and the Korean War gave a massive boost to the industry. During 1958–1964, the industry became less confident when, following a price collapse in 1958, prices refused to return to the levels of the early 1950s. During 1964–1977, prices collapsed more than in 1958, and two major attempts to reform the

D. Hall, *Emerging from an Entrenched Colonial Economy*, Palgrave Studies in Economic History, DOI 10.1007/978-3-319-53016-1_8

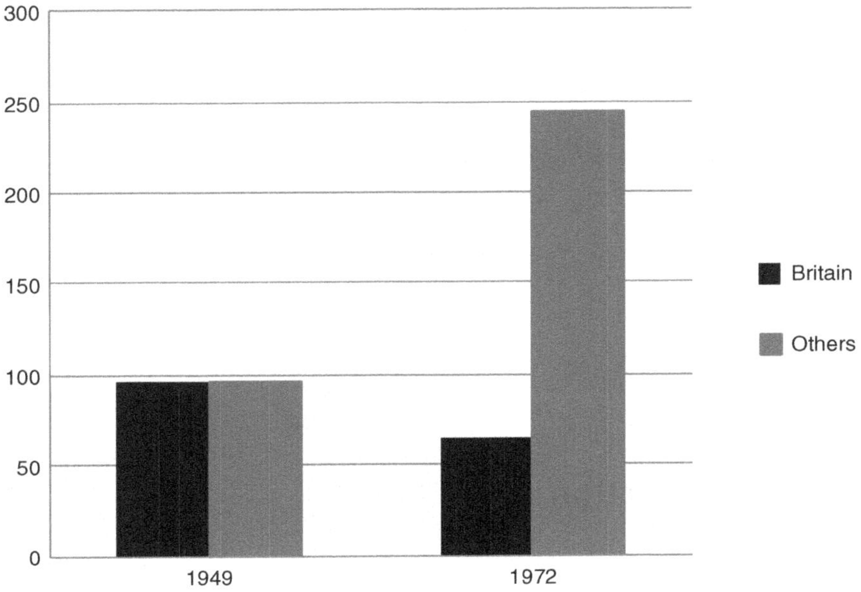

Fig. 8.1 New Zealand wool exports in tonnes (000) to Britain and others during 1949 and 1972 (NZDYB)

industry both failed. In the first period, schemes that protected growers from price collapse were introduced and welcomed by growers. That period created a generation of woolgrowers who saw little reason for change after clearance of wartime stockpiles and a reserve price scheme operated successfully. In the third period opposition within that generation held back the change seen by many, especially in the industry bureaucracy, as necessary to protect the industry's long-term future.

Unlike meat and dairy exports, wool exports were not threatened by British membership of the EEC but by competition from synthetics.[1] It was unclear how strong a threat synthetics posed but it was sufficient that it

[1] 'Synthetics' is used here as a convenient label for all types of man-made fibres and includes those adapted from natural polymers (artificial fibres) and those produced from synthetically produced polymers (synthetic fibres). Bill Carter and John MacGibbon, *Wool: A History of New Zealand's Wool Industry* (Wellington: Ngaio Press, 2003) give a very thorough description of the manufacture of man-made fibres, 186.

could not be ignored. The International Wool Secretariat (IWS) had been formed specifically in the 1930s by New Zealand, Australia and South Africa, to repel the growing threat from synthetics.[2] The IWS was set up coincidentally with the New Zealand Wool Committee, with IWS liaison an integral part of the Committee's activities. The activities transferred to the Wool Board when it replaced the Committee in 1945. The IWS operated remote from New Zealand, mainly in London, though nominally in support of New Zealand wool sales. IWS contact with New Zealand was through the Wool Board and its contact with farm-gate woolgrowers was extremely limited. Its role was never clearly understood by most growers. Growers paid for the IWS activities under the impression that it marketed their raw wool but that seems to have been a mistaken impression.

The threat from synthetics was stronger in New Zealand than other wool-producing countries because the dominant breed of sheep yielded coarse wool, the type most at risk from competition with synthetics. At first in the mid–nineteenth century, the breed on which the successful Australian industry had been established, merinos, dominated the New Zealand wool industry. But the New Zealand climate did not suit that breed, and onset of refrigeration in 1882 increased the importance of dual-purpose sheep that yielded coarser wools but gave better meat. Experience at the Mt Peel Station in Canterbury demonstrates why New Zealand moved to production of coarse wools. Merinos had problems with footrot and were replaced with cross-bred sheep that produced a 'faster maturing and better fleshed carcase for the frozen meat trade . . . did much better . . . and proved to be more profitable'. The last merino was sold off from Mt Peel in 1912.[3] The New Zealand Romney became by far the dominant breed in the mid–twentieth century, and by the mid-1960s merinos made up less than 2% of New Zealand's flock.[4]

[2] Malcolm Abbott, 'Promoting Wool Internationally: The Formation of the International Wool Secretariat', *Working Paper Series No. 9723*, December 1997, School of Economics, Victoria University Wellington; Carter and MacGibbon, 71–80.

[3] Robert Peden, *Making Sheep Country: Mt Peel Station and the Transformation of the Tussock Lands* (Auckland: Auckland University Press, 2011), 243.

[4] Iain Morrison, *New Zealand Sheep and Their Wool* (Wellington: New Zealand Wool Board, 1980); K. G. Ponting, *Wool Marketing* (Oxford: Pergamon Press, 1966), 28.

8.2 A Profitable Period

During World War II the British government purchased all New Zealand's exportable wool, an arrangement that finished within months of the War's end. After 1945 two organisations protected woolgrowers from price collapses. The first, the Joint Organisation (JO), in the late 1940s protected woolgrowers against prices being depressed by sale of stockpiles built up during World War II. The second, the New Zealand Wool Commission took over from the JO in 1952 and worked to mitigate, through a reserve price scheme, the domestic impact of price collapse. Through the 1940s and 1950s those organisations successfully enabled growers to exploit the favourable market conditions. After 1945 sales to Britain continued a decline that had started in the 1930s, but increased earnings from other countries more than compensated. In particular, prices surged at the start of the 1950s when the Korean War created an urgent need for wool in the USA. The profitability during the 1940s and early 1950s created a generation of woolgrowers who saw little reason for change.

Bulk purchase during wartime had been at prices higher than pre-war and stimulated increased production with the annual clip at the end of the war 30% higher than the average for the years 1934–1938.[5] But marketing could not return to the arrangements of pre-1939 immediately in 1945 because considerable stocks purchased by Britain during the war remained unused. Wool, unlike meat and dairy produce, did not perish and that made stockpiling an option rather than selling at low prices. Production during the War years exceeded requirements and wool stockpiled to an embarrassing extent.[6] There were fears that releasing those stocks onto the market would plunge prices for the new, post-war, clips. Consequently, a Wool Conference, held in London during April and May 1945 with representatives from New Zealand, Britain, Australia and South Africa, discussed how best to deal with the stockpiles. Edward Greensmith, a key figure in New Zealand's wool bureaucracy for three decades and in the New Zealand delegation, reports how the

---

[5] *Economist*, 9/11/1946, 758.

[6] John Baker, *The New Zealand People at War: The War Economy* (Wellington: Historical Publications Branch, 1965), 198.

stockpiles were 'a serious burden' and 'a cloud hanging over the market'.[7] The Conference's opening report warned that 'on reasonably optimistic assumptions the complete disposal of the stock, and of current clips in conjunction, may be expected to take 12 or 13 years'.[8] The Conference agreed to form a private company, UK-Dominions Wool Disposals Ltd., with the four governments nominating shareholders; that company became known as the Joint Organisation (JO). From June 1945 the JO replaced the wartime bulk purchase arrangements and attempted to prevent price collapse by an orderly disposal of stockpiles that avoided over-supply. The JO also protected woolgrowers from low prices by setting, at each season's start, a reserve price below which the organisation itself would purchase wool and hold it until prices rose.[9] Governments in each country needed to approve the reserve price but individual farmers, if they wished, could set their own reserve price above the JO's and withhold wool not sold at their own reserve.

The JO's main activities took place in London, and subsidiary bodies within the Dominions regulated selling their own surplus stocks and current clips. In New Zealand a Wool Disposal Account, set up at the Reserve Bank, received income from wool sales and funded the JO's activities – this fund became known as the Wool Industry Reserve Account.[10] For the Dominions' woolgrowers the JO ensured an orderly disposal of annual and stockpiled wool and avoided marked price fluctuations. According to Evans:

> By controlling the sale of such large quantities of wool, the JO had the effect of stabilizing the wool market during the crucial years of post–war reconstruction, and in so doing helped to prevent the economic chaos which the results of the war would undoubtedly have brought about.[11]

After World War II markets recovered from wartime disruption and created high demand for wool; the JO sold 40% of surplus stocks within

[7] Edward Greensmith, *The New Zealand Wool Commission* (Wellington: New Zealand Wool Marketing Corporation, 1996), 12.

[8] Greensmith, 12.

[9] Evans, B.L., *A History of Agricultural Production and Marketing in New Zealand* (Palmerston North: Keeling and Munday, 1969), 94.

[10] Wool Disposal Act, 1945.

[11] Evans, 96.

its first year, refuting estimates that it would take 13 years to clear stocks.[12] Changes in France demonstrated why demand soared. France needed to re-establish its export markets because its economy had been destroyed by 'the depredations of war', and by German requisition of materials and produce from France in support of its own war efforts.[13] France ran up 'massive trade deficits' to import 'essential foodstuffs, raw materials [including wool] and capital equipment'.[14] A similar situation to France held in other European countries. All significant markets for New Zealand wool were re-established before the 1940s ended (Table 8.1), and there was a significant new customer, the USSR, which had started buying wool from Britain during World War II. In the late 1940s growers had little difficulty in selling wool and prices doubled between 1945 and 1950 (Fig. 8.2).[15] New Zealand profited from the increased demand by more than £20 million.[16] When the 1940s ended New Zealand's combined sales to other countries had overtaken sales to Britain though Britain remained the strongest individual customer. In 1949 New Zealand exported tonnage 55% higher than in 1939 (Table 8.1).

In the early 1950s New Zealand sought to expand both existing markets and to expand into new markets. In 1954, New Zealand wool sold in more than 30 countries but in 1975 in only 23, perhaps telling us that in the 1950s New Zealand tried new markets but many did not become permanent, for instance, Mexico, Morocco, Syria and Turkey. The wool textile industry and its raw wool supplies by the mid–twentieth century were well established, and exports expanded during the 1950s within those well-established industries rather than to new customers.

The JO's success stimulated much discussion of a successor organisation.[17] The Federated Farmers Meat and Wool Section suggested a

[12] 'Contributory Charge on NZ Wool', *Straight Furrow*, 15/11/1946, 11, ATL.

[13] Roger Price, *A Concise History of France*, (Cambridge: Cambridge University Press, 1995), p274.

[14] Price, 277.

[15] Greensmith, 12.

[16] Evans, 96.

[17] Report to the Annual Conference of the Meat and Wool Section, 20/06/1950, Federated Farmers, 90 – 343 MSY–2730, M&W151/1950, 6–8, ATL.

Table 8.1 Pre-war and post-war wool exports (NZDYB)

	1939	1949
	Tonnes	Tonnes
Australia	6,643	2,991
Bulgaria	155	196
Belgium	8,153	5,607
Canada	3,845	6,469
China	559	27
Czechoslovakia	248	265
Denmark	368	1,424
Egypt	288	373
Finland	0	12
France	17,044	30,836
Germany	2,515	10,321
Greece	383	514
India	85	1,273
Ireland	0	196
Italy	16	3,320
Japan	3,771	2,574
Morocco	0	201
Netherlands	2,329	5,322
Norway	0	452
Poland	911	2,718
Portugal	166	0
South Africa	15	285
Sweden	1,463	1,080
Switzerland	0	19
USSR	0	10,901
UK	70,289	97,807
USA	6,545	9,352
Yugoslavia	10	257
Other countries	25	104
Total	125,825	194,893

permanent organisation to ensure orderly wool marketing – 'A future wool marketing plan is one of the most important matters concerning the sheep farmers at this present time'.[18] In late 1949 the New Zealand Wool Board agreed that the successor should be 'modelled on the present JO system' and based on 'the sale of wool at auction with the

[18] 'Activities of the Meat and Wool Section', *Straight Furrow*, 15/07/1949, 7, ATL.

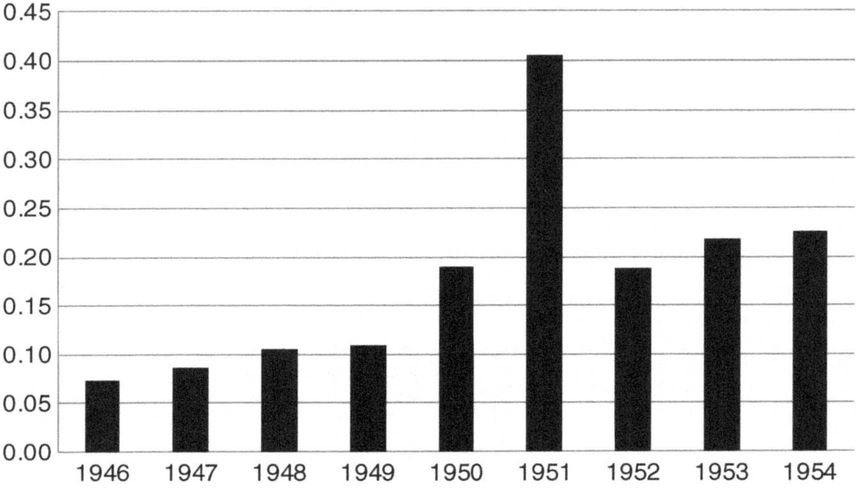

Fig. 8.2 Price of New Zealand wool in £/lb (NZDYB)

provision of a broad protective level by means of reserve prices'.[19] The Board suggested that profits from wartime bulk purchase and the post-war JO sales should be used to support a new organisation and the government agreed.

In 1949 the New Zealand Wool Board proposed a grower-controlled Commission that would purchase wool if it were not sold above a reserve price. That price would be set by the Commission at the selling season's start. Rather than farmers retaining wool that could not be sold at an acceptable price, the Commission would buy and hold the wool, anticipating selling wool later when prices rose. The Board proposed that the Commission would operate to 'set a limit to a major decline in the market'; it was a 'shock absorber on the rough road of fluctuating wool prices'.[20] Growers, justifiably, saw the money accumulated from wartime sales and disposal of post-war stockpiles as their funds. The government took a keen interest whenever the Commission stepped in to buy wool because that meant a reduction

[19] 'N.Z. Calls for Conference on Wool Marketing', *Straight Furrow*, 15/12/1949, 5, ATL.

[20] 'Post-J.O. Plan for Wool: Reserve Price Scheme Explained', *Straight Furrow*, 15/08/1951, 22, ATL; Evans, 97.

in overseas earnings if the Commission did not sell the wool quickly. But growers resented government interference; in setting up the Commission growers considered that they protected themselves using their own resources.

When choosing the appropriate reserve price the Commission took into account four main factors: current trends and prospects in international markets and in commodity prices; available financial resources; Wool Board's views; and, the need to maintain wool production in New Zealand. Also, the Minister needed to agree the prices proposed by the Commission.[21] The key periods would be times of low prices when the Commission would 'offer still greater resistance to any downward trend'.[22] Interference with the market would be minimised in open auctions, and provision would be made for a farmer to withdraw his wool if he disliked the reserve price set by the Commission. The later selling of wool purchased by the Commission would follow procedures adopted successfully by the JO – phasing sales so as not to disrupt prices. Federated Farmers discussed the plan with provincial representatives, and identified recommendations for improvements. In due course all Federated Farmers provinces but one supported the plan.[23]

In 1950/1951, two developments, over which New Zealand had absolutely no influence, came together to produce a threefold rise in wool prices (Fig. 8.2). First, the USA had become dependent on foreign wool; growing domestically only 40% of its needs.[24] Second, in June 1950 when war began in Korea, the USA needed wool stockpiles for military purposes; that wool needed to be bought overseas. New Zealand benefited as the tonnage purchased by the USA increased nearly fivefold.[25] At Parliament's opening in 1951, the Governor-

[21] Wool Commission Act 1951, 649.

[22] 'Post-J.O. Plan for Wool: Reserve Price Scheme Explained', *Straight Furrow*, 15/08/1951, 22, ATL.

[23] Annual Report of Meat and Wool Section Chairman, 25/06/1952, Federated Farmers, 90 – 343, MSY–2732, M&W118/1952, 6, ATL.

[24] 'Increasing Dependence By U.S. On Foreign Wool', *Straight Furrow*, 15/07/1950, 23, ATL.

[25] 'America Is Stockpiling Wool', *Straight Furrow*, 16/04/1951, 7, ATL.

General announced that 'great prosperity had come to New Zealand, mainly because of the prices received for our exports of primary produce, especially wool'.[26] Evans calls the early 1950s 'the golden age of wool farming'.[27] The high prices were a direct consequence of wool being sold on the open market, and the Chairman said, in his annual address to the Federated Farmers Meat and Wool Section, that 'New Zealand can rejoice that wool has been subject to world market competition'. That rejoicing coloured growers' preference for open and free marketing for at least two decades.[28] Later attempts at reform involved moves away from farmers having free choice; that produced emotional responses that reform, unacceptably, would take away farmers' freedom.

During the surge in prices brought on by the Korean War, the USA sought international control over raw materials including wool, possibly even suspending auctions.[29] At first, that had some appeal for New Zealand, South Africa and Australia, because prices might have been maintained at high levels for five years.[30] The New Zealand Minister for Agriculture, Keith Holyoake, together with officials from the Department of Agriculture, attended a conference in London to discuss the possibilities, but Federated Farmers became concerned that discussions were taking place without involving farmers. The Meat and Wool Section passed a resolution stating that any change to wool selling proposed under those circumstances would be strongly opposed.[31] Farmers urged the government to give all the information that it could before the forthcoming Meat and Wool Section annual meeting – 'Farmers generally are men of sound judgement who can be relied upon to look at the facts and come to a decision with both feet on the

[26] 'Close-up on Parliament', *Straight Furrow*, 15/11/1951, 34, ATL.

[27] Evans, 99.

[28] Address by Wool Board Chairman, 27/06/1950, Federated Farmers, 90 – 343 MSY–2730, M&W152/1950, 9, ATL.

[29] Has the Government decided to commandeer wool?, 25/06/1951, Federated Farmers, 90 – 343 MSY–2733, M&W41/1951, 2, ATL.

[30] Marketing Advisory Council Minutes, 25/08/1950, Keith Holyoake papers, MS–1814–06/5, 1, ATL.

[31] Greensmith, 34; Has the Government decided to commandeer wool?, 25/06/1951, Federated Farmers 90 –343 MSY–2733, M&W41/1951, 2, ATL.

ground'.[32] That remained a constant theme – decisions on matters associated with the wool industry should be left to woolgrowers.

The huge influx of money into New Zealand from the wool sale, unaccompanied by expansion of goods and services, threatened high inflation in 1951.[33] The government met with woolgrowers' representatives and they agreed that one-third of the farmers' income be held back and paid into accounts held for growers at the Reserve Bank. The Meat and Wool Section Chairman could claim that woolgrowers agreed to the proposals not for their own benefit but for 'the benefit of the country'.[34] In welcoming the agreement, Federated Farmers appreciated the 'true democratic way' that the Prime Minister had sought 'the opinion of a representative gathering of growers'.[35] That demonstrated the importance of making growers feel that they had a strong influence over government decisions; neglecting growers' views made opposition to change rife.

In autumn 1952 prices fell from the high level stimulated by the Korean War, and the Wool Commission operated for the first time and claimed to have mitigated the decline.[36] Federated Farmers Meat and Wool Council welcomed the steps taken by the Commission to 'strengthen the market'.[37] In 1953 the Commission set the floor price significantly lower than prices actually realised and that led to criticism that the floor price had been set too low. The Federated Farmers Meat and Wool Section Secretary suggested that a floor price should operate to 'maintain as far as is reasonably possible the purchasing power in New Zealand of growers' wool'.[38] Producers saw the 'floor price' as akin to

---

[32] 'Commodity Controls', *Straight Furrow*, 15/06/1951, 1, ATL.

[33] Address by Chairman Meat and Wool Section, 27/06/1951, Federated Farmers, 90 – 343 MSY–2733, M&W39/1951, 3, ATL.

[34] Address by Chairman Meat and Wool Section, 27/06/1951, Federated Farmers, 90 – 343 MSY–2733, M&W39/1951, 3, ATL.

[35] Address by Chairman Meat and Wool Section, 27/06/1951, Federated Farmers, 90 – 343 MSY–2733, M&W39/1951, 3, ATL.

[36] 'Commodity Controls', *Straight Furrow*, 01/06/1952, 21, ATL.

[37] Minutes of Meat and Wool Section Meeting, 30/04/1952, Federated Farmers, 90 – 343 MSY–2732, M&W105/1952, 8, ATL.

[38] Floor Price for 1953/54 Season, 06/1953, Federated Farmers, 90 – 343 MSY–2733, M&W204/1953, 2, ATL.

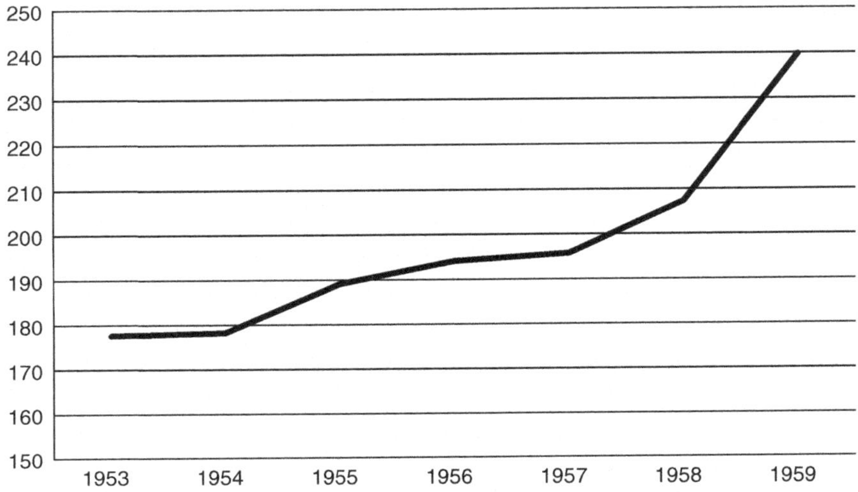

Fig. 8.3 New Zealand wool exports in tonnes (000) (NZDYB)

the 'guaranteed price' paid in the dairy industry – a means of guaranteeing them a reasonable standard of living. The Commission took the opportunity to stress that it sought only to protect against exceptionally low prices.[39] Ponting pointed out the reality that floor prices were 'regarded as a real bottom to the market and not a level designed to cover cost of production'.[40] Rather than guaranteeing a comfortable income for producers every season, the schemed aimed at preventing industry collapse during major collapse in overseas prices.

From 1953 to 1959 the wool tonnage sold by New Zealand increased by more than 40% (Fig. 8.3) because farmers were encouraged by Federated Farmers to improve their income by improving yield per acre and per man through applying science, exploiting machinery and better farming practices.[41] That improvement in productivity demonstrates growers' openness to change when change could be shown to have

[39] 'Explanation of Floor Price Scheme', *Straight Furrow*, 01/05/1953, 5, ATL.

[40] Ponting, 46.

[41] 'Reports to Conferences on Year's Activities', *Straight Furrow*, 01/07/1954, 33, ATL.

a direct impact on farming incomes. Sales increased to all significant customers apart from Britain. New Zealand's wool exports benefited from growth in textile trade amongst continental European countries, especially Western Germany, Italy and the Netherlands. Despite the New Zealand government's reluctance to recognise Communist China, wool sales to China by private sellers such as Dalgety increased ten times between 1956 and 1959. Also, Iron Curtain countries increased their consumption, especially the USSR.[42]

The long-term decline in New Zealand wool exports to Britain had started in the 1930s, caused by the decline in the British textile industry that demonstrated Britain losing its industrial pre-eminence of the late nineteenth and early twentieth centuries.[43] In addition to no longer being the world's banker, decline in the British textile industry demonstrated Britain losing its status as the world's workshop.[44] Britain's textile industry suffered partly through Britain's free trade with Commonwealth countries agreed at Ottawa in the 1930s. For textiles, imports into Britain from India, Pakistan and Hong Kong became important competitors in the domestic market, in a similar way in which imported food had become a competitor for British agriculture in the late nineteenth century.[45]

8.3 Doleful Days

After the surge during the Korean War, prices settled well above pre-World War II levels until a price collapse in 1957/1958. Prices recovered but not to the levels of the early 1950s. The Wool Board and, because of the impact on overseas earnings, the government, considered that change had become essential. Individual growers, who had farmed through the profitable and protected period of the 1940s and 1950s, complained about low

[42] 'World Summary of Wool Season's Prospects', *Straight Furrow*, 06/08/1958, 17, ATL.

[43] B. Toyne, and eleven others, *The Global Textile Industry* (London: George Allen and Unwin, 1984), 21.

[44] 'Britain Leads the World In Wool Textiles', *Straight Furrow*, 15/06/1948, 16, ATL.

[45] Geoffrey Owen, *From Empire to Europe* (London: Harper Collins, 1999), 66.

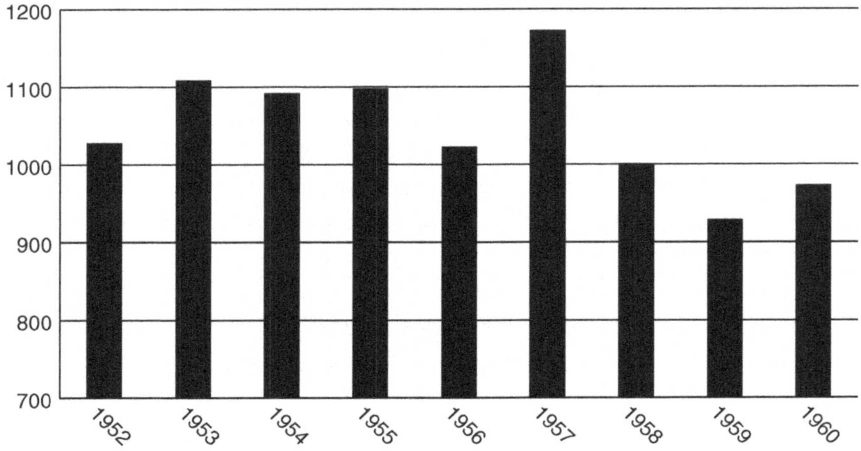

Fig. 8.4 Average wool price $/tonne (1971 prices) (NZDYB)

prices but did not want significant change. Britain's approach to the EEC in the early 1960s gave no major concern for New Zealand wool sales.

Falling demand in major wool consumers such as Britain, the USA, France and Japan caused a price collapse towards the end of the 1950s (Fig. 8.4).[46] In 1958, growing unemployment reduced sales to Britain, and in the USA wool consumption fell to the lowest level for 20 years.[47] For New Zealand wool, the tonnage sold still increased compared with previous years but the earnings fell to a level similar to pre-Korean war years. The stock and station agent, Dalgety, summarised the position best, noting that available financial resources had decreased but not the demand – prices fell until the wool was sold within the available resources.[48] The depression in prices led to calls for review of the 'chaotic' auction system for marketing wool.[49]

[46] Mr G A Duncan's Report to the Electoral Committee, 19/03/1958, Federated Farmers, 90 – 343 MSY–2736, M&W106/1958, 4, ATL.

[47] Mr G A Duncan's Report to the Electoral Committee, 19/03/1958, Federated Farmers, 90 – 343 MSY–2736, M&W106/1958, 3, ATL.

[48] '"Slump May Give Wool New Strength"', *Straight Furrow*, 16/07/1958, 12, ATL.

[49] 'Investigation of Wool Marketing Suggested', *Straight Furrow*, 07/01/1959, 5, ATL.

The fall in prices towards the end of the 1950s gave the Wool Commission its first major test; it purchased wool that otherwise would have sold below the reserve or remained unsold. The Commission later sold the wool, when prices had recovered, at a profit of $1 million.[50] The London *Economist* complimented the Commission saying that it had 'played its hand firmly and wisely'.[51] The Wool Board Chairman reported 'universal acclaim' within Britain and continental Europe for the 'support given to the market by the New Zealand Wool Commission'.[52] The Federated Farmers Meat and Wool Section Chairman identified 'one bright spot in an otherwise gloomy picture' – that was the Wool Commission operations; 'just how far prices would have gone if the Wool Commission had not been in existence no one can say'.[53]

Prices fell again by about 10% in 1958/1959 but earnings fell by only a few per cent because production increased considerably.[54] The low prices led to a discussion by the Federated Farmers Meat and Wool Section on wool marketing, which left the Southland District, for one, with 'a conviction that marketing seemed disorderly'. The District proposed changes for wool to be marketed in 'a method more in line with the requirements of the trade'. But the full Meat and Wool Section did not support the change proposed by Southland.[55] The Nelson District proposed that the Wool Board investigate if the 'auction system is the best means of selling our wool' but that, too, did not get support from the full Section.[56]

---

[50] Edward Greensmith, *The New Zealand Wool Commission* (Wellington: New Zealand Wool Marketing Corporation, 1996), 60.

[51] 'No Golden Fleece', *The Economist*, 23/08/1958, 614.

[52] 'Wool Board Chairman's Report on I.W.S. Executive Meeting', *Straight Furrow*, 03/09/1958, 11, ATL.

[53] Address by Chairman of the Meat and Wool Section, 25/06/1958, Federated Farmers, 90 – 343 MSY–2736, M&W114/1958, 2, ATL.

[54] Address by Chairman of the Meat and Wool Section, 24/06/1959, Federated Farmers, 90 – 343 MSY–2736, M&W23/1959, 1, ATL.

[55] Minutes of Meeting of Meat and Wool Section, 04/02/1959, Federated Farmers, 90 – 343 MSY–2736, M&W5/1959, 3, ATL.

[56] Minutes of Meeting of Meat and Wool Section, 24/06/1959, Federated Farmers, 90 – 343 MSY–2736, M&W26/1959, 4, ATL.

The long-term decline in Britain's textile industry was one incentive for it to join the EEC. Britain's reluctance to engage in European unification had stopped it benefiting from the growth in inter-European textile trade that took place in the 1950s.[57] But, even though wool earned 35% of New Zealand's overseas income, the prospect of British EEC membership gave the wool industry no major concern. The wool industry had little to contribute to McLuskie's Great Debate over British EEC membership. In 1960 New Zealand sold more wool to the EEC than to Britain and the Commonwealth combined. Dalgety reported the benefits of wool trade with the EEC countries: they were 'wool conscious' and prices were expected to 'make a spectacular come-back in the Common Market [EEC]' after the falls of the late 1950s.[58] *Life* reported that, should Britain join the EEC, 'there is no problem at all for the commodity [wool] which is . . . the biggest export product . . . the backbone of . . . New Zealand trade is not at stake'.[59]

New Zealand wool industry's isolation from the EEC debate is reflected further in a briefing paper prepared for Ministers, in July 1961, for the meeting with Duncan Sandys. Wool is barely mentioned apart from inclusion in one table illustrating New Zealand's trade with Britain.[60] Jack Marshall, the Minister responsible for New Zealand's EEC negotiations, says in his memoirs that:

> As time went on and it became clear that meat and dairy produce were our main concern, our consultations were usually confined to the meat and dairy boards.[61]

He rarely mentions wool when discussing EEC negotiations. Gustafson's biography of Keith Holyoake does not mention wool in

57 Owen, 57.

58 '1959 Wool Outlook More Hopeful', *Straight Furrow*, 21/01/1959, 13, ATL.

59 A Case of Butter: New Zealand Vs The Common Market, reprinted from Life Magazine, 13/07/1967, Federated Farmers 90–343 MSY–2720 D36/1967, 5, ATL.

60 Brief for the Sandys Meeting – July 1961, Cabinet Minutes 61(30) 3 July 1961 – AAFD W3738 807 Box 8, ATL.

61 John Marshall, *Memoirs Vol II; 1960–1988* (Auckland: William Collins Ltd., 1989), 62.

the chapter on Holyoake's contribution as Prime Minister to the EEC negotiations. Singleton and Robertson in discussing *Britain's First EEC Application* mention wool only when pointing out that the EEC had no plans 'to impose a tariff on raw wool'.[62]

The Wool Board Chairman, Jack (later Sir Jack) Acland, pointed out in 1967 that, for wool, synthetics threatened the industry far more than Britain joining the EEC. He said:

> Just as Britain's entry into the European Economic Community, if it occurs, will completely change our trading relationships, so has the rapid progress of the world's synthetic fibre industry already forced woolgrowers to reconsider their position'.[63]

The Wool Board noted the EEC discussions but took no strong view on New Zealand's approach.[64] Acland reported to the Federated Farmers Meat and Wool Section how the expansion of inter-European textile trade (excluding Britain), following the EEC formation, benefitted New Zealand, sales to Britain had remained static whilst sales to the EEC had increased by 30%. He said that 'the Common Market is benefitting the wool industry... if Britain joins the move may stimulate further demand'.[65] But he had reservations over Britain's membership, telling Wool Commission that 'wool was in happier position than the other products (meat and dairy)'. Nonetheless:

> Wool-growers' dependence on meat for about half their income impelled consideration of the problem of Britain and the European Common Market as a question for sheep farmers as a whole.

[62] John Singleton and Paul Robertson, *Economic Relations between and Australasia 1945–1970* (Basingstoke: Palgrave, 2002), 176.

[63] 'A Fight For Survival', *Straight Furrow*, 01/03/1967, 11, ATL.

[64] The Wool Board received reports at its meetings in 1961 but these were minor items on the Agenda. There seems to have been no major debate on the topic.

[65] Address by the Wool Board Chairman, Federated Farmers, 24/08/1961, 90 – 343 MSY–2738, M&W40/1961, 9, ATL.

The IWS, because it operated overseas and had no interest in the meat industry, had less reservation about stating how wool would benefit from British EEC membership. Immediately after Britain first sought to negotiate membership in 1961, the IWS Regional Director for Europe gave a particularly upbeat report to the Wool Board on the growing prospects for wool marketing within Europe. He noted

> a new spirit there, a Common Market spirit. There is immense prosperity. Britain has to go into the market. If the Common Market goes ahead without Britain she could outsell Britain [in textiles] within 10 years.[66]

The EEC was said to offer 'a tremendous potential for progressive trade expansion' and that proved to be the case.[67] In the early 1960s New Zealand wool sales to the EEC almost overtook sales to all other customers reaching 47% in value (Fig. 8.5).

In the early 1960s the high prices stimulated by post-war recovery and the Korean War had ended. The Wool Commission Chairman summarised in 1962 'the situation that has faced us in each year since 1957–1958 . . . has been quite different from that ruling in the earlier years of the 1950s'. He referred to the London *Economist* reporting that 'these are doleful days for commodities'.[68] The wool tonnages sold continued to increase but the earnings stabilised and even decreased. For the first time in two decades a steadily increasing output did not give a steady increase in earnings. Voices in favour of reform became stronger and the next decade was marked by two major attempts at reform led by Acland and the Wool Board.

---

[66] Address by Mr N.G.Lund, Wool Board Minutes, 21 October 1961, 1, ANZ.

[67] 'Wool – Barometer Of World Trade Prospects', *Straight Furrow*, 03/09/1958, 9, ATL.

[68] Report by the Wool Commission Chairman, 28/08/1962, Federated Farmers, 90 – 343 MSY-2738, M&W91/1962, 11, ATL.

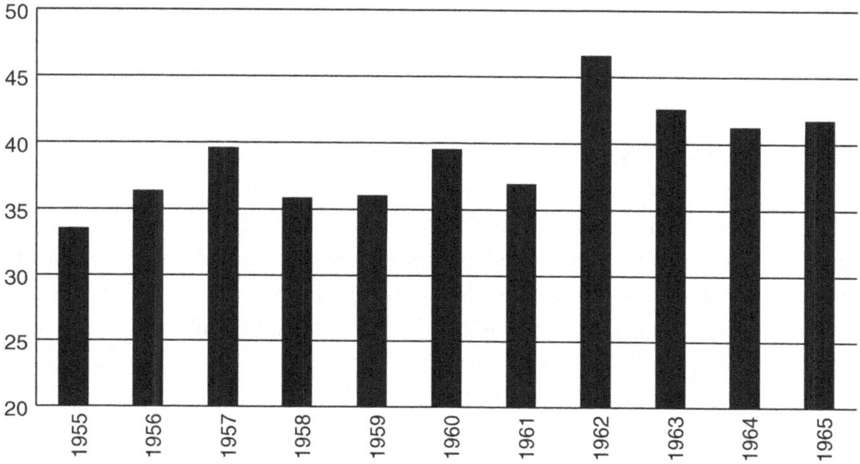

Fig. 8.5 Percentage of New Zealand wool exports sold to EEC countries (NZDYB)

8.4 An Attempt at Reform

Attempts at wool industry reform followed a fixed cycle: concern about major fluctuations in price especially decreases; studies of how to avoid the fluctuations and mitigate their impact; proposals for actual reform; and rejection of the proposals. An attempt at marketing reform started in 1964 when a sharp decline in prices followed an unexpected rise at the season's start. The Wool Board set up a Wool Marketing Study Group to investigate the causes of fluctuations and how those might be contained, including whether changes to marketing were needed.

Acland reported to the Electoral Committee in August 1964 that 'there was a ground swell of opinion . . . which is interested in methods of marketing our clip'.[69] In 1965 the Wool Board set up two groups to study wool marketing, one to consider causes of price fluctuations and

[69] Wool Marketing Study Group: Final Report, 01/11/1967, Federated Farmers, 90 – 343 MSY–2744, M&W85/1967, (iv), ATL.

the other to consider methods of selling wool other than by auction.[70] Early in 1966, the two groups became one, the Wool Marketing Study Group, when the Wool Board and the Wool Commission decided that there should be 'the first scientific study of major price fluctuations at auction' and the market situation that causes them.[71] Acland said in 1966 that finding ways to avoid fluctuations had become necessary because they made manufacturers fear that any profit made from woollen goods would be 'swallowed up by the losses caused by the fluctuations in the raw material price'. He had been warned by the US Carpet Wool Council 'that if New Zealand did not find a method of containing the price fluctuations ... the American industry would be forced to move out of wool as a carpet fibre'.[72]

Attitudes had started to change within the farming community following the low prices of the late 1950s and early 1960s, and some blamed the auction system for causing the significant wool price fluctuations. Federated Farmers Hawke's Bay branch pointed out that 'the younger farming generation was beginning to show its dissatisfaction with the method' and suggested that perhaps an appraisal system should be used with the wool price fixed by appraisers before sale. [73] The Federated Farmers North Canterbury executive also criticised auctions and Mr Uren told North Canterbury growers a negotiated price would be better.[74] He considered that the

> violent fluctuations in the price of wool were a condemnation of the present system. ... I am not happy about putting up a year's work ... for sale on a what–will–you–give–me–for–this basis. ... There was insufficient liaison between the producers and the buyers.[75]

---

[70] 'Wool Marketing Study Group', *Straight Furrow*, 07/07/1965, 12, ATL.

[71] 'Wool Auction Study', *Straight Furrow*, 02/03/1966, 10, ATL.

[72] Address by the Wool Board Chairman to the Electoral Committee, 02/03/1966, Federated Farmers, 90 – 343 M&W80/1966, 2, ATL; David Haslam, Proceedings of a Seminar on Wool Marketing in the 1980s, Agricultural Economics Research Unit, Lincoln College, Lincoln, 21 October 1976, 39.

[73] 'Wool Auction Instability', *Straight Furrow*, 16/09/1964, 38, ATL.

[74] 'Much Criticism of Auction System', *Straight Furrow*, 16/09/1964, 13, ATL.

[75] 'Farmer Criticises Wool Auctions', *Straight Furrow*, 02/06/1965, 24, ATL.

Mr Colquhoun told a Federated Farmers meeting in Wellington in 1965 that

> it should not be beyond the ingenuity of farmers . . . to devise a more up–to–date method of selling wool . . . it was hard to imagine a situation in which makers of cars, tractors or any other manufactured goods would dispose of their produce in the rough and tumble of a monthly auction, or of their increasing or decreasing their prices except in relation to their costs of production.[76]

F. G. Spackman, Chairman of the Federated Farmers Meat and Wool Section Council, said that auctions prevented manufacturers from budgeting for the season ahead with any sure knowledge of the cost of raw material. For synthetics, knowledge of the cost, and a lack of fluctuations in cost, made many textile manufacturers turn to synthetics.[77] But by 1966 the Wool Board and the Wool Commission had decided that the auction system should be kept because it was 'simple, widely supported and most effective in clearing each season's stocks of wool'. The Study Group now studied how 'big price swings might be contained' within the auction system.[78] A major price collapse in 1966–1968 encouraged reform.

8.5 The 1966/1968 Price Collapse

Prices collapsed dramatically between the end of 1966 and 1968 (Fig. 8.6). The Commission attempted to mitigate the impact for both woolgrowers and New Zealand's balance of payments but woolgrowers recognised only the need for the former. The reserve price had to be changed in mid-season because of the loss of overseas income and deficiency payments were introduced for woolgrowers. Federated

[76] '"Rough and Tumble" Wool Auctions', *Straight Furrow*, 19/05/1965, 5, ATL.
[77] 'Are Wool Auctions the Best System', *Straight Furrow*, 05/01/1967, 22, ATL.
[78] 'Wool Auction Study', *Straight Furrow*, 02/03/1966, p10, ATL.

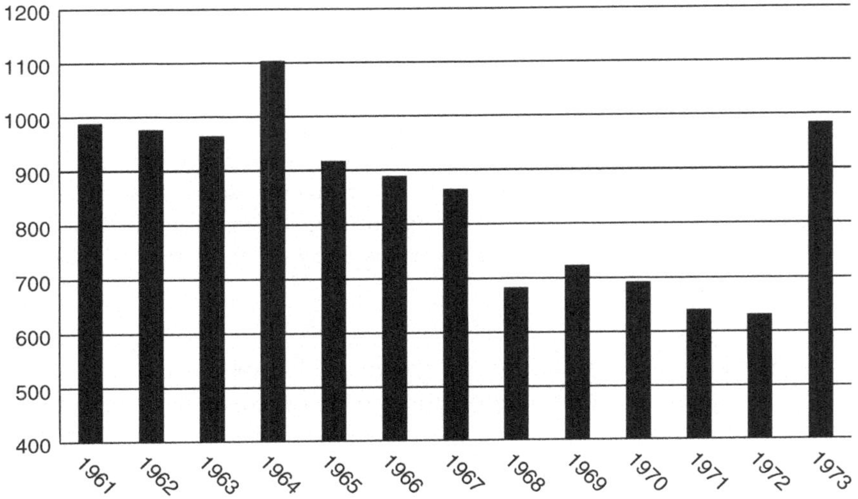

Fig. 8.6 Average wool price in $/tonne (1971 prices) (NZDYB)

Farmers sought to condemn the actions of the Commission and the government but eventually recognised the necessity of their actions.

The price collapse brought home to woolgrowers that their world had changed. Evans has given the most convincing explanations for the collapse, suggesting that severe economic restraints in Britain, France and Germany together with demand for carpet wool reduced by competition from synthetics.[79] Buchanan identifies the latter as a major cause not fully appreciated at the time; New Zealand had become over-dependent on selling coarse wool used mainly for carpets. [80] Coarse wool suffered more than other types in the competition with synthetics, especially in the USA. The USA, together with Britain, accounted for 75% of the world's carpet production and both markets for raw wool declined.[81]

[79] Evans, 99.

[80] Roger Buchanan, *The Last Shepherd: Anecdotes and Observations from five decades in the Wool Industry* (Wellington: Ngaio Press, 2012), 84.

[81] Wool Board Chairman' Address to the Electoral Committee, 02/03/1966, Federated Farmers, 90 – 343 MSY–2742, M&W80/1966, 4, ATL.

From the start of the price collapse in 1966 until June 1967 the Wool Commission spent more than £31 M buying wool which normally would have sold to overseas buyers.[82] Easton graphically describes the collapse and its longer-term impact:

> The great earthquake hit New Zealand in December 1966, in the Wool Exchange in Auckland. Bidding for wool was weak, prices collapsed, and the Wool Commission found itself buying in much of the clip – over a third by the end of the season. Except for the brief period of the international commodity price boom in 1972 and 1973, relative wool prices have never returned to their level of the 1960s – let alone the boom levels of the early 1950s.[83]

Evans concluded that it was 'only by dint of extensive purchases by the Wool Commission [that] . . . a situation . . . calamitous both for the industry and the nation was averted'.[84] The considerable quantities purchased by the Commission threatened to swamp the storage space in New Zealand. Even more importantly, the reduction in overseas sales intensified balance of payment difficulties and alerted the government to take more interest in the wool industry. Bill Carter and John MacGibbon describe the Wool Commission purchase of wool as 'woolgrowers depriving the rest of the country of the benefit of export income'.[85] Holyoake broadcast in Australia that New Zealand's floor price arrangement of buying in domestically at low prices had meant that the country had earned $100 M less than expected and Holyoake warned Australia against introducing such a plan.[86]

The need for New Zealand to change to production of finer wools increasingly became a topic discussed by producers. But in 1967 Acland

[82] Address to the Electoral Committee by the Wool Commission Chairman, 16/03/1967, Federated Farmers MSY–1944, M&W20/1967, 3–4, ATL.

[83] Brian Easton, *In Stormy Seas: The Post–War New Zealand Economy* (Dunedin: University of Otago Press, 1997), 48.

[84] Evans, 21.

[85] Carter and MacGibbon, 137.

[86] 'Incredible', *Straight Furrow*, 18/10/1967, 1, ATL.

saw no evidence 'yet to justify a shift to finer wools' and, in any case, if there was over-supply of coarse wools, 'our industry is sufficiently flexible to grow the finer wools'.[87] In May 1967, Bill Vines, the IWS Managing Director, had told 'woolbrokers, bankers and diplomats' in London that the time 'may' come when New Zealand needed to 'change its breeding policy... to produce finer wools'.[88] That led to major criticism by Spackman who ignored that Vines had said 'may'. Spackman said that the New Zealand investment in the IWS had been wasted and 'Mr Vines' statement is an admission of defeat for IWS' in failing to promote New Zealand's wools.[89]

During the price collapse Marshall sought advice on the causes and the future prospects for New Zealand wool. He met IWS representatives in London because it had 'better access to information' and held opinions 'likely to be more reliable than anyone else's'.[90] Vines gave his interpretation of the causes, saying that there were fewer end-uses for the coarse wools New Zealand produced. New Zealand wools, used mainly for carpets, had suffered most from global economic uncertainty. In addition, the demand for coarse wools for clothing had fallen with better heating of homes, transport and factories. The decline in prices for synthetic products that competed with New Zealand wool reduced wool prices. Finally, buyers' resources were inadequate to pay for increased wool production unless prices fell.

The day before meeting the IWS, Marshall had met synthetics industry's representatives and sought their views on future trends in fibre marketing. In 1966 Marshall had supported using synthetics in the New Zealand textile industry. They were 'part of life today... it would be short-sighted to deny manufacturers and consumers access to them'.[91] New Zealand woolgrowers disliked those remarks but Marshall

[87] 'No Evidence to Justify a Shift to Finer Wools', *Straight Furrow*, 05/04/1967, 18, ATL.

[88] 'The Story That Started it All', *Straight Furrow*, 03/05/1967, 7, ATL.

[89] 'Chairman's Statement Reflects Wool–growers Concern', *Straight Furrow*, 03/05/1967, 7, ATL.

[90] Transcript of Meeting in London 13 June 1967 at Wool House, AAQW – WW3379 Box 39 Part 1, 1–36, ANZ. The following five paragraphs are a summary of that transcript.

[91] 'Consumers Should Have Access to Synthetic Fibres', *Straight Furrow*, 16/11/1966, 19, ATL.

demonstrated that the government at least faced the reality of future textile production. Meeting with both the IWS and the synthetics industry showed Marshall sought a balanced view of the problems of New Zealand's wool industry during the mid-1960s.

The IWS reported clear trends against products that used New Zealand wool. New Zealand did not produce 'ideal carpet wool'; it lacked 'resilience and fullness'. Carpet manufacturers used New Zealand carpet wool only when blended with other wools. Marshall asked if New Zealand should change to producing finer wools. The IWS, aware of the criticism two months earlier, did not want to make a definitive statement on 'this highly contentious topic' but repeated that the fewer end-uses for coarse wool made the commercial situation 'more hazardous'. More than a year later, the Wool Board's Scientific Adviser proposed changing to new breeds but failed to persuade the Board, which responded that 'more benefit would probably be gained by reducing defects in wool rather than by encouraging growers to produce finer-wooled sheep'.[92]

During the 1966–1968 price collapse, the woolgrowers' reactions to attempts by the Wool Commission and the government to protect both growers and the national economy demonstrated woolgrowers' detachment from activities at a distance from the farm-gate. Growers put pressure on the Wool Commission to prevent it lowering the floor price for the 1967/1968 season and Spackman issued a press statement to emphasise growers' strong feelings.[93] He reported a resolution agreed at the May 1967 Federated Farmers Meat and Wool Section meeting: growers were 'gravely concerned at any suggestion of a reduced reserve (floor) price in the coming season'. Growers warned that lowering the floor price reduced farmers' incomes and led to a 'serious levelling off of production'. Marshall said at a press conference following his meeting with the IWS in London that 'it was important that we should fix a realistic price to ensure that next season's wool is sold [to overseas buyers]'.[94] Growers interpreted Marshall's remarks as the government

[92] New Zealand Wool Board: further records: Minute Book, MSY–5859, 02/10/1968, 2–3, ATL.

[93] Press Statement, 03/05/1967, Federated Farmers, 90 – 343 MSY–2744, M&W31/1967, ATL.

[94] 'Government Does NOT Fix Wool Price', *Straight Furrow*, 05/07/1957, 8, ATL.

trying to force a reduction in the floor price for the following season, and that triggered another press statement from Spackman complaining that Marshall's statement might be seen as 'direction to the Commission' on the price that should be set.[95]

The Commission set a reduced floor price for the 1967/1968 season against growers' wishes, and faced much criticism that stopped it setting an even lower price. Acland, in addition to being the Wool Board Chairman, was a Wool Commission member and in August 1967 had to defend the reduced price in his report to the Electoral College.[96] He told the College that he understood the 'bitter reaction' but the reduced floor price was 'the best that could be hoped for in the circumstances'. He understood that if the floor price became the market price there would be hardship for many farmers. But the price would 'get wool moving. . . . We can only trust that it holds good'. Acland advised growers to 'keep cool and keep busy'; the IWS would do 'everything that they can' to stimulate interest in New Zealand wools. That would not have given producers much comfort; the price collapse had followed the IWS operating for three years with a considerably increased budget for promotion.

At the 1967/1968 season's first auctions, the Commission purchased considerable quantities despite the reduced floor level; at the Dunedin sales the Commission found it needed to purchase more than 50%.[97] In August, before the main selling season, Greensmith, as Chairman of the Wool Commission, already feared that the floor price had been set too high: 'even now it is not certain whether the Commission's support is still somewhat high'.[98] *Straight Furrow* called Friday, 13 October 1967, 'Black Friday' when, after consultation with the government and the Wool Board, the Commission reduced the reserve price (but not the

[95] Press Statement, 15/06/1967, Federated Farmers, 90 – 343 MSY–2744, M&W34/1967, ATL.

[96] Wool Board Chairman's Report to the Electoral Committee, 24/08/1967, Federated Farmers, 90 – 343 MSY–2744, M&W64/1967, 10/12, ATL.

[97] Federated Farmers, 90-343, MSY–2744, M&W74/1967, *Wool – Survey of Floor Price Policy*, 31/10/1967, 1/4.

[98] Wool Commission Chairman's Report to the Electoral Committee, 24/08/1967, Federated Farmers, 90 – 343 MSY–2744, M&W65/1967, 10, ATL.

'floor price' paid to farmers) – a step that the Commission had been adamant would never happen to avoid future speculation driving down the reserve price.[99] Growers blamed government intervention for Black Friday. The initial low floor price together with the eventual need to reduce the reserve price produced a storm of protest, first directed at the government but eventually at the Commission and Greensmith, for giving way to government pressure. Rex Weber, a New Zealand wool-buyer and founder member of the Wool Merchants' Federation, illustrates the attitudes within the industry. In describing his experiences during 1967, Weber calls Greensmith 'a typical public servant of the kind so prevalent then'. Weber thought Greensmith 'knew little or nothing about our industry' – an unfair criticism of someone who had spent more than two decades in organisations protecting growers from price collapse.[100] Greensmith had been Secretary to the Treasury from 1955 to 1965 and Deputy Secretary before that, and well versed in the needs of New Zealand's export economy.

The reserve price reduction during the 1967/1968 season succeeded in reducing the tonnage that the Commission needed to buy and earned overseas exchange instead. To make up the difference for wool sold below the farmers' floor price, the Commission made supplementary (deficiency) payments for the first time. That brought criticism that the Commission made farmers feel degraded at having to accept subsidies, the lack of which the farming community in New Zealand always felt proudly distinguished their farming from agriculture elsewhere in the world. Greensmith understood the industry sufficiently well to say 'To many ruggedly individualistic growers anything savouring of a subsidy, even if from their own moneys, was obnoxious'.[101]

Spackman argued that the government should not interfere. He said that farmers' reserve funds financed the Wool Commission operations; taxpayers had not contributed. The government interference had 'delivered a death blow' to any future operation of the floor price scheme; a

---

[99] '"Black Friday" for Woolgrowers', *Straight Furrow*, 18/10/1967, 1, ATL.

[100] Rex Weber, *Wool Man* (Queen Charlotte Sound: Cape Catley Ltd, 1992), 70.

[101] Greensmith, 77.

complete Commission reorganisation would be needed. Spackman said growers' views on the Commission's future operation must be made known to the Meat and Wool Section Executive. In particular, would growers accept market realisation for their wool rather than see farmers' reserves run down through deficiency payments? Spackman said that Federated Farmers had always opposed deficiency payments in the past. He called a special Meat and Wool Council meeting, and the strength of feeling before the meeting is illustrated in the remit proposed by the Waikato District: 'this Section has lost confidence in the Wool Board, Wool Commission and the government as a result of the decision to reduce drastically the floor price scheme as understood by the farmer'.[102]

The special Council meeting had been called to oppose the Wool Commission actions. But the Council agreed that it 'reluctantly recognised' the steps taken and asked that the 'whole situation be reconsidered' before the next selling season. The Council concluded by 'supporting' the government finance loan at 1% interest agreed to allow the Commission to introduce its changes. Clearly, the Council did not want to approve the Commission and the government actions; but neither did it want to condemn steps that had been taken to make sure producers did not lose from the change forced on the Commission. Two weeks after 'Black Friday' it seemed less black to the Federated Farmers Executive and Meat and Wool Council. The remit declaring a loss of confidence in the Commission, Wool Board and government, together with a proposal that growers accept the market realisation with no deficiency payments, were dropped. Council members recognised that both farmers and overseas exchanges had been protected but it had taken considerable effort from the Commission and the Board to gain that recognition.

Five months later in March 1968 Greensmith could claim that growers now accepted the deficiency payments as satisfactory. Growers' incomes were 10% higher than if they had been paid the

[102] Agenda for the Special Meeting of the Meat and Wool Council, 31/10/1967, Federated Farmers, 90 – 343 MSY–2744, M&W74/1967, 2, ATL.

market realisation.[103] Greensmith pointed out that the Commission would not sell at loss wool purchased in the 1966/1967 season and would avoid conflict with sales of wool produced for 1967/1968. The Commission's decision to change the reserve price had been justified. But the episode left a prejudice against Greensmith and the Commission of which Weber's comments on Greensmith is one example. Prices increased sufficiently in 1968/1969 that the Commission could sell nearly half its stockpile at a profit without depressing the price for the new clip.[104] The Commission more than recovered its outlay through selling its stockpile in later years. The 1966/1968 hiatus spurred the marketing reform debate. Writing in 1969, Evans said that those responsible for production, processing and marketing 'must have no scruples about taking strong and imaginative – even drastic – action'.[105]

8.6 Prices Recover and Proposals for Reform are Rejected

The Wool Marketing Study Group finally reported at the depth of the price collapse between 1966 and 1968. But by the time specific proposals for reform were put forward in 1969 prices had recovered and the proposals were rejected.

The Study Group concluded that cyclical changes in the economies of wool-consuming countries caused fluctuations in raw wool consumption by woollen mills and those led to price fluctuations. Basically, economic changes outside New Zealand's control and not auctions caused fluctuations; mitigating the impact of price fluctuations within New Zealand was necessary.[106] The Group recommended that the system in place for

[103] Wool Commission Chairman's Address to the Electoral Committee, 19/03/1968, Federated Farmers, 90 – 343 MSY–2746, M&W15/1968, 1–14, ATL.

[104] Address to the Electoral Committee, 20/08/1969, Federated Farmers, 90 – 343 MSY–2747, M&W64/1969, 1, ATL.

[105] Evans, 103.

[106] Wool Marketing Study Group: Final Report, 01/11/1967, Federated Farmers, 90 – 343 MSY–2744, M&W85/1967, 26, ATL.

the dairy industry should be used for the wool industry, with a Wool Marketing Authority acquiring all wool grown in New Zealand at a price announced at the season's start. The Authority would then sell the wool through the existing auction system with the Authority's activities self-balancing over a period of years, as for the dairy industry. Standard wool types would be established within New Zealand, with the types standardised through objective measurement of fibre length, fibre diameter and staple length. The main difficulty for the Authority would be selecting the price to be paid to growers, and the report analysed thoroughly the many factors that would have to be taken into account.[107]

The Wool Board and the Wool Commission responded to the report by setting up a high-level Marketing Committee to assess the recommendations and propose legislation. The Marketing Committee included the Chairmen of the Board, the Commission, Federated Farmers Meat and Wool Section and the Electoral Committee. Delegates to the Meat and Wool Section meeting in February 1968 gave growers' views on the report. Most growers opposed compulsory acquisition by a monopoly organisation: they wanted to retain grower independence and to avoid government control. Growers demanded a referendum before adopting any plan. Only 5 of the 28 delegates expressed significant support for the overall plan.[108]

The government favoured establishing a marketing authority but left the decision to the wool industry. The Minister for Agriculture, Brian Talboys, said the government would not impose reorganisation but he thought the industry needed a centralised marketing operation similar to that in the dairy industry. In July 1968 he said that the real problem for wool marketing was

> our willingness or reluctance to accept change. . . . The present system was established in another age when journeys which today takes hours were

[107] Wool Marketing Study Group: Final Report, 01/11/1967, Federated Farmers, 90 – 343 MSY–2744, M&W85/1967, 70–82, ATL.

[108] Summary of views expressed by Delegates on the Wool Marketing Study Group Report, 14/02/1968, Federated Farmers, 90 – 343 MSY–2745, M&W8/1968, 1–4, ATL.

> measured in months and in an age when the romance of wool still carried emotional appeal. . . . The mystique of wool buying has been shattered by the cold-blooded logic that produces wool's competitors. But the emotional appeal is still strong.[109]

With hindsight, Talboys view aptly summarised the wool marketing reform debates between 1964 and 1977.

In November 1968 the wool textile industry emerged from the 1966–1968 price collapse and the sense of crisis stimulated by the collapse had passed. Buchanan describes how interest in market reform fluctuated in keeping with fluctuations in prices, and that woolgrowers lost their 'appetite for wool marketing reform when there is a substantial lift in wool prices'.[110] Neill notes a similar impact on New Zealand's trade policy more generally: 'When commodity prices enjoyed periods of high returns, change took a back seat'.[111] Wool prices advanced markedly at 1968/69 season's start and the Wool Commission no longer needed to buy wool.[112] The improvement coincided with the Marketing Committee giving its decision on the new marketing scheme – the scheme's implementation was important; growers would benefit from consistent pricing, objective measurement and collective marketing. But 'change would require strong support from a substantial majority of woolgrowers, and this is not apparent at present'. [113] Also, opposition from 'growers, brokers, buyers, merchants and processors' made it untimely to proceed with the proposed Authority.[114] The Committee showed their disappointment and included in their report that they considered that 'many of the criticisms arise from sectional interests. They have failed to take into account the over-riding national interest.'

[109] 'The Real Problem of Wool Marketing', *Straight Furrow*, 24/07/1968, 22, ATL.

[110] Buchanan, 296.

[111] Carol Neill, *Trading Our Way: Developments in New Zealand's Trade Policy 1930s to 1980s*, Doctoral Book, Massey University, Palmerston North, 2010, 292.

[112] 'Review Of The Wool Sales', *Straight Furrow*, 27/11/1968, 3, ATL.

[113] 'Marketing Authority for Wool Desirable but Not Timely', *Straight Furrow*, 08/01/1969, 1, ATL.

[114] 'One Wool Marketing Authority Plan Defended', *Straight Furrow*, 08/01/1969, 3, ATL.

The Wool Board and Wool Commission pussyfooted around the issues. They were convinced that change was necessary, but recognised that growers would not accept significant change. In a joint report the Board and Commission stated that it was not for them to propose a new marketing plan but they did exactly that, claiming 'merit in . . . having a comprehensive statement of present and proposed marketing activities'.[115] The joint report made several proposals for improvements but shied away from mentioning acquisition by a monopoly organisation. The nearest approach to that topic called for study of auctions to be compared with other selling methods. Many proposals were made for improving wool handling and preparation within New Zealand; the overall objective 'could be . . . to ensure that wool is sold . . . such that the preferences of users of wool is increased to the utmost', and to ensure that by 'keeping related costs to a minimum, growers obtain maximum net proceeds'. Another significant proposal called for extra promotion of New Zealand raw wool sales overseas.

In April 1969 the Federated Farmers Meat and Wool Council discussed thoroughly the Wool Marketing Study Report. Several delegates claimed that farmer 'apathy' and a 'lack of understanding of the factors behind the recommendations' caused opposition. There was dissatisfaction with the proposals but some saw 'a more evident dissatisfaction at the lack of progress in the industry making up its mind'.[116] Rangitikei wanted the Council to agree that there should be a growers' referendum before introduction of an acquisition scheme but the Council simply 'approved the recommendations of the Wool Marketing Committee'.[117] Spackman, as Meat and Wool Section Chairman, had been Wool Marketing Committee member and he, too, avoided using the word acquisition, but said that:

[115] Marketing Programme of the New Zealand Wool Board and the New Zealand Wool Commission, 26/11/1968, AALR W5427 873 Box 774, 1–13, ANZ.

[116] 'Ignorance And Apathy Colour Attitudes To Wool Marketing', *Straight Furrow*, 07/05/1969: 17, ATL.

[117] Minutes of the Meat and Wool Section Council Meeting, 30/04/1969, Federated Farmers, 90 – 343 M&W24/1969, 4, ATL.

> Major change could not be made until there was a greater grower understanding of the need for participation in marketing... growers should concern themselves with all aspects of wool marketing so that they can determine whether the present system is adequate for modern day business methods.[118]

Towards the end of 1969 a 'sheepfarmer', Mr Taylor of Windwhistle, summarised the objections to change in a letter to *Straight Furrow*. He objected to the 'propaganda' favouring reform proposals by the Wool Board and Wool Commission and concluded:

> Let us not, as sheep farmers, be deceived by the grandiose schemes designed either by the producer boards or government bureaucracies which in the end will destroy our freedom.[119]

Acland said that 'far too much emotion, deliberate misunderstanding and heat have been put into arguing the pros and cons of appraisal and purchase'.[120] But warning a farmer about a potential threat to his freedom raised far more interest than telling him that he should take more interest in modern business methods. Despite the opposition, some recommendations were implemented, for instance, objective wool measurement to standardise wool types. The reform attempt between 1964 and 1969 concluded with major marketing reform laid aside. But for the Wool Board only temporarily, the Board continued to develop its own marketing plan, working 'behind closed doors on ... legislation for the proposed wool marketing authority with powers of acquisition'.[121]

---

[118] Annual Address of the Chairman of the Meat and Wool Section, 18/06/1969, Federated Farmers, 90 – 343 MSY–2745, M&W31/1969, 1, ATL.

[119] 'Wool Marketing Authority, *Straight Furrow*, 03/09/1969, 21, ATL.

[120] Chairman's Report to the Electoral Committee, 28/08/1969, Federated Farmers, 90 – 343 MSY–2745, M&W61/1969, 13, ATL.

[121] Carter and MacGibbon, 206.

8.7 A Second Attempt at Reform Including Compulsory Acquisition

At first in the 1970s, reducing costs within New Zealand became the prime focus for improving the net return to farmers, but another attempt at major marketing reform quickly followed. At one point, the government, the Wool Board, the Wool Commission, the Electoral Committee and the Federated Farmers Meat and Wool Section, all supported the proposed reform. The continuing low prices during the early 1970s had gradually convinced the wool industry that marketing reform had become necessary. As part of the reform, the Wool Board wanted compulsory acquisition but, at first, disguised its intentions.

Wool production stabilised at the start of the 1970s with low and unchanging prices; increased income from higher production no longer compensated for increased costs.[122] Inefficiencies marked wool handling from the farm-gate to the auction to the dump store to the ship. According to S. G. Muir, the shipping coordinator for Auckland, fragmentation of the industry caused each New Zealand wool bale to be handled 47 times from the 'fall of the auctioneer's hammer to the ship's side'.[123] He said (no doubt describing the frustrations of his job) that there was no direct line from the wool shipper to the ship. Finding and assembling shipments was far more difficult than the loading at the dockside. The arrangements had grown haphazardly during the industry's development and steps were needed to improve their efficiency. The New Zealand Woolbuyers' Association suggested that 'the root cause' of the problems was the fragmented supply from 40,000 growers to 100 private merchants and 42 brokers' stores.[124]

The depressed earnings in the early 1970s once again stimulated a new reform cycle starting with demand by growers for significant reform. A Meat and Wool Electoral Committee member, Bruce Dryden, summarised woolgrowers' attitudes to marketing reform. He

[122] 'Season's clip will be down', *Straight Furrow*, 08/04/1970, 3, ATL.

[123] 'Handling of wool blamed for delays', *Straight Furrow*, 08/09/1971, 17, ATL.

[124] 'Woolbuyers Offer Marketing Plan', *Straight Furrow*, 06/10/1971, 10, ATL.

said that the Wool Study Group's proposals of the late 1960s provided the basis for future discussion but had suffered because over-enthusiastic supporters had pushed for immediate reform. Dryden thought wool-growers would be interested in any new scheme as long as it improved their share of the product's end value. But growers would refuse to consider any acquisition scheme outside grower control and would refuse to consider any scheme not accompanied by 'full working details'.[125] The Minister of Agriculture at the same meeting said that the present wool marketing system, unsatisfactorily, did not indicate clearly enough to growers the wool type required by consumers, and did not persuade buyers to meet consumers' demands. Also, in the present system the wool's value was assessed haphazardly. He asked rhetorically, what had become of the Study Group's report?[126]

The Federated Farmers Dominion Council asked the Wool Board formally to propose a plan for wool marketing claiming that 'nothing that the Board has implemented thus far has gone to the heart of the low-price problem'.[127] Wool leadership was 'on trial . . . the jury are getting restless'.[128] The Electoral Committee criticised the long wait since the Study Group reported and plans were 'well overdue'.[129] In April 1971 – for the first time – two Electoral Committee members proposed a no-confidence vote in the Wool Board because the Wool Board had not brought forward proposals for improved marketing procedures as had been expected in 1970. The proposal was heavily defeated but it was recognised that the proposers represented a significant number of farmers.[130]

In mid-1970 the Wool Board set up a Marketing Committee whose brief included studying 'further marketing improvements'. At least one

[125] 'Growers Claim They Are Not Getting Fair Share of Wool's Value', *Straight Furrow*, 27/05/1970, 6, ATL.

[126] 'Minister Claims Present System Not Satisfactory', *Straight Furrow*, 27/05/1970, 7, ATL.

[127] 'Federation Asks Wool Board to Present A Plan for Marketing', *Straight Furrow*, 30/07/1970, 4, ATL.

[128] 'Wool Leadership on Trial', *Straight Furrow*, 26/08/1970, 3, ATL.

[129] 'Wool Marketing Under Attack', *Straight Furrow*, 09/09/1970, 6, ATL.

[130] 'Wool Board Survives No Confidence Move', *Straight Furrow*, 07/04/1971, 8, ATL.

member thought that 'compulsory pools, or some form of acquisition, would be required ultimately'.[131] The Board hesitated on when to disclose its plans. It wanted to announce its intention to establish a 'marketing authority' in response to the questioning of whether the Board prepared for marketing reform but, nervously, hesitated because the plans were not finalised. 'Firm answers' to questions could not be given because that risked 'arousing fears in the trade which could be harmful to the market'. The Board decided that 'nothing should be said about a new authority'.[132] The Board would have been aware of the confusion in Australia where debate on a marketing authority, with powers of compulsory acquisition, demonstrated opposition from growers and banks, and the 'dissatisfaction' threatened the position of the Australian Wool Board's chairman.[133] Before 1970 ended 'the Australian Wool Scene' had become a 'jungle of bewilderment'.[134] New Zealand Wool Board members still thought 'the concept proposed by the Wool Marketing Study Group . . . was the right one' and the Marketing Committee recommended a 'compulsory pooling system'. The Board Member, Douglas Bremner, thought that the Board lacked the staff to convert the concept to an innovative marketing scheme and perhaps independent consultants were needed.[135]

In late 1970, when asked whether New Zealand's growers were sufficiently interested to support 'new, effective and wide-ranging changes', the Wool Board Manager mused that 'growers are ready to see improvements in the marketing system' and 'growers, brokers, dealers and buyers' all thought a wool authority as proposed in 1967 necessary. But the Wool Commission Manager remained unconvinced and saw apathy: 'Growers do not seem to be really aware of today's market realities . . . meat is relatively more important . . . growers have on

[131] New Zealand Wool Board: further records: Minute Book, MSY–5860, 01/07/1970, 6, ATL.

[132] New Zealand Wool Board: further records: Minute Book, MSY–5860, 10/08/1970, 2–3, ATL.

[133] 'Australian Wool Wrangle: Gunn to go?', *Straight Furrow*, 09/09/1970, 14, ATL.

[134] 'Australian Wool Scene: A Jungle of Bewilderment', *Straight Furrow*, 07/10/1970, 9, ATL.

[135] New Zealand Wool Board: further records: Minute Book, MSY–5860, 07/10/1970, 10, ATL.

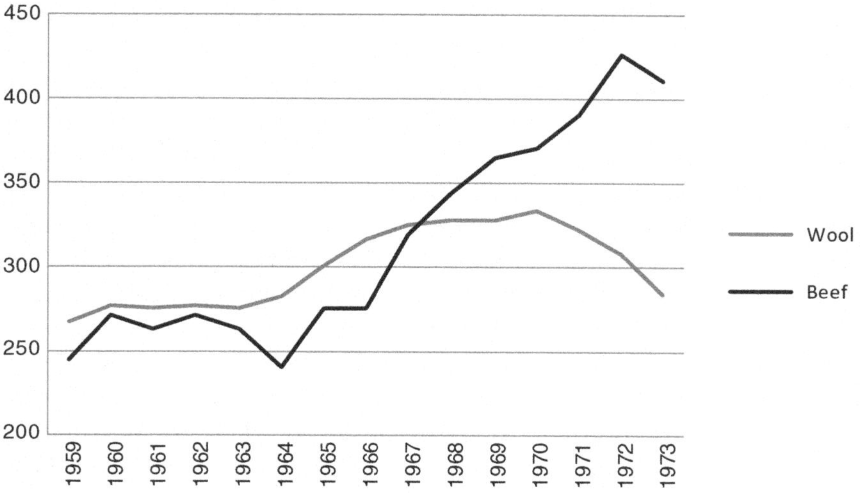

Fig. 8.7 Changes in production of wool and beef tonnages (000) (NZDYB)

the wool side . . . thrown in the sponge'.[136] The OECD noted New Zealand growers increasingly 'diversifying . . . into beef cattle', a change that can be seen in Fig. 8.7.

New Zealand produced high wool tonnages in the late 1960s but those began to fall as beef production accelerated.[137] The Acland family farm eventually changed sufficiently from woolgrowing to meat production that Jack Acland's son, John, became chairman of the Meat rather than the Wool Board. The Wool Board's Science Adviser concluded that 'sheep farmers' concentrated more on 'meat production rather than wool'.[138] The importance of meat production dissuaded growers from changing to sheep that produced finer wools but reduced meat productivity. The Wool Board anticipated that there would be change in the balance between breeds in the 1970s, with a reduction of Romneys, but not to sheep that gave fine wools but to

[136] 'Depressed Wool Prices and How to Improve Returns', *Straight Furrow*, 19/11/1970, 5, ATL.
[137] *Agricultural Policy in New Zealand*, OECD Report, February 1974, 26.
[138] New Zealand Wool Board: further records: Minute Book, MSY–5860, 01/07/1970, 8, ATL.

cross-breeds from Romneys, such as Coopworths and Perendales that gave better meat production.[139]

Acland reported to the Electoral Committee in April 1971 that the fall in prices and the increases in costs had changed attitudes towards reform. He noted a 'marked change . . . towards reform. . . . Woolgrowers, brokers, buyers and others are ready to accept more planning and control in most aspects of marketing'.[140] But the Board shied away from pushing through the reform that it saw as necessary. It sought additional ammunition to support change by engaging an organisation from outside New Zealand – the Battelle Memorial Institute from the USA – to investigate the organisation, structure and financial requirements of the wool growing industry in New Zealand; the effectiveness of the communication between the market and the producer; and the pricing mechanism and the marketing process after sale. The Board's marketing ideas became firmer but it postponed final decisions until after Battelle reported.[141] The Board decided it should let Battelle know 'the way in which its thoughts were developing' which suggests that the Board had already decided on the necessary reform and hoped that Battelle would provide independent support. Carter and MacGibbon suggest that the Battelle Report was 'clearly influenced by work done by the Board's planning group'.[142] But the Report's author, Dr Ivan Kinne, proposed a plan that he thought would be acceptable to all rather than proposing the major reform that the Board thought necessary.

Kinne reported in August 1971 and viewed New Zealand's market prospects pessimistically.[143] His report noted four major problems: the sales to Britain would continue to decrease over the next decade; the market was weak in the USA; Japanese wool use would increase but more slowly than in previous years; and carpet production, the largest

---

[139] New Zealand Wool Board: further records: Minute Book, MSY–5860, 01/03/1972, 4, ATL.

[140] 'A Changing Situation – Sir John Acland', *Straight Furrow*, 21/04/1971, 5, ATL.

[141] New Zealand Wool Board: further records: Minute Book, MSY–5860, 03/02/1971, 8, ATL.

[142] Carter and MacGibbon: 207, note 22.

[143] Final Report on The Marketing Of New Zealand Wool, 13/08/1971, Sir John Marshall Collection, MS–1403 121/05, ATL. The following two paragraphs are summaries from the Report. On the front page of Jack Marshall's copy his attention is drawn to the pages with comparisons with the synthetic fibre industry. The Report describes the synthetic fibre industry in as much detail as it describes the wool industry.

end-use, would increase but wool would not participate in that increase as firms, formerly using only wool, changed to using synthetics in addition. The report said that growers, remote from marketing, had little direct knowledge of marketing conditions and little bargaining power in the marketplace. The IWS was 'part of the marketing system' but had 'little contact with the raw wool using industry'. Battelle found that the auction system disadvantages outweighed advantages. It fostered a 'come and take it' attitude rather than aggressive marketing to industrial buyers. The seller had a short-sighted view of market conditions and the auction buyer was far removed from the actual user. The auction system worked best when demand exceeded supply and that was no longer the case.

Kinne's Report concluded that New Zealand wool moved to the market through non-coordinated and disjointed agencies with no central direction or decision making. Unlike wool's competitors, the synthetics' companies, strengths were not marshalled to combat competitive threats. The report said that the

> types of changes needed include . . . reduction in fragmentation . . . more direct contact with the marketplace . . . more centralization to provide the New Zealand wool industry (including the grower) with more bargaining power'. 'Replacement of the auction system' was another 'type of change needed'.

But the report rejected introduction of 'an acquisition scheme' because it would 'miss key marketing problems' and 'cost savings potential are not great enough to make up for market threats'. Kinne, in answering questions about acquisition, said that it 'would be completely unrealistic to walk in and completely take over the whole clip'.[144]

The Wool Board approved the Battelle Report and within a few days published a New Zealand Wool Board Marketing Plan which Acland outlined to the Electoral Committee and the Federated Farmers Meat and Wool Section Council.[145] Acland said that proposals included establishing a New Zealand Wool Marketing Corporation with power

[144] 'Grower Control Becomes Major Stumbling Block', *Straight Furrow*, 08/09/1971, 3, ATL.

[145] The New Zealand Wool Board Marketing Plan, August 1971, Acland Family papers, collection MB44, Macmillan Brown Library (MBL).

to buy wool and market it throughout the world. The Corporation would operate as a 'commercial organisation on a profit-making basis'.[146] In particular it would be 'free from domination by any one group' and would strive to reduce the 'fragmentation' of the present system of wool marketing. The Corporation would establish marketing units in key overseas areas to encourage the maximum use and most profitable sale of New Zealand wool. It would need considerable autonomy with broad powers. The Corporation would evaluate the most effective marketing system and might well decide that auctions needed to be replaced.

Initially, Federated Farmers responded positively but soon there were complaints that the Board had failed to distribute the Battelle Report 'promptly as promised'.[147] The report had been prepared in three sections, Findings and Conclusions, Recommendations, and Appendices which described the global wool trade. The Board distributed in full only the Findings and Conclusions; it decided not to distribute the Recommendations.[148] The Minister for Agriculture was asked in parliament one month after Battelle reported 'to give an assurance that the recommendations from the Battelle Report will be made available to the public'; the Minister gave no such assurance but said the recommendations were available 'in précis form'.[149] One month later Acland had to give his 'solemn assurance' to the Electoral Committee that the

> Battelle recommendations do not differ in any significant way from the Board's plan . . . It has been said that growers paid for the Battelle recommendations and are entitled to see them. . . . Believe me, the Board is acting in good faith.[150]

[146] 'Broad Powers for New Corporation', *Straight Furrow*, 25/08/1971, 3, ATL.

[147] 'Battelle: An information gap emerging', *Straight Furrow*, 08/09/1971, 3, ATL.

[148] Because the Recommendations were not distributed the copies of the Battelle Report in University and Public Libraries and Jack Marshall's papers are of only the 73 pages of the Findings and Conclusions. A copy of the Recommendations is amongst the Acland family papers, collection MB44, at the Macmillan Brown Library at the University of Canterbury. From the initials handwritten on the front page that copy is Jack Acland's personal copy.

[149] Hon. D. J. Carter, *NZPD*, 1971, Vol. 374, 3425, WCL.

[150] 'Solemn Assurance', *Straight Furrow*, 20/10/1971, 9, ATL.

Acland explained to the Electoral Committee and the Meat and Wool Section why the Recommendations were not distributed: the Board had responsibility for putting forward a marketing plan, Battelle were only advisers. Publishing the Battelle Recommendations at the same time as the Board's plan would have led to 'hopeless confusion' partly because the Recommendations contained 'some purely speculative ideas on the future operations of the corporation'.[151] The Board created suspicion by appearing to hide something, and that suspicion eventually grew into an intense opposition to the reform plans.

Carter and MacGibbon say that the Board's first proposals to the Electoral Committee and Federated Farmers 'were not drawn from the [Battelle] report's recommendations' but Carter and MacGibbon refer only to the Findings and Conclusions not the Recommendations. A comparison of the Board's proposals and the Battelle Recommendations shows considerable overlap with just a few, but important, differences.[152] In particular, the Board omitted the most controversial parts and added the possibility of compulsory acquisition whilst avoiding that loaded phrase.[153] The Battelle Recommendations included that the Corporation 'must operate at "arm's length" from grower domination' and growers should not have 'complete control'; the Board omitted those phrases from its proposals in favour of stating that growers would have 'adequate representation on the Corporation' through the Wool Board. Battelle recommended that government approval should be given for 'major actions . . . such as taking over major segments of the clip' but the Board omitted that definition of 'major actions'. Battelle recommended that future plans should include various options for growers to sell their wool not just to the Corporation but also to others.

[151] Address by the Wool Board Chairman to a Joint Meeting of the N.Z. Wool Board, the Electoral Committee and the Meat and Wool Section Council of Federated Farmers, 12/10/1971, 1–2, Acland Family papers, Collection MB44, MBL.

[152] Carter and MacGibbon, 207.

[153] This paragraph is based on comparing the document 'The New Zealand Wool Marketing Plan' approved by the Wool Board on 26/08/1972 with the Research Report 'The Marketing of New Zealand Wool: Recommendations' presented by the Battelle Columbus Laboratories to the Wool Board on 13/08/1972. John Acland's personal copies of the documents are available at the Macmillan Brown Library as part of the Acland Family papers, collection MB44.

Battelle insisted that the proposed options remain open to woolgrowers to give them an 'out' if they were unhappy with the Corporation's activities and to maintain competition for the Corporation to stop it becoming a 'bureaucracy'. In contrast, the Wool Board wanted the Corporation to have the power to abandon the options, and described the options as 'initially available to growers'. They should remain open only as long as the Corporation believed they were 'viable and beneficial to the marketing of New Zealand wool'. The Corporation 'should be as free from constraint as possible'. The Wool Board added the possibility of compulsory acquisition, but avoided that phrase, replacing it with 'the Corporation should . . . investigate a method of direct purchase making prompt or even immediate payment'.

Battelle had ruled out compulsory acquisition but the Wool Board wanted to keep the option open, leaving it to the proposed Corporation to decide on its importance. Battelle recommended that the specific operational procedures and activities of the proposed corporation should not be announced in advance but should be decided by an establishment company, set up to plan the proposed marketing Corporation in detail. The Board took up that proposal, that allowed it to be vague about exactly how the proposed Corporation would operate and whether there would be compulsory acquisition.

The experience of the late 1960s, when opposition put an end to reform, together with the 'bewilderment' and controversy in Australia over similar plans, made the Board avoid confronting the industry with a controversial plan. The Board hoped to dampen opposition by adding the controversial elements slowly over several months. But delay had the opposite impact by adding to the suspicion created by non-publication of the Battelle Recommendations. During those several month's delay opposition became far more organised. Battelle had warned that 'buyers and traders may react negatively . . . and try to destroy the corporation operations and the corporation should be prepared with contingency plans'. Because of the Wool Board's approach, growers tried to destroy the Corporation and succeeded.

Straight Furrow called the discussions of reform in the late 1960s/early 1970s the 'Great Wool Debate'. At first, the central issue in the debate following the Battelle Report became whether growers would control the proposed Corporation. But those in favour of the Corporation thought marketing efficiency would be best achieved with a Corporation free from interference by outside groups such as growers. The debate started with Federated Farmers warning that if the Wool Board continued with the proposal that the Corporation would have 'less than grower control . . . it is buying a fight which is not in the best interest of the industry'.[154] Federated Farmers insisted on its 'crystal clear' policy – grower control. The Federated Farmers Meat and Wool Council agreed on the necessity for reform, and for any new scheme to be commercially oriented, but insisted that control in any new organisation must stay with growers.[155] Bremner, possibly knowing he was a prime candidate for Corporation chairman, best expressed the Wool Board view; he stressed the importance of keeping the Corporation 'free from any political influence . . . if grower control was insisted upon the Corporation had absolutely no possibility of achieving the desired result'.[156] Mr Main of Manuwatu thought Federated Farmers mistaken in wanting greater grower representation in the Corporation and advised growers to 'think big and beyond the farm-gate'. The Wool Board had proposed three grower's votes in a directorate of seven, plus the Wool Board veto over the government's appointment of an independent chairman, Mr Main thought that would be sufficient to maintain grower interests. Mr Burbury of Waiau supported that view, saying the Corporation needed to be built around a business-like approach to wool marketing.[157]

Compulsory acquisition quickly overtook grower control as the Great Wool Debate's main topic. In his report to the meeting of the Electoral Committee and Federated Farmers immediately following Battelle reporting, Acland said 'some of you will be disappointed that the Board did not come down in favour of complete acquisition'.[158] Many

[154] 'Battelle: An information gap emerging', *Straight Furrow*, 08/09/1971, 3, ATL.
[155] 'Grower Control Becomes Major Stumbling Block', *Straight Furrow*, 08/09/1971, 3, ATL.
[156] New Zealand Wool Board: further records: Minute Book, MSY–5860, 08/09/1971, 5, ATL.
[157] 'Corporation Must Have Businessmen', *Straight Furrow*, 20/10/1971, 7, ATL.
[158] 'Sir John: Plan is Strong and Workable', *Straight Furrow*, 08/09/1971, 5, ATL.

saw that statement as the Wool Board rejecting the notion of complete acquisition, and Carter and MacGibbon's interpretation is that those words later caused personal criticism of Acland: they 'would return to dog him at growers' meetings some months later'.[159] Acland probably meant the Board had rejected the notion of immediate acquisition; a month later he said that the Wool Board proposed that the Corporation first concentrate on markets overseas and move towards acquisition when woolbuyers and users had confidence in the Corporation.[160] He tried to allay fears by outlining safeguards for grower interests; the Corporation could adopt certain powers only with agreement of the Wool Board and the government. Those powers included restricting the sale of wool by others; becoming the sole purchaser of wool; and becoming the sole exporter to any specific destination. He stressed again that the Directorate needed men of special skills able to establish trade confidence quickly.[161]

The government took the first steps towards legislation by setting up, as proposed by Battelle and the Wool Board, an 'establishment company' that would finalise plans for the proposed Corporation. A future chairman of the Board, John Clarke, foresaw difficulties in implementing legislation; he warned that 'factions opposing the Board's plan would marshal their strongest opposition and present it to the government at the Select Committee stages'.[162] H Ralph, formerly managing director of the Ford Motor Company of New Zealand, became Chairman of the establishment company.[163] In March 1972 Ralph reported to the Wool Board that, when writing the Battelle Report Kinne had been 'particularly careful . . . to tailor a scheme which would be acceptable'. Ralph said that on a recent visit 'he [Kinne] now favoured an earlier progression towards acquisition'.[164] Ralph said that the plan for the

[159] Carter and MacGibbon, 208.

[160] 'Acland – "Significant Change" by Woolbuyers', *Straight Furrow*, 06/10/1971, 10, ATL.

[161] 'Growers' Interests: Corporation Powers Qualified', *Straight Furrow*, 20/10/1971, 9, ATL.

[162] New Zealand Wool Board: further records: Minute Book, MSY–5860, 19/10/1971, 1, ATL.

[163] Proposed New Zealand Wool Marketing Corporation, 26/10/1971, AAFD W3738 811 Box 646, CAB 41/7/1, ATL.

[164] New Zealand Wool Board: further records: Minute Book, MSY–5860, 01/03/1972, 5, ATL.

Corporation to gradually prove itself before acquisition was introduced 'was not now deemed to be practical'; acquisition should be introduced as soon as possible.[165] The Wool Board recognised the sensitivity of changing to immediate acquisition and asked Ralph to 'enumerate the arguments' which had led the establishment company and Dr Kinne 'to change their minds about acquisition'.[166] The Board agreed that Ralph should, confidentially, inform the chairmen of the Electoral Committee and the Federated Farmers Meat and Wool Section. Ralph agreed to report to a joint meeting of those bodies 'in Committee' with no record of the meeting being released. The Chairman of the Meat and Wool Section said that the reasons for changing the Board's original plan should be given to 'all farming leaders'.[167] Ralph later told the Board that if growers would not support an early introduction of acquisition on a specific date 'it would be better not to establish the Corporation'.[168] To opponents outside the Board, the change confirmed their fears that the Board intended compulsory acquisition from the start, and the Board had acted in an underhand way in not stating that openly.[169]

In mid-1972, based on the Establishment Company's recommendations, the government announced plans for legislation and those included acquiring the whole of the wool clip, with acquisition introduced within two years, but subject to a growers' referendum.[170] The plans included that auctions and private selling methods would be abandoned 'because of their over-all inefficiency and short-term approach to wool marketing'. Acland said that the Board now accepted that instead of 'developing an acquisition scheme gradually' it should be launched within a year of the Corporation being established.[171]

[165] New Zealand Wool Board: further records: Minute Book, MSY–5860, 01/03/1972, 5, ATL.
[166] New Zealand Wool Board: further records: Minute Book, MSY–5860, 01/03/1972, 6, ATL.
[167] New Zealand Wool Board: further records: Minute Book, MSY–5860, 21/03/1972, 5, ATL.
[168] New Zealand Wool Board: further records: Minute Book, MSY–5860, 10/05/1972, 2, ATL.
[169] Carter and MacGibbon, 213.
[170] Wool Corporation Act, 1972.
[171] 'Wool At The Crossroads', *Straight Furrow*, 07/06/1972, 1, ATL.

The Board justified this by reporting the Establishment Company's decision that

> the conflict between grower choice and marketing efficiency had to be faced. . . . To fulfil its objectives of maximising long-term returns to the New Zealand woolgrowers . . . the Corporation has to come down on the side of marketing efficiency.[172]

Acland said that 'the power to acquire all wool has given teeth to the Corporation'. [173] He said that 'it was personally satisfying to see at last the principle of controlled wool marketing afloat' and announced that he would retire from the Wool Board in 1973.[174]

The legislation anticipated that the Corporation would absorb the Wool Commission and set prices in conjunction with the Wool Board, subject to approval by the Minister. The Corporation directors would be three grower representatives from the Wool Board, two men appointed by the Minister of Agriculture for their commercial expertise, and a Government Department official. The Chairman would be appointed jointly by the Wool Board and the Minister, but would not serve as a Wool Board member. After acquiring wool the Corporation would sell to private buyers who would ship the wool overseas. The Corporation sought a profit for growers not for itself, and intended 'to obtain maximum long-term returns for New Zealand woolgrowers'. The Corporation would pay a minimum price to growers at the season's start and a payment at the season's end if the season yielded a surplus.

A Select Committee reviewed the proposed legislation and Federated Farmers and the Electoral Committee sought approval from growers. The Federation sought approval at their Meat and Wool Section Conference and could report to the Select Committee that 51 delegates supported the proposals at the Conference with 6 against and 5 abstentions. The

[172] Address by Chairman of the New Zealand Wool Board to the Meetings of the Electoral Committee and the Dominion Meat and Wool Section Council of Federated Farmers with the New Zealand Wool Board, 23/05/1972, 9, Acland Family papers, collection MB44, MBL.

[173] 'Wool at the Crossroads', *Straight Furrow*, 07/06/1972, 1, ATL.

[174] 'Wool at the Crossroads', *Straight Furrow*, 07/06/1972, 2, ATL.

Southland delegate, Aubrey Begg, was typical of the minority opposition; he was 'implacably opposed' and demanded a 'national referendum so that if our freedom to sell wool is to be taken from us . . . it can only be done by a two–thirds majority'.[175] But overwhelmingly, the Conference accepted the need for the Corporation to operate in a commercial manner removed from direct grower influence. The decisions were made

> in full appreciation of the restrictions the new scheme would impose on the rights of the individual farmer . . . the fierce competition . . . from synthetic fibre monopolies offers woolgrowers no choice but to . . . band together.[176]

Federated Farmers believed 'firmly' that, to overcome 'fragmentation' and introduce 'greater efficiencies', the Corporation needed 'the powers of acquisition over the total New Zealand wool clip'.

Acland and the Wool Board seemed to be justified in the approach taken, and Acland congratulated the Conference on its decisions. He said 'today is the day we changed the future of the New Zealand wool industry'.[177] Sadly, that turned out to be wrong. For a few weeks it seemed that his retirement would be marked by the significant reform for which he had striven for several years.[178] But, during the next few months, opponents of acquisition subjected Acland to severe personal attacks on his honesty and judgement, forcing him to stand down early as Chairman in October 1972 because the attacks damaged his health.[179] Carter and MacGibbon say that 'it was . . . deplorable that, in the acrimony that developed within the wider wool industry . . . there was a tendency to play the man and not the ball'.[180]

---

[175] 'Overwhelming Majority: Wool Corporation Given Clear Mandate', *Straight Furrow*, 05/07/1972, 3, ATL.

[176] Submissions to the Land and Agriculture Committee by Federated Farmers, 03/08/1972, Federated Farmers, 90–343 MSY–90–343–05/4, 2, ATL.

[177] 'Overwhelming Majority: Wool Corporation Given Clear Mandate', *Straight Furrow*, 05/07/1972, 3, ATL.

[178] 'Sir John Acland Retiring', *Straight Furrow*, 07/06/1972, 13, ATL.

[179] 'Sir John Acland Stands Down', *Straight Furrow*, 20/09/1972, 6, ATL.

[180] Carter and MacGibbon, 219.

The Federated Farmers Meat and Wool Section demonstrated its support for urgent marketing reform in its submissions to the Select Committee. It included a list of positive resolutions adopted by the Section in the period 1967–1971. But the Section could not agree on 'the method and extent to which woolgrowers should be consulted' before the Section conveyed to the Select Committee 'growers' final views on the proposed Corporation'.[181] The uncertainty demonstrated disagreement within Federated Farmers, apparently led by the Dominion President, Alec Begg, who resigned. Begg complained that Acland and the Wool Board had changed their position on acquisition, and had either been naive or deceiving farmers deliberately on earlier occasions. The speed at which the proposals were being forced through deprived many members of the right to make their voices heard. Begg said he did not like the proposals but would go along with a majority decision, growers now had to organise outside the Federation.[182] Acland responded to the accusations that he had been 'naive or deceiving farmers deliberately' by pointing out that the Board's Marketing Plan issued in August 1971 'made no secret of the likely development scheme' and included the phrase 'the Corporation should investigate a method of direct purchase'.[183] He said, 'developing an acquisition scheme gradually' had simply been replaced by introducing it more quickly.

The question of who best represented farmers became important. Federated Farmers insisted in its submission to the Select Committee that there had been considerable consultation with its members, claiming to represent 80% of woolgrowers. At least 152 meetings had been held to discuss the proposals throughout the country, at which 124 meetings voted in favour, 18 against and 10 did not vote or expressed certain reservations. The Meat and Wool Section acknowledged that

[181] Minutes of the Meat and Wool Section Meeting, 26/04/1972, Federated Farmers 90–343–05/4, M&W25/1972, 7, ATL.

[182] 'Alec Begg's Decision: Objected to Speed of Wool Legislation', *Straight Furrow*, 27/07/1972, 3, ATL.

[183] Address by Chairman of the New Zealand Wool Board to the Meetings of the Electoral Committee and the Dominion Meat and Wool Section Council of Federated Farmers with the New Zealand Wool Board, 23/05/1972, 2, Acland Family papers, collection MB44, MBL.

some farmers wanted to retain their traditional individualism but there was 'an increasing awareness among the majority of growers that this individualism cannot be retained in the modern, intensely competitive, trading environment'.[184]

8.8 Opposition to Reform Grows and Stops the Reform

A major controversy erupted over whether the Corporation should have the power to purchase compulsorily all New Zealand's wool before selling it to overseas buyers. The lack of openness when the Wool Board first introduced the proposals made many woolgrowers feel they had been misled, and made a minority even more determined to oppose change unless a substantial majority of woolgrowers could be shown to support the proposal wholeheartedly. The National Government introduced legislation including a referendum but the Labour government elected soon afterwards abolished this requirement. When the Wool Marketing Corporation began operating early in 1973, the Wool Board and Federated Farmers tried to persuade growers to accept that the Corporation was a done deal. The controversy made growers take a strong interest in the elections for the Wool Board Electoral Committee, changing it to a majority against acquisition. In addition, a surge in prices in 1973 allayed the feeling of crisis in the wool industry and strengthened opposition to acquisition. The Wool Board and Federated Farmers accepted the outcome of the Electoral Committee elections and in 1973 abandoned the planned reform.[185]

Those opposed to compulsory acquisition formed a country-wide New Zealand Woolgrowers' Action Committee, outside Federated

[184] Submissions to the Land and Agriculture Committee, 03/08/1972, Federated Farmers 90–343–05/4, 12, ATL.

[185] Carter and MacGibbon describe the moves towards reform and the opposition giving a strong insight into the role of the many individuals involved, based, presumably, on Carter's experiences as the Executive Manager of the Woolbuyers' Association and working with those individuals, 202–228.

Farmers, to press for approval by a growers' referendum before introduction of acquisition. The Committee justified its approach by claiming that a majority of growers opposed acquisition, and based its campaign on rousing growers' fears of losing their freedom to sell as they wished. Carter and MacGibbon argue that a South Canterbury sheepfarmer, Herb Styles, became 'a prime catalyst for the anti-acquisition' movement by inviting those opposed to acquisition to contact him. Local South Island farmers responded strongly to the invitation, joining forces with a North Island 'ginger' group set up originally to 'oppose lethargy in the established order of Federated Farmers', which suggests that acquisition became the focal point for those with a series of grievances.[186] Styles had opposed acquisition at the September 1972 Electoral College meeting because 'the Wool Board had failed to discharge its duty to fully inform growers'.[187] The Action Committee intended to make the government 'withhold action on the Wool Marketing Corporation . . . until acceptable evidence is produced that the majority of growers accept the scheme as at present proposed'.[188] The Committee asked the Wool Board to conduct a referendum and if that were not implemented the Committee 'will take action ourselves'. The Committee wrote to the Jack Marshall, now in his short term as Prime Minister, and also made a strong anti-acquisition case to the Select Committee, rebutting specifically each point made in the Wool Board submission to the Committee.[189] The Action Committee felt justified because 'the majority of growers are opposed to compulsory acquisition' and it was 'not enough for the Wool Board to simply ask the opinion of the Electoral College, and the Meat and Wool Conference'.

The freedom for farmers to choose how to sell their wool remained the crux of the Great Wool Debate. Greensmith had described growers

[186] Carter and MacGibbon, 213.

[187] 'Tense Debate On Wool Marketing: Action Committee Soundly Defeated', *Straight Furrow*, 10, ATL.

[188] *Bulletin of the New Zealand Woolgrowers' Action Committee*, July 10 1972. ATL has a collection of the Action Committee Bulletins produced between July 1972 and January 1973. The quotes in this paragraph are taken from page 1 of the 10 July 1972 version.

[189] Letter to the Prime Minister, 29/09/1972, Sir John Marshall Collection, MS1403 479/05, ATL.

as 'ruggedly individualistic', and that rugged individualism led to an emotional response to acquisition on the grounds that it threatened farmers' freedom. Farmers were self-employed and responsible for all their own business decisions; they saw the threat that a government bureaucracy might become the sole buyer of their wool as a threat to the whole concept of individual, self-employed, farmers. Criticism of auctions in the late 1950s had briefly led to consideration that the Wool Commission should change to an acquisition scheme, and, at that time, Federated Farmers specified the overriding objection that such a scheme 'cut right across what has to be a fundamental principle, namely, the right of each grower to market his clip, how, when, and where he likes'.[190] Buchanan describes how farmers developed close relationships with the buyers who purchased their wool: 'loyalty featured strongly in rural communities'.[191] Easton in his review of stock and station agents sees such loyalty as a preference for known security over the uncertainty of changing to a new buyer ('the devil you know . . . ').[192]

Buchanan notes that during the reform controversy in the early 1970s change was 'anathema' to 'long-established and fiercely independent sheep farmers'.[193] He says that 'newer entrants, often with significant mortgage commitments' supported reform because that would 'provide greater security and income certainty'.[194] One example is Brian Chamberlin, a sheep farmer in the 1970s who later became President of Federated Farmers.[195] Chamberlin, as a new sheepfarmer with significant mortgage commitments, spoke in favour of the proposed Corporation and acquisition, calling the proposed reform the 'boldest attempt I have ever seen to gain the stability needed'.[196] Acland hoped

[190] Acquisition Scheme for Wool, Note to All Provincial Secretaries, 16/07/1960, Federated Farmers, 90–343 MSY–2737, M&W 81/1960, 1, ATL.

[191] Buchanan, 22.

[192] Easton, *Stock and Station Agents*, unpublished manuscript, 18.

[193] Buchanan, 114.

[194] Buchanan, 116.

[195] In conversation with the author on 11 August 2014.

[196] 'Overwhelming Majority: Wool Corporation Given Clear Mandate', *Straight Furrow*, 05/07/1972, p3, ATL.

to dampen controversy over acquisition but instead the Wool Board's actions stimulated more intense controversy. The controversy became more intense because, in addition to the doubts about acquisition, growers thought they had been misled. Perhaps, if the announcement of compulsory acquisition had been made immediately in August 1971, when all expected that to be the outcome, opposition would have been less. But the Battelle decision against acquisition had forced the Wool Board to hold back.

Acland's family had been long established in sheep farming in New Zealand, first sending wool to Britain in the mid-1850s, and he advocated reform against what Buchanan calls his 'fellow landed gentry'.[197] Acland's determination in pressing for reform, despite the considerable opposition, stemmed from his strong social conscience, a family tradition shared by the Acland family in Britain. During the 1940s Sir Richard Acland, Jack's contemporary in the British landed gentry, donated his estate to the British National Trust, and, in the 1950s, helped form the British Campaign for Nuclear Disarmament. Jack Acland was a sheep-farming establishment member but had a sufficiently strong social conscience that he had spoken against many in his party in the House of Representatives when a National MP in 1945 in favour of the financial support for young families that Labour introduced.[198] In 1968, Acland had been travelling to Wellington from the New Zealand South Island on the ferry *Wahine* when it sunk – Carter and MacGibbon described how 'in typical Acland fashion, he helped others into the lifeboats first'.[199] In the 1970s Acland recognised that it would be the new, younger, families, such as Brian Chamberlin's, that would suffer most in the long-term from the competition from synthetics. He saw the proposals for wool marketing reform protecting the livelihood of those families.[200] Just before retiring Acland said that 'small farms will

[197] Buchanan, 116.

[198] NZPD, 17/10/1945, Two hundreth and seventieth Volume, p244, WCL.

[199] Carter and MacGibbon, 154.

[200] I am grateful to John Acland, Jack Acland's son, for the additional insight into Jack's stand against the sheepfarming establishment, a stand that led to Jack being called a 'communist' and eventually damaged his health.

succumb to an uncontrolled marketing system', that formed the 'core of the matter'. He valued 'the independence of one and two-man farms' and had been 'alarmed . . . at a trend towards the amalgamation of properties'.[201] Acland saw compulsory acquisition as a means of maintaining the sheep farming tradition of family farms.

The Action Committee insisted it did not ignore the continuing competition from synthetics but competition would not be removed by compulsory acquisition 'putting the farmers of New Zealand in a straight jacket from which they cannot escape'.[202] The Committee claimed that those supporting the proposed legislation

> to take away freedom from the woolgrowers . . . are fearful of the results of their decision and are doing their best to suppress the free expression of woolgrower opinion.[203]

That had some truth; the Board had tried to suppress an outburst from growers by not openly proposing compulsory acquisition in the first publication of its Marketing Plan. The Action Committee said that the Wool Board has 'chosen to ignore you. . . . It's your wool and your future that is at stake. React accordingly. . . . You are not in a totalitarian state – Yet'.[204] The Action Committee asked woolgrowers whether they were 'in favour of monopolistic and socialistic control of any industry?'.[205] Weber, despite his role as a private buyer, strongly supported acquisition and broadcast his support in a radio programme; that led to a door being slammed in his face by a farmer's wife who accused him of being 'a bloody communist'.[206]

The Wool Board retaliated against the Action Committee by publishing an advertisement in *Straight Furrow*, encouraging farmers to support

---

[201] Address by the Wool Board Chairman to the Electoral Committee and the New Zealand Wool Board, 22/08/1972, 14, Acland Family papers, collection MB44, MBL.

[202] *Bulletin of the New Zealand Woolgrowers' Action Committee*, 10 July 1972, 2, ATL.

[203] *Bulletin of the New Zealand Woolgrowers' Action Committee*, 10 July 1972, 2–3, ATL.

[204] *Bulletin of the New Zealand Woolgrowers' Action Committee*, 10 July 1972, 2–3, ATL.

[205] *Bulletin of the New Zealand Woolgrowers' Action Committee*, January 1973, 6, ATL.

[206] Weber, 12.

their leaders within Federated Farmers. It said that those leaders unanimously supported the main issue – the need for a strong growers' Corporation with overall control of the handling, distribution and marketing. The Wool Board asked farmers to ignore those actively opposing the plan

> mainly on emotional grounds. . . . Protestors always seem to work harder than supporters and they get more headlines. The issue isn't settled yet, support the marketing plan, you should go to meetings, write to your MP, join the battle in the correspondence columns.[207]

Weber described the approach taken by the Action Committee – 'Acquisition means confiscation by a bureaucratic faceless body'. According to Weber the word acquisition became 'an ugly word . . . It sounded like dictatorship or a form of totalitarianism'. [208]

The furore raised by the Action Committee succeeded in making the Select Committee exclude acquisition from the Bill until it was agreed in a woolgrowers' referendum. The Wool Board reluctantly agreed to support that proposal because the Minister for Agriculture had advised the Board that the Bill 'did not have a sufficient majority of grower support'.[209] Federated Farmers expressed their disappointment that the original version of the Bill including acquisition might not be adopted, but agreed to support the referendum and abide by the decision.[210]

In October 1972, the government had passed the legislation, including that the Corporation would have powers of compulsory acquisition subject to a referendum of growers. The Wool Corporation took over the Wool Commission duties.[211] The Action Committee remained wary especially so when Labour replaced National in the General Election at the end of 1972. Labour had criticised National for its retreat from compulsory

[207] 'Wool Industry Leaders Deserve Your Support', *Straight Furrow*, 27/07/1971, 7, ATL.

[208] Weber, 125.

[209] Minutes of the Meat and Wool Council Meeting, 26/09/1972, Federated Farmers, 90–343–05/4, M&W65/1972, 8, ATL.

[210] 'Meat and Wool Section Reserved on Referendum', *Straight Furrow*, 04/10/1972, 3, ATL.

[211] Wool Marketing Corporation Act, 20/10/1972.

acquisition and the Action Committee wondered whether the new government would be 'bold enough . . . to deny growers the right to express their wishes'.[212] The Committee realised that it represented only a minority and insisted that any referendum should be decided not by only a 60% majority as proposed in the legislation but '70 or 75% should be the minimum for the imposition on woolgrowers of a socialistic form of marketing'. Aubrey Begg, the Southland delegate to the Federated Farmers Meat and Wool Section, decided to stand as a Labour MP, specifically to oppose acquisition in Parliament. He won the 1972 election in Awarua against Hugh Templeton, a National MP who supported acquisition. Begg told the Select Committee that if acquisition went ahead without an 'overwhelming majority . . . Federated Farmers will be stripped of farmers' trust' and 'it was not hard to envisage the Wool Board in the same position'.[213] But the new government boldly revoked the need for a referendum, with the new Minister, Colin Moyle, convinced that the Corporation needed power of acquisition to be effective. He announced that the government would introduce an Amendment to the Corporation Act, introducing acquisition without the need for a referendum.[214] Begg, as a Labour M.P., found himself opposed to his party on that key issue, and voted against the proposed Amendment at every stage.

In January 1973, the Wool Board member, Douglas Bremner, became the first Corporation Chairman.[215] Bremner, a farmer from Auckland, had considerable business experience because he had founded a carpet manufacturing business. The Action Committee decided to go ahead with its own unofficial referendum even though the Minister pointed out that the government had made its decision and would not be influenced by the referendum's outcome.[216] Tom McNab, who had replaced Spackman as the Federated Farmers Meat and Wool Section

---

[212] *Bulletin of the New Zealand Woolgrowers' Action Committee*, 5 December 1972, 1, ATL. The other quotes in this paragraph are on page 1 of that Bulletin.

[213] *Bulletin of the New Zealand Woolgrowers' Action Committee*, 5 December 1972, 1, ATL.

[214] Hon. C. J. Moyle, *NZPD*, 1973, 02/03/1973, Vol. 382, 453 WCL.

[215] Personnel of the Wool Marketing Corporation, 10/01/1973, Federated Farmers, 90–343–04/3, M&W1/1973, 1, ATL.

[216] 'Minister Emphatic: Agriculture Needs United Voice', *Straight Furrow*, 21/02/1973, 1, ATL.

Chairman, responded to the Action Committee by advising Section members that the Corporation had become 'an accomplished fact . . . farmers . . . should no longer debate its creation' but should now concentrate on influencing the Corporation.[217] He advised members that the Action Committee referendum, apart from the refusal of the government and Wool Board to accept its result, was too narrow to judge views effectively. Growers would reject acquisition with wool at 200 cents/kilo but what if it returned to 50 cents/kilo? McNab thought the issue far too complex for a simple referendum confined to yes or no without mentioning alternatives. Bremner issued a statement saying that the benefits from having the Corporation

> can only develop through a central body acting for growers with property over the clip . . . the Corporation is working towards a policy of acquisition. . . . This decision is taken on business grounds alone.[218]

Through the 1972/1973 season wool prices rose, lessening the sense of urgency for change and strengthening support for the Action Committee.[219] Unexpectedly, wool prices more than doubled thereby alleviating the feeling of crisis that had encouraged support for the Corporation's creation.[220] Weber described the change as 'Now the status quo seemed to be an attractive proposition' replacing the 'pessimism evident in the immediately preceding years'.[221] Moyle appealed to 'thinking' farmers to support a Corporation with powers of acquisition. He recognised that no 'thinking' farmer really wanted acquisition but they do recognise that it is good for the industry and the grower.[222] The Action Group claimed that their referendum showed 'over 14,000 farmers

[217] Wool Marketing Corporation Referendum on Acquisition, 01/02/1973, Federated Farmers, 90 – 343 M&W5/1973, 1, ATL.

[218] Statement by Mr W.M.D.Bremner, New Zealand Wool Marketing Corporation, 05/07/1973, Call–P Box q338.1763 NEW 1973, NZ Woolgrowers' Action Committee, 3, ANZ.

[219] Submissions to the Land and Agriculture Committee, 03/08/1972, Federated Farmers, 90–343–05/4, 12, ATL.

[220] 'Dramatic Rises for Wool But Experts are Cautious', *Straight Furrow*, 19/01/1972, 7, ATL.

[221] Weber, 125.

[222] 'No acquisition for the sake of acquisition', *Straight Furrow*, 04/04/1973, 2, ATL.

[about 30% of New Zealand woolgrowers] did not like what the Board was doing'.[223] Weber reports that 13,000 did not vote.[224] The Wool Board interpreted the result as meaning that '60 per cent either by voting or tacitly' favoured the proposed reform.[225] Eventually, the Meat and Wool Section achieved a compromise in a resolution calling for approval by a woolgrowers' majority before implementing compulsory acquisition, but the Section could not decide how to confirm a majority.[226]

The furore aroused by acquisition raised interest above the usual apathy in the Electoral Committee elections. Herman points out that usually less than 50% of growers voted, districts were rarely contested, and delegates rarely changed. For instance, in 1971, *Straight Furrow* reported that 'farmer apathy has once again shown itself in the dismal lack of competition for the 25 seats' on the Electoral Committee with only three contested.[227] But, in August 1973, 67.5% voted, all but one district were contested and 15 new delegates out of 25 were elected, giving the Committee an anti-acquisition majority.[228] *Straight Furrow* announced that the elections to the Committee had demonstrated that a majority opposed acquisition, and that made the matter a 'dead issue'; the Corporation could forget acquisition. The new Electoral Committee recommended that powers of the Corporation should not include acquisition.[229] McNab issued a press statement announcing that 'debate on the introduction of acquisition . . . should no longer divide woolgrowers. . . . The results of the recent Electoral Committee elections confirmed the change in woolgrower opinion'.[230]

[223] 'Members debate acquisition', *Straight Furrow*, 04/04/1973, 9, ATL.

[224] Weber, 126.

[225] New Zealand Wool Board Newsletter, February 1973, Wool (raw) – New Zealand Wool Marketing Corporation Officials Committee – Agendas – Minutes of Meetings 1971–1974, AAQW W3379 Box 41 8/5/1 Part 3, 1, ANZ.

[226] Minutes of the Meat and Wool Section Annual Conference, 27/06/1973, Federated Farmers, 90–343–04/3 M&W35/1973, 13, ATL.

[227] 'Electoral Committee Contest', *Straight Furrow*, 07/07/1971, 7, ATL.

[228] Phillip Herman, 'The Electoral Committee of the New Zealand Meat and Wool Boards', *Political Science*, June 1974, 26, 1, 61.

[229] 'Acquisition not needed', *Straight Furrow*, 05/09/1973, 12, ATL.

[230] Statement Re: Wool Marketing Corporation, 16/08/1973, Federated Farmers 90–343–04/3, M&W46/1973, 2, ATL.

John Clarke, who had taken over from Acland as Wool Board chairman, announced that the total marketing operation which the Board proposed had now been laid aside.[231] The Corporation investigated whether growers would voluntarily sell their wool to the Corporation.[232] The Corporation managing director reported the responses from canvassing farmer opinion – only two and a half percent were in favour. Some replies... 'beggar description'.[233] The Corporation's reduced powers made Bremner resign as Chairman, saying: 'Farmers and their leaders must take responsibility for solving their own problems.... Get on with it'.[234]

Owen McCarthy, Head of the Agricultural Economics and Marketing Department at Lincoln College, summarised in March 1974 the Great Wool Debate. He concluded that 'non-acquisition has reduced the Corporation to the status of a paper tiger' and it 'had only made timid steps in reform'. He expected the debate to 'drag on for some time yet with a wool marketing system of bygone days teetering precariously on an antiquated but oh so venerable foundation'.[235] Subsequent events justified his judgement. The Action Committee achieved its objective; it succeeded because it had the simple, single, objective of stopping acquisition. As the Committee's representatives had said when meeting the Wool Board, 'the Committee did not feel obliged to present an alternative plan'.[236]

The government remained convinced in 1974 that a Corporation needed the power of acquisition to be effective.[237] Much to Federated Farmers disgruntlement, the government introduced an amendment to the Wool Corporation Act, taking away the provision for agreement by

[231] 'Sheep and wool production falling far too short', *Straight Furrow*, 03/04/1974, 16, ATL.

[232] Notice to Woolgrowers: Voluntary Pooling Arrangement, 18/12/1973, Federated Farmers, 90–343–05/4, M&W79/1973, ATL.

[233] 'Farmers must solve the wool industry problems', *Straight Furrow*, 08/05/1974, 15, ATL.

[234] 'Farmers must solve the wool industry problems', *Straight Furrow*, 08/05/1974, 15, ATL.

[235] Owen McCarthy, 'The Wool Acquisition Controversy', *Canterbury of Chamber of Commerce Economic Bulletin*, no.577, March 1974, 2–4.

[236] New Zealand Wool Board: further records: Minute Book, MSY–5860, 013/09/1972, 6, ATL.

[237] Wool Corporation Amendment, 21/10/1974.

growers before the Corporation powers of acquisition could be used.[238] That led to suspicion immediately that the proposed Corporation would not be grower-controlled. The Prime Minister, Norman Kirk, told Parliament that he would 'accept a referendum of all those responsible, financially or otherwise for the production of wool.... It is not only the woolgrowers; it is the taxpayers of New Zealand'. He reported the financial assistance given by 'New Zealand taxpayers... to subsidise sheep farmers'.[239] The Federated Farmers Meat and Wool Annual Conference passed a resolution immediately expressing 'extreme concern at the Prime Minister's statement that the public has a right to be involved', and reaffirming 'its policy of effective grower control of the Wool Marketing Corporation'.[240]

Prices surged only temporarily during 1972/1973 and the return to low prices led to the Corporation 'acquiring' significant wool quantities, purchasing more than 50% in the New Zealand sales of January 1975.[241] Support through the Corporation ensured that farmers could still sell wool however low the prices, and there seemed no strong objection to acquisition in those circumstances. Yet again calls for wool marketing reform came from within Federated Farmers 'to ensure the future of the wool industry' but 'without any more committees, investigations or expense'; and there should be a poll of woolgrowers on the nature of the reform.[242]

Apart from prices increasing for a short period in 1973, New Zealand's earnings remained at the low levels of the late 1960s, spreading depression throughout the industry. In the 1970s Britain remained New Zealand wool's main customer but Britain's textile industry continued to decline rapidly: 85 firms had ceased weaving through the 1960s. New Zealand wool sales to the USA also declined and Clarke

[238] Press Statement, 31/05/1974, Federated Farmers, 90–343–04/4, M&W22/1974, 1, ATL; Hon. D. J. Carter, *NZPD*, 1974, Vol. 390, 1514, WCL.

[239] Right Hon. N. E. Kirk, *NZPD*, 1974, Vol. 391, 2508.

[240] Minutes of the Annual Conference of the Meat and Wool Section, 01/07/1974, Federated Farmers, 90–343–04/4, M&W29/1974, 114, ATL.

[241] 'Market support – Clarke', *Straight Furrow*, 03/04/1975, 10, ATL.

[242] 'Wool marketing reform', *Straight Furrow*, 05/03/1975, 14, ATL.

said in 1974 that the USA market 'could now almost be written off by New Zealand'. [243] Sales increased, however, to the USSR and Asian countries.[244] Clarke asked: 'Are we seeing a permanent swing from the markets of Western Europe and America to Eastern Europe, Japan, Hong Kong and the developing countries?'[245] The answer was – yes – earnings (at 1984 prices) had fallen by 1984 to 40% of the 1966 level with almost all the fall being in Western European countries and the USA (Table 8.2). Sales increased to Asia and Eastern Europe but insufficiently to make up the reduced sales elsewhere.

In 1975, Clarke again tried to encourage acceptance of the proposals made in 1972 for marketing wool: 'we must sell wool as our customers require it' and in a 'chiefly commercial way'.[246] He said that for 70 years 'we have said to the world: "here's our product . . . what'll you pay us for it?" . . . now we must say "this is the price we want for it"'. But the idea persisted that the best way to market wool should be decided by a referendum of 40,000 growers removed from contact with end users.

In 1977, with National back in power, the Corporation amalgamated with the Wool Board whilst arguments over acquisition continued. The Minister, Duncan MacIntyre, intended first to recommend to Cabinet that the amalgamated organisation should be allowed to introduce acquisition without the need for a growers' referendum. But, on the day of the Cabinet meeting, he reversed that recommendation after his Caucus Committee on Agriculture, meeting just before the Cabinet meeting, was 'strongly of the opinion that there should be a referendum'.[247] Legislation allowed the amalgamated organisation the power of acquisition but only if agreed in a growers' referendum. That agreement was never sought and acquisition never introduced; the antiquated marketing system teetered on. Weber summarises the consequences, he says that by the mid-1990s 'Sheep farming had lost is way, simply

---

[243] 'Wool Marketing Shifts', *Straight Furrow*, 08/05/1974, 14, ATL.

[244] 'China: A trade burst after the shut–off era', *Straight Furrow*, 17/09/1975, 3, ATL.

[245] 'Sheep and wool production falling too far short', *Straight Furrow*, 03/04/1974, 16, ATL.

[246] ''Stabilisation Questions and Answers', *Straight Furrow*, 02/07/1975, 13, ATL.

[247] Note to the Secretary of the Cabinet by the Minister for Agriculture, 01/03/1977, AAFD W3738 811 Box 24, ANZ.

Table 8.2 Changes in New Zealand wool export earnings 1966–1984 $(000) (at 1984 prices) (NZDYB)

UK	–30,661
USA	–23,773
France	–20,554
Belgium	–10,391
Italy	–3,316
Germany	–2,249
Sweden	–2,124
Spain	–1,995
Canada	–1,960
Denmark	–1,453
Portugal	–1,424
South Africa	–658
Norway	–434
UAR	–296
GDR	–283
Mexico	–206
Finland	–156
Japan	–102
Switzerland	–37
Yugoslavia	274
Ireland	791
Czechoslovakia	911
Poland	1,725
India	2,098
Pakistan	2,193
Egypt	2,515
Hong Kong	2,707
Greece	3,597
China (Taiwan)	4,246
Netherlands	4,865
Australia	6,627
Korea	7,053
Iran	11,099
China	12,897
USSR	14,352
Other countries	6,352
Total	**–74989**

because the 'old ways of marketing' had become 'anachronistic'; demand had 'collapsed', farms were in disrepair, sheep numbers had fallen from 70 million at the end of the 1970s to 58 million in the mid–1990s'.[248] Buchanan reported that those who 'led the crusade against acquisition in later years came to accept they may have backed the wrong horse'.[249] He points out also, looking back in 2012 on the attempts at reform in the 1960s and 1970s, that perhaps the wrong target had been chosen; rather than marketing reform, the underlying problem needed reform – New Zealand's main wool product losing out to synthetics, especially as carpet technology advanced.[250] But growers preferred to keep to dual-purpose sheep that yielded good productivity in wool and meat, rather than changing to sheep that gave finer wools but reduced meat productivity.

8.9 Conclusion

Neither a need to escape from over-dependence on the British market nor Britain's potential membership of the EEC drove change in the wool industry. Change was driven by the periodic price collapses caused by the threat from synthetics and the cyclic nature of trade amongst the major industrial nations. Britain's bulk purchase during World War II more than compensated New Zealand woolgrowers from suppression of their other markets by the war, and the relatively high prices paid by Britain stimulated increased production. The immediate World War II aftermath also profited New Zealand woolgrowers; wool sold well despite the considerable surplus stocks left over from wartime. Demand surged in markets that had been stifled during the war because countries, for instance, in continental Europe, recovered and restocked. Pre-war markets were quickly re-established. The stockpile left over from

[248] Weber, 127.

[249] Buchanan, 117.

[250] Buchanan, 86.

World War II sold far easier than had been expected, and did not disturb international markets.

The early 1950s proved even more profitable when the Korean War tripled prices. For most of the 1950s wool sold easily with virtually all markets expanding apart from Britain. New Zealand woolgrowers felt little pressure for change, except for the incentive to increase income by increasing productivity. New Zealand's production increased steadily through the period 1945–1975, and, by 1975, New Zealand exported 50% more tonnage than in the immediate post–war years. Earnings, at 1971 prices, increased steadily through the first part of the period as production rose, but by the end of the 1960s increased production did not translate into increased earnings as prices fell and remained low.

Britain purchased 56% of New Zealand wool exports in 1945 but less than 20% in 1975. The decline reflected an actual drop in quantities purchased by Britain and mirrored Britain loss of standing from being the world leader in wool textiles manufacture to no more than on par with others. New Zealand's wool industry had been established through its strong links with Britain, but, after 1945, wool exports to Britain's declined sufficiently slowly that growth in its other markets, notably, the EEC, the USSR and Japan, compensated for the reduced sales to Britain. The decline in the British market caused far less concern for the wool industry than for the meat and dairy industries. Growing sales to the original six EEC countries in the 1950s made the prospect of Britain entering the EEC much less of a concern for the New Zealand wool industry than for the dairy and meat industries. Indeed, there were reasons to expect that Britain's membership would benefit wool sales.

The profitable conditions of the 1940s and 1950s created a generation of woolgrowers in New Zealand for whom wool sale seemed not to be problematic. There were occasional dips in price but a 'floor price' scheme, introduced early in the 1950s, set a limit to how far prices could fall. In the 1930s there had been concern that synthetic fibres might replace wool but that seemed disproven through the 1940s and 1950s, when all wool sold even though production increased still further. Apart from the improvements to yield within the farm-gate, that generation of woolgrowers felt little pressure for change and insisted that, if there were to be change, they should control it.

Gradually through the 1960s realisation grew that economic factors, mainly outside New Zealand's control, dominated prices, making necessary domestic mitigation of the impact of low prices. That interested farmers directly, because it called for changes to the way in which their wool sold within New Zealand before being shipped overseas. The strongly fragmented industry had grown in an uncontrolled manner, first, in the vast numbers of small, individual, wool farms, and, second, in the many intermediary stages before wool reached the textile manufacturers. There seemed little consciousness of the fragmentation that the Woolbuyers' Association identified as the root cause of the problems – 'the fragmented supply from 40,000 growers to 100 private merchants and 42 brokers' stores'.[251] The growers in some ways resembled the cottage industries in Britain early in the Industrial Revolution – self-employed workers working at home passing their goods to agents and being told the prices they would receive.

The insistence that those many small growers should control the industry hindered change. Clearly, fragmentation that increased costs needed to reduce, but a strong minority of farmers insisted that they knew best how change should be implemented. The many other groups involved brokers, merchants, stock and station agents, dump store controllers, shipment controllers – all of whom sought to maintain their position in the industry, also forestalled change. In the late 1960s, the Wool Board, Wool Commission and Government agreed that changes to marketing had become necessary, but not by abandoning the auction system but by creating an Authority which purchased wool from growers before it went to auction. All elements in the chain from grower to consumer objected and prevented the change being introduced; the fear of interference in their own activities outweighed concern that change might be to the overall benefit for New Zealand.

The continuing low prices during the early 1970s convinced many in the New Zealand wool industry that reform had become essential. But, amidst a strong minority opposition, a Wool Corporation, introduced without its powers being defined fully, coincided with increased prices

[251] 'Woolbuyers Offer Marketing Plan', *Straight Furrow*, 06/10/1971, 10, ATL.

that strengthened opposition to change. Debate centred on whether the Corporation should have the power to compulsorily acquire all New Zealand's wool before marketing it overseas and whether such power should be in place only if agreed by a referendum of growers. The Wool Board, in the hope of avoiding controversy, held back from proposing openly compulsory acquisition, but, when the Board's intention became clear, a well-organised opposition, though not clearly a majority, stymied the proposed changes. After a decade of discussion, proposals for reform were laid aside.

It is difficult to identify what adaptation might have maintained wool as a high export earner for New Zealand. Perhaps changing to production of fine rather than coarse wool earlier might have slowed down the falling sales, but sheep that give fine wools are not high quality meat producers. Accepting and managing the decline, by finding replacements for the loss of earnings from wool, became the necessary task from the 1970s onwards. Meat exports provided those replacements. Many sheep farmers changed from wool production to meat, partly, by changing to beef production in addition to lamb.

9

Handling the Threat to Wool from Synthetics

9.1 Introduction

At first after World War II, New Zealand woolgrowers shared the attitude towards synthetics reported in *Straight Furrow* by F. J Collins in 1946. He said, 'a shrewd-headed, hard-thinking Yorkshireman, manager of one of Britain's biggest woollen mills' had told Collins:

> Artificial wool? Rubbish! There's no need to lose any sleep over that – now or ever. . . . They may in time succeed in making a more cheaply produced fibre . . . but, at best, it will only be a poor imitation. Take the health-giving properties of wool. Only nature can produce those. You'll never get those in any substitute.[1]

The threat from synthetics was first brought home to woolgrowers in the late 1940s by the need for greater quality control but other steps to deal with the threat were left to the IWS.

[1] 'The Threat of Synthetics', *Straight Furrow*, 15/06/1946, 35, ATL.

D. Hall, *Emerging from an Entrenched Colonial Economy*, Palgrave Studies in Economic History, DOI 10.1007/978-3-319-53016-1_9

Because the IWS's existence depended initially on the threat from synthetics, the organisation tended to stress the threat. Collins reported the views of the IWS Research Division head, a 'scientist interested only in facts and conscious of the possibilities of science':

> The superiority of wool in certain respects is no safeguard.... Synthetic fibres ... may nevertheless be successfully mixed with wool.... Such fabrics can retain some of the most important qualities of wool while, at the same time, cause a serious reduction in the amount of wool consumed. [2]

Concern about competition from synthetics lessened in the 1940s with wool markets stronger than in the 1930s and many doubted that the IWS helped New Zealand sales of raw wool. Growers paid a levy to support the IWS but only vaguely understood what the IWS did and how it helped them. When the Wool Board doubled the levy in 1964 that raised the IWS profile and woolgrowers began to ask questions about how their money was spent and how they benefitted. There were no clear answers. Following the price collapse of 1966–1968 woolgrowers questioned even more strongly the IWS's value. The Wool Board's financial weaknesses in the late 1960s persuaded the government to contribute to IWS costs but the government shared the woolgrowers' doubts. Eventually, in the 1970s, the Wool Board began to share those doubts and started, itself, to promote New Zealand wool sales overseas.

9.2 The Post-World War II Responses to the Threat from Synthetics

The government investigated possibilities for synthetics in New Zealand in 1945. The first change forced on woolgrowers was the increased importance of quality control. The IWS increased its coverage of wool-consuming countries through the 1950s but woolgrowers were sceptical about its impact. The Wool Board began a campaign to convince

[2] 'The Threat of Synthetics', *Straight Furrow*, 15/06/1946, 35, ATL.

woolgrowers of the importance of the IWS and, when the synthetics industry increased its promotion in the late 1950s, the Wool Board decided that the wool industry should respond with increased promotion.

In 1945 the New Zealand government recognised the eventual importance of synthetics as a complementary fibre to wool, and sought not to repel their growth but to establish a New Zealand foothold in their exploitation. The government allowed a delegation led by the Chairman of the British Rayon Federation, Sir Percy Ashley, to visit to discuss the possibilities.[3] New Zealand woolgrowers remained suspicious; Federated Farmers showed its hostility to developing rayon goods in New Zealand, but allowed Ashley to explain the rayon manufacturers' point of view through an interview with *Straight Furrow*. Ashley insisted that rayon would not compete with wool; joint wool/rayon textiles would expand wool consumption by introducing new products.[4] The woollen mills in New Zealand, supplying mainly the domestic textile market, had no reservations about using synthetics, keeping themselves 'abreast of developments' by manufacturing cloths that included synthetics 'in accordance with local demand'.[5] But a generation passed before woolgrowers in New Zealand accepted the advantages and inevitability of blending wool with synthetics.

Traditional farm-gate methods were disadvantageous for wool *vis-a-vis* synthetics and needed to change. Wool clips had to be handled more carefully to avoid dirt and foreign matter in wool; those were absent during fabric production using synthetic fibres and strengthened the incentive for fabric manufacturers to use synthetics rather than wool. The Wool Board advised farmers on how to handle their wool clip, for

[3] Visit: British Rayon Delegation, EA1, Box 243, 59/3/1/57, Part 1, ATL. The Delegation visited, between April and June 1945, woollen mills in Otago and met various trade organisations in addition to meeting Walter Nash, who was acting Prime Minister at the time.

[4] 'Rayon Manufacturing In New Zealand', *Straight Furrow*, 15/05/1945, 15, ATL. The article, whilst making clear the hostility of Federated Farmers, allows Ashley to make the case for rayon as a complement and not a competitor for wool. This is an example of the policy of *Straight Furrow* informing farmers even of views opposed by Federated Farmers.

[5] Woollen Milling in New Zealand, 24/10/1958, Federated Farmers, 90 – 343 MSY–2736, M&W140/1958, 3, ATL.

instance, by thoroughly cleaning shearing/wool sheds before use, to avoid loss through dirt acquired in shearing/handling.[6] The need to avoid contamination caused by branding became important because synthetics suffered no such contamination. British wool manufacturers complained about finding tar or paint in New Zealand wool; French, Dutch and Belgian manufacturers made similar complaints.[7] Tar and paint, traditional materials used in branding, could interfere with textile production – 'There is nothing that causes more trouble and expense', said a mill principal in Huddersfield, in Britain.[8] *The Press* in June 1952 reported that branding problems had been discussed 'with monotonous regularity for more than 100 years'; branding risked 'wholesale rejection of otherwise very desirable wool'.[9] It was illegal to use tar and paint in New Zealand but the debate over materials used in branding continued with monotonous regularity through the mid-twentieth century. Ridding farming of traditional methods took a long time; Buchanan describes this dependence on past tradition as 'the general rule had been 'do what father did' rather than rational consideration of what would most cost effectively meet market requirements'.[10]

In 1952, Dr Lipson of the Wool Textile Laboratory in Australia predicted accurately what happened in the next two decades. He believed that the advent of new synthetic fibres would not be catastrophic for wool. Each fibre type would play a role in overcoming the world's shortage of textile raw materials.[11] That proved to be the case; both wool and synthetics consumption increased, the growing needs for textiles globally could not be satisfied by either alone.[12] Man-made fibres took business away from other fibres such as cotton rather than wool. By

---

[6] 'Advice on Handling the Wool Clip', *Straight Furrow*, 15/02/1947. 26/7, ATL.

[7] 'Tar Branding of Wool', *Straight Furrow*, 15/12/1947, 37, ATL; 'Continental Textile Manufacturers Complain About Tarry Wool', *Straight Furrow*, 15/03/1949, 35, ATL.

[8] 'Tar Branding of Wool', *Straight Furrow*, 15/12/1947, 37, ATL.

[9] 'Spoilage through brands – Overseas Buyers Restive', *The Press*, 20/6/1952.

[10] Roger Buchanan, *The Last Shepherd: Anecdotes and Observations from five decades in the Wool Industry* (Wellington: Ngaio Press, 2012), 113.

[11] 'No Satisfactory Substitute: Wool Stands Supreme', *Straight Furrow*, 01/06/1952, 29, ATL.

[12] 'World Production of Chief Industrial Fibres', *Straight Furrow*, 01/06/1957, 50, ATL.

1961, man-made fibre production had increased, from 13% to 24% of world fibre production, but wool production did not change, remaining at 10%.[13]

In the early 1960s patents for synthetics were due to expire and chemical companies other than the original companies expected to enter the market, creating more competition with prices falling by 25%–30%. The IWS noted that synthetics sold more cheaply than wool; wool prices could not exceed synthetics by very much without risking reduced demand for wool. The IWS decided that it needed to break the link between wool and synthetics' prices by promoting wool as a superior product for which consumers would expect to pay more; to achieve that the IWS needed an increased budget.

In 1959, the Wool Board Chairman, Harry Wardell, warned that increased promotion by the synthetics industry needed to be matched by increased IWS promotion of wool.[14] Wardell took up the same theme six months later in his report to the Electoral Committee. After reporting that wool prices had fallen by 42% between the 1956/1957 season and the start of 1959, he said that that had led to criticism of the IWS. He saw the criticism as inevitable because the IWS acted on behalf of

> scores of thousands of individual woolgrowers who are situated many thousands of miles away with little or no knowledge or understanding of the Secretariat's activities.[15]

He did not see that lack of knowledge and understanding as a criticism of the Wool Board. The Board, as New Zealand's prime interface with the IWS, failed to make growers aware of IWS activities.

Wardell rejected criticism of the IWS. He said there was no evidence to show that the IWS promotion had deteriorated. The IWS's work since 1956 'has been better and more widespread than ever before'. But, to the remote woolgrowers that might be seen as condemning IWS

[13] 'More Man-Made Fibres, Less Demand For Wool', *Straight Furrow*, 23/08/1961, 23, ATL.

[14] Chairman's Address to the Electoral Committee, 19/03/1959, Federated Farmers MSY–2737, M&W10/1959, 11, ATL.

[15] Chairman's Address to the Electoral Committee, 27/08/1959, Federated Farmers MSY–2737, M&W39/1959, 3, ATL.

promotion, it had been 'better and more widespread' but prices for raw wool and woolgrowers' incomes had fallen significantly. Wardell demonstrated an ongoing separation between the Wool Board and growers over the IWS. The Wool Board judged the IWS by sale of woollen suits and not by the income reaching New Zealand woolgrowers. Wardell said that the 'severe financial losses' in which woolgrowers were 'unwilling partners' did not begin at the retail counter where the IWS had most impact, but in the 'pipeline' that fed raw wool to manufacturers. To Wardell and the Wool Board, IWS successfully promoted wool; unsurprisingly woolgrowers were more doubtful.

9.3 Increased Prominence for the IWS and Increased Questioning

In 1962, the IWS changed to the structure of a private enterprise, and one that gave Australia dominance, with the change being paid for by increasing the growers' levy. That increased the wariness with which New Zealand growers viewed the IWS. Through the 1960s, growers sought to understand better how the IWS supported them, but responses remained unclear. The Wool Board pressed the government to contribute financial support but that made growers and the Board hold back criticism of the IWS to avoid discouraging the government. Following the 1966–1968 price collapse, the government reluctantly agreed to financial support and that led to more direct questioning of the IWS activities, bypassing the Wool Board.

Acland, after taking over from Wardell as Wool Board Chairman in 1960, reported that IWS efficiency would be increased by Secretariat decisions being agreed no longer unanimously but by a majority vote of the Wool Boards of Australia, New Zealand and South Africa. Australia contributed 62% of the IWS budget and that now gave it a majority on the IWS Board (7 members with 3 each from New Zealand and South Africa). The New Zealand Wool Board agreed to the change 'readily' on the grounds that Board members would still think as 'woolgrowers rather than as nationals of any particular country'.[16] Through the 1960s and 1970s that change left lingering concerns amongst New Zealand producers that the IWS operated in Australia's interest rather than that of all three countries. When the Australian Wool Board Chairman William Gunn took over as the IWS Chairman in the early 1960s, and stayed on as Board Chairman, that encouraged those concerns.

In response to the growing concerns about synthetics amongst the Wool Boards of New Zealand, Australia and South Africa, Australia took the initiative and encouraged the IWS to adopt the structure used by a competitive private enterprise. In 1962, the IWS changed to that structure and engaged Bill Vines as Managing Director; Vines had been the World Manager for the Berger paint organisation and described as 'One of the best salesman in Britain'.[17] The Australian Wool Bureau Chairman claimed that 'woolgrower organisations . . . recognise the need for a fast-moving organisation capable of meeting the challenge of competing fibres'. But the IWS differed from a private enterprise in that it did not have to compete for income – income was from the levy paid by each woolgrower per bale of wool produced. The Australian Wool and Meat Producers Federation reflected scepticism amongst growers; the Federation expected to see growers reluctant to pay an increased levy at a time of economic difficulties, especially following a fall in wool prices even though there had been an increase in the IWS budget in previous years.

The New Zealand Wool Board decided that competition from synthetics needed a stronger response and agreed that the IWS promotion should be put on a footing more akin to the synthetics industry. That needed a vastly increased budget. The Board had its own promotion department, with a Director of Trade Promotion, but the department promoted wool sales within New Zealand rather than internationally.[18] The three IWS countries had agreed that individual countries should not

[16] Address by Chairman of the Wool Board to the Meat and Wool Section, 23/03/1961, Federated Farmers, 90 – 343 MSY–2737, M&W27/1961, 10, ATL.

[17] 'Bigger Spending for Research and Promotion', *Straight Furrow*, 15/02/1961, 21, ATL; 'Man Who Directs Battle for Wool's Future', *Straight Furrow*, 19/12/1962, 1, ATL.

[18] Wool Board Minutes, 31/01/1961, 9–10, ANZ.

promote their own wool separately overseas but leave international promotion to the IWS. New Zealand complained when the Australian Wool Bureau, an organisation separate from the Australian Wool Board, arranged an 'Australian Wool Awards display' in London.[19]

In 1963, the IWS had directors based in the USA, Canada, Switzerland, Norway, Sweden, Finland, Denmark, Belgium, Holland, Italy, France, Britain, Japan and India as well as units in Greece, Turkey, Spain and other Mediterranean countries.[20] In each consumer country the IWS promoted indigenous wool sales first, aiming to raise demand to a level at which it could not be satisfied by indigenous wool alone, and imports from IWS countries would be needed. The IWS sought 'not promote wool on a national basis but merely to promote wool as a commodity independent of its source of origin'. The IWS also undertook extensive consumer surveys and tried to persuade textile industries in each country to adopt new woollen products and new processes. Manufacturers, retailers and the IWS agreed to advertise wool products jointly on the understanding that advertisements stressed the wool content.

The IWS promoted products made only from pure wool, and not those manufactured from wool and synthetic fibre blends. One successful outcome for the IWS was the creation of Woolmark, a symbol used only on products made from pure wool. By distinguishing pure wool products from others the IWS tried to create an impression that the quality of pure wool products was superior. Blending was in its infancy in 1963 while improvements were still being made to pure wool's quality and performance. But the reduced effort in keeping synthetic products in good condition made them more attractive; for instance, washing woollen products needed greater care to avoid shrinkage. IWS research introduced new properties for woollen textiles such as 'drip-dry' and

[19] Wool Board Minutes, 01/03/1961, 2, ANZ.

[20] International Wool Secretariat, Dept. Industries and Commerce, 29/01/1963, AAQW–WW3379, Box39, 1/5, ATL. This paragraph and the next are a summary of a report of the meeting of the New Zealand Trade Commissioner in Delhi with the IWS Managing Director. The Commissioner produced a summary of the meeting for the Department of Industries and Commerce in Wellington. It seems that woolgrowers did not see that report.

'wash and wear', previously properties thought to be possessed only by synthetics. But manufacturers needed persuading to adopt those new techniques.[21]

IWS promotion encouraged consumer demand for woollen textiles with the intention that that would create demand for raw wool, but there seemed no attempt to make sure that increased demand would be satisfied by sale of raw New Zealand wool. The IWS focussed on persuading manufacturers to continue to sell woollen products, and not on where they bought their raw wool or the price they paid. The IWS had a conflict of interest because it sought to increase demand for woollen products sold by manufacturers but increased demand needed low prices and cheap raw wool, giving an incentive to reduce, not increase, growers' incomes. Measuring its success by woollen goods' sales gave the IWS a disincentive to act in a way that increased the price of raw wool. The 1971 Battelle Report had concluded that the 'posture of the IWS would be open to question' if it became involved in selling [raw] wool.[22] Vines rejected IWS involvement in raw wool promotion whilst 'he had no physical control over its quality or selling price'.[23] No one promoted the sale of raw New Zealand wool overseas.

New Zealand woolgrowers accepted warily that need for change in the IWS. The Federated Farmers Meat and Wool Section Chairman, Alec Begg, said that producers would watch 'with interest' the change in the IWS to an Australian-dominated Board and a 'highly paid managing director'.[24] Begg admitted that 'farmers, partly due to remoteness of situation and partly to the ties of their work', tended to 'lose sight of the many changes taking place around us'.[25] He argued that expecting the farmer alone to pay for promotion of wool was unfair

---

[21] '"Drip Dry Wool Will Take the Lead"', *Straight Furrow*, 16/09/1959, 8, ATL.

[22] Final Report on the Marketing of New Zealand Wool to the New Zealand Wool Board – Recommendations, 13/08/1971, Acland Family Papers, MB44, MBL.

[23] Carter and MacGibbon, 207.

[24] Address by Chairman of the Meat and Wool Section, 21/06/1961, Federated Farmers, 90 – 343 MSY–2736, M&W20/1961, 2, ATL.

[25] Chairman's Address to the Meat and Wool Section, 21/06/1961, Federated Farmers, 90 – 343 MSY–2738, M&W20/1961, 11, ATL.

> for the last 25 years successive governments had enforced the claim that overseas exchange received from exports belonged not to the producers but to New Zealand.

The farmer could justifiably ask whether 'the general public' through the government should also contribute.[26]

Through the 1940s and 1950s woolgrowers lost little sleep over synthetics, but eventually in the 1960s the Wool Board began to lose sleep. The Board had much difficulty in persuading woolgrowers that their nights should be disturbed also, Woolgrowers reluctant to see the levy increased were told 'they were living in the past' if they could not see the need for increased promotion.[27] But opposition persisted and Rangitikei sheep farmers criticised the IWS plans as being 'too big'.[28] Through the 1960s, the Wool Board spent 80% of its income on IWS activities. Rangitikei farmers felt that the IWS expenditure had not been explained and the IWS had been given a 'blank cheque'. Farmers wanted to know how the money was spent – 'as farmers we have too little say'.[29] But Acland, when asked by growers for details of the proposed IWS expenditure, had refused because 'it would give away secrets to the synthetic fibre industry... we don't see the balance sheets of our competitors'.[30]

Eventually the Wool Board decided that the levy on woolgrowers should be doubled, and that the increase should be matched using interest from the Wool Commission's Reserve funds up to the maximum allowed by legislation. Growers criticised the Wool Board for failing to consult them before making a decision to increase the IWS levy; the Federated Farmers Meat and Wool Section insisted that there should be no further increase 'without consultation with the grower'.

---

[26] Chairman's Address to the Meat and Wool Section, 21/06/1961, Federated Farmers, 90 – 343 MSY–2736, M&W20/1961, 5/6, ATL.

[27] 'Increased Wool Levy "Essential"', *Straight Furrow*, 07/11/1962, 19, ATL.

[28] 'Wool Scheme "Too Big"', *Straight Furrow*, 21/08/1963, 20, ATL.

[29] Wool Board Levy, 27/08/1973, Federated Farmers 90–343–04/3, M&W51/1973, 7, ATL; 'IWS Budget Explanation Wanted', *Straight Furrow*, 03/06/1964, 23, ATL.

[30] 'Big Rise In I.W.S Budget', *Straight Furrow*, 04/07/1962, 28, ATL.

The Federated Farmers Provincial Meat and Wool Chairman said that the Wool Board retained Federated Farmers support 'by a majority that was very slender indeed'.[31] Acland insisted that 'the final decision lay with the Board itself'.

After an increased levy had been agreed by the New Zealand Wool Board, Gunn described to the Boards of New Zealand, Australia and South Africa how the increased resources would be used.[32] Gunn said that the IWS had one objective – 'to make woolgrowing profitable for the 200,000 woolgrowers whom we represent'. The IWS had four elements: research, marketing, productivity and promotion. Research improved wool's performance as a textile fibre and also improved efficiency in wool production. Gunn had no doubt that the world market for textiles would grow and wool production needed to increase to stop wool's market share becoming smaller. The IWS Managing Director, Vines, reported on promotion.[33] Synthetics were 20% cheaper than wool and that threatened wool prices. Manufacturers who bought raw wool would sell woollen products at the higher price only if supported by promotion that created demand for the higher-priced product. The IWS provided promotion to support the manufacturers' own promotion. Vines said, confidently, that with the increased IWS budget, prosperity would be achieved for woolgrowers.

New Zealand woolgrowers could not see clearly how IWS promotion overseas helped them, and they had justifiable doubts; promotion most directly benefitted the overseas textile industries. The IWS claimed that IWS promotion stopped those industries changing to synthetics. How increases in their sales led to increased earnings from raw wool sales for New Zealand remained unclear. The IWS aimed at stimulating consumption but price instability stopped increased consumption

---

[31] 'Who Should Pay For IWS Work?', *Straight Furrow*, 17/06/1964, 4, ATL.

[32] Address by the Chairman of the international Wool Secretariat Board, 17/01/1964, International Wool Secretariat, Dept. Industries and Commerce, AAQW–WW3379, Box39, 1–8, ANZ. The two paragraphs summarise Gunn's speech.

[33] Address by the Managing Director of the International Wool Secretariat, 17/01/1964, International Wool Secretariat, Dept. Industries and Commerce, AAQW–WW3379, Box39, 1–5, ATL.

translating always into increased earnings for woolgrowers. Gunn had said that the IWS aimed at making wool growing profitable for producers but, perhaps, trying to keep them in business rather than pushing up their income seemed a more plausible outcome.

The Wool Board through the 1960s had no doubts that the IWS gave value for money. Buchanan says that even up to the 1980s the Wool Board reproduced 'IWS spin . . . without question and without editing'.[34] Carter and MacGibbon demonstrate how the IWS was an advertising agent in the glamorous world of high fashion in Europe and the USA, occasionally mixing with Royalty.[35] Possibly that glamour blinded the Wool Board, discouraging the Board from asking the more down to earth questions on IWS operations, for instance, how did they benefit New Zealand woolgrowers? Farmers were less susceptible to the glamour of royalty, and, in 1965, Begg reserved judgement on the expansion of IWS activities; he expected a full assessment to be made after a five-year 'trial period'.[36]

A full assessment did not take place. Instead, Acland as an IWS Board member and an integral part of the organisation wrote in 1969 a 'necessarily brief review' that he called 'personal and not meant to be definitive'.[37] The review reported how the IWS had spent its money with no attempt at measuring quantitatively the return from New Zealand's investment. IWS 'achievements' were described in vague generalities. Acland said that IWS promotion cannot control the market, it can only influence it. The IWS had 'led the way in a revival of the wool textile industry in many countries', but Acland did not identify those countries and whether New Zealand had benefitted from that revival. In Acland's review there is no attempt to demonstrate 'prosperity' being brought to New Zealand woolgrowers – the declared objective used to justify a vastly increased budget for the IWS. Three years later the IWS

[34] Buchanan, 124.

[35] Carter and MacGibbon, 228–241.

[36] Chairman's Address to the Meat and Wool Section, 23/06/1965, Federated Farmers, 90 – 343 MSY–2737, M&W18/1965, 2, ATL.

[37] The International Wool Secretariat: A Review, 30/04/1969, Federated Farmers, 90 – 343 MSY–2745, M&W23/1969, 1–10, ATL.

Managing Director said that the IWS did not have a means of assessing gains from promotion; that came out very clearly in Acland's review. Acland presented his review to the Federated Farmers Meat and Wool Council. But the Council gave priority to demanding that government should pay for IWS activities, not to the IWS's effectiveness.[38] Producers wanted the government to contribute to IWS support and avoided reinforcing government doubts by criticising IWS activities.

Through the 1960s, calls had continued for the government to contribute to reduce the woolgrowers' levy, and the Wool Board continued to try to find a politically acceptable way for the government to contribute. In 1969, when the depression in prices threatened the capital resources of the Wool Board and Wool Commission, the government found it increasingly difficult to refuse support. The Cabinet Secretary felt it necessary to remind the Cabinet of points made in earlier discussions on the topic. He reported three main points: there was no evidence wool producers needed support; sheep farmers' incomes had increased more than the average for farmers overall; and market trends made it inappropriate to encourage increased production rather than better export marketing.[39]

A C B Maiden, head of the Primary Industries Department in Australia, took over from Vines as the IWS Managing Director in 1969, and tried to justify the investment in the IWS to the New Zealand Electoral Committee in 1972.[40] His claimed that IWS promotion increased wool prices, but could support that only with

> you would have to search widely to find . . . a manufacturer prepared to offer a guarantee that wool prices would drop by less than one cent were IWS promotion to be stopped.

[38] Minutes of the Meat and Wool Section Council Meeting, 30/04/1969, Federated Farmers, 90 – 343 MSY–2745, M&W24/1969, 5, ATL.

[39] Financial Assistance for Wool Promotion, 31/03/1969, International Wool Secretariat, Dept. Industries and Commerce, AAQW–WW3379, Box39, 2, ANZ.

[40] Report to the New Zealand Electoral College, undated (probably March 1972), International Wool Secretariat, Dept. Industries and Commerce, AAQW–WW3379, Box39, ANZ. The following two paragraphs summarise Maiden's report.

He claimed also that IWS promotion, for instance, the introduction of Woolmark, had broken the link that tied wool prices to synthetics' prices, and wool prices had fallen through the 1960s by less than those for synthetics. Maiden said that the IWS sought a 'more academically acceptable assessment of the gains from promotion', but accepted that he could not give 'final or scientific proof that promotion pays off'.[41]

It was never made clear to farmers that the IWS promotion supplemented the textile manufacturers' own promotion rather than promoting raw New Zealand wool. Acland had become Wool Board Chairman when IWS expansion had been the key issue. He supported the IWS expansion and spent the 1960s defending that decision. Acland, justifiably, assessed that synthetics threatened wool in the long term, and that would eventually reduce wool consumption. But wool production continued to increase through the 1950s and 1960s, and New Zealand growers seemed to have no difficulty selling wool. Even during the price collapse of 1966/1968 wool still sold – to the Wool Commission. The increased wool consumption reflected increased consumption of all fibres. That seemed to give lie to the 1930s expectation that synthetic fibres would replace wool; both were needed to meet the increased demand for textiles in the 1940s, 1950s and 1960s.

As part of their proposed marketing plan that followed the Wool Study Group's report in 1968, the Wool Board and the Wool Commission proposed that New Zealand should introduce 'technical promotion . . . of the use of New Zealand raw wool in overseas markets' to increase 'the demand for New Zealand wools by keeping manufacturers fully informed' on the various New Zealand wools and their suitability. That attempted to plug the gap left by the IWS; the events of 1966–1968 had brought that gap increasingly to the attention of those outside the Wool Board.[42] The situation feared by Acland and the IWS became obvious in the 1970s, and the Battelle Report summarised well the threats. The demand for all fibres levelled off

[41] Report to the New Zealand Electoral College, undated (probably March 1972), International Wool Secretariat, Dept. Industries and Commerce, AAQW–WW3379, Box39, 18, ANZ.

[42] Marketing Programme of the New Zealand Wool Board and the New Zealand Wool Commission, 26/11/1968, AALR W5427 873 Box 774, 1–13, ANZ.

with wool consumption beginning to fall in absolute terms rather than just in relative terms. The textile industries stagnated or declined in most of New Zealand's main customers for raw wool. Only Asia-Pacific markets grew.[43]

In 1970 the government finally came round to contributing to the IWS levy, but in doing so demonstrated its doubts about IWS promotion, contributing only to IWS research and development.[44] Increased support followed in 1971, including a contribution to IWS promotion, but with the proviso that the Wool Board appointed the Director-General of Agriculture, or his nominee, as a Wool Board representative on the IWS Board, with full voting rights.[45] The government worried that the IWS proposed changes advantageous to Australian interests. Buchanan suggests that eventually the Wool Board also became concerned with the Australia-centric IWS stance.[46]

At the end of 1971 the Acting Minister for Agriculture, H. L. Pickering, asked the government's representative on the Wool Board, B S Trolove, to raise issues on the effectiveness of the IWS at its next Board meeting. In doing so, the Minister illustrated the specific long-term concerns of woolgrowers on the worth of investment in the IWS.[47] Pickering wanted Trolove to question how the IWS policies would benefit New Zealand directly. Also should the IWS increase expenditure on research at the expense of promotion? Would the IWS 'give consideration to an independent assessment of its activities' because of the frequent complaints about its role? He questioned also whether more IWS funds should be spent on promoting New Zealand wool to manufacturers rather than promoting sales from manufacturers to

[43] B. Toyne, and eleven others, *The Global Textile Industry* (London: George Allen and Unwin, 1984), 88–90.

[44] IWS Grant for Research and Development, 02/11/1970, Wool (raw) Administration, International Wool Secretariat Constitution Function Reports, AAQW – WW3379 Box 39 Part 1, 8/1/18, ANZ.

[45] Wool Board Finance, Wool (raw) Administration, 24/05/1971, International Wool Secretariat Constitution Function Reports, AAQW – WW3379 Box 39 Part 1, 8/1/18, 2, ANZ.

[46] Buchanan, 124.

[47] Minister of Agriculture to B S Trolove, 04/11/1971, Wool (raw) Administration, International Wool Secretariat Constitution Function Reports, Wool (raw) – Administration – International Wool Secretariat Constitution Function Reports, AAQW – WW3379 Box 39 Part 2, 8/1/18, ANZ.

consumers. Finally, he questioned spending considerable IWS resources in the declining USA market rather than spending in the potential growing markets of Eastern Europe. Wool Board members now questioned the IWS effectiveness and 'its relevance to the future marketing of New Zealand Wools'; two members 'pressed for assurances that the IWS was giving New Zealand value for money'.[48]

9.4 Doubts about IWS Effectiveness Grow and Those Are Justified

Trolove reported that it remained unclear whether IWS priorities were in New Zealand's best interests, and New Zealand began its own promotion of raw wool sales overseas. Gunn wanted more money for the IWS but the New Zealand Wool Board now opposed increased support and came close to withdrawing. Governments commissioned an independent review of IWS management but that did not assess the return to woolgrowers. The justification for the many doubts about the IWS is demonstrated by comparing New Zealand wool exports to countries with IWS promotion and those without. That demonstration supports Buchanan's judgement that New Zealand did not benefit from IWS generic promotion of wool product sales.

Trolove could not report any direct IWS support for sale of raw New Zealand wool. He said the IWS now promoted blends of wool and synthetics whilst still investigating the possibilities for carpets, the product of most interest to New Zealand.[49] To Trolove, the IWS did not want to see resources diverted from promotion to research because promotion, financed jointly by manufacturers and the IWS, persuaded manufacturers to 'include wool merchandise in their lines'; Acland called that 'the bait of promotional moneys'.[50] Trolove said that the IWS

[48] Carter and MacGibbon, 210.

[49] B S Trolove to the Minister of Agriculture, 09/11/1971, AAQW – WW3379 Box 39 Part 2, 8/1/18, ANZ.

[50] Chairman's Address to the Electoral Committee, 28/08/1969, Federated Farmers, 90 – 343 MSY–2745, M&W61/1969, 14, ATL.

Constitution did not allow it to promote raw wool sales to manufacturers. Ministers and growers outside the Wool Board had clearly been unaware of that point through the whole of the IWS life. Trolove continued that the IWS agreed that it would increase spending on technical activities in Eastern Europe but found it impossible to spend on promotion in the Communist bloc. Trolove agreed that an independent assessment would be desirable, but the marketing reform discussions in the member countries made it inappropriate to carry out such a review at present. The Battelle Report at this time dismissed the role of the IWS in five short sentences including: 'it was part of the marketing system . . . but is not a marketing organisation . . . it has relatively little contact with the raw wool using industry'.[51] The Battelle recommendations dismissed marketing through the IWS because it was 'inappropriate for actually conducting [raw] wool marketing'.[52]

In 1969 even the Wool Board began to doubt IWS's effectiveness, and began to send 'technical officers' overseas to promote the sale of raw New Zealand wool.[53] New Zealand became more active in promoting sale of its raw wool rather than leaving overseas promotion almost exclusively to the IWS. Buchanan took part in that increased promotion and calls those activities 'developing the religion of New Zealand wool'.[54] Rather than relying on the IWS alone to organise a stand at the Frankfurt Carpet Fair as in previous years, the New Zealand Wool Board shared the stand specifically to promote New Zealand wool.[55]

Increasingly, the New Zealand wool industry recognised that it had remained oriented more to the traditional pure-wool users whose importance declined relative to the modern multi-fibre firms. The New Zealand industry had remained too focussed on pure wool and put up

---

[51] Final Report on the Marketing of New Zealand Wool, 13/08/1971, Sir John Marshall Collection, MS–1403 121/05, 52, ATL.

[52] Final Report on The Marketing Of New Zealand Wool, 13/08/1971, Sir John Marshall Collection, MS–1403 121/05, 1, ATL. 1.

[53] Wool Board Chairman's Address to the Electoral Committee, 28/08/1969, Federated Farmers, 90 – 343 MS–Y2747, M&W61/1969, 11, ATL.

[54] Buchanan, 156.

[55] Address by the Chairman of the Wool Board to the Meeting of the Electoral Committee and the New Zealand Wool Board, 22/08/1972, 3, Acland Family papers, collection MB44, MBL.

barriers against participation in the modern textile developments. The Wool Board's General Manager, J D Fraser, began to talk about 'moving with the times in the textile trade – even promoting blends of wool with other fibres when this is advantageous to us'.[56] As Trolove had reported, the IWS Board had agreed that promoting blends should be started.[57] Maiden said that working with blends had been a 'subject of constant . . . agonising review' within the IWS. Assessment of the possibilities 'is infinitely more complex than many people appear to appreciate'. But the IWS staff thought 'blend promotion is an exciting development. . . . A realistic programme of blend promotion . . . will give us the experience . . . to react more effectively to future market developments'. In 1973, 27 years after the President of the British Rayon Federation had proposed during his visit to New Zealand that blended products would encourage wool use in new products, the IWS and the Wool Board accepted that proposal.[58]

In 1972 the New Zealand IWS board members would not agree the future IWS budget because growers did not want the IWS levy raised. Also, the New Zealand Wool Board was 'clearly divided in its attitude to IWS', and in the Board's assessment of what New Zealand 'obtained from its contribution'.[59] Horrified Wool Board staff responded that 'the spirit of criticism is endangering our ties with the IWS'. The staff feared that the Board might withdraw from the IWS which they considered would be a mistake. The staff pressed for an increase in the Board's income because

> the Board lacks the proper machinery for oversight of the IWS. . . . If the board had expert staff with full knowledge of IWS policies, expenditure, accounting and market research, a great many doubts would be resolved.[60]

[56] 'Depressed Wool Prices: How to Improve Returns', *Straight Furrow*, 19/11/1970, 4, ATL.

[57] Report to the New Zealand Electoral College, undated, International Wool Secretariat, Dept. Industries and Commerce, AAQW–WW3379, Box39, 13–15, ANZ.

[58] 'Secrecy Will Surround Woolblendmark Symbol', *Straight Furrow*, 06/01/1972, 3, ATL

[59] Meeting of the Wool Boards and the IWS, 02/03/1972, AAQW – WW3379 Box 39 Part 2, 5, ANZ.

[60] The Wool Board and the IWS – The View of Board Staff, 01/03/1972, No.335, Acland family papers, Collection MB44, MBL.

In 1973 the New Zealand, Australian and South African governments commissioned independent management consultants to review the IWS. The review questioned whether the management structure was appropriate for the scale, scope and nature of its operations, and whether the Managing Director was 'assisted by the most appropriate staffing arrangements' and 'assisted... by a board of the most suitable size and composition'.[61] But the review did not ask the key question that producers and the government had been asking for more than a decade: what financial return New Zealand woolgrowers received in return for their investment in the IWS? The report focussed almost entirely on maintaining the demand for woollen products, taking for granted that that would benefit IWS growers. The review made no attempt to review how past activities had benefitted woolgrowers, and made no recommendation on how that might be assessed.

The obvious test for IWS effectiveness is to review how New Zealand earnings changed in countries with IWS operations. In 1951 the IWS offices were in France, Italy, Belgium, Sweden, Switzerland, the Netherlands, Denmark, Sweden and Norway and an office was about to open in West Germany. The IWS impact remains unclear: over the next decade New Zealand wool exports went up in the first four of those countries and in West Germany but decreased in the other five. Vines said in 1961 that the IWS had directors in the USA, Canada, Switzerland, Norway, Sweden, Finland, Denmark, Belgium, Holland, Italy, France, Britain, Japan and India as well as units in Greece, Turkey, Spain and Mediterranean countries. Between 1961 and 1971 wool exports from New Zealand fell by about 20% in the countries named by Vines; for the countries, without support from the IWS, exports increased by about 50% (Fig. 9.1). By the end of the 1960s, New Zealand sales had fallen to insignificant levels in seven countries named by Vines (Switzerland, Sweden, Finland, Norway, India, Denmark and Turkey). The IWS had put its efforts into declining markets rather than identifying those with the best prospects for growth.

[61] Integrating Strategic Management and Control, March 1974, P338.176314 MACK 1974, (i), ATL.

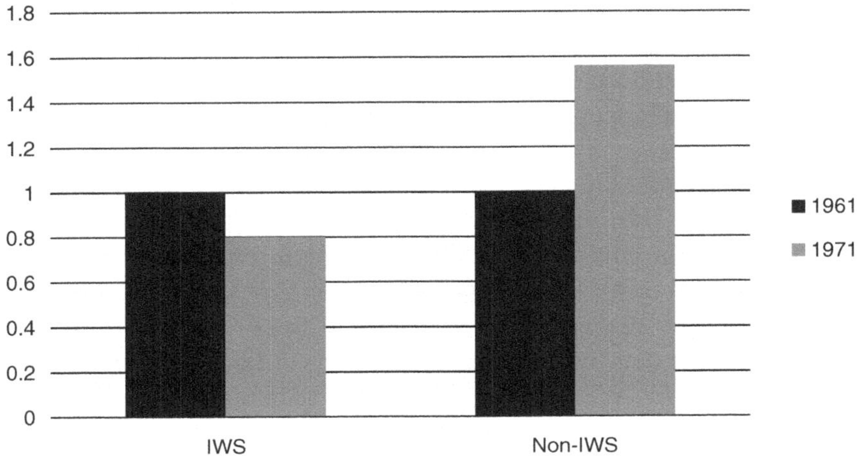

Fig 9.1 Relative wool tonnages sold to IWS and non-IWS countries (NZDYB)

Vastly increased promotion by the IWS in the 1960s led to only one permanent new market between 1960 and 1970: Spain, which accounted for only 0.3% of New Zealand exports. India ceased to be a customer despite being a country identified specifically by Gunn in 1962 as an Asian country in which a 'vast new market' might open up with increased promotion.[62] Gunn seemed unaware that, at the end of 1960, New Zealand's Trade Commissioner in Delhi had warned the Department of Industries and Commerce in Wellington that the IWS increased its budget for wool promotion in India fivefold with unfortunate timing as foreign exchange difficulties made India reduce licences for wool imports.[63] As warned by the Trade Commissioner, New Zealand earnings from wool sales in India dropped from more than £800,000 in 1963 to insignificant levels from 1964 onwards, whilst IWS operations continued until 1969. Such a complete falling off in raw wool sales accompanied by a considerable increase in IWS promotion fully justified doubts about the IWS.

[62] 'I.W.S., With Finance, Will Boost Wool', *Straight Furrow*, 06/06/1962, 17, ATL.

[63] Note on the International Wool Secretariat, 07/12/1960, International Wool Secretariat, Dept. Industries and Commerce, AAQW–WW3379, Box39, 1–2, ANZ.

In 1969 Acland reported that in the 1960s the IWS had opened branches in Austria, Finland, Mexico and Portugal. None showed any significant increases in buying New Zealand wool, especially the first, Austria, for which Statistics New Zealand shows no purchase in the late 1960s and early 1970s. Acland also identified Europe and North America as areas that received the greatest IWS resources; the IWS had 'greatly increased its promotional work on carpets in the USA, Britain and the rest of Europe' at the start of 1966.[64] But sales to Britain continued to decline whilst sales to the other Western European countries stagnated. The North American market began to decline from the mid-1960s to the point in the 1970s when Acland's successor said it could be written off.

Buchanan, and Carter and MacGibbon, point out a major concern over the IWS effectiveness for New Zealand. New Zealand's cross-bred wool, used mainly for interior textiles, represented only one-third of the wool used globally for those textiles. The IWS's generic promotion promoted the cause of all who supplied wool for interior textiles, including New Zealand's competitors.[65] But those competitors were 'freeloaders' who did not contribute to the IWS budget, thereby benefitting from the promotion funded by New Zealand woolgrowers. Buchanan argues strongly against the generic promotion, the whole essence of the IWS programmes.

New Zealand woolgrowers justifiably questioned the IWS value. There is no evidence that the IWS achieved the 'prosperity' for the growers that Vines expected to be generated by the increased budget for the IWS in the early 1960s. The existence of the IWS prevented New Zealand promoting its own overseas sales through the 1940s, 1950s and 1960s. If that promotion had been in place it would have brought home to New Zealand much earlier that its raw wool end-uses were shrinking, and, as pointed out by Buchanan, more than just marketing methods needed change. The International Wool Secretariat

[64] Wool Board Chairman's Address to the Electoral Committee, 02/03/1966, Federated Farmers, 90 – 343 MSY–2742, M&W80/1966, 4, ATL.

[65] Buchanan, 265–267, Carter and MacGibbon, 304.

demise began when New Zealand finally withdrew in 1994/1995 followed by South Africa soon afterwards and the remnants of the IWS lingered as an Australian wool promotion organisation, eventually splitting into separate organisations, Australian Wool Innovation and The Woolmark Company.[66]

9.5 Conclusion

By 1960 the Wool Board and the IWS had become far more aware of the potential long-term difficulties and the need for change. They were well aware of the concerns of wool consumers and the strength of competition from synthetic fibres, whose growth through the mid–twentieth century seemed, at one extreme, to threaten wool's eventual extinction as an essential raw material for textiles. The IWS had been set up to promote wool in its competition with synthetic fibres but the profitable period of the 1940s and 1950s argued against the IWS importance. The IWS needed to stress the threat from synthetics to justify its existence because a growers' levy paid partly for the IWS. The levy paid by woolgrowers to support IWS promotion subsidised the advertising budgets of textile manufacturers on the grounds that otherwise they would use synthetics rather than wool. That promotion could not have been more remote from actual woolgrowers in New Zealand, and it is not surprising that woolgrowers had strong doubts about contributing to significant increases in the IWS levy. It is unclear whether the IWS achieved its stated objective of enhancing growers' income. Perhaps the strongest claim, in retrospect, is that the IWS kept some New Zealand woolgrowers in business by encouraging textile manufacturers to maintain products made from pure wool for longer than might otherwise have been the case.

[66] Buchanan, 283.

10

Conclusion

This book has set out to understand how primary production in New Zealand coped with enforced change during the period 1945–1975, change enforced by changes in the financial position of its dominant customer, Britain, and by the New Zealand government's moves towards increased independence from Britain. New Zealand's comparative advantage as an efficient producer of agricultural produce made it dependent on primary production for export, it did not have sufficient advantage in other areas to move easily away from that dependence. Changes were needed within primary production and the markets for primary produce.

For meat and dairy exports at the end of World War II, Sinclair's description of New Zealand being 'paralysingly dependent on Britain' and McAloon's comment that New Zealand's 'colonial economy' remained 'entrenched' are very appropriate. In 1945, the high percentage of meat and dairy exports sold to Britain made the economy difficult to change, and it resembled a service to Britain ('Britain's Offshore Farm') rather than an economy free to choose its customers. During the period of bulk purchase, New Zealand needed British permission to sell elsewhere and it depended on British shipping to overcome the disadvantage of a

D. Hall, *Emerging from an Entrenched Colonial Economy*, Palgrave Studies in Economic History, DOI 10.1007/978-3-319-53016-1_10

geographic location distant from its main markets. The dependence on the British market had been strong at the start of the twentieth century though doubts about relying on that market had started to appear during the Depression years of the 1930s. Bulk purchase by Britain during and after World War II restored that dependence. Even through the 1950s and 1960s, meat and dairy sales to Britain remained entrenched and relying on British favour through agreements for 'free and unrestricted' access that New Zealand producers and government viewed as essential for keeping exports sufficiently high to maintain New Zealand's standard of living.

A reluctance to move away from the British market for meat and dairy exports is not surprising. Not only sentiment and loyalty encouraged continuation of the bulk purchase contracts for meat and dairy produce into the 1950s. Retaining strong links with the British market made commercial sense, especially in the immediate aftermath of war, when markets outside Britain, and the shipping needed to take goods to those markets, would have been extremely difficult to find. Britain's need for essential meat and dairy imports made exports from New Zealand profitable and created a secure financial base for New Zealand primary producers for at least three decades after the war.

Attitudes in New Zealand changed in the late 1940s and early 1950s, when Britain still set meat and dairy prices based on producer costs. New Zealand's more favourable climate made costs less than those of other countries, for instance, Denmark, and Britain paid higher prices for Danish produce. New Zealand producers, remote from the price negotiations, saw only the bottom line and not the factors that led to the bottom line. When Ormond wanted to 'twist the lion's tail' that captured what many producers thought privately, but had been reluctant to say publicly. Those concerns about prices paid by Britain grew during the Korean War when wool sold on the open market at substantial profit. The concerns encouraged New Zealand to end the bulk purchase contracts early but it was soon clear that dependence on Britain remained essential; retention of the meat agreement for free and unrestricted access remained a prime consideration for producers until the end of the 1960s. Also, dairy producers and the New Zealand government sought in 1957 and secured an agreement with Britain for free and unrestricted access. Retaining that agreement, even though it was temporarily set aside when a quota system was introduced, remained a political cornerstone for dairy exports until the end of the 1960s. The importance given to those agreements was not an illustration of a reluctance to change; it made commercial sense to retain that access to the British market as long as possible as a sheet anchor whilst markets elsewhere were built up. The absence of a catastrophic collapse in the New Zealand economy when restrictions were imposed by Britain in the 1960s, and then by the EEC in the 1970s, demonstrated that, by that time, New Zealand was no longer over-dependent on the British market. When exports fell after 1973 it was not because Britain had joined the EEC but because the oil price shock damaged the economies of most of New Zealand's major customers. The biggest fall was in wool, a commodity whose sales were independent of British EEC membership.

Meat and dairy producers comprised a force for change; diversification started as soon as Britain agreed that it no longer needed the full exportable surpluses in the 1950s, well before Britain first applied to join the EEC. Producers, represented by Federated Farmers, recognised the need for change and encouraged the boards and the government to take the necessary steps. Those steps needed to be taken cautiously as for any business venturing into new markets, weighing carefully expected benefits against the additional investment needed. Change was slowed down not by endemic conservatism but by the barriers that protected the subsidised agriculture of others, subsidisation that led to dumping and further inhibited New Zealand's moves into new markets. Also, markets had to be built warily at first in Asia where lack of finance and unfamiliarity with New Zealand's meat and dairy produce slowed progress in building new markets.

The producer boards and the government recognised, reluctantly, until Norman Kirk pointed it out in 1969, the strong conflict of interest with American producers. Federated Farmers led by their General Secretary Alec O'Shea were well aware of those difficulties and tried to overcome the conflict by working with American producers. But the American market proved illusory once the Korean War ended, apart from a niche in the American beef market. The export of beef succeeded, against the protectionism of the USA, because the New Zealand contribution, although significant for New Zealand, represented a small fraction of American beef consumption, and did not threaten domestic producers in the USA. New Zealand tried to replace the threat of declining sales to Britain by growing its economic relationship with the USA, but it had the wrong basic industries to develop a strong economic relationship; apart from beef, the USA did not need New Zealand's agricultural exports. In addition to its agricultural protectionism, the USA slowed down New Zealand's market diversification by its frequent dumping of agricultural surpluses. The USA was not a good substitute for Britain as a customer for New Zealand produce, despite its considerably stronger consumer base than Britain.

By the end of the 1950s most meat and dairy producers accepted that Britain could no longer go on taking increases in exports, though it did carry on maintaining existing quantities. No other country wanted New Zealand's lamb and butter in anything like the tonnages sent to Britain; that hindered diversification of markets. Producers clung to the British market because it provided a relatively secure and remunerative income. Meat and dairy had become prime export products for New Zealand because of the British market's security and profitability. New Zealand relied on favourable treatment by, first, Britain, and then, by Britain and the EEC, for sale of lamb and butter. New Zealand could not afford major decline in selling those items to Britain even into the twenty-first century. Fortunately, Britain continued to take significant quantities well after it had joined the EEC, belying the fears of the 1960s when British membership of the EEC was seen as major threat to New Zealand's living standards.

John Ormond's well-publicised pronouncements on the continuing importance of the British market leave an impression of endemic conservatism in the meat industry, but were made in parallel with less well publicised diversification in meat markets, especially by independent exporters, apparently encouraged by other Meat Board members. Meat producers responded to the need for change, increasing their output of meat at the expense of wool, partly, by introducing beef cattle in addition to sheep. Dairy farmers also increased their production of beef. The changes had to be made slowly so that farmers could be convinced that sales of the changed product would be permanent. Achievement of the necessary change is demonstrated by the success of meat sales at the end of the 1960s and early 1970s. Freezing factories achieved change by introducing higher levels of hygiene and new products – originally simply producing carcasses but eventually turning carcasses into selected products presented in ways suitable for supermarkets.

Dairy farmers responded to the need for change by changing their herds from Jerseys to Friesians, as milk products based on solids rather than butterfat became more important. Also, they improved herd productivity through selective breeding and mechanisation of dairying. The dairy industry overall recognised the need for change from the 1950s, especially the need for companies to amalgamate to give increased flexibility in products, and farmers to increase their herd sizes at the expense of less efficient producers. Dairy benefitted by the diversification into what originally were called by-products but eventually became significant products in their own right, for instance, milk powder and casein. For dairy exports there was also a market diversification by provision of technical support, especially for processing milk powder into fresh milk in countries new to the processing. The industry recognised early the need to engage with Asia, and that that called for a far different approach to marketing from that for the long-established markets of Europe. There were barriers to change: the unfamiliarity of Asians with milk products; the lack of income in Asia to afford dairy products at prices that covered producers' costs; the protectionism that restricted New Zealand's dairy sales outside Britain; and, the dumping of surpluses by others, especially the USA, in New Zealand's potential new markets. But despite those obstacles to diversification, in addition to the increased productivity of dairy farmers, dairy factories successfully diversified their produce in response to market needs and the Dairy Board successfully adapted its marketing to suit the produce. Markets were expanded successfully to the extent that, by the early 1970s, production could not keep up with the increasing market opportunities.

New Zealand had successfully emerged from an entrenched colonial economy in meat and dairy produce by 1975 because it had reduced its dependence on Britain considerably; the trade relationship with Britain developed into a relationship no different to those with other countries. New Zealand producers were not 'compulsory decolonised' in the 1970s but had recognised even in the 1950s that they needed to move away from being Britain's dairy farm and begin a voluntary decolonisation. Establishing markets in other major economies (the original six EEC countries, the USA and Japan) made that change possible. There is a myriad of other markets but those would be insufficient by far without the exports to those major economies. Through the mid-twentieth century the growing economic weakness of its main customer forced New Zealand to become more aware of its geographical neighbours and to adapt. There is an obvious dominant power, China, which in the twenty-first century has the same need for agricultural imports that Britain had in the late nineteenth and early twentieth centuries. Whilst the farming community in New Zealand remains its backbone for overseas trade, New Zealand needs a strong economic relationship with a dominant economic power that needs agricultural produce. The relationship with Britain benefitted New Zealand up to the 1970s at least; China is now filling the economic role previously played by Britain. But the relationship is different because there are not [yet?] Belich's 'strong familial and sentimental links' that strengthened the relationship with Britain; lack of those links may stop [postpone?] New Zealand becoming China's dairy farm.

The wool industry was not entrenched and colonial; even before World War II New Zealand already had a diverse range of customers for its wool exports. Britain contracted to purchase New Zealand's wool during World War II but did not need the tonnages; bulk purchase ended as soon as the War finished leaving a considerable unused stockpile. Producers and the government were far less concerned at the loss of the British market for wool than for meat and dairy produce. Wool sales to Britain declined from the 1930s with the cause well understood – Britain's textile industry losing its competitive advantage. New Zealand coped easily with that decline by selling wool to others. Rather than losing the British market, synthetics had become the main threat in the long term. But the successful continuation of wool sales into the 1960s masked the threat from synthetics. Changes in the economies of the major wool-buying countries that caused price collapses remained a more immediate threat to woolgrowers' incomes than the impact of synthetics.

For woolgrowers, the success of wool exports through the 1940s, 1950s and 1960s discouraged change. Exports produced a steady income for woolgrowers despite the considerable fluctuations in price. Soon after World War II, the New Zealand wool industry easily re-established the diversity of markets that had been in place before the War. The global wool market recovered quickly and enabled farmers to return to earning a steady income despite occasional price collapses. The profits from wartime sales, and from selling the stockpile accumulated during the War, provided a safety cushion that mitigated the impact of those collapses.

New Zealand's wool, produced mainly from cross-bred sheep, suffered more than other wools from competition with synthetics, but woolgrowers' produce continued to be sold remuneratively, disguising the potential impact from synthetics. New Zealand wool bodies were more pre-occupied with how wool was handled and marketed within New Zealand rather than learning lessons from contact with end-users because they saw the latter as the IWS's role. The perception that the IWS handled the need for change outside New Zealand masked the need for change within New Zealand. New Zealand's wool exports might have been greater if the growing difficulty of selling cross-bred wool had been realised earlier; but changing to production of fine wools would have been at the expense of dual-purpose sheep and would have damaged sheep-meat sales. For most sheep farmers income from meat sales were on a par, at least, with wool sales.

It is not clear how the IWS benefitted New Zealand's woolgrowers. Its strongest benefit seemed to be to the textile manufacturers in the consumer countries. Increasing textile manufacturers' sales presumably led to increased wool buying but not necessarily New Zealand wool. The IWS was set up at a time of considerable fear that synthetics would replace wool but as that fear receded in the 1950s the justification for the IWS receded. The IWS failed to establish new markets and there is a noticeable lack of improvement in raw wool sales by New Zealand in countries in which the IWS had operations. Also, the IWS possibly retarded the collaboration between the pure wool and the synthetics industry; collaboration that eventually benefitted both.

The many thousands of small producers well separated from the wools' end-users constrained the industry. Proposals for marketing reform attempted to make the industry a more coherent and efficient entity but even the main proponent, Jack Acland, saw the reform as protecting the many small producers rather than changing the nature of the woolgrowing farms. The reforms aimed at marketing the growers' wool more efficiently but not at the growers themselves, except for how they sold their wool. Proposals for reform foundered partly because, even with its fragmented nature, international economics had made the industry prosperous in the 1940s and 1950s. Through the 1960s, the generation of wool farmers who farmed during the twenty years between the end of the 1930s and the end of the 1950s dominated the wool industry. That generation found the need for change within New Zealand difficult to comprehend. Fluctuations in price stimulated calls for reform but few reform proposals successfully carried through to implementation, especially when proposals for reform were delayed and coincided with upturns in the economies of the major wool buying nations. The rejection of reform in the early 1970s is a clear example of how a short, intensive, emotional, minority, campaign, targeted at farmers can succeed against rational proposals developed over many years.

Through the three decades after World War II wool had its established and diverse markets, and those continued without major need for change. There were no potential new customers that might have been secured with a more dynamic approach to diversifying markets. Woolgrowers did change in response to market pressures but to meat production rather than diversifying wool markets.

The reduction in the percentage of primary produce exports going to Britain simply continued the long-term reduction that had started in the 1930s. The percentage reduction did not demonstrate the 'nemesis' of British–New Zealand trade; it demonstrated the successful increase in New Zealand trade with countries in addition to trade with Britain – the percentage reduction should be celebrated rather than mourned. New Zealand acquired customers with growing economies in addition to its main customer whose affluent days were over. Britain could no longer afford increases in exports from New Zealand but did afford to carry on accepting significant quantities of lamb and butter. The breaking away from the British market was not driven by an eagerness to establish an independent identity but by the realisation that whilst Britain could not take increases Asia could. Ormond summarised well in 1972 that, despite the growing gap in trading interests, the strong bonds of sentiment and sympathy remained between New Zealand and the people of Britain.

The threat that Britain's EEC membership would be the 'hardest economic blow ever struck' encouraged New Zealand's diversification. John Ormond's warnings probably had far more impact in New Zealand than in Britain and the EEC countries. That threat of Britain's engagement with European unification gave an additional impetus to New Zealand's acceptance from 1957 that Britain could not continue to take the increases in exports necessary for New Zealand to maintain its living standards. Fear of Britain joining the EEC encouraged steps that were already in place rather than starting the search for new markets. Britain's membership of the EEC did not speed up significantly the decline in the percentage of New Zealand exports going to Britain and did not provoke a crisis in New Zealand's economy. The more significant impact was from Britain deciding in the 1940s to rebuild its indigenous agriculture which had been seriously weakened by its policy of free trade. The rebuilding took place partly to stave off starvation during wartime, but more significantly to stave off balance of payments problems after the war. Britain needed to reduce its imports considerably and food imports were a substantial item that, either, had to be reduced, or, at the least, not allowed to grow. Britain's increased production of dairy produce contributed to making the market over-supplied in the 1960s, and to the introduction of quotas that protected New Zealand from price collapses through the 1960s. Britain's reduced need for meat exports led to the levy on New Zealand lamb exports at the end of the 1960s.

Free and unrestricted access for meat and dairy produce had been the keynote of New Zealand's vital interests that it insisted should be preserved if Britain became an EEC member. But free and unrestricted access for both meat and dairy produce ended in the 1960s before Britain joined the EEC. The EEC took over dairy quotas that had been introduced by Britain in the 1960s partly to protect New Zealand. That takeover by the EEC gave additional benefits to New Zealand in that

Britain alone could no longer set prices and, for instance, EEC regulations made Britain pay compensation for sterling's depreciation. New Zealand's diversification to new markets made the EEC dairy quota more than sufficient and New Zealand did not at first fill the quota. For the wool industry there was never a threat from Britain's EEC membership; the original six EEC countries were significant customers for New Zealand wool as soon as markets were restored after World War II and by 1960 sales to those six had become stronger than those to the Commonwealth including Britain.

The special arrangements agreed by the EEC for New Zealand substantially met the assurance given to New Zealand in 1961 by the British Secretary for Commonwealth Affairs, Duncan Sandys. New Zealand succeeded in being treated as a special case because it adopted a clear strategy of not opposing British membership, whilst demonstrating to EEC countries the importance of continuing access for its meat and dairy products. The decade, between Britain's first application and EEC acceptance of British membership, enabled New Zealand to put in place the representation in EEC capitals, and support teams in New Zealand, to ensure a clear and persuasive strategic narrative with the EEC countries. Jack Marshall's quiet, gentlemanly, nature made him the ideal leader at the forefront of that support. New Zealand gained from British EEC membership also because Imperial Preference ended, and New Zealand no longer had to give preference to imports from Britain, more easily negotiating trade agreements with others. The impact of Britain's membership of the EEC on New Zealand is best described by Easton's statement – it was an emotional rather than an economic shock. Emotionally, for the generations, described by Barnes, that had grown up as British, the apparent rejection by the Motherland was, undoubtedly, an emotional disaster, but not for their economics; it injured their hearts but not their pockets. The introduction of satisfactory EEC sheepmeat regulations in 1980 finally confirmed that New Zealand had dealt successfully with the economic threats expected at the start of the 1960s when Britain first applied to join the EEC.

Over the 10 years of negotiations before the EEC accepted Britain as a member, the fears mutated into a myth, well established in the twenty-first century, that British membership was disastrous for New Zealand's economy, irrespective of what actually happened. Marshall's quiet diplomacy in Europe received far less attention in New Zealand than Ormond's well-publicised jeremiads. Even in 2016, the view remained that Britain had 'unceremoniously dumped' New Zealand when joining the EEC. The myth is perpetuated by Lind who calls the EEC negotiations 'machinations' [OED definition – 'malicious intrigue']. Further examples of that mutation are Belich's interpretation that the day Britain joined the EEC was a 'black letter day' for New Zealand and Brownie and Dalziel's conclusion that 'the potentially disastrous impact of Britain's entry . . . recognised . . . when it was first mooted . . . was amply justified'. Belich, and Brownie and Dalziel, have been misled by looking at changes over too restricted a period. Singleton and Robertson's conclusion that the Anglo–New Zealand nexus was 'brutally snapped' in 1973 is inconsistent with Britain remaining a prime customer for New Zealand meat and dairy produce into the twenty-first century. Mein Smith's interpretation that Britain 'abandoned' its Commonwealth food producers is inconsistent in New Zealand's case, with the Sandys assurance, the Luxembourg protocol, and the Dublin re-negotiation of that protocol in New Zealand's favour. Easton's comments that 'the common perception of the impact of Britain joining the EEC is an exaggeration' and there are still 'those who [wrongly] blame that event for the subsequent difficulties of the New Zealand economy' has been shown to be well justified by the studies reported in this book.

Personalities had a strong influence on how change was manifested. There is a clear distinction between the nature and impact of the main producer leaders during the period of change. Ormond, from a family that transplanted a part of England into New Zealand, seemed to want to remain a part of England. That encouraged him to cling to the British market but the contribution of others, for instance, independent exporters and other meat board members, enabled the niche markets of beef in the USA and mutton in Japan to become significant diversification. Acland was also from a family that transplanted a part of England but was more concerned with maintaining the financial standing of New Zealand woolgrowing families. There was little scope for expanding markets and wool industry reform was needed, but Acland tried to introduce it by consent whilst easing the impact on growers rather than bringing them sharply up against the need for change. He achieved consent but that was overturned by a minority, vociferously wanting to maintain the status quo. Linton was a manager rather than a farmer and, though strong willed, was less driven by emotional attachment to farming. He stood up to Britain as much as Ormond but in the quiet of meeting rooms rather than on the pages of the media. He quietly, but persuasively, led the dairy industry through change, for instance, realistically recognising the importance of quotas being used in the British market well before their acceptance by other producers. The introduction of quotas before Britain succeeded in joining the EEC eased the potential difficulties when Britain successfully achieved membership. Linton's annual negotiation of quotas with Britain and other Europeans through the 1960s prepared the ground well for the final, satisfactory, EEC negotiations of quotas in 1971.

The importance of primary production as an earner of overseas income made the meat, wool and dairy industries of prime importance for, and hence with considerable influence on, government. But overseas income was only one of many balls that governments had to juggle, primary production contributed less than 10% of GNI and employed less than 15% of the workforce. Ormond was wrong in claiming that farmers ran the country, but because of its importance as an earner of overseas income, earning more than 75% even at the end of the period analysed in this book, farming was the ball the government could least afford to drop and had to pay more attention to than others. Undoubtedly for the New Zealand government primary production had to be a priority; producers remained the backbone of the economy throughout the whole of the period from 1945 into the 1970s, and adapted through the many difficulties of breaking away from being Britain's offshore farm to keep that backbone strong and able to survive through the buffeting of the oil price shocks of the 1970s.

Bibliography

Primary Sources

Alexander Turnbull Library

Federated Farmers, 90–343, MSY2708–2723, Dairy Section Circulars.
Federated Farmers, 90–343, 03/03–03/06, Dairy Section Papers.
Federated Farmers, 90–343, MSY2730–2747, Meat and Wool Section Circulars.
Federated Farmers, 90–343, 04/03, 04/04, 05/04, Meat and Wool Section Papers on Wool.
New Zealand Wool Board, Further Records – Minute Book, MSY5858–5860.
P338.176314 MACK 1974, *Integrating Strategic Management and Control [review of IWS organisation]*, March 1974.
Sir Keith Holyoake papers, MS1814.
Sir John Marshall Papers, MS1403.
Sir John Marshall Collection, MS1403 479/05, Woolgrowers Action Committee.
Sir John Marshall Collection, MS1403–121/05 *The Marketing of New Zealand Wool, Findings and Conclusions*, Battelle, Columbus Laboratories, Ohio, Aug 1971.
Wellington Woolbrokers' Association Minutes, MSY–4140.

D. Hall, *Emerging from an Entrenched Colonial Economy*, Palgrave Studies in Economic History, DOI 10.1007/978-3-319-53016-1

NZ Woolgrowers Action Committee/Bulletin - Call number - Per NZ WOO
New Zealand Woolbrokers' Association – Minute Book – MSY 4140.
The Agricultural Development Conference 1963–64 (Wellington: Government Printer, 1966).

Archives New Zealand

Dairy

Dairy Industry Bulletin 1958–1963, ABBU W4244 Box 33 7/2/2.
Dairy - Dairy Industry - Policy, Agency Arrangements, Export of Dairy Products, AAQW WS3379 Box 11 4/1/4.
Dairy Industry and General 1960, ADRK 17391 T1/274 40/648/8.
Dairy Products Marketing - World Butter Market Situation, ADRK 17391 T1W2591/38 40/648/13.
Dumping of Dairy Produce in United Kingdom 1958–1961, AAFZ W5705 7174 Box 64 3288.
Dumping of Dairy Produce on the United Kingdom Market 1962–1967, AAFZ W1318 7174 Box 189 3288.
Foreign Trade - Dairy Produce – General, AAFD W3738 811 Box1141 CAB130/2/1.
Industry and Commerce - Primary Industries - Dairy Industries, AAFD W3738 811 Box 1033 CAB 123/10/1.
Industry and Commerce - Primary Industries - Dairy Industries 1960-1969, AAFD W3738 811 Box 1032 CAB 123/10/1.
Marketing of New Zealand Dairy Produce in United Kingdom and Elsewhere 1959–1972, AAFZ W1710 7174 Box 15.
New Zealand Trade - United Kingdom - Dairy Produce: Butter 1968–1970, ABHS W4268 7148 Box 13.
New Zealand Trade - United Kingdom - Dairy Produce: Butter, 1973–1988, ABHS W5503 7148 Box 42 LONB 37/1/2.
New Zealand Affairs: Economic Relations - Japan - Dairy Products, ABHS 950 W4627/1304 40/12/9.
Overseas Projects - Milk Products (New Zealand) Ltd. - Minutes of Meetings 1953–1984, ABBU W4244 Box 328 26/53/1-5.
Overseas markets - Exports and enquiries - Japan - Casein (Nissei-Kyoeki Co), ABBU W4244 Box 143 11/8/13.

Press Statements on butter dumping in United Kingdom - 4/11/58 - 10/10/63, ABBU W4244 Box 33.
Statutory Boards and Committees - Dairy Board – General, AAFD W3738 811 Box 645 CAB41/3/1.
United Kingdom - Export - Dairy Products - Policy and Information 1971–1985, AATJ W4838 7428 Box 284 162/3/1.
Trade: United Kingdom: Dairy Produce 1971-1972, C 324 075 C1W2358 54 955/UK/1.

Meat

Meat Export Development Company (New Zealand) Limited – General, AAFZ W1318 7174 Box 228.
Meat Export Development Company (New Zealand) Limited, AAFZ W1710 7174 Box 120.
Importation of Meat into Japan, AAFZ W1714 7174 Box 36.

Wool

International Wool Secretariat Constitution Function Reports, AAQW W3379, Box39.
Statutory Boards and Committees – Wool Board and Wool Commission, AAFD W3738/646 811 CAB 41/7/1.
Wool Industry, AALR W5427 873 Box 774 40/772/2/3–5.
Wool Marketing Committee AALR W5427 873 Box 774 40/772/2/7–8.
Wool Marketing Committee – report of the Wool Marketing Committee, AALR W5427 873 Box 774, 40/772/2/7.
Visit: British Rayon Delegation, 1945, ACIE 8798/EA1/243 Box 243, 59/3/1/57.

European Economic Community (EEC)

Agricultural Commodities UK EEC (European Economic Community) Discussions - Dairy Products, AALR W3158 873 Box100 T61/7/1/15.
Commonwealth Economic Consultative Council - Finance Ministers Meeting London 1960, AALR W3158 873 Box 80 T61/3/31.

Discussions, Mr D Sandys (United Kingdom Secretary of State) for Commonwealth relations on United Kingdom and Europe - July 1961, AEFN 19147 IC22.
E.E.C. [European Economic Community] – 1971–supplementary cuttings (newspaper clippings), ABOT W2670 6787 Box 2.
E.E.C. [European Economic Community] – The Agreement – statements and papers, ABOT W2670 6787 Box 2.
EEC–UK negotiations: Consultations with Producers - Feb 1962 - Sept 1966, T1 W2666 33 61/5/4/1/1.
GATT and European Economic Community, T1 526 52/904/20/1.
Newspaper Clippings Commonwealth and Common Market June 1961 to February 1962, AAFZ W1318 7174 223.
New Zealand's Economic Relations - European Economic Community – General, T1 W2666 41 75/4.

Trade in General

Cabinet Meetings 1951–1961, AAFD W3738 807.
Committee on Economic and Financial Questions, E(61)M.18.
Economic Affairs - Monetary and Economic Council - General 1961–1971, AAFD W3738 811 Box 962 CAB 121/7/1.
New Zealand Trade – United Kingdom – Discussions 1957: Documents, ABHS W4628 7148 Box 12 LONB 37/1/1E.
Review of New Zealand Trade Policy 1957, ADRK 17391 T1/424 61/3/21.
Statutory Boards and Committees - Apple and Pear Marketing Board – General, AAFD W3738/645 811 CAB 42/2/1.
United Kingdom Foreign Trade – General, AAFD W3158/76 873 CAB 502/2/1.
United Kingdom and New Zealand Trade Discussions 1958, AALR W3158 873 Box 79 T61/3/25/1.

Other Primary Sources

Acland Family Papers, Collection MB44, Macmillan Brown Library, University of Canterbury.
Appendix to the Journal of the House of Representatives, Economic Surveys, B5–6.
Appendix to the Journal of the House of Representatives 1934–1935 Session, H–30, Dairy Industry Commission.

Awahuri Co-operative Dairy Factory Company Ltd – Campbell Series 1 and 2 – Massey University Dairy Archives, Palmerston North.

Dominion Post

Evening Post

Final Report on the Marketing of New Zealand Wool – Battelle Columbus Laboratories – Recommendations – Collection MB44, Macmillan Brown Library, University of Canterbury.

John Ormond Papers, Hawke's Bay Museum-Theatre-Gallery.

New Zealand Acts as Enacted, Parliamentary Counsel Office, http://www.nzlii.org/nz/legis/hist_act/

New Zealand Digital Yearbook, www.stats.govt.nz/yearbooks.

New Zealand Herald

New Zealand and the European Economic Community, paper presented to the House of Representatives by Leave, Government Printer, Wellington, 1971.

New Zealand Listener

New Zealand Parliamentary Debates (NZPD)

Organisation for Economic Co-operation and Development (OECD), *Agricultural Policy in New Zealand*, February 1974.

PRO FO371/158322 XC21689, New Zealand: Visit of the Secretary of State for discussions about possible United Kingdom Association with EEC, 23/08/1961, Public Records Office, London.

Reserve Bank Bulletin, http://rbnz.govt.nz/research_and_publications/reserve_bank_bulletin/1981/1981oct44_9meatindustryreview.pdf

Straight Furrow, the Journal of Federated Farmers of New Zealand inc., 1945–1980, at the National Library of New Zealand.

The Economist Historical Archive

The New Zealand Dairy Exporter

The Press

The Times Historical Archive

United Nations Conference on Trade and Development database – http://unctadstat.unctad.org/wds/TableViewer/tableView.aspx

Secondary Sources

Books

Abernethy, David, *The Dynamics of Global Dominance* (Yale: Yale University, 2000).

Baker, John, *The New Zealand People at War: The War Economy* (Wellington: Historical Publications Branch, 1965).

Barnes, Felicity, *New Zealand's London: A Colony and its Metropolis* (Auckland: Auckland University Press, 2012).

Bassett, Michael, *Coates of Kaipara* (Auckland: Auckland University Press, 1999).

Bassett, Michael, *Sir Joseph Ward: A Political Biography* (Auckland: Auckland University Press, 1993).

Bassett, Michael, *The State in the New Zealand: Socialism without Doctrines?* (Auckland: Auckland University Press, 1998).

Bassett, Michael, with King, Michael, *Tomorrow Comes the Song* (Auckland: Penguin Books (NZ) Ltd., 2000).

Belich, James, *Making Peoples; A History of New Zealanders* (Auckland: Penguin Books (NZ), 1996).

Belich, James, *Paradise Reforged: A History of New Zealanders from the 1880s to the Year 2000* (Auckland: Penguin Books (NZ), 2001).

Belich, James, *Replenishing the Earth: The Settler Revolution and the Rise of the Anglo-World, 1783–1939* (Oxford: Oxford University Press, 2009).

Brendon, Piers, *The Decline and Fall of the British Empire 1781–1997* (London: Vintage Books, 2008).

Brooking, Tom, *Lands for the People? The Highland Clearances and the Colonization of New Zealand: A Biography of John Mackenzie* (Dunedin: University of Otago Press, 1996).

Buchanan, Roger, *The Last Shepherd: Anecdotes and Observations from Five Decades in the Wool Industry* (Wellington: Ngaio Press, 2012).

Bullock, Alan, *Ernest Bevin: Foreign Secretary, 1945–1951* (London: William Heinemann Ltd., 1983).

Butler, L. J., *Britain and Empire. Adjusting to the Post-Imperial World* (London: I. B. Tauris, 2002).

Cain, Peter, and Hopkins, Anthony, *British Imperialism: 1688–2000* (Harlow: Pearson Education Ltd, 2002).

Cairncross, Alec, *The British Economy since 1945* (Oxford: Blackwell, 1992).

Calder, Mick, and Tyson, Janet, *Meat Acts: The New Zealand Meat Industry 1972–1997* (Wellington: Meat New Zealand, 1999).

Callaghan, James, *Time and Chance* (London: Collins, 1987).

Carter, Bill, and MacGibbon, John, *Wool: A History of New Zealand's Wool Industry* (Wellington: Ngaio Press, 2003).

Clarke, Peter, *The Last Thousand Days of the British Empire* (London: Penguin, 2007).

Condliffe, James, *New Zealand in the Making: A Study of Economic and Social Development* (London: George Allen and Unwin Ltd., 1959).

Darwin, John, *Britain and Decolonisation. The Retreat from Empire in the Post-War World* (Basingstoke: MacMillan Education Ltd., 1988).

Dedman, Martin, *The Origins and Development of the European Union: 1945–95* (Abingdon: Routledge, 2000).

Donaldson, Peter, *Guide to the British Economy* (Harmondsworth: Penguin Books, 1976).

Douglas, R., *Liquidation of Empire; The Decline of the British Empire* (Harlow: Palgrave Macmillan, 2002).

Easton, B., *The Nationbuilders* (Auckland: Auckland University Press, 2001).

Easton, Brian, *In Stormy Seas: The Post-War New Zealand Economy* (Dunedin: University of Otago Press, 1997).

Evans, B.L., *A History of Agricultural Production and Marketing in New Zealand* (Palmerston North: Keeling and Munday, 1969).

Ferguson, Niall, *Empire* (London: Penguin Books, 2007).

Fieldhouse, D., *The Colonial Empires: A Comparative Survey from the Eighteenth Century* (London: Macmillan, 1982).

Gould, John, *The Rake's Progress? The New Zealand Economy since 1945* (Auckland: Hodder and Stoughton, 1982).

Greensmith, Edward, *The New Zealand Wool Commission* (Wellington: New Zealand Wool Marketing Corporation, 1996).

Gustafson, Barry, *His Way: A Biography of Robert Muldoon* (Auckland: Auckland University Press, 2001).

Gustafson, Barry, *Kiwi Keith: A Biography of Keith Holyoake* (Auckland Auckland University Press, 2007).

Hawke, Gary., *The Making of New Zealand: An Economic History* (Cambridge: Cambridge University Press, 1985).

Hayward, Dai, editor: *Golden Jubilee: The story of the First Fifty Years of the New Zealand Meat Producers Board 1922–1972* (Wellington: Universal Printers, 1972).

Heath, Edward, *The Course of my Life: My Autobiography* (London: Hodder and Stoughton, 1999).

Horne, Alastair, *Macmillan: 1894–1956: Volume One of the Official Biography* (London: Macmillan, 1988).

Hunt, Graeme, *The Black Prince: The Biography of Fintan Patrick Walsh* (Auckland: Penguin Books (NZ) Ltd., 2004).
King, Michael, *The Penguin History of New Zealand Illustrated* (North Shore: Penguin Books, 2007).
Lacquer, Walter, *Europe Since Hitler* (Harmondsworth: Penguin Books, 1972).
Lind, Clive, *A Cut Above: Early History of the Alliance Freezing Company (Southland) Ltd, Alliance Freezing Co.* (Invercargill: Southland Frozen Meat Ltd., Invercargill, 1985).
Lind, Clive, *The Keys to Prosperity: The Centennial History of Southland Frozen Meat Ltd.* (Invercargill: Southland Frozen Meat Ltd., 1981).
Lind, Clive, *Till the Cows Came Home* (Wellington: Steele Roberts, 2013).
Livingstone, J.M., *Britain and the World Economy* (Harmondsworth: Penguin Books, 1971).
MacKenzie, Francine, *Redefining the Bonds of Commonwealth 1939–1948* (New York: Palgrave Macmillan, 2002).
Macmillan, Harold, *At the End of the Day: 1961–1963* (London: Macmillan, 1973).
Mangold, Peter, *The Almost Impossible Ally: Harold Macmillan and Charles de Gaulle* (New York: I.B Tauris, 2006).
Martin, J.E., *The Forgotten Worker* (Wellington: George Allen and Unwin, 1990).
Marshall, John, *Memoirs Vol II; 1960–1988* (Auckland: William Collins Ltd., 1989).
McAloon, Jim, *Judgements of All Kinds* (Wellington: Victoria University Press, 2013).
McKinnon, Malcolm, *Independence and Foreign Policy: New Zealand in the World since 1935* (Auckland: Auckland University Press, 1993).
McKinnon, Malcolm, *Treasury: The New Zealand Treasury 1840–2000* (Auckland: Auckland University Press, 2003).
McLuskie, R.B., *The Great Debate: New Zealand, Britain and the EEC: The Shaping of Attitudes, 1960–63* (Wellington: Decision Research Centre, Victoria University of Wellington, 1986).
Mein Smith, Philippa, *A Concise History of New Zealand* (Cambridge: Cambridge University Press, 2011).
Moon, Paul, *Fatal Frontiers: A New History of New Zealand in the Decade before the Treaty* (Auckland: Penguin Books (NZ), 2006).
Morrison, Iain, *New Zealand Sheep and Their Wool* (Wellington: New Zealand Wool Board, 1980).

Muldoon, Robert, *The New Zealand Economy: A Personal View* (Auckland: Endeavour Press, 1985).

Owen, Geoffrey, *From Empire to Europe* (London: Harper Collins, 1999).

Palmer, Geoffrey, *Reform: A Memoir* (Wellington: Victoria University Press, 2013).

Pawson, Eric, and Tom Brooking, *Environmental Histories of New Zealand* (South Melbourne: Oxford University Press, 2002).

Peden, Robert, *Making Sheep Country: Mt Peel Station and the Transformation of the Tussocks* (Auckland: Auckland University Press, 2011).

Pimlott, Ben, *Harold Wilson* (London: HarperCollins, 1972).

Ponting, K. G., *Wool Marketing* (Oxford: Pergamon Press, 1966).

Rhodes James, Robert, *Anthony Eden* (London: Weidenfield and Nicholson Ltd., 1986).

Robbins, Keith, *The Eclipse of a Great Power: Modern Britain 1870–1992* (Harlow: Longman, 1994).

Schama, Simon, *A History of Britain: The Fate of Empire 1771–2000* (London: BBC Worldwide, 2002).

Sinclair, Keith, *Walter Nash* (Auckland: Auckland University Press, 1976).

Singleton, John, and Robertson, Paul, *Economic Relations Between Britain and Australasia 1945–1970* (Basingstoke: Palgrave, 2002).

Stewart, Michael, *Keynes and After* (Harmondsworth: Penguin Books, 1975).

Sutch, William, Colony or Nation? in Michael Turnbull, (ed.), *Economic Crises in New Zealand from the 1860s to the 1960s* (Sydney: Sydney University Press, 1968).

Tait, Peter, *In the Chair: The Public Life of Sir John Ormond* (Waipukurau: CHB Print, 1989).

Templeton, Malcolm, *An Eye An Ear and A Voice: 50 Years in New Zealand's External Relations 1943–1993* (Wellington: Ministry of Foreign Affairs and Trade, 1993).

Thomas, Hugh, *The Suez Affair* (Harmondsworth: Penguin Books, 1970).

Thomson, David, *The Pelican History of England: England in the Nineteenth Century* (Harmondsworth: Penguin Books, 1977).

Toyne, B. and eleven others, *The Global Textile Industry* (London: George Allen and Unwin, 1984).

Urwin, D., *A Political History of Western Europe since 1945* (Harlow: Pearson Education, 1997).

Wallace, Neal, *When the Farm-gates Opened* (Dunedin: University of Otago, 2014).

Ward, Arthur, *A Command of Co-operatives* (Wellington: New Zealand Dairy Board, 1975).

Ward, Stuart, *Australia and the British Embrace: Demise of the Imperial Ideal* (Victoria: Melbourne University Press, 2001).

Weber, R., *Wool Man* (Queen Charlotte Sound: Cape Catley Ltd, 1992).

Woodfield, Ted, *Against the Odds: Negotiating for New Zealand's Future* (Wellington: Dunmore Publishing Ltd., 2008).

Zeiler, T.W., *Free Trade, Free World; The Advent of GATT* (Chapel Hill: The University of North Carolina Press, 1999).

Articles

Abbott, M., 'Promoting Wool Internationally: The Formation of the International Wool Secretariat', *Australian Economic History Review*, Vol. 38, no. 3, 1998, pp. 258-279.

Badly, John, 'A Wairoa Farmer's View of Wool Marketing in the 1980s', *Proceedings of a Seminar on Wool Marketing in the 1980s*, ed. Owen McCarthy and John Pride, Agricultural Economics Research Unit, Lincoln College, Lincoln, 21 October 1976, pp. 19-25.

Bewley, Joyce, A Survey of Changes in Production, Manufacturing and Marketing in the New Zealand Dairy Industry, 1947-48 to 1967–68, *New Zealand Geographer*, Vol. 26, no. 1, 1970, pp. 36-49.

Brands, Henry, 'From ANZUS to SEATO: United States Strategic Policy towards Australia and New Zealand,1952-1954', *The International History Review*, Vol. 9, no. 2, May 1987, pp. 250-270.

Brownie, Shane, and Dalziel, Paul, 'Shift-share analyses of New Zealand exports, 1970–1984', *New Zealand Economic Papers*, Vol. 27, no. 2, 1993, pp. 233-249.

Carter, Bill, 'Some Thoughts on Wool Marketing in the 1980s', *Proceedings of a Seminar on Wool Marketing in the 1980s*, ed. Owen McCarthy and John Pride, Agricultural Economics Research Unit, Lincoln College, Lincoln, 21 October 1976, pp. 26-36.

Curtis, Bruce, and Reveley, James, 'Producers, Processors and Unions: The Meat Producers Board and Labour Relations in the New Zealand Meat Industry 1952-71', *Australian Economic History Review*, Vol. 41, no. 2, July 2001, pp. 135-138.

Dalton, D.C., 'Merino Romney Crossbreeding', *New Zealand Journal of Agriculture*, Vol. 120, no. 1, January 1970, pp. 46-49.

Dobbs, Fred, 'How Would My Organisation Market Wool in the 1980s?', *Proceedings of a Seminar on Wool Marketing in the 1980s*, ed. Owen McCarthy and John Pride, Agricultural Economics Research Unit, Lincoln College, Lincoln, 21 October 1976, pp. 70–88.

Easton, Brian, Stock and Station Agent Industry, unpublished manuscript.

Fleming, G.A., 'Agricultural Support Policies in a Small Open Country: New Zealand in the 1920s', *Economic History Review*, Vol. LII, no. 2, 1999, pp. 334–354.

Greasley, David, and Oxley, Les, 'The Pastoral Boom, the Rural Land Market and the Long Swings in New Zealand's Economic Growth, 1873–1939', *Economic History Review*, Vol. 62, no. 2, 2009, pp. 324–349.

Guest, John, and Singleton, John, 'The Murapara Project and Industrial Development in New Zealand 1945–65', *Australian Economic History Review*, Vol. 39, no. 1, 1999, pp. 52–71.

Haslam, David, 'The View of a Canterbury Farmer (and Ex-Wool Board Employee) on Wool Marketing in the 1980s', *Proceedings of a Seminar on Wool Marketing in the 1980s*, ed. Owen McCarthy and John Pride, Agricultural Economics Research Unit, Lincoln College, Lincoln, 21 October 1976, pp. 37–48.

Herman, P.G., 'The Electoral Committee of the New Zealand Meat and Wool Boards', *Political Science*, Vol. 26, no. 1, 1974, pp. 56–67.

Kuipers, Victor, 'The GATT stumbling block', *New Zealand International Review*, Vol. 18, no. 1, 1993, pp. 11–12.

Lewis, K.H.C., Davies, G.H., and Scales, G.H., 'Merinos or Corriedales on the High Country?', *New Zealand Journal of Agriculture*, Vol. 123, no. 6, December 1971, pp. 22–23.

Lewthwaite, Gordon, 'Commonwealth and Common Market: The Dilemma of the New Zealand Dairy Industry', *Geographical Review*, Vol. 61, no. 1, 1971, pp. 72–101.

McCarthy, Owen, 'An Academic's View of Wool Marketing in the 1980s', *Proceedings of a Seminar on Wool Marketing in the 1980s*, ed. Owen McCarthy and John Pride, Agricultural Economics Research Unit, Lincoln College, Lincoln, 21 October 1976, pp. 60–69.

McCleod, David, 'The Condition of Sheep Farming in New Zealand', *New Zealand Geographer*, 6, 1, April 1950, pp. 72–78.

Moran, Warren, Greg Blunden, and Adrian Bradly, 'Empowering Family Farms through Cooperatives and Producer Marketing Boards', *Economic Geography*, Vol. 72, no. 2, 1996, pp. 161–177.

Ogawa, Hiroyuki, 'Britain's Commonwealth Dilemma: Discussions with Australia, Canada and New Zealand and Transition of British Trade Policy 1956–59', *Contemporary British History*, Vol. 17, no. 3, 2003, pp. 1–28.

Robertson, Paul, and Singleton, John, 'The Old Commonwealth and Britain's First Application to join the EEC: 1961–3', *Australian Economic History Review*, Vol. 40, no. 2, 2000, pp. 159–177.

Rooth, Tim, 'Imperial Self-Insufficiency Rediscovered: Britain and Australia, 1945–51', *Australian Economic History Review*, Vol. 39, no. 1, 1999, pp. 29–51.

Schedvin, C.B., 'Staples and Regions of the Pax Britannica', *Economic History Review*, Vol. 43, no. 4, 1990, pp. 533–59.

Singleton, John, and Robertson, Paul, 'Britain, Butter and European Integration, 1957–1964', *Economic History Review*, Vol. L, no. 2, 1997, pp. 327–347.

Singleton, John, 'New Zealand, Britain and the Survival of the Ottawa Agreement, 1945–77', *The Australian Journal of Politics and History*, Vol. 43. no. 2, 1997, pp. 168–182.

Ward, Lionel, 'Wool Marketing: The Australian Experience', *Proceedings of a Seminar on Wool Marketing in the 1980s*, ed. Owen McCarthy and John Pride, Agricultural Economics Research Unit, Lincoln College, Lincoln, 21 October 1976, pp. 49–59.

Wilding, Peter, 'A Southland Farmer's View of Wool Marketing in the 1980s', *Proceedings of a Seminar on Wool Marketing in the 1980s*, ed. Owen McCarthy and John Pride, Agricultural Economics Research Unit, Lincoln College, Lincoln, 21 October 1976, pp. 11–18.

Wilkinson, The Hon. Peter, 'The New Zealand Economy in the 1980s', *Proceedings of a Seminar on Wool Marketing in the 1980s*, ed. Owen McCarthy and John Pride, Agricultural Economics Research Unit, Lincoln College, Lincoln, 21 October 1976, pp. 1–10.

Willis, Richard, 'Farming in New Zealand and the EEC–the case of the Dairy Industry', *New Zealand Geographer*, Vol. 40, no. 1, 1984, pp. 2–11.

Young, J., 'The Parting of the Ways'?: Britain, the Messina Conference and the Spaak Committee, June – December 1955', in *British Foreign Policy, 1945–56*, ed. M Dockrill and J Young, (London: Macmillan Press Ltd., 1989).

Theses

Bartley, C.M., The Accountability of the New Zealand Meat Producers Board to Famers from 1922–1985, Masters Book, University of Canterbury, 1987.

Herman, Phillip, *A History of Federated Farmers*, Doctoral Book, Victoria University of Wellington, Wellington, 1974.

McKinnon, Malcolm, *The Impact of War: A Diplomatic History of New Zealand's Economic Relations with Britain, 1939–1954*, Doctoral Book, Victoria University Wellington, 1981.

Neill, Carol, *Trading Our Way: Developments in New Zealand's Trade Policy 1930s to 1980s*, Doctoral Book, Massey University, Palmerston North, 2010.

Other

Abbott, Malcolm, 'Promoting Wool Internationally: The Formation of the International Wool Secretariat', *Working Paper Series 9723*, December 1997, School of Economics, Victoria University Wellington.

Encyclopedia of New Zealand – Biographies, www.teara.govt.nz/en/biographies, accessed 15 February 2014.

Index

D. Hall, *Emerging from an Entrenched Colonial Economy*, Palgrave Studies in Economic History, DOI 10.1007/978-3-319-53016-1

J

K

L

M

The manufacturer's authorised representative in the EU is Springer Nature Customer Service Centre GmbH, Europaplatz 3, 69115 Heidelberg, Germany. If you have any concerns regarding our products, please contact ProductSafety@springernature.com

Printed and bound by CPI Group (UK) Ltd, Croydon, CR0 4YY

05/10/2026

02228422-0002